WALTER RALEGH'S *HISTORY OF THE WORLD*
AND THE HISTORICAL CULTURE OF THE LATE RENAISSANCE

WALTER RALEGH'S *HISTORY OF THE WORLD* AND THE HISTORICAL CULTURE OF THE LATE RENAISSANCE

NICHOLAS POPPER

THE UNIVERSITY OF CHICAGO PRESS

CHICAGO AND LONDON

Publication of this book has been aided by a grant from the Bevington Fund.

The University of Chicago Press, Chicago 60637
The University of Chicago Press, Ltd., London
© 2012 by The University of Chicago
All rights reserved. Published 2012.
Paperback edition 2014
Printed in the United States of America

23 22 21 20 19 18 17 16 15 14   2 3 4 5 6

ISBN-13: 978-0-226-67500-8 (cloth)
ISBN-13: 978-0-226-21396-5 (paper)
ISBN-13: 978-0-226-67502-2 (e-book)
DOI: 10.7208/chicago/9780226675022.001.0001

Library of Congress Cataloging-in-Publication Data

Popper, Nicholas Seth, 1977–
    Walter Ralegh's History of the world and the historical culture of the late
Renaissance / Nicholas Popper.
        pages. cm.
    Includes bibliographical references and index.
    ISBN 978-0-226-67500-8 (hardcover : alkaline paper) — ISBN 0-226-67500-9
(hardcover : alkaline paper) — ISBN 978-0-226-67502-2 (e-book) —
ISBN 0-226-67502-5 (e-book)   1. Raleigh, Walter, Sir, 1552?–1618. History of
the world.   2. Historiography.   I. Title.
    D57.RI84P67 2012
    907.2—dc23

                                                              2012001096

♾ This paper meets the requirements of ANSI/NISO Z39.48-1992 (Permanence
of Paper).

TO AMY

AND TO HAZEL

AND CELIA

CONTENTS

ILLUSTRATIONS

ACKNOWLEDGMENTS
=====================

I have undertaken this project at four locations, and at each, beginning at Princeton, I have been privileged to join communities of brilliant scholars. I have no doubt (indeed, I hope) that many scholars feel that they have been blessed to find the very best mentor on the planet; I have had the good fortune to be right in this sentiment. For many years, Anthony Grafton has devoted to me his substantial energy and incalculable erudition, an honor that I'm not sure how I deserve. His interventions during the shaping of this book have come at perfectly chosen moments, while his kindness has been unrelenting.

Peter Lake has liberally offered his time and expertise, exhibiting an innate sense of when to grant me independence and when to provide more forceful direction. It has been a privilege to observe his scholarly rigor and creativity. The late Mike Mahoney taught me with great intelligence and patience, and I am thankful to have received his advice. I am grateful to Nancy Siraisi for the meticulous attention and care that she gave my manuscript; her criticisms and suggestions have been instrumental at several stages during its development.

All scholars should have a foundation for their experience as rigorous as Princeton's Program Seminar in the History of Science, and I thank everyone in the program for their advice and criticism. It has been a source of enduring happiness for me that my time at Princeton coincided with that of James Byrne, who I deeply admire as a man and as a scholar. Bill Bulman's openness and enthusiasm have been an irreplaceable source of comfort and help. For years, Elizabeth McCahill has been a giving friend, providing exceptional encouragement and advice. Alexander Bick's levity and intellectual appetite have reinvigorated me at down moments for years. I thank Will Slauter for his incomparable ability to bring clarity to and offer distraction from this experience. I count myself lucky to have been introduced to Daniela Bleichmar, Sara Brooks, Angela Gleason, Brendan Kane, Rupa Mishra, Tania Munz, Jane Murphy, Cat Nisbett, Renee Raphael, Jeff Schwegman, Dan Schwartz, Alastair Sponsel, Jeris Stueland, Antoinette Sutto, and Matt Wisnioski.

In London, Lisa Jardine generously brought me into the Centre for Editing Lives and Letters at Queen Mary, University of London. Her kindness was amplified by Robyn Adams, Jan Broadway, Warren Boutcher, Rosanna Cox, Harriet Knight, and Alison Wiggins, whose advice and good humor made me want never to leave. Brent Sirota and James Vaughn, along with Andrea Coleman, Mark Forsyth, Phil Roe, and Martin Svedman, provided indispensable debate, inspiration, and distraction during that most productive time.

At Caltech, Mordechai Feingold sponsored me as the Mellon Postdoctoral in the Humanities, enabling me to discover the amazing vitality of early modern studies in Southern California. During my stay there, he, John Brewer, Matthew Hunter, Noel Swerdlow, and, most especially, Gideon Manning were wonderful colleagues whose insights pushed the project along at a moment when my own sense of it was stagnating. Susan Davis's generosity enabled an incredibly fruitful year. Nicholas Dew, Juan Gomez, and Craig Martin were no less vital to my time there; I can only hope we will all have fellowships at the Huntington at the same time again.

The History Department at the College of William and Mary has been an incredibly enjoyable and vibrant place to work; I cannot imagine a more productive and congenial environment. I am grateful to all my colleagues, though it would be ungracious not to single out Chandos Brown, Fred Corney, Cindy Hahamovitch, LuAnn Homza, Kathy Levitan, Paul Mapp, Leisa Meyer, Brett Rushforth, and Ron Schechter for their attention and guidance. Jonathan Eacott, Amanda Herbert, Daniel Livesay, Elena Schneider, and Molly Warsh at the Omohundro Institute of Early American History and Culture have also created an immeasurably stimulating academic community during my time in Williamsburg.

I have also been the recipient of much encouragement—often for reasons totally opaque to me—from many senior scholars from early in my academic career. As an undergraduate at Haverford College, Lisa Jane Graham and Susan Stuard devoted encouragement and attention to me that I can never repay. Ann Blair, Tom Cogswell, Michael Gordin, Robert Goulding, Deborah Harkness, Randolph Head, Adrian Johns, William Chester Jordan, Paulina Kewes, Peter Mancall, Margaret Meserve, Mark Nicholls,

Joad Raymond, David Sedley, Simon Shaffer, William Sherman, Nigel Smith, Malcolm Smuts, and Jacob Soll have been unaccountably supportive. Most notably, Lauren Kassell has devoted a measure of hospitality, kindness, and consideration to me that I can only hope to one day return, and I thank her in particular for her detailed comments on the final draft of the book.

This project could not have been completed without generous support from a wide range of institutions. Funding has been supplied by the College of William and Mary Faculty Summer Research Grant Program, the Mrs. Giles M. Whiting Foundation, the Andrew Mellon Foundation, and the North Caroliniana Society. I particularly thank the staffs at the Swem Library, the College of William and Mary; Firestone Library, Princeton University; the British Library; the Cambridge University Library; the Bodleian Library; the Henry E. Huntington Library; the Folger Library; the Walter Ralegh Collection at the University of North Carolina; the Small Special Collections Library, the University of Virginia; the Houghton Library, Harvard University; the Beinecke Library, Yale University; and the Public Record Office in Kew for their assistance.

Doug Mitchell, Tim McGovern, Sandy Hazel, and Joseph Brown have made the terrifying process of pushing this curiosity through to print feel almost natural. I am deeply grateful to them for their patience and guidance, and I am extremely appreciative of the efforts of the two anonymous reviewers, who contributed to shaping the final product as much as anybody.

My parents have been indescribably sympathetic and understanding. The intelligence and suitability of their encouragement and advice always remind me of how fortunate I am to have the insuperable advantage of my family. My sister and my grandmother have stimulated enthusiasm and provided support at vital times. Ari Form and Gabe Boylan have been extraordinarily generous friends. Emma has allowed me to take her for walks when I've needed to escape from my imprisonment at the hands of Ralegh.

Finally, this book would be a shell of itself without the presence, since the first day of graduate school, of Amy Haley. It has been shaped by her unwavering love, brilliance, and encouragement, and I thank her for being my best friend and most incisive critic. To her I also owe Hazel and Celia, sources of unspeakable, exuberant joy. It is with great happiness and relief that I dedicate this book to her.

The reader should note several decisions that I have made in preparing this work. First, I have spelled Ralegh's last name according to the current scholarly convention. Second, I have cited the *History* by book, chapter, section, subsection (where applicable), and page of the 1614 edition (e.g., *HW*, 1.12,2.3.214; *HW*, 3.3.6.38). Please note that a second pagination commences at the beginning of book 3. Third, where the original version of the text used a macron to substitute for letters, I have added and italicized the missing letters. Finally, all translations are mine unless otherwise noted. In some cases, I have elected to use pre-1700 English translations, though Ralegh probably owned the texts in their original languages. This is done as a nod to the stylistic conventions and flavor of the period. For the same reason, my own translations are intended to convey some degree of the rhetorical aesthetic of the originals. Many of the authors, like Ralegh, were masterful stylists, and I apologize for what might appear clumsy and laborious efforts to replicate their elegant and economical prose.

Frequently Used Abbreviations

BJRL	*Bulletin of the John Rylands Library*
BL	British Library
EHR	*English Historical Review*
HJ	*Historical Journal*
HLQ	*Huntington Library Quarterly*
HR	*Historical Research*
HW	Walter Ralegh, *History of the World* (London, 1614)
JBS	*Journal of British Studies*
JEMH	*Journal of Early Modern History*
JHI	*Journal of the History of Ideas*
JMH	*Journal of Modern History*

JWCI	*Journal of the Warburg and Courtauld Institutes*
MLN	*Modern Language Notes*
NB	Walter Ralegh's manuscript notebook, BL Add. MS 57555
P&P	*Past and Present*
RQ	*Renaissance Quarterly*
SCJ	*Sixteenth Century Journal*
TRHS	*Transactions of the Royal Historical Society*

INTRODUCTION

The captive explorer had been condemned to death. Aging and scorned, Sir Walter Ralegh spent his declining years in the Tower of London a convicted traitor, his life preserved only by the grace of his captor, King James I.[1] The old adventurer limped from shrapnel buried in his leg during the 1596 naval victory at Cadiz, and a stroke shortly after his 1603 imprisonment had further hobbled the physical gifts that delighted Elizabeth I's court, endured Amazon expeditions, and withstood European combats. Now, painfully ascending the stairs to the promenade above his White Tower quarters, he could only look out over the Thames at the playhouses and shacks of Southwark or gaze on the cold northern skies that had disappeared behind him as his ships plunged down the New World coastline into the tropics.

Deprived of his corporeal strength and his mobility, with little audience for the wit and poetry that had endeared him to Elizabeth, Ralegh set himself to new tasks. In the Tower, he received visitors, set up a still, and, aided by the collection of over five hundred books in his chambers, began

---

1. For Ralegh's biography, see Mark Nicholls and Penry Williams, *Sir Walter Raleigh: In Life and Legend* (London: Continuum, 2011), and their recent entry on Ralegh in the *Dictionary of National Biography*. The most significant earlier biographies are Pierre Lefranc, *Sir Walter Raleigh, écrivain, l'oeuvre et l'idées* (Paris: Librarie Armand Colin; Quebec: Les presses de l'Université Laval, 1968); and Edward Edwards, *The Life of Sir Walter Ralegh*, 2 vols. (London: Macmillan, 1868). See also Edward Thompson, *Sir Walter Ralegh: Last of the Elizabethans* (New Haven, CT: Yale University Press, 1936); Willard M. Wallace, *Sir Walter Raleigh* (Princeton, NJ: Princeton University Press, 1959); A. L. Rowse, *Ralegh and the Throckmortons* (London: Macmillan, 1962); Stephen Greenblatt, *Sir Walter Ralegh: The Renaissance Man and His Roles* (New Haven, CT: Yale University Press, 1973); and Raleigh Trevelyan, *Sir Walter Raleigh* (New York: Henry Holt, 2002). The recent biography of Ralegh's wife is also essential: Anna Beer, *Bess: The Life of Lady Ralegh, Wife to Sir Walter* (London: Constable, 2004).

working on a universal world history.[2] As was customary, he began with the Creation, intending to proceed to his present in three lengthy volumes. In seven years of work, he produced only one volume, a massive fifteen-hundred-folio tome that examined nearly four millennia from Creation to 168 BC. In 1614, sensing that volatility within James's regime offered the hope of restoration to the king's favor, he rushed the *History of the World* into print. Though only a portion of the original project, this book enjoyed immense popularity for a century after its publication, boasting over a dozen editions, reprints, and abridgments.[3]

2. For when the *History* was written, see Lefranc, *Sir Walter Raleigh*, 638–42. For the library catalog, see Walter Oakeshott, "Sir Walter Ralegh's Library," *The Library*, 5th ser., 23 (1968): 285–327.

3. Editions or reprints were published in 1614, 1617, 1621, 1628, 1634, 1652, 1666, 1671, 1677, 1687, and 1736; abridgments or excerpts in 1636, 1647, 1650, 1698, 1700, 1702, and 1708; and a continuation by Alexander Ross in 1652. See John Racin Jr., *Sir Walter Raleigh as Historian* (Salzburg: Universität Salzburg, 1974), 5–21, and "The Early Editions of Sir Walter Ralegh's *History of the World*," *Studies in Bibliography* 17 (1964): 199–209, which revise T. N. Brushfield, "Sir Walter Ralegh and His 'History of the World,'" *Report and Transactions of the Devonshire Association* 19 (1887): 398–418; and Sir Charles Firth, "Sir Walter Raleigh's *History of the World*," in *Proceedings of the British Academy* (London, 1917–18), 427–46. Other notable works containing studies of the *History* include Ernest A. Strathmann, *Sir Walter Ralegh: A Study in Elizabethan Skepticism* (New York: Cambridge University Press, 1959); F. Smith Fussner, *The Historical Revolution: English Historical Writing and Thought, 1580–1640* (London: Routledge & Kegan Paul, 1962); Raleigh Ashlin Skelton, "Ralegh as Geographer," *Virginia Magazine of History and Biography* 71 (1963): 131–49; P. M. Rattansi, "Alchemy and Natural Magic in Raleigh's *History of the World*," *Ambix* 13 (1965–66): 122–38; F. J. Levy, *Tudor Historical Thought* (San Marino, CA: Huntington Library, 1967); C. A. Patrides, ed., *The History of the World* (London: Macmillan, 1971); Leonard Tennenhouse, "Sir Walter Raleigh and the Literature of Clientage," in *Patronage in the Renaissance*, ed. Guy Fitch Lytle and Stephen Orgel (Princeton, NJ: Princeton University Press, 1981), 235–58; Steven W. May, *Sir Walter Ralegh* (Boston: Twayne, 1989); D. R. Woolf, *The Idea of History in Early Stuart England: Erudition, Ideology, and the "Light of Truth" from the Accession of James I to the Civil War* (Toronto: University of Toronto Press, 1990); Joseph Levine, "Sir Walter Ralegh and the Ancient Wisdom," in *Court, Country and Culture: Essays on Early Modern British History in Honor of Perez Zagorin*, ed. Bonnelyn Young Kunze and Dwight D. Brautigam (Rochester, NY: University of Rochester Press, 1992), 89–108; Anna Beer, *Sir Walter Ralegh and His Readers in the Seventeenth Century: Speaking to the People* (New York: St. Martin's, 1997), and "'Left to the World without a Maister': Sir Walter Ralegh's *The History of the World* as a Public Text," *Studies in Philology* 91 (1994): 432–63; Charles G. Salas, "Ralegh and the Punic Wars," *JHI* 57 (1996): 195–215; Eleri Larkum, "Providence and Politics in Sir Walter Ralegh's *History of the World*" (Ph.D. diss., University of Oxford, 1997); Jenny Wilson, *Ralegh's History of the World: Its Purpose and Political Significance* (Durham, NC: Thomas Harriot Seminar, 1999); Lauren Kassell, "'All This Land Was Full Fill'd of Faerie'; or, Magic and the Past in Early Modern England," *JHI* 67 (2006): 107–22; and Benjamin Schmidt, "Reading Ralegh's America: Texts, Books, and Readers in the Early Modern Atlantic World," in *The Atlantic World and Virginia, 1550–1624*, ed. Peter C. Mancall (Chapel Hill: University of North Carolina Press, for the Omohundro Institute of Early American History and Culture, 2007), 454–88.

The following study asks why Ralegh devoted so much of himself to the project of the *History* and why the book continued to command such attention well after his execution in 1618. It answers these questions by placing Ralegh's work within an early modern European culture that increasingly assigned profound value to historical analysis. The study and composition of history served as a laboratory for responding to the instability that battered European culture between 1400 and 1700. Early modern scholars faced the urgent problem of interpreting and addressing violent ruptures in the world around them—a world distanced from its past by theological division, jarring discoveries, technological innovation, and political upheaval. During this period, a growing number of scholars and erudite political counselors argued that worldly authority optimally derived from expertise in observing and analyzing the past. Their struggle to decode meaning in contemporary events propelled them to develop new techniques for identifying historical precedents and new ways of applying knowledge gleaned from the past to interpretations of the present. Kings, popes, nobles, and statesmen read and responded to scholarly histories written by public figures such as Niccolò Machiavelli, Johannes Goropius Becanus, and Justus Lipsius and devoted considerable energy to applying or refuting their counsels. The impact of the culture of historical counsel was not confined to the pages of books or the council chambers of princes, for the dissemination of the practices constitutive of such expertise wrought widespread intellectual, political, and theological change throughout Europe.

At the outset of this period, history was considered a species of rhetoric primarily valued for its ability to inflame auditors to virtue.[4] This

4. The best general works on historical scholarship in the early modern period are Anthony Grafton, *The Footnote: A Curious History* (Cambridge, MA: Harvard University Press, 1997); and the relevant chapters in Donald R. Kelley, *The Faces of History: Historical Inquiry from Herodotus to Herder* (New Haven, CT: Yale University Press, 1998). See also Hendrik Johannes Erasmus, *The Origins of Rome in Historiography from Petrarch to Perizonius* (Assen: Van Gorcum, 1962); Peter Burke, *The Renaissance Sense of the Past* (New York: St. Martin's, 1970); and Arnaldo Momigliano, *The Classical Foundations of Modern Historiography* (Berkeley and Los Angeles: University of California Press, 1990). For early modern British historiography, see T. D. Kendrick, *British Antiquity* (London: Methuen, 1950); Levi Fox, ed., *English Historical Scholarship in the Sixteenth and Seventeenth Centuries* (London: Dugdale Society, for the Oxford University Press, 1956); May McKisack, *Medieval History in the Tudor Age* (Oxford: Clarendon, 1971); Fussner, *The Historical Revolution*; Levy, *Tudor Historical Thought*; Kevin Sharpe, *Sir Robert Cotton, 1586–1631: History and Politics in Early Modern England* (Oxford: Oxford University Press, 1979); Joseph Levine, *Humanism and History: The Origins of Modern English Historiography* (Ithaca, NY: Cornell University Press, 1987); G. J. R. Parry, *A Protestant Vision: William Harrison and the Reformation of Elizabethan England* (Cambridge: Cambridge University Press, 1987); Timothy Hampton, *Writing from History: The Rhetoric of*

classical characterization drove learned statesmen to embrace history as the learning most conducive to their aspirations. Over the sixteenth century, scholars reconfigured the study of the past, portraying the reading of histories as a form of experience that generated wisdom by revealing the processes of causation underlying earthly events. The rhetorical and philosophical traditions that have been so richly examined by modern scholars gave way to a lesser-known intellectual culture in which erudition and governance went hand in hand, in which expertise in analyzing causes outweighed virtue or sophisticated oratory. As scholars and statesmen turned to histories for precedents and patterns that would help them establish order, they transformed the methodological foundations of their discipline. These new prescriptions required consultation of all relevant sources for the event under examination, from the reports of contemporary eyewitnesses to the works of later commentators and even to ruins and physical artifacts. Whether text or object, each source was subjected to minute parsing, reduced to shards of evidence that were then recombined in an overarching narrative reconstituted by, and accounting for, each fragment. This movement cleaved history from rhetoric and, instead, defined it in terms of a specific methodology that demanded an erudite, antiquarian, empirical, and inductive approach to explaining causation. As history emerged as the master discipline of early modern Europe, these methods structured the European elite's foundations of learning, and all other disciplines were subject to its canons.

Early modern scholars believed that the proper deployment of historical analysis would ameliorate the uncertainty sundering their world by establishing a single, certain vision of the past that could then be used to resolve the striations of the present. This conviction increasingly was

---

Exemplarity in Renaissance Literature (Ithaca, NY: Cornell University Press, 1990); Richard Helgerson, *Forms of Nationhood: The Elizabethan Writing of England* (Chicago: University of Chicago Press, 1992); Graham Parry, *The Trophies of Time: English Antiquarians in the Seventeenth Century* (Oxford: Oxford University Press, 1995); Thomas Betteridge, *Tudor Histories of the English Reformations, 1530–83* (Aldershot: Ashgate, 1999); D. R. Woolf, *Reading History in Early Modern England* (Cambridge: Cambridge University Press, 2000), *The Social Circulation of the Past: English Historical Culture, 1500–1730* (Oxford: Oxford University Press, 2003), and *The Idea of History in Early Stuart England*; Paulina Kewes, ed., *The Uses of History in Early Modern England* (San Marino, CA: Huntington Library, 2006); Jan Broadway, *"No Historie So Meete": Gentry Culture and the Development of Local History in Elizabethan and Early Stuart England* (Manchester: Manchester University Press, 2006); Jennifer Summit, *Memory's Library: Medieval Books in Early Modern England* (Chicago: University of Chicago Press, 2008); Angus Vine, *In Defiance of Time: Antiquarian Writing in Early Modern England* (Oxford: Oxford University Press, 2010); and Adam Smyth, *Autobiography in Early Modern England* (Cambridge: Cambridge University Press, 2010).

invested with theological significance. As the authority of this culture spread and both Protestant and Catholic Reformations pressured governments, ecclesiology and politics became inseparable. Scholars viewed the production of counsel from historical analysis as itself providential, reflecting divine control over terrestrial events. To many participants in this culture, counselors were ministers, and historians were prophets. The reading of histories constituted a form of illumination and the application of historical methodology a pious labor imbued with divine approval.[5]

To the horror of most of these men, the implementation of the methods of historical analysis exacerbated disputes rather than eliminating them, and the practices developed to reveal causation themselves challenged the political and intellectual regimes they had been devised to strengthen. The emphasis on integrating an expansive range of sources undermined the autonomy and preeminence of sacred texts, while the importance of reconstituting evidentiary fragments celebrated the work of the modern commentator at the expense of the credibility of venerable authorities. Integrating new evidence, moreover, generated controversial visions of the past that contradicted revered perceptions about ancient communities. Early modern scholars projected flickering specters of their present back through time, hoping by illumination and evidence to grasp the true nature of Providence and stimulate the pursuit of their ideal futures; instead, they discovered that their methods intensified instability rather than reestablishing a previous golden age of their own ideals. And those learned counselors who performed their duties according to this regime found that the pursuit of virtue gradually shaped their counsels less than did intelligence gleaned from the correspondence of shady informers and the obscure gleanings of clients dispatched to provincial archives. The historical

5. For this special place of Providence in early modern British thought, see Alexandra Walsham, *Providence in Early Modern England* (Oxford: Oxford University Press, 1999). This relation between prophecy and history did not break from medieval traditions. See R. W. Southern, "Aspects of the European Tradition of Historical Writing: 3, History as Prophecy," *TRHS*, 5th ser., 22 (1972): 159–80; and Julia Crick, "Geoffrey of Monmouth: Prophecy and History," *Journal of Medieval History* 18 (1992): 357–71. For this relation under the Tudors and Stuarts, see A. N. McLaren, "Prophecy and Providentialism in the Reign of Elizabeth I," in *Prophecy: The Power of Inspired Languages in History, 1300–2000*, ed. Bertrand Taithe and Tim Thornton (Stroud: Sutton, 1997), 1–30; Kevin Sharpe, *Reading Revolutions: The Politics of Reading in Early Modern England* (New Haven, CT: Yale University Press, 2000), and "Reading Revelations: Prophecy, Hermeneutics and Politics in Early Modern Britain," in *Reading, Society and Politics in Early Modern England*, ed. Kevin M. Sharpe and Steven N. Zwicker (Cambridge: Cambridge University Press, 2003), 122–63; and Thomas S. Freeman, "Providence and Prescription: The Account of Elizabeth in Foxe's *Book of Martyrs*," in *The Myth of Elizabeth*, ed. Susan Doran and Thomas S. Freeman (Basingstoke: Palgrave, 2003), 27–55.

turn transformed Europe, but not because scholarly reflection on ancient and medieval communities precipitated a sense of historicist difference from the past.[6] The methods constitutive of historical analysis wrought unexpected and unwanted change on early modern Europe, for they eroded the authority of the Bible, posed modern commentators as challengers to ancient traditions, elevated the scientific method as an alternative to textual exegesis, and succored the growth of the early modern information state.

Ralegh's *History of the World* emerged during this tumultuous process, and it can be used to reveal the mechanics of the transformation wrought by the deployment of historical analysis. The decision to write the *History* revealed Ralegh's participation in a venerable, vibrant culture of politics, polemic, and erudition, and his implementation of the canons of this culture thus highlights the limitations of studying English scholarship and politics in an insular vein. His work exemplified the scholarly regime that valued historical training as the foundation of proper rule and that viewed scholarship and politics as intertwined and reinforcing. Ralegh believed that transmitting this culture to an English-reading audience in a massive universal history would benefit both himself and the realm by illuminating the operation of divine Providence on earth. He appears a curious representative of this world, for he is known better as a provincial pirate–cum–royal courtier than as an industrious scholar, attributed international significance as a British sea dog rather than as a member of a pan-European class of learned politicians. But, though he wrote in a vernacular language unfamiliar to most European scholars, the texts in his library and the ways in which he manipulated them to portray an uncertain past reveal a deep immersion in the expansive culture of applied historical scholarship.

Ralegh took on himself a daunting enterprise, but one with familiar precedents. Late antique Christian, and before that Jewish, polemicists composed such universal histories to argue that all events occurred under the custody of a single divine creator. And Ralegh well knew that, throughout contemporary Europe, learned statesmen were reading, analyzing, and composing histories. Despite his limited personal acquaintance with contemporary English scholars such as William Camden, Rob-

6. Pace J. G. A. Pocock, *The Machiavellian Moment: Florentine Political Thought and the Atlantic Republican Tradition* (Princeton, NJ: Princeton University Press, 1975), and "England," in *National Consciousness, History and Political Culture in Early-Modern Europe,* ed. Orest Ranum (Baltimore: Johns Hopkins University Press, 1975), 98–117. See Zachary Sayre Schiffman, "Renaissance Historicism Reconsidered," *History and Theory* 24 (1985): 170–82.

ert Cotton, and William Lambarde, his universal world history engaged sophisticated works of contemporary Continental scholars and venerable traditions. Analyzing his text requires understanding the European republic of letters and recognizing that early modern England's participation in this community enabled individuals such as Ralegh to navigate its arcane waters without local guides. His experience of incarceration while he produced the *History* may have been unusual, but the work itself represented a practice widespread from Scotland to Naples to Gdansk.

That Ralegh responded to his grievous circumstances with the exacting manipulation of sources in sustained historical analysis testifies to the depth of this culture's penetration into European affairs while also revealing the channels by which it spread. Though Ralegh was not a towering intellect or a paradigm-shifting innovator, neither was he a derivative hack. He may best be described as part of the rank and file of a movement, a node weaving together the crackling strands of a network, or a prism refracting unique patterns from external illumination. He ranks as one of the many practitioners of historical analysis who flung themselves into resuscitations of the past, adapting the methods for their immediate contexts, expecting to yield certain wisdom that would assuage the jagged and discordant present. And the unique contours of his vision reflect this culture's capacity to spawn a spectacular bazaar of narratives, each drenched with distinctive detail and inimitable argumentation. Viewing the early modern world through Ralegh's *History* uncovers a culture consciously experiencing rapid transformation, captivated and distressed by its own history, inventive with methods and creative with sources, chaotic and alien, but recognizable—a wholly confusing palimpsest of a world that spawned another more familiar.

What follows is a study of the book Ralegh produced, a book whose composition and circulation exemplified the early modern regime of processing the past. My methodology has been to decipher his scholarly techniques and discern how he would have understood his practices. I have thus read his sources with the *History* and his lone extant notebook at hand, determining how he interacted with them by deducing what captured his attention and what he overlooked, what he subscribed to and what he dismissed. Such close scrutiny of his relation with his sources— epitomized by my use of his largely neglected geographical notebook— supplies a different model for analyzing the *History* than that deployed by most previous scholars, who have focused on the balms of his rhetoric and philosophy and ignored the allergen of his erudition. This focus has allowed me to trace closely the circulation—and stagnation—of visions of the past and the scholarly methods that permeated early modern historical culture and, in turn, to place their impact in sharp relief.

Accordingly, the framework organizing my study reflects the stages of the *History*'s production and circulation. Successive chapters are devoted to the contexts that led Ralegh to conceive the project, the sources he used, the methods with which he elicited evidence, his recombination of this material into a narrative, the presentation he gave to this account, and, finally, the reception of the work in the seventeenth and eighteenth centuries. All but the first and last chapter are centered on Ralegh's text and the specific sources that provided the bulk of his evidence; my sources with few exceptions have been those he used in producing his work, and, for readers' convenience, in my bibliography I have identified sources in his library or cited in the *History* with an asterisk. All but the last chapter, furthermore, center their analysis on one apposite strand of early modern learning that Ralegh addressed in producing the *History*. This framework enables a closer look at his engagement with particular aspects of historical culture—its prescriptive methods, its practitioners, its range of political orientations—to situate him in proper intellectual perspective while also illuminating the broad transformations provoked by those aspects' methods. It also reveals how the culture of historical analysis infused each stage in the book's life, from Ralegh's absorption of its canons in conceptualizing the project to his dissemination of them by the *History*'s publication.

Chapter 1 focuses on the contexts supporting Ralegh's decision to commence the project of a universal history, beginning with a treatment of his life and career. It then examines how learned statesmen had come to view the synthesis of narrow evidence culled from a broad range of sources as a mode of developing prudent counsel and suggests why Ralegh, like many of his contemporaries, held the image of the historian as a methodical prophet of the past, present, and future. It thus explains why he believed implementing the practices of historical counsel would remedy a crisis he perceived as unfolding from the flawed policies propagated by the Jacobean regime. The following four chapters build on this by focusing on one methodological aspect of historical culture. The study of Ralegh's sources in chapter 2 investigates his chronology, a demanding, technical early modern subject. While at the outset of the sixteenth century ancient chronology had predominantly been a mode of scriptural exegesis, Ralegh participated in a wave of scholars who fleshed out biblical testimony by consulting ancient pagan historians and astronomical evidence. In their pursuit of sources that would reinforce the sanctity of the Bible, these chronologers unwittingly devised ways of evaluating evidence that eroded Scripture's singular authority. Chapter 3 uses Ralegh's geographical note-book to examine the methods of reading that scholars directed at their expanded set of sources. Like that of many of his contemporaries, Ralegh's practice of reading isolated the most irreducible fragments of evidence from his sources, a system of producing knowledge that prized the collec-tion and collation of individual observations over the traditional empha-sis on authorial credibility. Chapter 4 examines how Ralegh reanimated such historical particulars into a coherent elaboration of divine causation by emphasizing the wisdom he had gained through his experience as an explorer. Focusing on travels as a means to explain change in the ancient world, he exalted a facet of his expertise while also generating a revisionist narrative that subtly admonished James for his continuing incarceration. In chapter 5, I examine the presentation of Ralegh's counsels by investi-gating his histories of political institutions and of warfare. These treat-ments sought to affirm his loyalty to his sovereign while suggesting his ability both to quell parliamentary dissatisfaction and to coordinate the anti-Spanish policy he hoped that James would finally embrace. Ralegh's manipulation of sources, moreover, projected his skill in compiling and deploying information. This expertise increasingly was required by early modern European governments, but it gradually obscured the possession of virtue as the basis of political authority and, in certain circumstances, could foment radical political theories.

Chapter 6 assesses the reception of the *History*, using evidence left by readers in marginal annotations in their copies, loose-leaf notes, letters, and poems to show how Ralegh's personal and political motivations for the work were eclipsed by the polemical and pedagogical imperatives that readers brought to the text from their own contexts. And, in the reception of the *History*, we can observe how the regime of historical analysis in which Ralegh was a participant gradually faded, yielding to a neoclassical culture again categorizing history within the field of rhetoric. Finally, a brief conclusion suggests that, when systematized as a philosophical ori-entation, the practices constitutive of historical analysis became central to the scientific revolution that challenged the preeminence of the culture of historical counsel. This episode exemplifies the process by which Ralegh's work advanced methods and practices that, though seeking to restore his place and strengthen existing authorities, transformed European politics, scholarship, and religion.

That argument is the largest embedded in this work, and it revises the long-held depiction of the early modern historical revolution as precipitating modernity by generating a historicist consciousness. This book consolidates recent scholarship that has emphasized early modern scholarly practices rather than disembodied ideas, the assertion of expertise rather than the unfurling of genius, and the circulation of historical knowledge throughout European society rather than the origination of the modern historical method. It has also drawn on work that has shown that early modern scholars mediated new and unexpected observations through books rather than by passively yielding to experience and that the generation of many radical innovations transpired, not at Europe's intellectual margins, but within established contexts.[7] Directing this work toward historical culture, I advance the argument that the widespread implementation of practices devised to refine the study of the past exerted a profound impact on all aspects of European intellectual and political life. As I will show,

7. For prominent recent examples of such work, see Anthony Grafton, with April Shelford and Nancy Siraisi, *New Worlds, Ancient Texts: The Power of Tradition and the Shock of Discovery* (Cambridge, MA: Harvard University Press, 1992); William H. Sherman, *John Dee: The Politics of Reading and Writing in the English Renaissance* (Amherst: University of Massachusetts Press, 1995); Ann Blair, *The Theater of Nature: Jean Bodin and Renaissance Science* (Princeton, NJ: Princeton University Press, 1997), and *Too Much to Know: Managing Scholarly Information Before the Modern Age* (New Haven, CT: Yale University Press, 2010); Lorraine Daston and Katharine Park, *Wonders and the Order of Nature, 1150–1750* (New York: Zone, 1998); Adrian Johns, *The Nature of the Book: Print and Knowledge in the Making* (Chicago: University of Chicago Press, 1998); Adam Fox, *Oral and Literate Culture in England, 1500–1700* (Oxford: Clarendon, 2000); Sharpe, *Reading Revolutions*; Woolf, *Reading History in Early Modern England*, and *The Social Circulation of the Past*; Alastair Bellany, *The Politics of Court Scandal in Early Modern England: News Culture and the Overbury Affair, 1603–1660* (Cambridge: Cambridge University Press, 2002); Jonathan Sheehan, *The Enlightenment Bible: Translation, Scholarship, Culture* (Princeton, NJ: Princeton University Press, 2005); Jacob Soll, *Publishing the Prince: History, Reading, and the Birth of Political Criticism* (Ann Arbor: University of Michigan Press, 2005); Brian Ogilvie, *The Science of Describing: Natural History in Renaissance Europe* (Chicago: University of Chicago Press, 2006); Grafton, *What Was History? The Art of History in Early Modern Europe* (Cambridge: Cambridge University Press, 2007); Nancy Siraisi, *History, Medicine, and the Traditions of Renaissance Learning* (Ann Arbor: University of Michigan Press, 2007); Tara Nummedal, *Alchemy and Authority in the Holy Roman Empire* (Chicago: University of Chicago Press, 2007); Margaret Meserve, *Empires of Islam in Renaissance Historical Thought* (Cambridge, MA: Harvard University Press, 2008); Summit, *Memory's Library*; Jean-Louis Quantin, *The Church of England and Christian Antiquity: The Construction of a Confessional Identity in the 17th Century* (Oxford: Oxford University Press, 2009); Leah DeVun, *Prophecy, Alchemy, and the End of Time: John of Rupescissa in the Late Middle Ages* (New York: Columbia University Press, 2009); Smyth, *Autobiography in Early Modern England*; and Eric Ash, ed., *Expertise: Practical Knowledge and the Early Modern State*, Osiris 25 (Chicago: University of Chicago Press, 2010). For a broader emphasis on historicizing studies of method, see Peter Becker and William Clark, eds., *Little Tools of Knowledge: Historical Essays on Academic and Bureaucratic Practices* (Ann Arbor: University of Michigan Press, 2000); and David Womersley, "Against the Teleology of Technique," *HLQ* 68 (2005): 95–108 (reprinted in Kewes, ed., *The Uses of History*, 91–104).

history's role as the preeminent discipline of early modern Europe stimulated the production and circulation of antiquarian, empirical, inductive, and experiential methods of making knowledge, and the adoption of these methods undergirded the remarkable transformations of the seventeenth and eighteenth centuries. This recalibration of the authority of sources and intensified interest in exotic sources led scholars to devise historicist interpretations that undermined the sacrality of Scripture. Similarly, the inductive synthesis of observations collected from esoteric sources into coherent temporal narratives emerged as the most celebrated mode of intellectual inquiry, abetting the reconsideration of conceptions about the ancient world, and spurring the triumph of the moderns over the ancients. The widening range of acceptable sources also heightened the authority of learning gleaned from consideration of natural phenomena, while the application of these methods reconfigured natural philosophy into natural science. And statesmen who directed these practices of making knowledge and exercising power toward their own domains succored the emergence of information states whose intellectual basis for authority depended more on the compilation and preservation of state records than on the enduring ideology of virtue.

Early modern scholars described unprecedented modern empires as reinstating venerated ancient kingdoms and innovative natural philosophy as reinvigorating Abraham's knowledge. They struggled to reassert order by prophesying the New World in ancient Palestine, the true revelation of Christianity among ancient Chaldeans, modern warfare among the ancient Hebrews, and their emerging world in ancient Mesopotamia. Yet the scholarly techniques they devised to evoke these apparitions of the past hastened the demise of the order they labored to strengthen. As the revolution of the historical turn emanated throughout Europe, implementation of the constellation of methods demanded by this scholarly regime failed to restore an idealized preexisting state of harmony. Instead, these methods coalesced to transform and sunder the shared culture of their practitioners, radiating throughout Europe, not the light of stability they cherished, but its darkening gloom.

CHAPTER ONE

Context:
Ralegh and Historical Culture

RALEGH'S LIFE AND CAREER

R alegh's participation in the culture of historical counsel illuminates the vast scope of this movement's influence. As the following chapter will show, the canons of historical culture were shaped in an array of intellectual and political contexts, resulting in an enterprise deemed prophetic and prudential, whose practices demanded the microscopic analysis of a broad range of sources. The Elizabethan elite absorbed its dictates into their political experience, and Ralegh's ascendancy took place in an environment that prized the collection and manipulation of historical texts. By invoking this multilayered conception of the past, Ralegh orchestrated the *History* both to meet the needs of a realmwide crisis and to address highly personal apprehensions concerning his own life.

Little in Ralegh's background portended a future role as a prophetic scholar proffering learned counsel. His early career suggests a desire to use military experience and education to establish qualification for provincial administration. Ralegh was born in 1554 to a fiercely Protestant gentry family of Devon.[1] The West Country produced many of England's foremost sailors and soldiers, and many of Ralegh's maternal relatives had careers in these fields that embedded them within the local power structure. His father, similarly, had served as deputy vice admiral of Devon. Ralegh himself spent 1569–70 fighting for the Huguenot cause as a mercenary in France. In 1572, he matriculated at Oriel College, Oxford, where he was one of the older students among the growing number of gentry and

---

1. Ralegh's mother was mentioned in Foxe's *Book of Martyrs*. See John Foxe, *Acts and Monuments* (London, 1563), 1737.

aristocrats attending university. There is no record that he took a degree, and, in 1575, he was admitted to the Middle Temple. For the next few years he gadded about London, composing verse, brawling, serving short terms in prisons, and associating with poet-ruffians such as his maternal half brothers Adrian and Humphrey Gilbert. From 1580 to 1581, he served as a captain in Ireland under Lord Grey de Wilton as part of the effort to suppress the second Desmond rebellion. During this time, he presided over the brutal massacre of Continental Catholic reinforcements at Smerwick. It has been conjectured that he discovered significant letters among the possessions of the slaughtered that he used to gain entry to court in 1580.[2]

By 1581, Ralegh had captured Elizabeth's favor. His rise was swift and spectacular, grounded in his mastery of the idiom of chaste love of his sovereign expressed through the courtier's tools of wit, verse composition, dancing, and disciplined self-presentation.[3] The court buzzed with rumors about the queen's new favorite, and his ascent spurred malicious gossip and ridicule of the accent that betrayed his provincial origins. But Ralegh was more than a glittering ornament in Elizabeth's court. He quickly became a powerful administrator of the military and maritime affairs associated with the West Country and the region's most prominent representative at court.[4] After Humphrey Gilbert's death in 1583, he was given the patent for exploration in the New World, an enterprise performed by Cornwall's and Devon's sailors. In 1584, he was elected a member of Parliament for Devon, and he represented various West Country constituencies during Elizabeth's reign. He was knighted in January 1585 and shortly thereafter became vice admiral of the West, lord warden of the Stanneries, and lord lieutenant of Cornwall. His highest appointment came in 1591, when he succeeded Christopher Hatton as captain of the guard. That same year, he published his *Last Fight of the Revenge*, an account of a recent naval defeat mythologizing the bravery of a foolhardy kinsman and fostering anti-Spanish sentiment.[5] The favorite was also Elizabeth's chief agent for Devon and Cornwall affairs, and his military and maritime expertise

---

2. See Steven W. May, "How Ralegh Became a Courtier," *John Donne Journal* 27 (2008): 131–40.

3. Paul E. J. Hammer, "'Absolute and Sovereign Mistress of Her Grace'? Queen Elizabeth and Her Favourites, 1581–1592," in *The World of the Favourite*, ed. J. H. Elliot and L. W. B. Brockliss (New Haven, CT: Yale University Press, 1999), 38–53.

4. Joyce Youings, *Ralegh's Country: The South West of England in the Reign of Queen Elizabeth I* (Raleigh: America's Four Hundredth Anniversary Committee, North Carolina Department of Cultural Resources, 1986).

5. See Peter Earle, *The Last Fight of the Revenge* (London: Collins & Brown, 1992).

was directed toward both shaping public opinion and implementing crown policy.

But, though Ralegh acquired highly coveted offices, he failed to reach the loftiest heights of Elizabethan government and was not appointed a privy counselor. The fall ensuing from his 1591 secret marriage to Elizabeth Throckmorton, a maid of honor, foreclosed this possibility. This marriage undermined Ralegh's purported singular love of his aging queen, who angrily banned the couple from court and ordered their imprisonment in the Tower of London. After their release, Ralegh and his wife relocated to his estate at Sherborne. In fact, his disgrace did not lead to his exile from politics; rather, he performed duties appropriate to a provincial governor and was returned for the 1593 parliament. But salacious rumors followed him, and, in 1593, the Court of High Commission was convened to investigate rumors of his atheism that, as we will see in the next chapter, spread from the pages of confessional pamphleteering to provincial gossip. The commission disbanded after satisfactorily establishing his orthodoxy, and he continued to pursue Elizabeth's favor. In 1595, he convinced her to let him lead an expedition seeking El Dorado in Guiana. After this enterprise failed, his enemies accused him of feigning the voyage while hiding in Devon. He responded in his exculpatory 1596 *Discoverie of the Large, Rich and Bewtiful Empire of Guiana*, an eyewitness account urging English exploration of this uncolonized region.[6] Gradually, these efforts persuaded the queen to again bestow her favor. After performing a significant role in the assault on Cadiz later that year, Ralegh regained a prominent place at court, and the next year he privateered in the Azores against the Spanish treasure fleet. He and his sovereign were reconciled in her last years.

Ralegh's position, however, remained fragile. Like all counselors in the 1590s, he struggled to decipher the queen's intentions while negotiating an environment marked by hostility between aspirants to her favor. By 1591, the old guard of Elizabethan counselors such as Robert Dudley, Earl of Leicester, Francis Walsingham, and Christopher Hatton had died, and only William Cecil, Baron Burghley, remained from Elizabeth's remarkably stable group of long-term advisers.[7] The new generation of counselors lacked

6. See the excellent edition *Sir Walter Ralegh's* Discoverie of Guiana, ed. Joyce Lorimer (Aldershot: Ashgate, for the Hakluyt Society of London, 2006).

7. Wallace T. MacCaffrey, *The Shaping of the Elizabethan Regime* (Princeton, NJ: Princeton University Press, 1968), *Queen Elizabeth and the Making of Policy, 1572–1588* (Princeton, NJ: Princeton University Press, 1981), and *Elizabeth I: War and Politics* (Princeton, NJ: Princeton University Press, 1992). For this group, see, above all, Patrick Collinson, "The Monarchi-

the earlier group's capacity for collaborative action and compromise and, instead, operated with a ruthless fractiousness that had previously been reserved for those outside the regime. Burghley's son Robert Cecil and Robert Devereux, Earl of Essex, spent the 1590s maneuvering in pursuit of favor, seeking control of appointments, and plunging the precarious power structure into factional tumult.[8] Though Essex had emerged as the queen's favorite during Ralegh's disgrace, the early 1590s saw him and Ralegh periodically in a tenuous alliance. But they fell out permanently in the wake of the Cadiz expedition, when each claimed primary credit for the successes of the assault and blamed the other for the treasure fleet's escape.[9] Ralegh and Cecil allied after 1596, and Cecil's son William was educated at Sherborne.[10] The two recoiled at Essex's ill-fated rebellion, and Ralegh was slandered as cheerfully laughing through Essex's execution in 1601.

The demise of their common enemy and a dispute in the 1601 parliament weakened the Ralegh-Cecil alliance, and it fully unraveled after Elizabeth's death in 1603. During the 1590s, Cecil had been preparing for the likely ascent of James VI of Scotland. He and Henry Howard, Earl of Northampton, secured James's favor, and they held the sovereign's trust when he ascended the English throne. The cryptopapist Howard despised Ralegh for his anti-Spanish and anti-Catholic politics. He convinced James that Ralegh would not accept him as king, and Ralegh exacerbated matters by making only clumsy attempts to endear himself. Within a year of James's ascent, Ralegh was implicated in the nebulous Main Plot.[11] The prosecutor, Edward Coke, accused Ralegh of conspiring with the Spanish to depose the new monarch and promote James's cousin Arabella Stuart.

cal Republic of Queen Elizabeth I," *BJRL* 69 (1987): 394–424, and "The Elizabethan Exclusion Crisis and the Elizabethan Polity," *Proceedings of the British Academy* 84 (1994): 51–92; and Simon Adams, *Leicester and the Court: Essays on Elizabethan Politics* (Manchester: Manchester University Press, 2002).

8. For the factionalism of the 1590s, see Christopher Haigh, ed., *The Reign of Elizabeth I* (Athens: University of Georgia Press, 1985); John Guy, ed., *The Reign of Elizabeth I: Court and Culture in the Last Decade* (Cambridge: Cambridge University Press, 1988); and Paul E. J. Hammer, *The Polarisation of Elizabethan Politics: The Political Career of Robert Devereux, 2nd Earl of Essex, 1585–1597* (Cambridge: Cambridge University Press, 1999).

9. See Paul Hammer, "Myth-Making: Politics, Propaganda and the Capture of Cadiz in 1596," *HJ* 40 (1997): 621–42.

10. Walter Ralegh to Robert Cecil, Sherborne, 27 March 1600, in *The Letters of Sir Walter Raleigh*, ed. Agnes Latham and Joyce Youings (Exeter: University of Exeter Press, 1999), 188.

11. See Mark Nicholls, "Sir Walter Ralegh's Treason: A Prosecution Document," *EHR* 110 (1995): 902–24, "Treason's Reward: The Punishment of Conspirators in the Bye Plot of 1603," *HJ* 38 (1995): 821–41, and "Two Winchester Trials: The Prosecution of Henry, Lord Cobham, and Thomas Lord Grey de Wilton, November 1603," *HR* 68 (1995): 26–48.

Scheduled for execution, Ralegh was spared at the last moment, legally dead, but alive in the Tower.

Though Ralegh allegedly tried to commit suicide early in his Tower stay, before long he again assumed activities that might benefit himself and the state. Indeed, confinement kept him near the center of Jacobean affairs in a way that exile to Devon would not have. Less than two weeks after his reprieve, he had already requested a trunk containing valuable papers.[12] Early in his incarceration, he wrote discourses on potential matches for James and Anne of Denmark's children, developed a curative salve, and wrote position papers that captured the attention of Henry, Prince of Wales, whose militant anti-Spanish Calvinism stood in marked contrast to his father's ecumenical pacifism.[13] Though the chronology of these works is uncertain, Ralegh's production of such advices appears to have increased after 1607 as Cecil's effort to reform crown finances incurred growing public and royal hostility. It was at this time that Ralegh began work on the *History*.[14] Printing likely began in April 1611, when the *History* was entered in the Stationer's Register, quite possibly with Prince Henry's encouragement. Ralegh's best hope for release from the Tower seemingly perished with the prince's death in 1612, but he did not cease working on the *History* or producing counsel for Prince Charles.[15]

Two years later, Ralegh perceived the regime's descent into crisis as an opportunity. In early 1614, death and scandal unsettled the Jacobean government in both its political and its polemical ranks. Howard, who after Cecil's 1612 death became James's foremost adviser, had further alienated large swaths of the political nation, and his credibility was destroyed by his implication in the Overbury affair and his mismanagement of the "Addled Parliament."[16] When the disgraced Howard died that June, James's

---

12. Robert Cecil to George Harvey, 20 December 1603, CP MS 102/84.

13. For Prince Henry, see J. W. Williamson, *The Myth of the Conqueror: Prince Henry Stuart, a Study of 17th Century Personation* (New York: AMS, 1978). For Ralegh and alchemy, see Rattansi, "Alchemy and Natural Magic in Raleigh's *History of the World*"; and J. W. Shirley, "The Scientific Experiments of Sir Walter Ralegh, the Wizard Earl, and the Three Magi in the Tower, 1603–17," *Ambix* 1–2 (1949): 52–66.

14. Pauline Croft, "The Reputation of Robert Cecil: Libels, Public Opinion and Popular Awareness in the Early Seventeenth Century," *TRHS*, 6th ser., 1 (1991): 43–69.

15. For Ralegh's relationship with Henry, see Tennenhouse, "Sir Walter Raleigh and the Literature of Clientage"; and the important criticisms in Beer, "'Left to the World without a Maister.'"

16. For Northampton and this context, see Linda Levy Peck, *Northampton, Patronage and Policy at the Court of James I* (London: Allen & Unwin, 1982); Bellany, *The Politics of Court Scandal in Early Modern England*; and Stephen Clucas and Rosalind Davies, eds., *The Crisis of 1614 and the Addled Parliament* (Burlington, VT: Ashgate, 2002).

government found itself in the position of exceptional uncertainty. Unsuccessful efforts to manipulate Parliament had left the king impoverished and distrusted. Moreover, James's Anglican polemical apparatus was tottering no less than the political. Isaac Causabon, James's prized polemicist and conversant, had increasingly drawn public slights for his inability to speak English and association with the king's unpopular ecclesiastical settlement. He died that July while still at work on his effort to refute Cardinal Cesare Baronius's *Annales Ecclesiastici*.[17] The king was, thus, in short order deprived of his foremost scholarly and political counselors.

In England, James had always relied heavily on one powerful counselor, but the Overbury affair and Howard's recent failures compromised his ability to fill the conspicuous opening at the top of the regime with someone from the pro-Spanish, peace faction. Perceiving the possibility of regaining James's favor, Ralegh produced two works highlighting his ability to proffer learned counsel. First, he brought the *History* to an abrupt close and then pressed William Stansby, on behalf of the bookseller Walter Burre, to publish the completed portion. The work was for sale in early November 1614.[18] The decision to issue this work at this moment recognized that James was an active participant in a pan-European learned political culture and that he ascribed grave value to the moderating effect of erudite debates.[19] Ralegh hoped that the *History*'s displays of prudence and erudition would convince the king to install him at the center of a reconfigured regime, synthesizing the roles of Howard and Casaubon.

James was not swayed, recoiling instead at the intensity of Ralegh's criticism of kings.[20] The court observer John Chamberlain noted Ralegh's

---

17. William Stenhouse, "Thomas Dempster, Royal Historian to James I, and Classical and Historical Scholarship in Early Stuart England," *SCJ* 35 (2004): 397–412; Anthony Grafton and Joanna Weinberg, with Alastair Hamilton, *"I Have Always Loved the Holy Tongue": Isaac Causabon, the Jews, and a Forgotten Chapter in Renaissance Scholarship* (Cambridge, MA: Belknap Press of Harvard University Press, 2011).

18. The precise date of publication has been widely debated, but Racin (*Sir Walter Ralegh as Historian*, 11–12) definitively establishes November 1614 as the earliest possible date. Henry Broughton recorded in his copy of the *History* that he had purchased it on 11 November 1614 while imprisoned in the Fleet (UNC CSWR A4, 145), establishing the firmest ground for fixing a precise publication date in early November.

19. Compare W. B. Patterson, *King James VI and I and the Reunion of Christendom* (Cambridge: Cambridge University Press, 1997); and Anthony Milton, *Catholic and Reformed: The Roman and Protestant Churches in English Protestant Thought, 1600–1640* (Cambridge: Cambridge University Press, 1995); Paul Nelles, "The Uses of Orthodoxy and Jacobean Erudition: Thomas James and the Bodleian Library," *History of Universities* 22 (2007): 21–70; and Quantin, *The Church of England and Christian Antiquity*.

20. Beer (*Sir Walter Ralegh and His Readers*, 37–38) definitively demonstrates that James objected, not to Ralegh's project, but rather to, as James himself put it, the one-sided "de-

severe disappointment when the *History* was recalled later that year by the crown for being "too sawcie in censuring Princes."[21] Frustrated, Ralegh abandoned his historical project, but he continued to work to secure release from the Tower. He produced his "Dialogue between a Counsellor of State, and a Justice of the Peace," which suggested that he could ably manage an unruly parliament by honoring the institution's historical privileges while still implementing James's agenda.[22] In the following two years, he wrote tracts on the history of navigation and the history of warfare that contained skeletal treatments of the centuries after the end point of the *History*. At last, in 1616, the impoverished James granted Ralegh temporary freedom to seek El Dorado's gold under the proviso that he not attack the Spanish. With Ralegh abroad, the confiscated copies of the *History*, as well as a reprinting, were sold for crown profit. But the voyage proved disastrous: Ralegh neither found gold nor prevented his crew from destroying a Spanish fort, and his son Wat was killed during the raid. Ralegh may have considered fleeing to the Continent to avoid his king's ire, but instead he chose to return to England, where he was seized, tried, and, in 1618, beheaded.

Ralegh was the last surviving Elizabethan favorite and the last major statesmen from the pre-Essex period at the Jacobean court, and in his scaffold speech he idealized the queen's reign by expressing deep sympathy and love for Essex.[23] He quickly became a symbol of bygone Elizabethan glory for Englishmen dissatisfied with the Stuarts. Within a decade of his death, he had become a hero for anti-Stuart Puritans and Parliamentarians, revered as a symbol of halcyon days.[24]

But, in his own time and his own estimation, Ralegh was no Puritan

---

scription of the kings that he hates, whomof he speaketh nothing but evil" (*Letters of King James VI and I*, ed. G. P. V. Akrigg [Berkeley and Los Angeles: University of California Press, 1984], 388).

21. John Chamberlain to Dudley Carleton, London, 5 January 1615, in *The Letters of John Chamberlain*, ed. Norman Egbert McClure, 2 vols. (Philadelphia: American Philosophical Society, 1939), 1:568.

22. See Anna Beer, "Sir Walter Ralegh's Dialogue betweene a Counsellor of State and Justice of Peace," in Clucas and Davies, eds., *The Crisis of 1614 and the Addled Parliament*, 127–41, and "'Left to the World without a Maister'"; and Jan Broadway, "Political Appropriation: Reading Sir Walter Ralegh's 'Dialogue between a Counsellor of State and a Justice of Peace,'" Centre for Editing Lives and Letters, 2006, http://www.livesandletters.ac.uk/papers/SOTC_2006_01_001.pdf.

23. For his scaffold speech, see Greenblatt, *Sir Walter Ralegh*; Beer, *Sir Walter Ralegh and His Readers*, 82–108; and Andrew Fleck, "'At the Time of His Death': Manuscript Instability and Walter Ralegh's Performance on the Scaffold," *JBS* 48 (2009): 4–28.

24. See esp. Christopher Hill, *The Intellectual Origins of the English Revolution Revisited* (Oxford: Clarendon, 1997); and Beer, *Sir Walter Ralegh and His Readers*, 109–38.

or monarchomach. He was a courtier, a crown servant, and an administrator whose practices were determined by his experience in the Elizabethan regime—and he remained committed to these activities even as a captive counselor under James.

RALEGH AND TEXT IN ELIZABETHAN POLITICAL CULTURE

The bulk of Ralegh's surviving prose writings date from his Jacobean incarceration. Verse composition had been the appropriate medium to express his courtly love to Elizabeth, but he did not use poetry to appeal to his male sovereign. Rather, when seeking to attract James's favor, he composed analyses of contemporary affairs considering policy alternatives and firmly advocating a particular course of action. These texts indicate the implementation of a political practice increasingly characteristic of European governments, one grounded in the recording, circulation, and preservation of counsel and policy.[25]

Elizabethan privy counselors voraciously collected letters supplying intelligence on conditions in Britain and abroad, position papers analyzing actions available to Elizabeth and foreign princes, historical tracts offering

25. For learned counselors in early modern Europe, see Anthony Grafton and Lisa Jardine, *From Humanism to the Humanities: Education and the Liberal Arts in Fifteenth- and Sixteenth-Century Europe* (London: Duckworth, 1986); Blair, *The Theater of Nature*; John Headley, *Tommaso Campanella and the Transformation of the World* (Princeton, NJ: Princeton University Press, 1997); Howard Louthan, *The Quest for Compromise: Peacemakers in Counter-Reformation Vienna* (Cambridge: Cambridge University Press, 1997); Antonio Barrera-Osorio, *Experiencing Nature: The Spanish American Empire and the Early Scientific Revolution* (Austin: University of Texas Press, 2006); Siraisi, *History, Medicine, and the Traditions of Renaissance Learning*; Nummedal, *Alchemy and Authority in the Holy Roman Empire*; Jacob Soll, *The Information Master: Jean Baptiste Colbert's Secret State Intelligence System* (Ann Arbor: University of Michigan Press, 2009), and *Publishing the Prince*; and Alexandra Kess, *Johann Sleidan and the Protestant Vision of History* (Aldershot: Ashgate, 2008). For the English context, see Sharpe, *Sir Robert Cotton*, and *Reading Revolutions*; Anthony Grafton and Lisa Jardine, "'Studied for Action': How Gabriel Harvey Read His Livy," *P&P* 129 (1990): 30–78; Lisa Jardine, "Encountering Ireland: Gabriel Harvey, Edmund Spenser and English Colonial Ventures," in *Representing Ireland: Literature and the Origins of Conflict, 1534–1660*, ed. Brendan Bradshaw, Andrew Hadfield, and Willy Maley (Cambridge: Cambridge University Press, 1993), 60–75; Lisa Jardine and William Sherman, "Pragmatic Readers: Knowledge Transactions and Scholarly Services in Early Modern England," in *Religion, Culture and Society in Early Modern England: Essays in Honour of Patrick Collinson*, ed. Anthony John Fletcher and Peter Roberts (Cambridge: Cambridge University Press, 1996), 102–24; Sherman, *John Dee*; Hammer, *The Polarisation of Elizabethan Politics*; Thomas F. Mayer, *Reginald Pole: Prince and Prophet* (Cambridge: Cambridge University Press, 2000); and Alexandra Gajda, "The State of Christendom: History, Political Thought and the Essex Circle," *HR* 81 (2008): 423–46.

precedents legitimizing political maneuvering, and polemics imploring specific policies. Their collections teemed with considerations of the most sensitive issues of Elizabeth's reign, such as her relationships with the monarchs of France and Spain, action in the Low Countries, the presence of recusants, the proper structure and practice of the Anglican Church, the strained relations with Scotland, and, above all, the question of the succession. The surfeit of surviving evidence of their collecting such works— as well as the surge in publications patronized by powerful statesmen— testifies to the rise of a textually based mode of political practice.[26]

Ralegh did produce several written advices during Elizabeth's reign, including a 1592/93 tract on the succession, his 1596 account of the action at Cadiz, and two papers concerning war with Spain.[27] Many of his letters from this period offer counsel on military matters for correspondents such as Walsingham and Cecil.[28] He thus was one of the scores of men in Elizabeth's regime who lent their pens to evaluating policies that were then evaluated by the queen and the Privy Council. He also received manuscript position papers from those with less access than him, though in notably smaller numbers than the most powerful Elizabethan statesmen.[29]

26. See Dale Hoak, *The King's Council in the Reign of Edward VI* (Cambridge: Cambridge University Press, 1976); Mervyn James, *English Politics and the Concept of Honour, 1485–1642*, suppl. 3, *P&P* (1978); Patrick Collinson, "Puritans, Men of Business and Elizabethan Parliaments," *Parliamentary History* 7 (1988): 187–211; Michael A. R. Graves, *Thomas Norton: The Parliament Man* (Oxford: Blackwell, 1994); Markku Peltonen, *Classical Humanism and Republicanism in English Political Thought, 1570–1640* (Cambridge: Cambridge University Press, 1995); H. R. Woudhuysen, *Sir Philip Sidney and the Circulation of Manuscripts, 1558–1640* (New York: Clarendon, 1996); Stephen Alford, *The Early Elizabethan Polity: William Cecil and the British Succession Crisis, 1558–1569* (Cambridge: Cambridge University Press, 1998); Paul E. J. Hammer, "The Uses of Scholarship: The Secretariat of Robert Devereux, Second Earl of Essex, c. 1585–1601," *EHR* 109 (1994): 26–51, "Essex and Europe: Evidence from Confidential Instructions by the Earl of Essex, 1595–6," *EHR* 111 (1996): 357–81, and *The Polarisation of Elizabethan Politics*; Warren Boutcher, "Humanism and Literature in Late Tudor England: Translation, the Continental Book, and the Case of Montaigne's *Essais*," in *Reassessing Tudor Humanism*, ed. Jonathan Woolfson (Basingstoke: Palgrave Macmillan, 2002), 243–68; Natalie Mears, *Queenship and Political Discourse in the Elizabethan Realms* (Cambridge: Cambridge University Press, 2005); and Peter Beal and Grace Ioppolo, eds., *Elizabeth I and the Culture of Writing* (London: BL, 2007).

27. Others likely have been lost; in all probability, his papers were seized after his attainder and then again after his execution. They may have been lost in one of the Whitehall fires of the 1620s. The canon of Ralegh's prose writings has been much discussed. See May, *Sir Walter Ralegh*.

28. See Latham and Youings, eds., *The Letters of Sir Walter Ralegh*, passim. Compare also, e.g., the advice solicited by Walsingham from John Norris, Ralegh, and others concerning the defense of Plymouth in November 1587 (BL Add. MS 48162, fols. 4rff.).

29. Many of his waste papers were burned after his death by his clients, while those of Walsingham et al. survived with remarkable frequency. See J. W. Shirley, "Sir Walter Raleigh's

This reflected his lesser power within the governing elite—a status epitomized by his frustrated pursuit of the position of privy counselor.

Ralegh's publication of the *Last Fight of the Revenge* and the *Discovery of Guiana* similarly indicates that his role in the administration differed from that of the privy counselors, who infrequently published under their own names. The Elizabethan elite carefully orchestrated the circulation of texts intended to intervene strategically in moments of tension. But, when men such as Burghley, Walsingham, or Leicester wished to shape public opinion, they generally encouraged clients to produce polemical tracts or historical admonitions. Lesser figures within the regime, such as Thomas Norton, were among those encouraged to author texts manipulating broader sentiment. These men operated with varying degrees of independence to issue print or manuscript publications that articulated crown policy to a broader public or framed the popular interpretation of recent events.[30]

There were risks inherent in this system, however. Authors of such works hoped to pressure Elizabeth toward specific actions by mobilizing a public sphere to foment demonstrations of loyalty, but Norton, John Hales, and many others closely connected to prominent counselors were disgraced when their counsels were deemed overly aggressive. This danger prompted privy counselors to establish at least the pretense of distance from polemical publications, not wishing to hazard their participation in the formation of policy. There is no question that Ralegh aspired to achieve the place of privy counselor and was exasperated by Elizabeth's refusal. But his record of publication reveals that his position as closely resembled Norton's as it did Burghley's. Though he performed vital work for the regime through the duties associated with his crown offices, his occasional

Guiana Finances," *HLQ* 13 (1949): 55–69. BL Sloane 1133, a detailed consideration of the colonization of Guiana, is an exception.

30. See Collinson, "Puritans, Men of Business and Elizabethan Parliaments"; Graves, *Thomas Norton*; Peter Lake and Michael C. Questier, "Puritans, Papists, and the 'Public Sphere' in Early Modern England," *JMH* 72 (2000): 587–627; Natalie Mears, "Counsel, Public Debate, and Queenship: John Stubbs's *The Discoverie of a Gaping Gulf, 1579*," *HJ* 44 (2001): 629–50; Peter Lake, with Michael Questier, *The Anti-Christ's Lewd Hat: Protestants, Papists and Players in Post-Reformation England* (New Haven, CT: Yale University Press, 2002); Peter Lake, "The Politics of 'Popularity' and the Public Sphere: The 'Monarchical Republic' of Elizabeth I Defends Itself," in *The Politics of the Public Sphere in Early Modern England*, ed. Peter Lake and Steven C. A. Pincus (Manchester: Manchester University Press, 2007), 59–94, and "'The Monarchical Republic of Queen Elizabeth I' (and the Fall of Archbishop Grindal) Revisited," in *The Monarchical Republic of Early Modern England: Essays in Response to Patrick Collinson*, ed. John F. McDiarmid (Aldershot: Ashgate, 2007), 129–47; and Ethan Shagan, "The Two Republics: Conflicting Views of Participatory Local Government in Early Tudor England," in McDiarmid, ed., *The Monarchical Republic of Early Modern England*, 19–36.

role as conduit to the public suggests his inhibited ability to shape policy within the regime.

The 1603 trial cast Ralegh's position in stark relief. A central issue in the case concerned his right to possess dangerous written material.[31] Ralegh was accused of giving to a purported coconspirator a book by the anti-Scottish member of Parliament Robert Snagge denying James's right to the crown. When asked how he acquired this material, Ralegh replied that he had taken it from Burghley's house after his death in 1598. Robert Cecil claimed that he had known that Ralegh had taken geographical works but expressed disappointment that such a controversial work was taken without his approval. Cecil made clear that he "need not make any Apology on the behalfe of his father considering how usuall and necessary it is for counsellers & those in his place to interpret & keepe such kinde of writings." Cecil noted that he too possessed many texts that rightfully would be considered treasonous in the hands of others. Ralegh tried to seize support from this admission "and affirmed that as my lord Cecyll had sayd, he thought a man might fynde in his house also all the libells almost that had been made against the late Queene." But he was rebuffed: "Mr Attorney sayd he [Ralegh] was noe privy Counsellor nor he hoped ever should be. My Lo[rd] Cecyll sayd he was noe Counsellor of state but he had been called to consultation."[32] Ralegh asked how privy counselors could acquire such texts unless through the hands of trusted colleagues and why Cecil had allowed him to peruse libels were his mere knowledge of them treasonous. But the prosecution's point had been made. Ralegh did not belong to the innermost circle of Elizabethan statesmen. He was a client, trusted enough to be consulted at their discretion, but barred from the elite chambers of Elizabethan government.[33] This role was reprised shortly after Ralegh was spared execution, when Cecil surveyed the contents of his books before allowing them to the prisoner.[34]

---

31. See Rosalind Davies, "'The Great Day of Mart': Returning to Texts at the Trial of Sir Walter Ralegh in 1603," *Renaissance Forum* 4, no. 1 (1999), available at http://www.hull.ac.uk/renforum/v4no1/davies.htm.

32. BL Cotton Titus C VII, fol. 8r.

33. For example, in 1599, Cecil requested that Ralegh peruse Edward Blount's translation of Jeronimo Castenaggio's *Historie of the Uniting of the Kingdom of Portugall to the Crown of Castile* to confirm that the Catholic bias of the original text was appropriately muted. Walter Ralegh to Robert Cecil, London, 15 March 1599, in Latham and Youings, eds., *The Letters of Sir Walter Ralegh*, 187.

34. Cecil to Sir George Harvey, 20 December 1603, CP MS 102/84. Cecil was most concerned with Ralegh's copies of Philip III's will, "a discourse of SP [Spanish] government and a little collection of commonplaces."

Nevertheless, Ralegh had absorbed the textual mode of counsel, and during his imprisonment he persisted in providing written advices for royal readers. He perceived the formation of such counsel to be both his responsibility and evidence of the expertise that might win back James's elusive favor. Far from causing his political exile, then, his disgrace and incarceration forced him to engage with the Jacobean government and to orient his own activities toward advancing Stuart interests in the hope of regaining his liberty.

A BRIEF OVERVIEW OF *THE HISTORY OF THE WORLD*

The manuscript advices that Ralegh produced in the Tower demanded up-to-date information and, in some cases, a wide range of sources. But none required the effort or resources of the *History*. In order to understand his labor, the rest of the chapter will first outline the content of the massive tome, then supply an overview of how he produced it, before delineating the intellectual context that explains both the intensity of his devotion and why he constructed the *History* as he did.

The *History* begins with an allegorical frontispiece that combines a providential view of history with the Ciceronian maxim that history is "the teacher of life, the witness of times, the herald of antiquity, the light of truth, and the life of memory"[35] (see fig. 1a). The eye of Providence watches over a globe held aloft by Clio, who is labeled the "teacher of life." Icons on the globe mark significant events or places from Scripture, such as the Garden of Eden and Noah's Ark, and from Ralegh's own life, such as the Tower of London and Guiana. Clio tramples the figures of skeletal Death and emaciated Oblivion. Fama Mala and Fama Bona—one leprous, the other angelic—sound trumpets on either side. Clio is also flanked by withered Experience and flawless Truth. These figures are recessed in a temple supported by four ornamented columns. The first is adorned with images of books and labeled "times witness"; hieroglyphs representing the "herald of antiquity" ornament the second; rays engraved on the third depict the "light of truth"; and overgrown ivy festoons the fourth, "the life of memory." On the facing page, verses by Ben Jonson entitled the "Mind of the Front" explicate the image (see fig. 1b).

The text of the *History* begins with a preface in which Ralegh evokes God's omnipotence and omniscience, explaining that everything that

35. Cicero, *De oratore*, Loeb Classical Library (Cambridge, MA: Cambridge University Press, 1942), 2.9.36.

Figure 1. Frontispiece (a) and "Minde of the Front" (b) of the 1614 *History of the World*, with annotations by Henry Broughton. Sir Walter Raleigh Collection, North Carolina Collection at the University of North Carolina at Chapel Hill, UNC CSWR A3.

THE MINDE OF
THE FRONT.

FRom Death and darke Obliuion (neere the same)
The Mistresse of Mans life, graue Historie,
Raising the VVorld to good, or Euill fame,
Doth vindicate it to Æternitie.

High Prouidence would so: that nor the good
Might be defrauded, nor the Great secur'd,
But both might know their wayes are vnderstood,
And the reward, and punishment assur'd.

This makes, that lighted by the beamie hand
Of Truth, which searcheth the most hidden springs,
And guided by Experience, whose streight wand
Doth mete, whose Line doth sound the depth of things:

Shee chearefully supporteth what shee reares;
Assisted by no strengths, but are her owne,
Some note of which each varied Pillar beares,
By which as proper titles shee is knowne,

Times witnesse, Herald of Antiquitie,
The light of Truth, and life of Memorie.

transpires on earth reflects a divine pattern. After discussing Creation, he demonstrates the operations of Providence by drawing from recent historians evidence of the vicissitudes of medieval and contemporary European kingdoms that would otherwise have escaped the *History*'s temporal purview. In particular, he details how the tyrannies, violence, and theological missteps of the worst kings were divinely avenged on their successors. These accounts constitute model historical analyses linking earthly iniquity to providential retribution. The study of the past, they make clear, reveals the terrible majesty of God's infinite power, expressed above all through the creation of the world ex nihilo and then through alterations visited on humanity's faulty kingdoms.

The five books of the *History* meld two providential models of world history. The first two books each include two of the six ages, a schema best known from Augustine that divides the past into periods from Creation to the Flood, to Abraham, to David, to the Babylonian Captivity, to Christ, to the Apocalypse. Book 1 begins with Creation, then traces the settlement of the earth after Adam and Eve's expulsion from Paradise. Ralegh here narrates the sin of Cain and the corruption of the line of Seth that precipitated the Flood with which God nearly eliminated humanity. He then chronicles the repopulation of the earth, including the establishment of government under Nimrod, ending the book just before Abraham's birth. Book 2 resumes with the story of Abraham, speeding past Isaac, Jacob, and Joseph to Pharaoh's enslavement of the Israelites. Ralegh carefully works through their miraculous escape and Exodus before giving a detailed analysis of the establishment of the twelve tribes in the Holy Land. Their adoption of kingship and flourishing under Solomon gave way to decline into wickedness and idolatry, leading to the divine retribution of the Babylonian Captivity and the scattering of the tribes. Interspersed with this narrative are accounts of contemporaneous events such as the Battle of Troy and the foundation of Rome.

The organization of the subsequent three books departs from the pattern of the six ages, instead following the schema of the four monarchies, an exegetical theory derived from the Book of Daniel that traces the *translatio imperii* from the Assyrians to the Persians to the Macedonians to the Romans. Book 3 begins with the decline of the Assyrian Empire after the Captivity, then traces the meteoric rise of the Persian Empire before Xerxes' disastrous effort to subdue Greece led to its collapse. Ralegh then turns his attention to the Hellenic world, closely examining how the Athenian-led resistance to Persian encroachment sparked the Peloponnesian War. The last section examines the late fifth-century BC maneu-verings of Persia, Sparta, Athens, and Thebes, concluding in 362 BC with the Battle of Mantinea, which dissolved Hellas into weak disunity.

Book 4, like book 3, is compact by Ralegh's standards. It begins with the rise of Philip of Macedon and the emergence of Macedonia, before de-voting considerable space to Alexander the Great's military expeditions that established dominance over the entirety of the known world. After Alexander's death, as Ralegh explores in detail, his generals engaged in treachery and warfare, seeking to control regions of Alexander's dissolv-ing empire. Their chaotic wars enabled the strengthening of Rome, and Ralegh concludes the book by describing Pyrrhus's ephemeral victory over that emerging republic.

Book 5—the lengthiest of all—traces Rome's transformation from small farming community to global superpower, concentrating on its se-ries of victorious wars. The chapter begins with the First Punic War, when Rome's naval dominance of Carthage established its control of the Medi-terranean, moving then to the annihilation of Hannibal and Carthage in the Second Punic War. Ralegh then turns to the reemergence of Macedonia and the rise of the Seleucid Empire before narrating Rome's destruction of these regimes. He concludes with the Second Macedonian War in 168 BC, after which Rome reigned from Spain to Persia.[36]

Ralegh's narrative of the ancient world shifts focus over time from the Hebrews to the Persians, Greeks, and Romans. He also treats the histories of less powerful peoples and kingdoms such as the Tyrians and Sicanians within the broader framework of the largest empires. The *History*'s organi-zation firmly established it within the tradition of the universal history, a venerable genre that traced the whole of mankind as a single, interrelated narration comprehending all known peoples and cultures.[37] Not all uni-

---

36. Numerous theories have been advanced for why Ralegh terminated the narrative at this point. Tennenhouse ("Sir Walter Ralegh and the Literature of Clientage") claimed that he stopped working on the *History* in 1612 after the death of his anticipated patron, Prince Henry. Beer ("Left to the World without a Maister") saw his task as public historian as al-ready completed. I propose two nested theories. As noted above, the urgency of the moment forced him to publish what he had completed. Second, Polybius had terminated his narrative with this last triumph, signaling that it culminated Rome's domination of the known world. (See Katherine Clarke, *Between Geography and History: Hellenic Constructions of the Roman World* [Oxford: Clarendon, 1999].) Ralegh likely accepted this as a suggestive terminus since he believed that Rome still maintained tyranny over his own world.

37. Adalbert Klempt, *Die Säkularisierung der universalhistorichen Auffassung: Zum Wandel des Geschichtsdenkens im 16. und 17. Jahrhundert* (Göttingen: Musterschmidt, 1960).

versal historians commenced with the beginning of time. Early modern scholars recognized Herodotus and Polybius as practitioners of this tradition, and even Eusebius, its greatest Christian representative, began his history with Nimrod. Most Christian historians, however, had absorbed Paulus Orosius's criticism of Eusebius and chose to honor divine judgment by beginning their narratives from Creation. Otherwise, they continued to adhere to the method used by Eusebius, who emphasized literal and historical exegesis of Scripture while placing the appearance of Christ and rise of his church within pagan and Jewish historical narratives. His work and methods had, in turn, become sources and models for later church historians, and universal histories were produced, augmented, and read throughout medieval and early modern Europe.[38]

Like many sixteenth-century practitioners of universal history, Ralegh devoted immense attention to questions of technical scholarship that had arisen in the previous century. Interspersed within the stories of the Hebrews and the rise and fall of empires lay numerous labyrinthine scholarly digressions—erudite discussions of sources, explications of toponyms, and ruminations on the various names by which individual figures were known. Especially in the earlier books, Ralegh interrupted his chronological narrative with sprawling considerations of the location of the Garden of Eden, analyses of the shape and size of Noah's Ark, arguments concerning Egypt's political structure, investigations of the ancient geography of Canaan, inquiries into the antiquity of the Sicyonians, and debates concerning whether Alexander could have defeated the Romans. While most universal historians submerged their intellectual labor within the production of a steady narrative, Ralegh used the chronological narrative as a framework not only to discuss the events of the past but also to consider the authority of ancient historians and intervene in antiquarian and historical debates. The *History* was not only a narrative but also a commentary on the merits of previous interpreters. It was universal not only in narrative scope but also in the effort to adjudicate claims made about the historical workings of Providence that Ralegh found in his collection of sources. His expertise in managing this past, he hoped, would provide evidence of his prudence and of divine approbation, thus persuading his sovereign to accept his counsels.

---

38. See Don Cameron Allen, *Mysteriously Meant: The Rediscovery of Pagan Symbolism and Allegorical Interpretation in the Renaissance* (Baltimore: Johns Hopkins University Press, 1970); and Anthony Grafton and Megan Williams, *Christianity and the Transformation of the Book: Origen, Eusebius, and the Library of Caesarea* (Cambridge, MA: Belknap Press of Harvard University Press, 2006).

HOW DID RALEGH PRODUCE THE *HISTORY*?

As following chapters will demonstrate, Ralegh pieced his narrative together by synthesizing evidence from the staggering collection of sources
he kept in his Tower quarters. The five hundred volumes of his library are
known from a catalog he recorded in a notebook around 1607 as well as
from references in the *History*.[39] It is not known whether he had a preexisting library transported from Sherborne or his London lodgings to the
Bloody Tower or whether he accumulated the collection while imprisoned.
The catalog listed books according to their places on shelves that lined his
rooms, and, since it dates from his first year working on the *History*, the
library may have been accumulated deliberately for this task.[40] The works
were in six languages: Latin, English, French, Spanish, Italian, and Greek
(though he could not read the last). Few were pamphlets or short tracts.
The collection largely consisted of massive Latin folios and heavy quartos,
printed on the Continent, and arguing historical, theological, antiquarian,
and natural philosophical intricacies. Ralegh, as we will see, was at ease
in this world of erudite disputation.

It is difficult to characterize the contents of the library briefly, and the
names and titles listed below are representative rather than exhaustive.
The collection will be illuminated by further chapters, and, as Ralegh's
reading practices form the core of this book, they will not be discussed
in this brief summation. Ralegh owned works ancient and modern, celebrated and obscure. His library included plentiful historical, chronological, and geographical material to extend his universal history beyond
168 BC, suggesting the sincerity of his claim that he had "hewn out" the
contents of the two ensuing volumes that would have brought the *History*
up to his present.[41] His wide range of histories produced over the course of
literate history included those by ancient historians such as Livy and Taci-

---

39. Oakeshott, "Sir Walter Ralegh's Library." The list should not be taken as a comprehen-
sive catalog of his sources—references in the *History* to later works by Casaubon and Agostino
Tornielli, e.g., and citations in the notebook to Laelio Bisciola's 1611 *Horarum subsicivarum
Tomus* demonstrate that Ralegh continued to borrow or acquire items for his library. John
Aubrey later reported that Ralegh was a voracious reader: "He studied most in his sea voyages,
where he carried always a trunk of books along with him, and had nothing to divert him."
John Aubrey, *Brief Lives*, ed. Richard Barber (Woodbridge: Boydell, 1982), 263.

40. For a related depiction of early modern libraries, see Paul Nelles, "The Library as an
Instrument of Discovery: Gabriel Naudé and the Uses of History," in *History and the Dis-
ciplines: The Reclassification of Knowledge in Early Modern Europe*, ed. Donald R. Kelley
(Rochester, NY: University of Rochester Press, 1997), 41–57.

41. *HW*, 5.6.12.776.

tus, early medieval historians such as Jordanes and Paul the Deacon, late medieval historians such as Enguerrand de Monstrellet and Jean Froissart, and contemporaries and near contemporaries such as Jacques Auguste de Thou and Cesare Baronio. The scope of the historical works ranged from universal histories to studies of individual cities, families, or peoples, from examinations of ancient civilizations to newsbooks of contemporary events. He owned numerous works illuminating the ancient and medieval histories of other European peoples, such as those by Jean Le Maire de Belges, Robert Coenalis, Ubbo Emmius, and Wolfgang Lazius, and contemporary European histories by Nicolas Vignier and Ludovico Guicciardini. He also possessed an impressive assortment of chroniclers and historians concerned with the British past: Bede, Nennius, Gildas, Geoffrey of Monmouth, Polydore Vergil, John Leland, John Bale, William Lambarde, John Twyne, William Camden, Francis Godwin, and John Stow. He also had works by Juan de Acosta, Leo Africanus, Juan Gonzalez de Mendoza, Levinus Apollonius, and others examining ancient and modern African, Asian, and New World history.

The collection extended well beyond histories. The proverbial two eyes of history—chronology and geography—were represented by Johann Funck, Gerard Mercator, Agostino Tornielli, Daniel Angelocrator, Jean Matal, Sebastian Münster, and Heinrich Bünting, among many others. Ralegh owned theoretical tracts on the reading and writing of history by Christopher Mylaeus, David Chytraeus, Matthaeus Dresserus, Lancelot-Voisin, sieur de La Popelinière, and Johann Rosa. He had antiquarian studies by Johannes Rosinus, Claude Fauchet, Johann Wilhelm Stucki, and Paulo Manuzio. He owned at least four editions of the Bible. His collection of scriptural commentaries ranged from works by the Italian Cardinal Thomas de Vio to the Anglican controversialist Andrew Willet, from the Wittenberg Lutheran Polycarp Leyser to the French Calvinist Jean Mercier. Indeed, the collection was notably more ecumenical than its collector—Catholics, Lutherans, Calvinists, Anglicans, and pagans were all well represented. He had dictionaries, patristic classics, legal works, medical and natural philosophical compendia, commentaries on warfare, and travel narratives. And he had astronomical and astrological texts, polemics from the doctrinal conflict raging within the Anglican Church, collections of sayings and jokes, Catholic polemics, and printed commonplace books.

The collection was, however, by no means a representative sample of early modern books. Little trace can be found of the technical rhetoric with which the Renaissance is often associated—Quintilian and Erasmus are not listed, and Cicero is represented only by *De natura deorum* (though he was cited more broadly in the *History*). The library list contained only two poetic works (Petrarch and Palingenius), though Ralegh clearly was familiar with many others. Several other points about the collection merit notice. Ralegh did own a broad set of philosophical sources, though far fewer by scholastic authors than by Renaissance Neoplatonists such as Marsilio Ficino, Pico della Mirandola, and Johann Reuchlin or Mosaic philosophers such as Levinus Lemnius and Otto Casmann.[42] His theological holdings were similarly slanted toward the historical or material dimensions of these traditions; for example, though he owned several of Melanchthon's works, he owned none by Luther, and the catalog lists Calvin's Genesis commentary but not the *Institutes*.

Though Ralegh owned texts that had been composed over the entire span of the known past, the plurality of the library dated from the prior century—his was a modern collection. Most of the works that he owned are now unknown to all but a few scholars. For every work by Machiavelli or Copernicus, there were more by forgotten scholars like the Toulousain historian Antoine Noguier, who claimed that Virgil had once studied in his birthplace; or the Zurich pastor Stucki, whose *Antiquitatum Convivialium Libri* devoted nearly four hundred folio leaves to the feasts of the ancient Hebrews, Greeks, and Latins; or the Erfurt Carthusian Johannes de Indagine, whose treatise on prophetic hand reading went through at least twenty-three editions and reprints before 1676; or the Frieslander Gellius Snecanus, an early covenant theologian and precursor of Arminius.[43] Ralegh's *History* was a response to these works just as much as it was to Melanchthon or Pico, and the following chapters will repeatedly exhibit the significance of his readings of forgotten histories, chronologies, and geographies to the *History*'s construction.

In fact, while Ralegh consulted a remarkable range of sources in producing the *History*, he repeatedly referred to a core of modern authors to substantiate his points or provide convenient straw men. These included

---

42. Sachiko Kusukawa, *The Transformation of Natural Philosophy: The Case of Philip Melanchthon* (Cambridge: Cambridge University Press, 1995); and Ann Blair, "Mosaic Physics and the Search for a Pious Natural Philosophy in the Late Renaissance," *Isis* 91 (2000): 32–58.

43. Antoine Noguier, *Histoire Tolsaine* (Toulouse, 1556); Johann Wilhelm Stucki, *Antiquitatum Convivialium Libri* (Zurich, 1597); Johannes de Indagine, *Introductiones Apotelesmaticae* (Frankfurt, 1522); Gellius Snecanus, *Methodica Descriptio, et fundamentum trium locorum communium sacrae Scripturae* (Leiden, 1584).

the fifteenth-century Dominican Annius of Viterbo, the Vatican librarian Agostino Steuco, the French Calvinist Matthieu Béroalde, the Antwerpian Catholic Joannes Goropius Becanus, the Antwerpian antiquarian Abraham Ortelius, the Spanish Jesuits Benedicto Pererius and Benedicto Arias Montano, the Röstock Lutheran David Chytraeus, and the French polymath Joseph Scaliger. Only in the fourth book did ancient works supply the majority of his sources, and even then their assertions were tempered by modern commentators'. His *History* reflects his encounters with these modern scholars as much as his redaction of ancient authorities.

The extent to which Ralegh was personally responsible for composing the *History* from these sources has been questioned, largely because William Drummond reported that Ben Jonson claimed: "The best wits in *England* were imployed in making his History. *Ben* himself had written a Piece to him of the *Punick* War, which he altered, and set in his Book."[44] Jonson contributed a verse to the frontispiece of the *History*, served as tutor to Ralegh's son Wat in 1613–14, and may have acted as liaison between Ralegh and the printer Burre. If he did provide Ralegh with an account of the Punic War, it is undoubtedly possible that Ralegh took it under consideration. The same applies to contributions from Henry Percy, ninth Earl of Northumberland. In 1605, Percy was imprisoned for complicity in the Gunpowder Plot, and he brought to the Tower a sizable library, alchemical interests complementary to Ralegh's, and a retinue including former Ralegh clients, notably Thomas Harriot.[45] Harriot produced extracts of chronological works and studies of the postdiluvian settlement of the world that Ralegh may have consulted, though he did not follow them, and studies of population growth that Ralegh did use.[46] Ralegh also received visitors who may have helped him—he wrote a letter to Robert Cotton while in the Tower, for example, requesting to borrow thirteen books on British antiquities, of which two were listed in his library catalog.[47] What help he received from his chaplain, Robert Burhill, and his Tower servant,

44. William Drummond, *The Works of William Drummond* (Edinburgh, 1711), 225.

45. Compare Shirley, "The Scientific Experiments of Sir Walter Ralegh"; and G. R. Batho, "Thomas Harriot and the Northumberland Household," in *Thomas Harriot: An Elizabethan Man of Science*, ed. Robert Fox (Aldershot: Ashgate, 2000), 28–47. For Harriot more broadly, see John W. Shirley, ed., *Thomas Harriot: Renaissance Scientist* (Oxford: Clarendon, 1974); and Fox, ed., *Thomas Harriot*.

46. See BL Add. MSS 6782–89, esp. MS 6782, fols. 311r–v; MS 6786, fols. 246ff.; MS 6788, fols. 507ff.; and MS 6789, fols. 469ff. See also Barrett J. Sokol, "Thomas Harriot—Sir Walter Ralegh's Tutor—on Population," *Annals of Science* 31 (1974): 205–12.

47. Walter Ralegh to Robert Cotton, London, n.d. [ca. 1610], in Latham and Youings, eds., *The Letters of Sir Walter Ralegh*, 319.

John Talbot, similarly cannot be identified precisely.[48] But strikingly little evidence remains linking Ralegh with Camden, Cotton, Lambarde, Stow, Foxe, Verstegan, Holinshed, Dempster, Wheare, Bacon, or other British scholars associated with historical practice during Ralegh's life. And no evidence aside from Jonson's late complaint suggests that Ralegh was not, in fact, the final author of the *History*, of its many elegant passages brimming with brilliantly vivid prose as well as its endless pages of dull disputation and tedious citation. Jonson's boasting should not excite conspiracy theories of secret authorship or plagiarism in anyone aware of the expectation of collaboration among preromantic authors. The following analysis will suggest that, even if he himself did not compose—or, as we will see, translate—every last passage in the *History*, the text depended on the works he had amassed in his penal library, and the act of synthesizing these sources constituted the intellectual labor producing the text. If the *History* was a collaborative effort, it was above all a collaboration between Ralegh and the sources he collected.

RALEGH AND JAMES IN BRIEF

Excavating Ralegh's motivations in producing the *History* requires the shedding of many preconceptions concerning the work. Most previous commentators have been interested primarily in using the text to gauge the extent of Ralegh's antipathy toward James I. To modern historians, the predominant question, proceeding from the knowledge that Charles I's opponents in the Civil War perceived Ralegh as a key precedent, has been whether his criticisms amounted to license to rebellion. A vision of Ralegh as inchoately modern has been most fully expanded by Christopher Hill, who apotheosized Ralegh as a scientific, secularist, Parliamentarian republican.[49]

However much Ralegh disliked his royal captor, the following study does not support the argument that his criticisms intended either to incite rebellion or to dismantle the basis of James's rule. His position papers were, as has been noted above, for James as well as for Prince Henry, and he was disappointed by the king's response to the *History*. He never ceased

48. For the potential contributions of these last two, see May, *Sir Walter Ralegh*, 86. Burhill almost certainly performed the limited amount of Hebrew scholarship that Ralegh required. Note Ralegh's reference to a "skilfull *Hebritian*" (*HW*, 2.7.3.2.335).

49. Compare Hill, *The Intellectual Origins of the English Revolution Revisited*, 131–224. Lefranc (*Sir Walter Ralegh*), Greenblatt (*Sir Walter Ralegh*), and Beer (*Sir Walter Ralegh and His Readers*) also subscribe to a more nuanced version of this position.

his efforts to secure James's approval and release from the Tower, and, indeed, in 1616 he succeeded. A distinguished lineage of admiring royalist readers contradicts the claim that Ralegh's work was necessarily oppositional.[50] As will become clear, his discussions of kingship offer persuasive arguments for absolutism and no support for republicanism or monarchomachia. The *History* did not represent a stage of escalation toward Civil War; rather, it supports a postrevisionist argument that participants in Jacobean political life expected consensus. They were deeply disquieted at its breakdown, and, accordingly, they labored to reassert what they considered the proper traditional order rather than pressing for innovations. Efforts to alleviate conflicts often exacerbated them, but those few who did agitate for revolution incurred malicious severity. Ralegh's criticisms of James never questioned the constitutional or genealogical basis of his kingship but rather enacted well-established conventions of critical counsel to reproach the king for his conduct, the way in which he managed his court, and his pacifism. Ralegh was unquestionably seized on as a predecessor by later generations of oppositional dissidents, but he himself did not compass revolution.

Instead of viewing the *History* as motivated by antipathy toward James, scholars must examine the significance of the historical writing that Ralegh encountered in his library and articulated in the text. Ralegh possessed a majestic view of the study of the past. History, he wrote,

> hath carried our knowledge over the vast and devouring space of so many thousands of yeares, and given so faire and peircing eies to our minde, that we plainly behold living now (as if we had lived then), that great World . . . *the wise work* (saith Hermes) *of a great GOD*, as it was then, when but new to it selfe. By it I say it is, that we live in the very time when it was created: we behold how it was governed: how it was covered with waters, and againe repeopled: How Kings and Kingdomes have florished and fallen; and for what vertue and piety GOD made prosperous; and for what vice and deformity he made wretched, both the one and the other. . . . In a word, wee may gather out of History a policy no lesse wise than eternall; by the comparison and application of other mens fore-passed miseries, with our owne like errours and ill deservings.[51]

50. See chapter 6 below.
51. *HW*, A2r–v.

Histories made present the entire theater of divine creation. They allowed readers to live cognitively in all times of the world, to use the past as a providential mirror reflecting divinely approved conduct and beliefs.[52] They revealed how events had unfolded and offered a salve for an experienced reader to quell the disorder and strife searing his world. They offered a body of wisdom from which sacred principles could be elicited and emulated. And this was, to Ralegh, undoubtedly a divine gift: "GODS iudgments upon the greater and greatest, have been left to posterity; first by those happy hands which the Holy Ghost hath guided; and secondly, by their vertue, who have gathered the acts and ends of men, mighty and remarkable in the world."[53] Ralegh's text, like those of his predecessors, would complement Scripture to reform and educate humanity.

Ralegh's decision to publish in English was not a confident pronouncement that his countrymen would embrace his representation of Providence. In his preface, Ralegh made clear that he wrote despite the ill-treatment he had received, and expected to encounter again, from a hostile multitude: "Unto me it will not seeme strange, though I finde these my worthles papers torne with Rats: seeing the slothfull Censurers of all ages have not spared to taxe the Reverend Fathers of the Church, with Ambition, the severest men to themselves, with Hypocrisie, the greatest lovers of Iustice, with Popularity; and those of the truest valor and fortitude."[54] Ralegh placed himself within a martyrological tradition of despised prophets reviled in their homelands by cruel, ungodly contemporaries. The evil nature of men drove him to write. The *History*'s purpose was to edify out of existence that iniquitous mass of persecutors by constructing a guide to piety drawn from the divine meaning dimly visible in terrestrial events.

Ralegh presented the *History* as a divinely sanctioned project that directed his learning toward interpreting providential judgment and adumbrating for his readers pious truths. As such, he clearly hoped that it would allay any residual fears concerning his religious commitments. But his devotion does not provide the only explanatory context for the *History*. The text also emerged from his experience as a counselor within a European-wide political culture highly reliant on the use, circulation, and manipulation of texts. If the labor was extraordinary, the task was not. The foundations for studying the *History* consist not only in examining Ralegh's

52. See Natalie Kaoukji, "Flying to Nowhere: Mathematical Magic and the Machine in the Library" (Ph.D. diss., University of Cambridge, 2008).
53. *HW*, A2v.
54. *HW*, A2r.

personal circumstances but also in tracing the unfolding of Ralegh's context for historical study, showing how transformations in the practices of early modern historians and historical readers stimulated his project and structured his endeavors.

THE EARLY MODERN PRACTICE OF HISTORICAL COUNSEL

Understanding how Ralegh perceived the study of the past requires investigating the intellectual trajectories that reinforced each other within the culture of historical counsel of early modern Europe. Historical expertise emerged over the fifteenth and sixteenth centuries as the most treasured knowledge for aspiring counselors and practicing statesmen. This section will examine how, during this period, such individuals directed a shifting set of modes of historical analysis toward political, religious, and scholarly questions, transforming a potent humanist enterprise into an innovative, layered species of learned counsel. It will show how erudite counselors reconfigured the historically oriented culture of advice first patterned in the wreckage of fifteenth-century Italy as they spread its practices throughout Europe in the following century. While an earlier generation of Italian scholars had seen the church as one of many governments in which they might gain employment, later learned counselors, especially in Northern European governments after the Reformation, conceived of their labor as state administrators as itself ministerial. Examining the shifts in how scholars produced and wrote about histories will reveal how historical analyses became acts of state prophecy characterized by a distinct set of practices. The methods and organization of the *History* reveal Ralegh's particular inflection of this culture.

⋙

Throughout Italy in the fifteenth century, counselors, aristocrats, and civic leaders avidly read histories as guides to conduct. Their investigations addressed the instability that disrupted the peninsula as aristocratic warlords battled each other, republican city-states, and the papacy and political structures collapsed and reorganized with disorderly celerity. As larger, territorially based governments emerged from this carnage, statecraft was reconfigured. Florence, Venice, Naples, Milan, and the papacy developed sophisticated bureaucracies that collected and preserved documents to provide administrative continuity against the ravages of war. A permanent state of diplomacy required ambassadors stationed at adminis-

trative centers who were required to send frequent missives home, conveying news and information gleaned at rival courts. Learned secretaries read,
processed, and replied to these communications or devoted their mastery
of classical Latin to compose persuasive public statements.[55] These transformations in political practice stimulated the production and preservation of thickening volumes of written materials.

The counselors who staffed these governments were trained in the humanistic disciplines in schools for nobles and well-born civic leaders run
by famed teachers such as Guarino da Verona and Pier Paolo Vergerio.[56]
These teachers supplemented grammar and rhetoric with moral philosophy and history, studies considered generative of virtue. Their schools
prioritized ancient historians such as Livy and Plutarch who viewed history as a species of rhetoric. *History* in this view was predominantly understood as a Plutarchan and Ciceronian theater of exempla—a hortatory,
moral device. By observation of past particulars, the student theoretically
developed the prudence necessary to apply virtuous moral philosophy to
governance.

These humanists depicted model aristocrats as surrounded by learned
counselors, thus providing historical precedents for their own employment. Such was the logic behind the Sienese humanist Francesco Patrizi's
1450 *De regno et regis institutione*, which was dedicated to Alfonso V of
Aragon. Alfonso was reputed to remunerate historians spectacularly, and
his Neapolitan court was the setting for Lorenzo Valla's historicist debunking of *The Donation of Constantine* and Bartolommeo Facio's *De rebus gestis ab Alphonso*, an imitation of Caesar's *Commentaries*. Alfonso
himself had purportedly been cured of illness by reading a brief passage of

55. See Garrett Mattingly, *Renaissance Diplomacy* (London: Cape, 1955); Vincent Ilardi,
"Fifteenth-Century Diplomatic Documents in Western European Archives and Libraries
(1450–1494)," *Studies in the Renaissance* 9 (1962): 64–112; Gary Ianziti, *Humanistic Historiography under the Sforzas: Politics and Propaganda in Fifteenth-Century Milan* (Oxford:
Clarendon, 1988); Peter Burke, "Early Modern Venice as a Center of Information and Communication," in *Venice Reconsidered: The History and Civilization of an Italian City State,
1297–1797*, ed. John Martin and Dennis Romano (Baltimore: Johns Hopkins University Press,
2000), 389–419; Marcello Simonetta, *Rinascimento segreto: Il mondo del segretario da Petrarca a Machiavelli* (Milan: F. Angeli, 2004); Elizabeth McCahill, "Humanism in the Theater
of Lies: Classical Scholarship in the Early Quattrocento Curia" (Ph.D. diss., Princeton University, 2005); Paul M. Dover, "Deciphering the Diplomatic Archives of Fifteenth-Century Italy,"
Archival Science 7 (2007): 297–316; and Filippo de Vivo, *Information and Communication in
Venice: Rethinking Early Modern Politics* (Cambridge: Cambridge University Press, 2007).

56. Grafton and Jardine, *From Humanism to the Humanities*; Robert Black, "The New
Laws of History," *Renaissance Studies* 1 (1987): 126–56; and Paul Grendler, *Schooling in Re-
naissance Italy: Literacy and Learning, 1300–1600* (Baltimore: Johns Hopkins University
Press, 1989).

Quintus Curtius's history of Alexander. He sent special envoys to collect the alleged relic of Livy's arm bone and listened to passages from Caesar and Livy alongside his soldiers while on campaign.[57] He was, thus, receptive to Patrizi's characterization of history as "the learning which must be considered thoroughly necessary to Kings, Dukes, Emperors, and all Princes. For from it examples of all kinds of virtue can be drawn, as well as imitations of the most famous actions."[58] Patrizi cataloged the illustrious ancient kings, emperors, and commanders who heeded the counsels of learned men—thereby displaying his own suitability for the role he was praising. He concluded: "The first companions of kings and princes are learned and wise men, who help them by counsel and authority, and who illuminate royal dignity."[59]

Patrizi's ideal prince depended on expert scholars whose wisdom provided a guide to virtue and prudence. His view challenged an aristocratic, feudal model of governance in which fitness to govern derived from noble birth. Similarly, Giovanni Pontano's 1493 *De Principe*—dedicated to Alfonso's grandson Alfonso II, Duke of Calabria—praised the elder king's patronage of learned men. Like Patrizi, Pontano argued that those who disparaged erudition were dangerous: "What is so necessary as to know many things and to firmly remember them, whether the knowledge is of natural and occult things, or is the memory of past things and the examples of famous men? Unless it is thought unnecessary to know the difference between the honest and the corrupt, the good and the bad, what must be sought and what must be fled."[60] His ideal prince emanated prudence derived from moral philosophical knowledge and reinforced through interaction with learned men in counsel.

Patrizi and Pontano belonged to a reemerging Latin and Greek tradi-

---

57. See Eric Cochrane, *Historians and Historiography in the Italian Renaissance* (Chicago: University of Chicago Press, 1981); and Jerry Bentley, *Politics and Culture in Renaissance Naples* (Princeton, NJ: Princeton University Press, 1987).

58. Francesco Patrizi of Siena, *De regno et regis institutione* (Strasbourg, 1608), 105–6. "Cuius cognitio Regibus, Ducibus, Imperatoribus, & omnibus Principibus perquam necessaria habenda est. Ex ea namque omnium virtutum exempla depromuntur, & imitationes quaeque clarissimarum actionum."

59. Ibid., 25. "Sed hoc demum concludendum censeo, primos Regum ac principum comites esse doctos ac sapientes viros, qui & consilio & auctoritate adjuvant & regiam dignitatem illustrant."

60. Giovanni Gioviano Pontano, *De Principe* (1493; Roma: Salerno, 2003), 29. "Quid est enim, per Christum, tam necessarium quam multa scire atque ea tum in cognitione naturae et rerum occultarum, tum in memoria rerum praeteritarum et clarorum virorum exemplis posita? Nisi si quid honestum quid turpe, quid bonum quid malum, quid expetendum contra quid fugiendum."

tion that sought to imitate Cicero and Plutarch. In their formulation, historical exempla directed attentive readers to philosophical truth, which, in turn, stimulated virtuous action. Their past consisted of a disarrayed catalog of acceptable and disreputable behavior. It was an instrument for those whose function was to incite virtue.

As the practices of humanism circulated beyond the Italian peninsula from the late fifteenth century, so too did the model of the learned counselor. Over the sixteenth century, European governments increasingly operated with the assumption that kings were best served when surrounded by individuals whose education ensured prudence. Ralegh's *History* sought to evoke this tradition as he hoped that the learning and virtue displayed in it would convince James to mobilize his considerable imprisoned wisdom.

ANNIUS OF VITERBO AND THE PROPHESYING OF NEW PASTS

Humanist reverence of pagan antiquity within the political culture of the Italian Peninsula, however, alarmed many who believed that Christians erred when they imitated those not blessed with knowledge of revelation. Well before Erasmus and Luther decried papal Rome's paeans to Jove, at least one partisan of the papal curia revolted against the humanists by challenging the validity of their historical narrative and scholarly methods. This attack came from the notorious Dominican Annius of Viterbo.[61]

Annius was convinced that his Etruscan ancestors had been favored with divine approval to rival that of the Jews, a belief that he bulwarked through a series of forgeries. He distrusted the works of classical antiquity prized by contemporary scholars, for the ancient Greeks and their pagan Roman inheritors, Annius maintained, had occluded the true past

---

61. There is a wonderful range of literature on Annius. See Walter Stephens, "Berosus Chaldaeus: Counterfeit and Fictive Editors of the Early Sixteenth Century" (Ph.D. diss., Cornell University, 1979), *Giants in Those Days: Folklore, Ancient History, and Nationalism* (Lincoln: University of Nebraska Press, 1989), and "When Pope Noah Ruled the Etruscans: Annius of Viterbo and His Forged *Antiquitates*," *MLN* 119, suppl. (2004): S201–S223; C. R. Ligota, "Annius of Viterbo and Historical Method," *JWCI* 50 (1987): 44–56; Anthony Grafton, "Invention of Traditions and Traditions of Invention in Renaissance Europe: The Strange Case of Annius of Viterbo," in *The Transmission of Culture in Early Modern Europe*, ed. Anthony Grafton and Ann Blair (Philadelphia: University of Pennsylvania Press, 1990), 8–38, and *Forgers and Critics: Creativity and Duplicity in Western Scholarship* (Princeton, NJ: Princeton University Press, 1990); Ingrid Rowland, *The Scarith of Scornello: A Tale of Renaissance Forgery* (Chicago: University of Chicago Press, 2004); and Brian Curran, *The Egyptian Renaissance: The Afterlife of Ancient Egypt in Early Modern Italy* (Chicago: University of Chicago Press, 2007).

by disparaging their neighbors as barbarians, taking credit for admirable arts that they did not invent, and corrupting arts that they had inherited. To uncover their lies, Annius forged extracts that he attributed to ancient chroniclers such as Berosus the Chaldean or Megasthenes the Persian— whom he called Metasthenes—who were dimly known from surviving sources to have worked from official records. These forgeries gave detailed accounts of periods of ancient history that had previously seemed utterly irretrievable. He invented descendants of Noah to populate these shadowy pasts, creating a family tree for all peoples from Creation onward. After the Flood, Annius's forgeries showed, Noah had maintained the true religion while coordinating his descendants' plantation of the world from his seat in Etruria. Though heterodoxy ceaselessly sprung up in disparate locales, many communities in the ancient world adhered to the true religion, and Annius praised ancestors of prominent European dynasties— especially his Borgia patron—for the defense of orthodoxy. He equipped these concocted sources with commentaries written in his own name, in which he cited both authentic and forged sources to corroborate his interpretations. When published in 1498 as *Vetustissimi Auctores*, the whole was a vertiginous, self-supporting labyrinth of citation that was proof that Etruria had been the capital of a proto-Christian civilization that had been inherited by Christian Rome and was more glorious and ancient than the Hebrew, pagan Roman, or Greek traditions it subsumed.[62] Though within a decade of their publication Raffaele Maffei and others rejected his textual recoveries as forgeries, Annius exerted an impact well into the seventeenth century.

For all the novelty of his vision, Annius reconfigured existing practices to create his glimmering apparition of the past.[63] Above all, he invented what contemporaneous philologists analyzed, fabricating spurious etymologies and historical figures. Many in the ancient world, he argued, were known by different names to different communities, and identifying the single figure behind multiple names allowed local myths to be synthesized into a unified history. On this principle, he creatively correlated the names of Noah's forged progeny with the names of regions and cities, thus making the plantation progress as he wished.

62. Annius of Viterbo, *Berosi Sacerdotis Chaldaici, Antiquitatum Italiae ac totius orbis libri* (1498; Antwerp, 1552).

63. For Annius's medieval precedents, see Grafton, *Forgers and Critics*; Andrew Jotischky, *The Carmelites and Antiquity: Mendicants and Their Pasts in the Middle Ages* (Oxford: Oxford University Press, 2002); and Alfred Hiatt, *The Making of Medieval Forgeries: False Documents in Fifteenth-Century England* (London: BL/University of Toronto Press, 2004).

Annius also adapted the approaches of previous historians who had questioned the accuracy of surviving records. While he may have known of Geoffrey of Monmouth and similar dubious chroniclers, his forged texts subsumed ancient sources rather than ignoring them, and his commentaries brimmed with references to authentic citations from Diodorus Siculus, Dionysius of Halicarnassus, and others. Citing legitimate sources to corroborate his falsehoods constituted one of his most effective strategies and marked his work as distinct from those of medieval fabulists. His efforts more closely followed the example of Leonardo Bruni's *Historiae Florentini Populi*. Bruni had conjured a legendary advanced civilization of Etruria by alleging flaws in Roman sources and magnifying the significance of fragmentary evidence of Florence's past.[64] The rhetorical style and construction of Bruni's history, however, unmistakably sought to honor Florence with a masterful Livian history. Though adversarial, the history produced by this paragon of humanism was firmly imitative. Annius's work, on the other hand, consisted of rhetorically thin forgeries of ancient annals engulfed in thick commentaries, compilations more reminiscent of scholastic teaching tools than Aldine editions. Both in format and in narrative, Annius sought to discredit humanist scholarship as modeled on pagan liars and intellectual thieves while absorbing their sources into his own idiosyncratic vision.[65]

Annius's work utterly unsettled the historical understanding of early modern scholars. It questioned the uniqueness of God's relationship with the Jews. It disparaged the learning of the Greeks and attributed to the Italian Peninsula theological magnificence a millennium before Christ. It gave solid historical foundations to mythological dynastic origins. Above all, it suggested that the history in Scripture could not be fully understood unless supplemented by his texts. His vision dramatically altered the practices and debates of the next generations of historians. The most substantial historical work of the sixteenth century addressed his claims as much as those of Livy, Polybius, Tacitus, or any genuine ancient. Scholars wrote new histories expanding his narrative as well as vilifying condemnations. While many admirers explicitly acknowledged their Annian debt, others

---

64. See Riccardo Fubini, "Osservazioni sugli *Historiarum florentini populi libri xii di Leonardo Bruni*," in *Studi di storia medievale e moderna per Ernesto Sestan*, 2 vols. (Florence: Leo S. Olschki, 1980), 1:429–32; and Gary Ianziti, "Challenging Chronicles: Leonardo Bruni's *History of the Florentine People*," in *Chronicling History: Chroniclers and Historians in Medieval and Renaissance Italy*, ed. Sharon Dale, Alison Williams Lewin, and Duane J. Osheim (University Park: Pennsylvania State University Press, 2007), 249–72.

65. For this point in particular, see Stephens, "Berosus Chaldaeus."

tacitly embedded his work in their histories. Even scholars who knew his texts were forged cited them when they offered support, and others defended Annius by claiming that his conjectures likely reproduced the authentic texts.[66]

Though Annius's texts compromised the credibility of ancient Roman and Greek histories, they did not detract from the value of historical knowledge. On the contrary, his spidery narrative of world settlement became a robust instrument for propagandists praising the antiquity of crowns and peoples. While his forged sources were cited frequently, more often poached was his account of postdiluvian European plantation. Throughout Europe, scholars used his vision—though minimizing his glorious Etruscan past—to conjure illustrious pasts for their royal patrons. In France, for example, his texts were a fertile source for the royal historiographer, Jean Le Maire de Belges, who saw the simultaneous diffusion of orthodox practices as supporting a conciliarist, Gallican church politics, in which Rome was only one of a number of nodes of divinely licensed religious practice. Many French historians after Le Maire further developed this vision, combining Annian evidence with adversarial readings of Livy, Caesar, and Ammianus Marcellinus to depict an ancient Gaul characterized by a pious citizenry, political sophistication, military prowess, and advanced forms of learning.[67]

Annius's claims could be manipulated to support all manner of ecclesiastical and political belief. For example, the Braunschweig court historian Reinier Reineck's 1594–97 *Historia Julia*, a gargantuan universal history, foretold a Lutheran Holy Roman Empire as the apocalyptic summation of world history. Reineck continued the project of Melanchthon's 1532 *Chronica Carionis*, which had also drawn from Annius information about ancient civilizations—especially the forefathers of the Germans—

66. See esp. ibid.; Grafton, *Forgers and Critics*; and Ligota, "Annius of Viterbo and Historical Method."

67. Compare Stephens, *Giants in Those Days*. For early modern French historiography, see Donald R. Kelley, *The Foundations of Modern Historical Scholarship: Language, Law and History in the French Renaissance* (New York: Columbia University Press, 1970); George Huppert, *The Idea of Perfect History: Historical Erudition and Historical Philosophy in Renaissance France* (Urbana: University of Illinois Press, 1970); Claude-Gilbert Dubois, *Celtes et Gaulois au XVIe siècle: Le développement littéraire d'un mythe nationaliste* (Paris: J. Vrin, 1972), and *La conception de l'histoire en France au XVIe siècle* (Paris: A.-G. Nizet, 1977); Orest Ranum, *Artisans of Glory: Writers and Historical Thought in Seventeenth-Century France* (Chapel Hill: University of North Carolina Press, 1980); R. E. Asher, *National Myths in Renaissance France: Francus, Samothes and the Druids* (Edinburgh: Edinburgh University Press, 1993); and Marie-Dominique Couzinet, *Histoire et méthode à la Renaissance* (Paris: J. Vrin, 1996).

unmentioned in Scripture but disparaged by the Greeks.[68] Annius's histories were used for local histories as well. Perhaps his most faithful successor was the Antwerpian Catholic physician Johannes Goropius Becanus. In his 1569 *Origines Antwerpianae*, Goropius attacked Annius as a forger, but he himself invented and manipulated philological and archaeological evidence to recalibrate the resting spot of Noah's Ark, the progress of the plantation, and the subsequent history of his Frisian ancestors. He demonstrated that they had been uniquely absent from the Tower of Babel and were, thus, exempt from the confusion of languages. This divine favor, he argued, was a sign that the Antwerpians were God's chosen people, which he hoped would compel his work's dedicatee, Philip II, to sweep into the Low Countries in defense of the besieged city.[69]

Annius had British proponents too. Geoffrey of Monmouth's defenders used Annian sources and techniques to depict a vibrant pre-Roman Britain that challenged the conception of the barbaric wasteland that Polydore Vergil had seen no reason to describe in his *Historia Anglica*. These advocates included the Henrician antiquarians John Leland and John Bale and the Canterbury schoolmaster John Twyne. Twyne drew evidence from the genealogies in Annius's Berosus that Britain had been called *Albion* after its first settler, who, before Troy's foundation or the birth of Moses, crossed an isthmus connecting Gaul and Britain that had since eroded.[70] He believed that Caesar had unfairly disparaged a civilized, pious people descended from Phoenicians who had colonized the island to control Cornwall's tin mines.[71] Annius continued to shape the production of Brit-

---

68. For early modern German and Holy Roman imperial historiography, see Gerald Strauss, *Sixteenth Century Germany: Its Topography and Topographers* (Madison: University of Wisconsin Press, 1959); Frank L. Borchardt, *German Antiquity in Renaissance Myth* (Baltimore: Johns Hopkins University Press, 1971); Marie Tanner, *The Last Descendant of Aeneas: The Hapsburgs and the Mythic Image of the Emperor* (New Haven, CT: Yale University Press, 1993); and Asaph Ben-Tov, *Lutheran Humanists and Greek Antiquity: Melanchthonian Scholarship between Universal History and Pedagogy* (Leiden: Brill, 2009).

69. For Spanish and Habsburg historiography, see Robert Brian Tate, *Ensayos sobre la historiografía peninsular del siglo XV* (Madrid: Gredos, 1970); Richard Kagan, "Clio and the Crown: Writing History in Hapsburg Spain," in *Spain, Europe, and the Atlantic World: Essays in Honour of John H. Elliot*, ed. Richard L. Kagan and Geoffrey Parker (Cambridge: Cambridge University Press, 1995), 73–100, and *Clio and the Crown: The Politics of History in Medieval and Early Modern Spain* (Baltimore: Johns Hopkins University Press, 2009); and A. Katie Harris, *From Muslim to Christian Granada: Inventing a City's Past in Early Modern Spain* (Baltimore: Johns Hopkins University Press, 2007).

70. John Twyne, *De Rebus Albionicis, Britannicis atque Anglicis, commentariorum libri* (London, 1590), 9, 15ff., 93–94.

71. Ibid., 41–43.

ish histories—the early history of Britain in Holinshed's *Chronicle* drew
primarily on Annius's works, Richard Lynche published a free translation
of Annius in 1601, and George Owen Harry's 1604 genealogy of James used
Annius to trace James's ancestry to Noah.[72]

Ralegh owned many Annian histories, including aforementioned works
by Le Maire de Belges, Goropius, Twyne, Reineck, Bale, and Leland as well
as Franz Irenicus's 1518 *Exegesis historiae Germaniae*, Antoine Noguier's
1556 *Histoire Tolsaine*, Robert Coenalis's 1557 *Gallica Historia*, Wolfgang
Lazius's 1557 *De gentium aliquot migrationibus*, Jean Chameau's 1566
Histoire du Berry, and Pierre de Sainct Julien's 1581 *De l'Origine des Bour-*
gongnons. He also owned numerous critics. Confutations of Annian materials lace scriptural commentaries such as Pererius's omnicompetent Genesis commentary, the *Hexapla* of the Anglican controversialist Willett,
and the intensely literalist commentary of the French Calvinist Mercier.
Ralegh also owned the 1598 *Historia Antiqua* of Gaspar Varrerius, which
Camden complimented as the most systematic dismantling of Annius's
credibility.[73]

The extent and significance of Annian influence should now be clear.
Scholars wrested Annius's forged sources to support all religious positions,
retell local or global histories, and, thus, challenge the Greek and Roman
traditions or integrate them into grander syntheses. Annius's claim to
have unearthed new sources spurred others to hunt for lost sources. But,
above all, this flourishing scholarly industry generated controversies. For
those such as Ralegh seeking to depict the deep past, the ancient world
was not strictly that described in the Bible and authentic Latin and Greek
works. Historians did not share a consensus on what had taken place in
the past or on the best means of establishing a stable narrative. The most
illuminating texts to some were dangerous forgeries to others. What had
taken place in the ancient world was a source of widespread contention
and little agreement.[74] The task assumed by Ralegh demanded the judi-
cious evaluation of a bewildering array of histories that proclaimed the
mendacity of their rivals while proposing wildly discordant visions of the
ancient world.

---

72. George Owen Harry, *The Genealogy of the High and Mighty Monarch, James* (London,
1604); Richard Lynche, *An Historical Treatise of the Travels of Noah into Europe* (London,
1601).

73. See T. C. Skeat, "Two 'Lost' Works by John Leland," *EHR* 65 (1950): 507.

74. For the consequences of this environment, see my "Ocean of Lies: The Problem of
Historical Evidence in the Sixteenth Century," *HLQ* 74 (2011): 375–400.

HISTORY BECOMES EXPERIENCE

The model of the learned counselor thrived in various forms in the sixteenth century. Most famously, Erasmus's 1516 *Institution of the Christian Prince* became the manual of the virtuous counselor renowned for moral philosophical rigor, and James I's *Basilikon Doron* later emerged from this Christian humanist tradition.[75] Despite—or perhaps because of—the Annian challenge, the study of history increasingly assumed a central role, aided by shifts in the preferences that scholars and politicians demonstrated toward ancient historians. Though Polybius was still not widely read, his historical methodology was gaining traction.[76] Polybius subscribed to the Greek definition of history as "inquiry," focusing on the investigation of causes and motivations by disciplined analysis of material factors. He identified three tools for the historian: the study and collation of documents, geographical knowledge, and experience in political matters.[77] Application of these tools, he explained, enabled the construction of narratives that accurately portrayed processes of causation, rather than merely supplying moral exempla. Masterful knowledge of the material ways in which actors and influences shaped events constituted the primary lode of the investigator of the past.[78]

In Polybius's depiction, recognizing causation in the past supplied experience for evaluating the present.[79] Several influential scholars began in the 1530s to disseminate this conception of the utility of historical knowledge. In his 1531 *De tradendis disciplinis*, the Spanish humanist and theo-

75. For the endurance of this tradition in England, see John Guy and Alistair Fox, *Reassessing the Henrician Age: Humanism, Politics and Reform, 1500–1550* (New York: Blackwell, 1986); and Margo Todd, *Christian Humanism and the Puritan Social Order* (Cambridge: Cambridge University Press, 1987).

76. For the Renaissance reception of Polybius, see George H. Nadel, "Philosophy of History Before Historicism," *History and Theory* 3 (1964): 291–315; Peter Burke, "A Survey of the Popularity of Ancient Historians, 1450–1700," *History and Theory* 5 (1966): 135–52; Arnaldo Momigliano, "Polybius' Reappearance in Western Europe," in *Essays in Ancient and Modern Historiography* (Middletown, CT: Wesleyan University Press, 1987), 79–98; and the introduction to Gianna Pomata and Nancy G. Siraisi, eds., *Historia: Empiricism and Erudition in Early Modern Europe* (Cambridge, MA: MIT Press, 2005).

77. Polybius 12.25e.442.

78. Polybius 12.25h.446–47.

79. Similarly, some contemporaries conceived of history as a form of social medicine. See Nancy Siraisi, "Anatomizing the Past: Physicians and History in Renaissance Culture," *RQ* 53 (2000): 1–30, and *History, Medicine, and the Traditions of Renaissance Learning*; Jacob Soll, "Healing the Body Politic: French Royal Doctors, History and the Birth of a Nation, 1560–1634," *RQ* 55 (2002): 1259–86; and Pomata and Siraisi, eds., *Historia*.

logian Juan Luis Vives explained: "Practical wisdom is increased by experience. . . . Experience is either our own individually, or that obtained by others, which may serve to warn us, by the example of past occurrences such as are contained in histories, fables, stories, and similitudes. Briefly, experience may be gained from all accounts of things which are handed down as having been said or done, or, again, from those writings which have been composed and are suited to instruct men in wisdom." Study of the past retained an exemplary function, but it was primarily a school of experience supplying material to be archived in the prudent counselor's memory. Vives described this function repeatedly: "We gain our experiences by course of time in the pursuit of practical affairs. What has happened to others, we get to know from the memory of past ages, which is called history. This brings about the state in which we seem to be not less interested in past ages than in our own, and we can continually make use of their experience as well as that of our own times."[80] He thus transformed history from a collection of moral exemplars to a repository of experience in practical affairs. It was no longer primarily a method for acquiring virtue but had become the basis for experiential prudence.

Across the Channel that same year, Thomas Elyot's *The Boke of the Governour* also disseminated the notion that history constituted surrogate experience. The *Boke* went through eight editions in the sixteenth century and articulated in the vernacular ideas that learned humanists gleaned from Latin texts. Though Elyot complimented Erasmus, his description of the education befitting noble sons drew more substantially from Patrizi's and Pontano's emphasis on historical counsel. But he did not rehash their view of the past as a repository of moral exempla. Like Vives, he depicted history as a theater of experience, claiming that of "suche persons, as do contempne auncient histories reputing them amonge leasinges and fantasies . . . it may be sayd, that they frustrate Experience."[81] History, rather than moral philosophy or theology, provided the bedrock of noble education because it revealed the causes of events. He emphasized that "counsaylers garnished with learning, and also experience, shall there-by consider the places, times and personages, examining the state of the mat-

---

80. Juan Luis Vives, *On Education: A Translation of the De tradendis disciplinis of Juan Luis Vives*, trans. Foster Watson (Cambridge: University Press, 1913), 38, 230.

81. Thomas Elyot, *The Boke Named the Governour* (London, 1580), 203v. Elyot may have read Vives or come into contact with him during one of Vives's many stays in England. For Elyot, see F. W. Conrad, "The Problem of Counsel Reconsidered: The Case of Sir Thomas Elyot," in *Political Thought and the Tudor Commonwealth: Deep Structure, Discourse and Disguise*, ed. Paul A. Fideler and T. F. Mayer (London: Routledge, 1992), 75–107.

ter, than practised, and . . . revolving longe and oftentimes in their mindes, things that be passed, and conferring them to the matters that bee in their experience, studiously doe seeke out the reason and manner, how that which is by them approved may be brought to effect."[82] The study of the past furnished a method of increasing experience to better observe events and discern causation, and the experience gained by knowledge of past events, rather than virtue inherited by blood or conduct, distinguished those fit to govern. Empirical analysis of both texts and events supplied the expertise most suited to advise princes.

Vives's and Elyot's vision was shared by many contemporaries; Machiavelli's *The Prince* and *The Discourses on Livy*, both first published in 1531, represented its most extreme forms.[83] The function of history that such men espoused made historical analysis of causation the primary source of wisdom. Accordingly, Ralegh used the *History* to showcase his expertise in discerning causation, rather than reducing it to studies of the virtue and vice of ancient figures—though he did include these too in his work. This consonance of historical study and experience also supplied him with a lucid explanation for why his role in Elizabeth's government qualified him to engage in minute analyses of the ancient past. His historical acumen was, in turn, taken to magnify his considerable personal experience in daily affairs, a percussive logic that allowed him to substantiate his claims to wisdom and prudence.

CAUSATION, ANTIQUARIANISM, AND ECCLESIASTICAL HISTORY

Scholars soon began composing histories that prioritized exposing the causal process of events over narrative description. In their efforts to do so, they expanded the range of sources they consulted. To produce his *Storia d'Italia* (completed between 1537 and 1540 but unpublished until 1561), explaining Italy's descent into chaos after Charles VIII of France's invasion, the Florentine aristocrat Francesco Guicciardini rooted through the letters, proclamations, and treaties in the houses of the Florentine nobility.[84] This technique was directed at ecclesiastical history as well.

---

82. Elyot, *The Boke Named the Governour*, 214v.

83. See Felix Gilbert, *Machiavelli and Guicciardini: Politics and History in Sixteenth-Century Florence* (Princeton, NJ: Princeton University Press, 1965); and Victoria Kahn, "Reading Machiavelli: Innocent Gentillet's Discourse on Method," *Political Theory* 22 (1994): 539–60.

84. See Gilbert, *Machiavelli and Guicciardini*.

For example, the Rhineland diplomat Johannes Sleidan's 1556 *Commentariorum de statu religionis et republicae libri* narrated the course of
the Reformation using records compiled and obtained from friends made
during his two decades of service to various political and ecclesiastical
entities.[85] In the latter half of the sixteenth century, ecclesiastical historians directed this document-oriented methodology at the deeper past.
The Reformation and Counter-Reformation ecclesiastical histories of Flacius Illyricus, Baronius, and Foxe assembled both narrative and nonnarrative sources to map transformations in the ancient and medieval worlds.
While their practices may have resembled those of Guicciardini's secular
history, however, they derived from methods internal to the tradition of
ecclesiastical history.

Sixteenth-century ecclesiastical historians perceived church history
as in disarray.[86] They were particularly suspicious of the monastic chroniclers who constituted their medieval authorities.[87] These monks exercised
an older, philosophical convention of describing the past as the writer
felt it ought to have transpired. The Carmelites, for example, devised a
celebratory lineage for their order that extended back to Elijah. This convention prompted widespread forgeries of official documents and had supported Annius's histories as well.[88] Interpreting the chronicles of medieval
monks was a foremost concern of Protestant ecclesiastical historians, who
traced the corruption of the true church through these sources. But, despite their distrust of monks, they eagerly adopted other elements of monastic historical practice.

In fact, the ex-Carmelite John Bale was one of the foremost produc-

85. Donald Kelley, "Johann Sleidan and the Origins of History as a Profession," *JMH* 52
(1980): 573–98; Kess, *Johann Sleidan*. Sleidan knew other methods for producing histories. His
De quattuor summis imperiis derived from the four monarchies tradition given currency by
Melanchthon's *Chronica Carionis*, and both exclusively drew on historical narratives for their
sources.

86. John M. Headley, *Luther's View of Church History* (New Haven, CT: Yale University
Press, 1963); William McCuaig, *Carlo Sigonio: The Changing World of the Late Renaissance*
(Princeton, NJ: Princeton University Press, 1989); Simon Ditchfield, *Liturgy, Sanctity and His-
tory in Tridentine Italy: Pietro Maria Campi and the Preservation of the Particular* (Cam-
bridge: Cambridge University Press, 1995); Irena Backus, *Historical Method and Confessional
Identity in the Era of the Reformation (1378–1615)* (Leiden: Brill, 2003); Alison Knowles Fra-
zier, *Possible Lives: Authors and Saints in Renaissance Italy* (New York: Columbia University
Press, 2005).

87. See Beryl Smalley, *English Friars and Antiquity in the Early Fourteenth Century*
(New York: Barnes & Noble, 1961); Jotischky, *The Carmelites and Antiquity*; and Chris Given-
Wilson, *Chronicles: The Writing of History in Medieval England* (London: Hambledon Con-
tinuum, 2004).

88. See Hiatt, *The Making of Medieval Forgeries*.

ers of document-based Reformation ecclesiastical histories. On leaving the Carmelites around 1536, Bale became one of England's most ardent reformers. But, both before and after his conversion, he traveled to monasteries throughout England, France, and the Low Countries, transcribing into duodecimo volumes extracts from chronicles, charters, and letters pertaining to the Carmelite order.[89] Though after his conversion he used these notes as sources for antipapal polemics, while still in the order he was already performing such archetypal antiquarian activities as recording materials that he encountered in monastic cartularies.[90]

After his conversion, Bale was joined in antiquarian activities by the royal chaplain, John Leland.[91] They believed their task to be the divinely sponsored reconstitution of England's past—a necessary step in reformation that had been hindered, paradoxically, by the plundering of monastic

89. BL Cotton Titus D X. See Andrew Jotischky, "Gerard of Nazareth, John Bale and the Origins of the Carmelite Order," *Journal of Ecclesiastical History* 46 (1995): 214–36.

90. For antiquarianism, see Arnaldo Momigliano, "Ancient History and the Antiquarian," *JWCI* 13 (1950): 285–315; Anthony Grafton, "The Ancient City Restored: Archaeology, Ecclesiastical History, and Egyptology," in *Rome Reborn: The Vatican Library and Renaissance Culture,* ed. Anthony Grafton (Washington, DC: Library of Congress, 1993), 87–124; Leonard Barkan, *Unearthing the Past: Archaeology and Aesthetics in the Making of Renaissance Culture* (New Haven, CT: Yale University Press, 1999); Peter N. Miller, *Peiresc's Europe: Learning and Virtue in the Seventeenth Century* (New Haven, CT: Yale University Press, 2000), and "The 'Antiquarianization' of Biblical Scholarship and the London Polyglot Bible (1653–57)," *JHI* 62 (2001): 463–82; William Stenhouse, *Reading Inscriptions and Writing Ancient History: Historical Scholarship in the Late Renaissance* (London: Institute of Classical Studies, University of London School of Advanced Study, 2005); Martin Mulsow, "Antiquarianism and Idolatry: The *Historia* of Religions in the Seventeenth Century," in Pomata and Siraisi, eds., *Historia,* 181–210; Jonathan Sheehan, "Sacred and Profane: Idolatry, Antiquarianism and the Polemics of Distinction in the Seventeenth Century," *P&P* 192 (2006): 35–66, and "Temple and Tabernacle: The Place of Religion in Early Modern England," in *Making Knowledge in Early Modern Europe: Practices, Objects, and Texts, 1400–1800,* ed. Pamela H. Smith and Benjamin Schmidt (Chicago: University of Chicago Press, 2007), 248–72; Peter N. Miller, ed., *Momigliano and Antiquarianism: Foundations of the Modern Cultural Sciences* (Toronto: University of Toronto Press, 2007); and Carina L. Johnson, "Stone Gods and Counter-Reformation Knowledges," in Smith and Schmidt, eds., *Making Knowledge in Early Modern Europe,* 233–48. For Bale in this context, see McKisack, *Medieval History in the Tudor Age;* Honor C. McCusker, *John Bale: Dramatist and Antiquary* (Bryn Mawr, PA, 1942); and Jotischky, *The Carmelites and Antiquity.*

91. Leland had traveled to France, where he earned the praises of such luminaries as Guillaume Budé and Jacques Lefevre d'Etaples. While there, he was likely exposed to the antiquarian movement exemplified by the Italian antiquarians Poggio Bracciolini, Flavio Biondi, and Cyriac of Ancona, who recorded the ruins, landscapes, and appellatives of places they visited. See James Patrick Carley, "John Leland in Paris: The Evidence of His Poetry," *Studies in Philology* 83 (1986): 1–50; and Jennifer Summit, "Leland's *Itinerary* and the Remains of the Medieval Past," in *Reading the Medieval in Early Modern England,* ed. Gordan McMullan and David Matthews (Cambridge: Cambridge University Press, 2007), 159–78, and *Memory's Library.*

libraries sparked by Henry VIII's 1534 Dissolution of the Monasteries.[92] As Bale explained in his 1549 commentary on Leland's *New Year's Gift*, their assiduous pursuit of dispersed sources had revealed the process by which Rome usurped supremacy over the English church. Analyzing earlier English histories, Bale explained, clarified which rites were superstitious corruptions introduced by the pope and which were properly orthodox. He argued that the works of virtuous British writers ought to be printed, and he claimed the occlusion of such valuable monuments of Christian practice accounted for religious practices infected by popishness.[93] He attempted to bring this process to light in his 1548 *Illustrium Maioris Britanniae Scriptorum . . . Summarium*, a chronological dictionary of British writers modeled on the biobibliographic tradition of Saint Jerome's *De viris illustribus*.[94]

Bale had clear precedents in mind for scholarly and pious travel, pursuing long-buried ancient texts that would reveal obfuscated Christian ortho-

92. For the impact of the dissolution, see Neil R. Ker, "The Migration of Manuscripts from the English Medieval Libraries," *The Library*, 4th ser., 23 (1942): 1–11, and "Sir John Prise," *The Library*, 5th ser., 10 (1955): 1–24; and J. P. Carley, "Monastic Collections and Their Disposal," in *The Cambridge History of the Book in Britain*, vol. 4, *1557–1695*, ed. John Barnard and Donald F. McKenzie, with the assistance of Maureen Bell (Cambridge: Cambridge University Press, 2002), 339–47, and "The Dispersal of the Monastic Libraries and the Salvaging of the Spoils," in *The Cambridge History of Libraries in Britain and Ireland*, vol. 1, To 1640 (Cambridge: Cambridge University Press, 2006), 265–91.

93. John Bale, "New Year's Gift" (1549), in *John Leland's Itinerary*, ed. John Chandler (Thrupp: Sutton, 1993), 2–4.

94. John Bale, *Illustrium Maioris Britanniae Scriptorum . . . Summarium* (Wesel, 1548). Note that Bale himself later obscured the origins of his antiquarian practice by implying that the Reformation prompted his travels: "The sweetness of histories, the desire for letters, and a vehement love towards my homeland first compelled me to the labor assumed in this volume. For when I saw with surety in 1533 that the Dissolution of the Monasteries loomed on account of the iniquities of the inhabitants and their contempt of truth, I rushed to those of their libraries which by the singular gift of God were then most familiar to me, those of the Carmelites and Augustinians. I labored in these for nearly three years in collecting the authors, titles, and incipits of diverse books. I would have done so too in the libraries of the Dominicans, Minorites, Carthusians and Brigidines, if they had not uncivilly denied me entrance." Ibid., 247v. "Utque causam suscepti in hoc volumine laboris explicem, ad id me in primis coegerunt historiarum dulcedo, literum cupiditas, atque vehementer naturalis officiosus ergo patriam amor. Nam cum certis argumentis praevidissem anno Christi Mdxxxiii Anglorum coenobiis iustissimam, ob nefanda inhabitantium scelera ac veritatis contemptum, imminere destructionem. Ad eorum statim singulari Dei dono, me contuli Bibliothecas, qui mihi tunc magis erant familiares ac benevoli, utpote Carmelitarum & Augustinensium. Apud illos triennio fore laboravi in colligendis diversorum librorum autoribus & titulis, cum quorundam eorum initiis. Quod & apud Dominicanos ac Minoritas, Carthusianos, Brigidanos, aliosque sectarios fecissem quoque, si non inciviliter introitum mihi negassent."

doxy. As he explained: "[Leland] is here unto us in Englande, in these hys frutefull labours, as was Joannes Annius to the Italienes."[95] Leland's restoration of antiquities evoked for Bale the notorious Dominican. The inscrutable Benedictine abbot of Sponheim Trithemius joined Annius as inspiration, for he too had traveled to libraries to collect materials for a national biography of authors. Among the other precedents Bale identified were the fourteenth-century Carmelite John Trisse and the fifteenth-century Carmelite Arnold Bostius, while Leland and the Swiss encyclopedist Conrad Gesner were the only nonmonastic precedents in the postclassical world. Bale recognized his Protestant biobibliographic mission as exposing the lies perpetrated by corrupt monks, but his conviction that the textual pilgrim's life was the proper way to pursue knowledge not only predated his conversion but also resulted from his experience examining Carmelite history while still in the order.[96] If Bale condemned the monastic historians who had strengthened Rome's control over his realm, he continued to deploy their antiquarian methods.

Such antiquarianism constituted the foundation for ecclesiastical history in the sixteenth century. Bale, in fact, was a member of the community that most fully developed the practices of traveling to repositories, extracting and copying chronicles, writs, and charters, and synthesizing this material into a coherent whole. He may have met the Croatian theologian Matthias Flacius Illyricus, the head of the consortium of Lutheran scholars who compiled the behemoth seven-volume *Magdeburg Centuries*, as early as 1540.[97] Flacius contended that the papacy had assumed tyrannical control over the record keeping of the church, and he believed it imperative to establish a true administrative church history from the textual records preserved throughout Christendom.[98] Like Bale, Flacius published a biobibliography, his 1556 *Catalogus testium veritatis*. He also published

95. Bale, "New Year's Gift," 1.

96. For Trithemius, see Borchardt, *German Antiquity in Renaissance Myth*; and Anthony Grafton, *Worlds Made by Words: Scholarship and Community in the Modern West* (Cambridge, MA: Harvard University Press, 2009), 56–79.

97. For various positions on the relationship between Bale and Flacius, see McCusker, *John Bale*; Oliver K. Olson, *Matthias Flacius and the Survival of Luther's Reform* (Wiesbaden: Harrasowitz, 2002); and Norman L. Jones, "Matthew Parker, John Bale, and the Magdeburg Centuriators," *SCJ* 12 (1981): 35–39.

98. For Flacius's criticism of the papal library, see Paul Nelles, "The Renaissance Ancient Library Tradition and Christian Antiquity," in *Les humanistes et leur bibliothèque*, ed. Rudolf De Smet (Leuver: Peeters, 2002), 159–74. For his opponents, see Jean-Louis Ferrary, *Onofrio Panvinio et les antiquités romaines* (Rome: École française de Rome, Palais Farnèse, 1996).

editions of medieval chronicles and documents collected from libraries visited during his movements from Venice to Wittenberg to Jena that illustrated papal pollution of the church.

At the outset of their project, the Centuriators elected to structure the *Centuries* systematically rather than chronologically, dividing church history into hundred-year units. Within each century they presented their evidence under a rigid list of methodically chosen categories, such as *doctrine, heresies, ceremonies, councils, martyrs,* and *miracles.* Evidence was compiled strictly according to these same headings. Flacius and his collaborators assembled a team of correspondents and scholars from whom he borrowed rare works and whom he also paid to go to archives and copy extracts.[99] These scholars were instructed to read histories with the lists of the above topoi at hand and extract relevant passages as appropriate. These collections were then passed to the project's central readers, who integrated the materials into a systematic whole. The *Centuries* thus required a specific method of observation utilized by excerpting researchers.[100] Bale remained one of these men after Johannes Wigand assumed control of the project from Flacius.[101]

These ecclesiastical historians, then, applied sophisticated antiquarian means to collect little-known documents that they methodically read for evidence within strict categories. Their enterprises, furthermore, were not directed toward the erection of a theater of theological exempla. Rather, they sought to unveil processes of change and corruption in the church, integrating the antiquarianism of medieval monks with the causal conception of history formulated by Vives and Elyot. And, above all, they invested this historical practice with a theological significance, describing their labor of methodically recovering the past as suffused with divine blessing, sanctifying historical analysis as itself a providential act. Ralegh, as we have seen, embraced this notion of the historian as divine

---

99. For the Centuriators' methods, see Ronald Diener, "The Magdeburg Centuries: A Bibliothecal and Historiographical Analysis" (Ph.D. diss., Harvard University Divinity School, 1978); Anthony Grafton, "Where Was Salomon's House? Ecclesiastical History and the Intellectual Origins of Bacon's *New Atlantis*," in *Die europäische Gelehrtenrepublik im Zeitalter des Konfessionalismus,* ed. Herbert Jaumann, Wolfenbüttler Forschungen 96 (Wiesbaden, 2001), 21–38; and Gregory Lyon, "Baudouin, Flacius, and the Plan for the Magdeburg Centuries," *JHI* 64 (2003): 253–72.

100. For a different intellectual endeavor deploying similar methods, see J. R. Christianson, *On Tycho's Island: Tycho Brahe and His Assistants, 1570–1601* (Cambridge: Cambridge University Press, 2000).

101. Joannes Wigandus to John Bale, Magdeburg, 2 March 1559, in McCusker, *John Bale,* 70.

instrument entrusted with reforming humanity's depravity and restoring the true knowledge of terrestrial events; as we shall see, he also adapted their practices of assembling and analyzing texts to his own venture.

THE *ARTES HISTORICAE* AND THE RISE OF THE LEARNED COUNSELOR

Among the Centuriators' most trusted correspondents was the French jurist and historian Francois Baudouin, whom they consulted early in the project for advice about their systematic organization. In fact, their project resembled a work he had been preparing, a guide for the production and interpretation of universal histories. While the Centuriators' methods and organization owed much to Baudouin's advices, his 1561 *De institutione historiae universae* extended ecclesiastical antiquarianism to redefine the sources appropriate for developing political expertise.

Baudouin's work was the first tremendous success in the genre of the *artes historicae*.[102] As training in history became central to governance, scholars produced methodological works instructing how to profitably read histories. Such texts were printed in increasing numbers from the 1530s, plateauing at around one new title per year from 1560 to 1640. Baudouin's work and Jean Bodin's 1566 *Methodus ad Facilem Historiarum Cognitionem* were the primary catalysts for the popularity of this genre as well as two of its most provocative representatives.

The boom in *artes historicae* represented an intellectual response to a decade of turmoil. The Habsburg-Valois conflict enveloped every European government in the 1550s, and the larger states waged near-constant warfare. When uneasy peace descended in 1559, the Habsburg Empire, cleaved into the Spanish and the Holy Roman Empires, exerted a broad dominance that other governments struggled to limit. In the ensuing decades, European governments constantly engaged in war and machination, seeking to expand influence and control political affairs. Their efforts were hindered by internal strife as the confessional conflict that propelled foreign policy also threatened to rend states from within.

---

102. For Baudouin and the *ars historica*, see the works of Donald Kelley, esp. "Historia Integra: Francius Baudouin and His Conception of History," *JHI* 25 (1964): 35–57; Astrid Witschi-Bernz, "Bibliography of Works in the Philosophy of History, 1500–1800," *History and Theory* 12 (1972): 3–50, and "Main Trends in Historical-Method Literature: Sixteenth to Eighteenth Centuries," *History and Theory* 12 (1972): 51–90; Couzinet, *Histoire et méthode*; Lyon, "Baudouin, Flacius, and the Plan for the Magdeburg Centuries"; and Grafton, *What Was History?* 62–122.

In this troubled context, the learned counselor thrived. Faced with a crisis defined in theological terms, these advisers embraced the ministerial elements of their labor and argued that learning alone could salve Europe's wounds.[103] In his dedicatory epistle to the chancellor of France, Michel de l'Hôpital, Baudouin urged that studying the universal history of humanity would reveal a devout juridical framework to guide France out of contemporary perturbations. He did not distinguish between ecclesiastical and political history and observed no geographical or chronological borders; rather, he demanded that his historian examine the present, medieval, and ancient pasts and peoples near and far, thriving and extinct. This full reconstitution of universal history, he maintained, would reveal the universal legal and political principles necessary for ideal governments.

To accomplish this goal, Baudouin demanded a reassessment of the sources appropriate for historical knowledge. He rejected the anticipated criticism that a paucity of evidence rendered the construction of a universal history impossible. Despite the destruction of ancient monuments, he marveled, authentic histories produced in the ancient world flowed one after another, enabling a continuous history of all time. As he explained: "Those remnants which are remaining to us can be fused well enough into a history, if we investigate all things by correcting each particular in every writer, and we appropriately unite what each of them offers."[104] Baudouin insisted that the materials for histories should not be limited to a small set of canonical texts:

> As from the books of Cicero great and fruitful material for history can be found: thus the testimonies of many great things can be excerpted from the commentaries of other writers, even if these do not claim to be historians, that otherwise are lost to us. Therefore, I cannot fail to reprehend the negligence of those who, when they demand histories, do not look there. Why should I say this only about books and papers?

103. Compare J. H. M. Salmon, *Renaissance and Revolt: Essays in the Intellectual and Social History of Early Modern France* (Cambridge: Cambridge University Press, 1987); and William J. Bouwsma, *The Waning of the Renaissance, ca. 1550–1640* (New Haven, CT: Yale University Press, 2000). See also, though in a slightly different vein, Siraisi, *History, Medicine, and the Traditions of Renaissance Learning.*

104. Francois Baudouin, "De institutione historiae universae, et eius cum iurisprudentia coniunctione," in *Artis Historicae Penus*, ed. Joannes Wolfius (Basel, 1579), 655. "Qualescunque reliquae nobis relictae sunt (hoc enim dicendum iterum est) historiam satis integram conflare utcunque possunt; si ab singulis scriptoribus singulae corrogando, omnia pervestigemus, & quod singuli conferent, apte colligamus atque coniungamus."

Is it not the case that ancient statues and pictures, and inscriptions sculpted on stones and coins, and embroidered on tapestries and wall hangings, also supply material for histories? And therefore, as I said before, we ought to seek a history both universal and true.[105]

Baudouin thus encouraged scholars to seize evidence from any available source, expanding the techniques used by Bale and Flacius to allow the construction of a universal history revealing the diverse effects that God used to control the world.

Baudouin perceived one frequently neglected type of source as possessing considerable value. He wrote: "I truly grieve that the ancient custom of the Christians is not observed. The ancient church had its chosen (in the legal idiom) notaries, who collected diligently and with good faith and authenticated with public authority the memory of things, and they preserved in their Archives such monuments of uncorrupt faith."[106] He noted that the Romans too had observed this custom. Baudouin, then, recommended both the use of archival study for the writing of history and the production of archives to certify the memory of worthwhile acts.[107] He made archival research a cornerstone of the historical method that was crucial to the education of statesmen.

Bodin too was deeply concerned with the proper evaluation of past his-

---

105. Ibid., 646–47. "Ut autem ex Ciceronis libris dico amplissimam & uberrimam historiae materiam repeti posse: sic etiam ex aliorum scriptorum, etsi historicos se esse non profiteant, commentariis excerpi multarum maximarum rerum testimonia possunt, quae alioqui nos fugiunt. Itaque non possum non eorum reprehendere negligentiam, qui cum historias requirunt, eo non respiciunt. Quid de libris aut chartis loquor? Nonne & veteres statuae ac picturae, & lapidibus aut nummis insculptae inscriptiones, & denique quae aulaeis vel peristromatibus intexta sunt, historiae argumentum undique nobi suppeditant? Ergo, ut antea dixi, historiam & universam & veram debere nos quaerere: sic iam dico, consequi posse."

106. Ibid., 650. "Ego vero in earum rerum historia conservanda magis doleo veterem Christianorum morem non esse observatum. Habuit enim vetus Ecclesia delectos suos (ut Iuris verbo utar) actuarios, qui & diligenter & bona fide colligerent, publicaque auctoritate consignarent illarum rerum memoriam: & in suis Archivis talia incorruptae fidei monumenta, quae tamen omnibus paterent, adservavit."

107. Baudouin's injunctions likely furthered an incipient trend. Between 1565 and 1568, the papacy, Philip II, Cosimo de Medici, and the French crown organized or ordered centralized archives. Baudouin certainly knew the clerk of the Parliament of Paris, Jean du Tillet, who had used crown archives to derive precedents and titles for the king and royal counselors, and whose researches were posthumously published in 1578. See Donald Kelley, "Jean du Tillet, Archivist and Antiquary," *JMH* 38 (1966): 337–54, and *The Foundations of Modern Historical Scholarship*, 226–49; and Elizabeth A. R. Brown, "Jean du Tillet et les Archives de France," *Histoire et archives* 2 (1997): 29–63.

torians, and he recommended that readers judge the credibility of histories by their authors' fidelity to official sources.[108] But he drew from an unexpected source to press his argument. As he explained: "Here we ought to revert to the words of Metasthenes, who said, 'It is true that all authors who write about kings need not be accepted, but only the priests to whom is entrusted preservation of the public annals. An illustration is Berosus, who restored the whole history of the Assyrians from the annals of the ancients.'"[109] The passage cited was not from the authentic scraps of Megasthenes known to Bodin's contemporaries; rather, he found it in Annius's forgery. When Bodin sought a clinching affirmation of the utility of public records, he cited a work he knew was forged that emanated from an ecclesiastical history tradition of hunting for concealed ancient records in monastic archives. The turn to archives was substantiated by a monastic, antiquarian ideal of analysis expressed in fabricated official records.[110]

While both Bodin and Baudouin recommended close inspection of public records, however, they did not endorse the use of all official evidence. As Bodin tartly noted: "Of course the actual historical truth ought not to be sought from the commentaries of kings, since they are boastful about their many exploits."[111] He thus distinguished the records worth consulting from state-sponsored plaudits that served propagandistic ends, for he saw these officially approved texts as full of deliberate exaggerations and occlusions. Rather, he preferred documents produced in the course of daily legal and political business.

Baudouin's and Bodin's advocacy of the use of archives gave further impetus to an emerging method of producing historical narratives. From at latest the 1460s, scholars creating propagandistic histories had used archival sources.[112] But, in the wake of Baudouin's recommendations, archives became the very locus of the *arcana imperii*, as counselors diligently collected and preserved nonnarrative records as aids to the production of

108. For Bodin, see Kelley, *The Foundations of Modern Historical Thought*; Couzinet, *Histoire et méthode*; and Julian H. Franklin, *Jean Bodin and the Sixteenth-Century Revolution in the Methodology of Law and History* (Westport, CT: Greenwood, 1977). See also, by contrast, T. C. Price Zimmermann, *Paolo Giovio: The Historian and the Crisis of Sixteenth-Century Italy* (Princeton, NJ: Princeton University Press, 1995).

109. Jean Bodin, *Method for the Easy Comprehension of History* (1566), trans. Beatrice Reynolds (New York: Norton, 1969), 47.

110. See Grafton, *What Was History?*

111. Bodin, *Method*, 47.

112. Compare Ianziti, *Humanistic Historiography*.

counsel and often without the goal of composing narrative histories.[113] Archives were envisioned as comprehensive centers of political information, collections of political experience to be scrutinized by elite learned counselors intent on discerning—and controlling—causation in the world around them.[114] The counselor's ability to assess circumstances accurately and devise prudent counsel depended on placement at the center of government, which enabled him to microscopically survey the range of factors that potentially determined the unfolding of events.[115] This context altered the reading preferences of learned counselors. They gravitated toward histories that explained events through decisions made by cabals and committees secreted within royal courts, and Tacitus and Polybius, with their focus on the small coterie of counselors maneuvering in the courts of the ancient world, supplanted Plutarch and Livy as favored reading.[116]

113. The earlier commission for Jean du Tillet to reorganize the crown archives may have dated from 1562, which would indicate that Baudouin's text might have prompted immediate action. Kelley, "Jean du Tillet," 344; and Brown, "Jean du Tillet." For medieval and early modern archives, see Ilardi, "Fifteenth-Century Diplomatic Documents"; Robert-Henri Bautier, "La phase cruciale de l'histoire des archives: La constitution des dépôts d'archives et la naissance de l'archivistique," *Archivum* 18 (1968): 139–49; Rosamond McKiterrick, ed., *The Uses of Literacy in Early Medieval Europe* (Cambridge: Cambridge University Press, 1990); Thomas Noble, "Literacy and the Papal Government in Late Antiquity and the Early Middle Ages," in ibid., 82–108; Elizabeth Hallam, "Nine Centuries of Keeping the Public Records," in *The Records of the Nation*, ed. G. H. Martin and Peter Spufford (Woodbridge: Boydell, 1990), 9–16; M. T. Clanchy, *From Memory to Written Record: England, 1066–1307* (London: Blackwell, 1993); Olivier Guyotjeannin, "Les méthodes de travail des archivistes du roi de France (fin XIIIe–début XVIe siècle)," *Archiv für Diplomatik* 42 (1996): 295–374; Adam J. Kosto and Anders Winroth, eds., *Charters, Cartularies and Archives: The Preservation and Transmission of Documents in the Medieval West* (Toronto: Pontifical Institute of Mediaeval Studies, 2002); and Randolph Head, "Knowing Like a State: The Transformation of Political Knowledge in Swiss Archives, 1450–1770," *JMH* 75 (2003): 745–82. See also Dover, "Deciphering the Diplomatic Archives of Fifteenth-Century Italy"; Randolph Head, "Mirroring Governance: Archives, Inventories and Political Knowledge in Early Modern Switzerland and Europe," *Archival Science* 7 (2007): 317–29; and "Archival Knowledge Cultures in Europe, 1400–1900," ed. Randolph Head, special issue, *Archival Science* 10 (2010).

114. de Vivo, *Information and Communication in Venice*; Maria Portuondo, *Secret Science: Spanish Cartography and the New World* (Chicago: University of Chicago Press, 2009); Soll, *The Information Master*.

115. See, above all, Peter Burke, "Tacitism: Scepticism and Reason of State," in *The Cambridge History of Political Thought, 1450–1700*, ed. J. H. Burns and Mark Goldie (Cambridge: Cambridge University Press, 1996); and Richard Tuck, *Philosophy and Government, 1572–1651* (Cambridge: Cambridge University Press, 1993).

116. See Burke, "A Survey of the Popularity of Ancient Historians." In the British context, see A. T. Bradford, "Stuart Absolutism and the Utility of Tacitus," *HLQ* 46 (1983): 127–55; David Womersley, "Sir Henry Savile's Translation of Tacitus and the Political Interpretation of Elizabethan Texts," *Review of English Studies* 42 (1991): 313–42; J. H. M. Salmon,

Ralegh's collection of *artes historicae* did not include Baudouin or Bodin. But their works exerted powerful significance on those Ralegh did possess and the context in which he operated, and the *History* reveals the imprint of their methods for analyzing and producing histories. The massive library he compiled strove to achieve Baudouin's injunction to amass a universal collection of evidence. As will become clear, Ralegh at times placed great significance on material evidence. And, as we shall see, he enthusiastically implemented Baudouin's prescription to identify "each particular in every writer" by using notebooks to organize fragments of evidence that he then sought to integrate into a cohesive whole. Ralegh approached his library as an archive of the ancient world, supplying him with an overwhelming collection of evidence with which he could perform the project of historical causal analysis on a universal scale. And his methods in performing this task fulfilled the demands placed by the most rigorous methodical thinkers on historically-minded learned counselors.

HISTORICAL ANALYSIS IN ELIZABETHAN ENGLAND

Though the Henrician Reformation was founded on the claim of historical independence from Rome and supported by the collection of precedents drawn from chronicles known as the *Collecteana Satis Copiosa*, it did not spur many besides Bale and Leland to pursue detailed investigations into the English past. But, over the course of Elizabeth's reign, the upper echelon of her regime was infiltrated by a dynamic culture of historical practice that characterized study of the past as a school of experience and demanded the methodical reading of a broad range of sources according to precisely enumerated categories.[117]

"Seneca and Tacitus in Jacobean England," in *The Mental World of the Jacobean Court*, ed. Linda Levy Peck (Cambridge: Cambridge University Press, 1991), 169–88; Ronald Mellor, "Tacitus, Academic Politics, and Regicide in the Reign of Charles I: The Tragedy of Dr. Isaac Dorislaus," *International Journal of the Classical Tradition* 11 (2004–5): 153–93; and Paulina Kewes, "Henry Savile's Tacitus and the Politics of Roman History in Late Elizabethan England," *HLQ* 74 (2011): 515–51.

117. The standard account of the culture of Elizabethan counselors depicts a conflict between those counselors who felt that authority derived from lineage and those who felt that it derived from virtue. Rhetoric and moral philosophy were the humanist studies that ostensibly advanced virtue. Compare James, *English Politics and the Concept of Honour*; Quentin Skinner, *The Foundations of Modern Political Thought*, 2 vols. (Cambridge: Cambridge University Press, 1978), and *Reason and Rhetoric in the Philosophy of Hobbes* (Cambridge: Cambridge University Press, 1996); Tuck, *Philosophy and Government*; Peltonen, *Classical Humanism and Republicanism in English Political Thought*; and John Guy, *Politics, Law and Counsel in Tudor and Early Stuart England* (Aldershot: Ashgate, 2000).

The archbishop of Canterbury, Matthew Parker, was the first elite royal counselor in Tudor England with specific expertise in uncovering and interpreting historical records. Parker, in fact, learned his methods from the Centuriators. Six months after Elizabeth's coronation, Flacius's emissaries arrived in England to request texts and collections of extracts within the categories they supplied to their researchers, and Elizabeth directed Parker to this task.[118] In 1561, Flacius's emissary returned to collect any books accumulated, bearing a letter in which Flacius urged: "It would be very useful if in your reign and in Scotland, all books and manuscripts that you judge to be very rare or at least unknown by name, were collected from remote and obscure places into the open."[119] He explained that private men possessed many valuable monuments of the English past, and he pressed Parker to borrow and copy significant passages of these works. Supplementing this letter was a volume containing extracts from Matthew Paris's *Historia Anglorum* and other chronicles, a list of desired sources, and an impressive catalog of works by British authors already in Flacius's possession.[120] Flacius intended this package to function as a model for training Parker in ecclesiastical antiquarianism, teaching him how to locate, acquire, and organize evidence gleaned from dispersed works.

Parker responded by apologizing for procuring little of value. He marveled that Flacius's knowledge of English materials exceeded his own and stressed the difficulty of finding the requested materials. As he explained, monastic libraries had been "pillaged before it was realized how much inconvenience this would cause the church of Christ from this clandestine plundering and casting away of books."[121] This devastation was compounded during Mary's reign when valuable books had been burned. The queen's library thus was of little use to the Centuriators, and Parker con-

118. Jones, "Matthew Parker, John Bale, and the Magdeburg Centuriators." See also Benedict Scott Robinson, "'Darke Speeche': Matthew Parker and the Reforming of History," *SCJ* 29 (1998): 1061–83.

119. *Correspondence of Matthew Parker*, ed. John Bruce and the Reverend Thomas Thomason Perowne (New York: Johnson Reprint, 1968), 140. "Valde utile esset tuam Rev. P. id agere ut est istic in vestro regno et in Scotia, ex locis remotioribus et ignobilioribus, in certa quaedam et illustriora comportarentur, omnes libri manuscripti et qui rariores esse existimarentur, aut etiam quorum nomina plane ignorarentur."

120. BL Egerton 3790. Many thanks to Professor Norman Jones for sharing this discovery with me.

121. Bruce and Perowne, eds., *Correspondence of Matthew Parker*, 288. "Certe Academiae, et quaecunque fuerunt religiosum aedificia, prius diripiebantur, quam animadvertebatur quantum incommodi rediturum esset ecclesiae Christi ex hac librorum clandestine direptione et iactura."

tritely admitted that he had yielded fewer materials than he had hoped, "before I was taught by experience."[122]

Experience and Flacius's advice, however, would have a salutary effect on Parker's ability to locate valuable materials. Over the 1560s, his implementation of Flacius's prescriptions resulted in the recovery of many medieval chronicles. Like the Centuriators, Parker cultivated collaborators whom he dispatched to dispersed locales to obtain desired sources.[123] Lawrence Nowell, his most trusted correspondent, traveled throughout England and to the Continent in the late 1560s, purchasing texts, and filling notebooks with extracts of sources.[124] Many of these works were in Anglo-Saxon, and Parker patronized Nowell's and Lambarde's efforts to master this language. He also oversaw the publication of many of these histories. While his 1572 *De Antiquitate Brittanicae Ecclesiae* was prefaced with an idiosyncratic *ars historica*, most of these publications were equipped with prefaces explaining how they justified the Church Settlement, of which he was the architect. This strategy also bore the imprint of Flacius, who appended similar introductions to medieval sources he guided into print.

Parker's expertise in locating records was recognized as a powerful instrument and applied beyond the reconfiguration of the Anglican Church. In July 1568, the archbishop received a commission from the Privy Council instructing him to collect documents pertaining to the queen's rights to Scotland.[125] The task was of particular moment since, two months prior, Mary Stuart had fled to England, resigning the crown to her infant son, James VI. Acquiring these documents required application of the antiquarian methods introduced to Parker by Flacius. As Parker's commission explained: "Most of the same writings and records so kept in the monasteries are now come to the possession of sundry private persons, and so partly remain obscure and unknown: in which said records be mentioned such historical matters and monuments of antiquity, both for the eccle-

---

122. Ibid., 288. ". . . priusquam experientia eram edoctus."

123. For the Parker circle's antiquarian practices, see Robin Flower, "Lawrence Nowell and the Discovery of England in Tudor Times," *Proceedings of the British Academy* 21 (1937 for 1935): 48–73; P. M. Black, "Matthew Parker's Search for Cranmer's 'Great Notable Written Books,'" *The Library*, 5th ser., 29 (1974): 312–22, and "Laurence Nowell's 'Disappearance' in Germany and Its Bearing on the Whereabouts of His Collectanea, 1568–1572," *EHR* 92 (1977): 345–53; Timothy Graham, "Matthew Parker's Manuscripts: An Elizabethan Library and Its Use," in *The Cambridge History of Libraries in Britain and Ireland*, vol. 1, *To 1640*, 322–44; and Summit, *Memory's Library*.

124. See Flower, "Lawrence Nowell." Most of Nowell's collections are in the British Library, but see also HEH MS 26341.

125. For the medieval use of chronicles for political ends in England, see Given-Wilson, *Chronicles*.

siastical and civil government."[126] In this case, Parker was entrusted, not with narrating a history, but with unearthing politically charged evidence that resuscitated a past connecting Elizabeth to Scotland.

Parker's work demonstrated the utility of historical expertise, showing how the collection and control of historical evidence could provide powerful instruments for his queen. Over the course of Elizabeth's reign, scholars were increasingly to help statesmen interpret historical sources. Indeed, the culture of historical counsel supplied the most powerful stimulant for the culture of textual counsel. Gabriel Harvey's readings of Livy are the best-known instance of this sort of knowledge transaction, and John Dee's career revolved around his ability to render his astonishing library—overflowing with chronicles, histories, and records—usable to powerful individuals. The careers of Henry Wotton, Henry Cuffe, Robert Naunton, Thomas Norton, Thomas Digges, and Lambarde reveal how fundamental the role of the "facilitator" engaged in interpreting historical works was to Elizabethan political culture.[127] Appropriately, histories of all sorts poured off the presses in Elizabethan England—editions of medieval chroniclers such as Matthew Paris and national histories such as those of Holinshed and Camden, ancient works by Livy, Plutarch, and Eusebius alongside modern histories by Guicciardini and Jean de Serres, while scholars like William Harrison and Francis Thynne devoted countless hours to producing exacting manuscript histories.[128]

126. Archbishop Matthew Parker to William Cecil, Croydon, July 1568, in Bruce and Perowne, eds., *Correspondence of Matthew Parker*, 327–28.

127. See Grafton and Jardine, *From Humanism to the Humanities*, and "'Studied for Action'"; Collinson, "The Monarchical Republic of Queen Elizabeth I," and "Puritans, Men of Business and Elizabethan Parliaments"; Jardine and Sherman, "Pragmatic Readers"; Hammer, "The Uses of Scholarship," and "Essex and Europe"; Sherman, *John Dee*; Eric Ash, *Power, Knowledge and Expertise in Elizabethan England* (Baltimore: Johns Hopkins University Press, 2004); and Robyn Adams, "A Spy on the Payroll? William Hearle and the Mid Elizabethan Polity," *HR* 83 (2010): 1–15.

128. See Parry, *A Protestant Vision*; and David Carlson, "The Writings and Manuscript Collections of the Elizabethan Alchemist, Antiquary, and Herald Francis Thynne," *HLQ* 52 (1989): 203–72. For Elizabethan historical production, see the works cited in introduction n. 4 above along with Keith Thomas, *The Perception of the Past in Early Modern England*, Creighton Trust Lecture, 1983 (London: University of London, 1984); Fritz Levy, "Hayward, Daniel, and the Beginnings of Politic History in England," *HLQ* 50 (1987): 1–34; Stuart Piggott, *Ancient Britains and the Antiquarian Imagination* (London: Thames & Hudson, 1989); D. R. Woolf, "The Power of the Past: History, Ritual and Political Authority in Tudor England," in Fideler and Mayer, eds., *Political Thought and the Tudor Commonwealth*, 19–49; Christiane Kunst, "William Camden's *Britannia*: History and Historiography," in *Ancient History and the Antiquarian: Essays in Memory of Arnaldo Momigliano*, ed. M. H. Crawford and C. R. Ligota (London: Warburg Institute, 1995), 117–31; J. D. Alsop, "William Fleetwood and Elizabethan Historical Scholarship," *SCJ* 25 (1995): 155–76; Patrick Collinson, "One of Us? William

The extent of this culture has not been fully appreciated. A short overview of Burghley's and Leicester's historical activities will demonstrate that prominent statesmen in Elizabeth's regime had absorbed the imperatives of historical analysis. Burghley was the dedicatee of a large number of histories, and he accepted rare copies of medieval chronicles from hopeful clients.[129] He was also consulted by at least one aspiring author with a proposal for a universal history, which he revised extensively.[130] He corresponded with esteemed Continental scholars, and Sleidan, Johannes Sturm, and David Chytraeus all consulted him or sent him copies of their histories.[131] Like these men, Burghley grasped the political uses of antiquarian scholarship, and he had headed the Privy Council that composed Parker's 1568 commission while also frequently composing recommendations for policy rooted in modes of historical counsel.[132] Moreover, he often sent clients to the depositories in the Tower of London or Westminster to seek extracts of official records that he then annotated.[133] As we shall see, Robert Beale most frequently performed the responsibility of collecting documents, but Burghley occasionally visited the archives himself, recording notes that he would use in crown administration.[134] He consulted contemporary histories, collecting, for example, evidence from Flavio Biondi and Marcantonio Sabellico that popes had frequently condoned assassinations and genealogical notes from Commines.[135] Similar notes in his hand remain examining scriptural genealogies, chronological analyses

---

Camden and the Making of History," *TRHS*, 6th ser., 8 (1998): 139–63; Richard Cust, "Catholicism, Antiquarianism, and Gentry Honour: The Writings of Thomas Shirley," *Midland History* 23 (1998): 40–70; Ian Gadd and Alexandra Gillespie, eds., *John Stow (1525–1605) and the Making of the English Past: Studies in Early Modern Culture and the History of the Book* (London: BL, 2004); and Kewes, "Henry Savile's Tacitus."

129. See, e.g., Burghley's copy of Higden's *Polychronicon*, HEH 28561, with a few annotations in his hand. Such books were commonly exchanged as gifts for those seeking patronage in the Elizabethan regime. For example, John Foxe presented his annotated copy of Lambarde's *Archaionomia* (HEH 2649A-B) to the bishop of Salisbury, John Jewel, in 1568, and, when seeking the patronage of Thomas Egerton, Baron of Ellesmere, in 1587, Lambarde sent him a copy of the twelfth-century "Black Book of the Exchequer" with corrections and an index (HEH EL 62136).

130. BL Lansdowne 101, fols. 1–3.

131. See Johannes Sleidanus, *Sleidans Briefwechsel*, ed. Hermann Baumgarten (Strassburg: Trübner, 1881), 251–60. For Chytraeus, see CP MS 203/6. For Sturm, see SP 70/114/16, fol. 854.

132. For example, see the attack on papal usurpation of temporal authority in CP 171/35.

133. See, among many other instances, BL Lansdowne 479.

134. Examples include BL Lansdowne 48, fols. 77v and forward; and CP 165/29.

135. BL Lansdowne 94, fols. 186–87; and CP 230/5.

for the dating of Easter, extracts from medieval English histories, investigations of the structure of Roman armies, and more.[136] On at least one occasion, he recommended Eusebius to a recusant, trusting in the evangelizing power of ecclesiastical history.[137] Like so many other counselors, he collected axioms from Sallust and Tacitus.[138] Throughout his life, finally, he inscribed in notebooks and printed almanacs long-running annals of events of both personal and political impact and meticulous studies of his own genealogy.[139]

Like their Continental counterparts, Elizabethan counselors agreed that reading histories without method was insufficient to develop prudence. Accordingly, Elizabethan scholars produced *artes historicae*. Leicester was the recipient of several of these, including Thomas Danett's preface to his 1565 translation of Commines's *Memoires*. Danett explained that, "by conferinge tymes past wth the present estate, a wise man is able to divine what is hereafter like to happen," before querying: "But how can we beholde as it weare in a glasse the tymes past, unlesse we know the deedes of our auncestors? And how can we knowe the deedes of our auncestors unlesse we reade histories?" He continued: "But those wch minde to take profitt by the readinge of histories . . . consider not so much what was done as by what meanes it was done . . . To be shorte they make the historie to be a paterne of all their doings both private and publiqe & studie not onelie to have speculacion of histories, but also to practise."[140] Danett thus provided for Leicester a classic exposition of the conviction that prudent men should use study of the past to guide their actions.

In 1564, Leicester received a manuscript copy of the Swiss Calvinist and London emigré Jacopo Aconcio's "Delle osservationi, et avvertimenti che haver si debbono nel legger delle historie."[141] Leicester's client Thomas Blundeville drew heavily on this work in producing the first published English *ars historica*, his 1574 *The True Order and Methode of Wryting and Reading Hystories*, which synthesized Aconcio's treatise with the *ars*

---

136. For scriptural genealogies, see SP 12/235/82, fol. 180; and SP 12/255/79, fols. 116–30. For the chronological notes, see BL Lansdowne 103, fols. 29v–31v. For one example of Burghley's notes on Roman armies, see ibid., fols. 293r–v. For examples of notes from medieval chronicles, see ibid., fol. 313; and cf. BL Lansdowne SP 12/255/80, fols. 131–33.

137. Thomas Tresham to Burghley, 22 September 1582, CP 162/70.

138. For one set of political maxims, see BL Lansdowne 103, fol. 303r.

139. Examples include CP 140/1, CP 140/3, CP 140/4, CP 140/8, CP 140/13, CP 333/1, and CP 334/2.

140. BL Add. MS 21579, fols. 3v, 4r–v.

141. SP 12/34/53, fols. 136–52.

historica of Francesco Patrizi of Cherso.[142] Blundeville had already demonstrated a keen appreciation for the use of history four years earlier in his *A Very Briefe and Profitable Treatise*, which he claimed to have translated from the Aragonese political philosopher Fadrique Furio Ceriol.[143] Blundeville here explained: "A dyligent Hystoriographer, which readeth to further his knowledge, and not please his eares, can be ignoraunt in nothing that appertaines to governement, be it in time of warre or peace. For he seeth & knoeweth al the sleytes & fine pollicies that hath been used in eyther of both tymes. Neyther is it possible for anye man, live hee never so long, to get by hys owne experience, the tenth part of that knowledge which a diligent reader of Hystories shall obtayne in fewe yeres." He lucidly described history as surrogate experience that enabled the discernment of contemporary causes for the benefit of the state. He even suggested that the prince quiz prospective counselors on the histories of France, Spain, and England, explaining: "If the counseler can aunswere readily, there is no doubt but he is a good Hystoriographer, and can use hys knowledge to good purpose, when tyme and occasion shall serve." And he proclaimed: "Nothing is more necessary for a counseler, than to bee a diligent reader of Hystories."[144]

Leicester also recognized the value of historical records as much as he did that of the histories themselves. In 1567, on the recommendation of William Paulet, Marquess of Winchester, he commissioned the keeper of the Tower records, William Bowyer, to produce a heraldic volume celebrating his genealogy. Winchester had been impressed by a volume Bowyer had produced for him, which combined conventional heraldic analyses of coats of arms with eulogistic humanist poems and extracts from Tower records, and Bowyer produced for Leicester an even more exceedingly sumptuous volume.[145] Winchester also recommended Bowyer to Burghley, raving that his method would "grow a greater Reformacion among the heraulds that

142. It should be clear that I am concerned, not with the intellectual innovation of British participants in the culture of historical counsel, but with their application of its structures. For evaluations of their scholarship, see D. R. Kelley, "History, English Law, and the Renaissance," *P&P* 65 (1974): 24–51; and Christopher Brooks and Kevin Sharpe, with rejoinder by D. R. Kelley, "History, English Law and the Renaissance," *P&P* 72 (1976): 133–46.

143. Blundeville's goal in describing these works as translations was to draw the luster of Continental learning to his work, which faintly resembles his sources.

144. Thomas Blundeville, *A very breife and profitable Treatise declaringe howe many counsels, and what maner of Counselers a Prince that will governe well ought to have* (London, 1570), F1v, F2v, F1r–Fiir.

145. The Paulet genealogy is BL Add. MS 21923; the Leicester genealogy is HEH MS HM 160. The records selected for this genealogy provided strong evidence that Leicester should be appointed lord steward, a position he sought for several decades before receiving it in 1587.

maketh ther books at adventure and not by the records."[146] Burghley too
seems to have appreciated Winchester's argument, for he relied on clients
in the College of Arms such as Robert Glover to provide him with records
of England's past—a task aided when Glover inherited some of Nowell's
and Leland's books.[147]

Virtually all notable Elizabethan counselors after the 1570s used historical analyses. They also advocated this practice to aspiring counselors
as a means to augment experience. In particular, they recommended to
well-born young men traveling abroad the observation of historical evidence in sets of instructions that drew on the *artes apodemicae*, or "arts
of travel," developed by Continental Ramist scholars in the 1560s and
1570s.[148] The English counselors' versions of such instructions enjoined
historical knowledge as a significant product of travel. Burghley's 1571 letter preparing Edward Manners, third Earl of Rutland, for a tour to France,
for example, directed Rutland to antiquarian observations.[149] Among prescriptions that Rutland observe military organization and installations,
geography, and court culture, Burghley insisted: "What notable antiquities
ar to be seene of ye Romans tyme or since being of value and uppon yt
what thereof it shall be good to confer them wt the description of ye old
authors as Cesar, Livy, Suetonius etc or wt the modern."[150] Rutland should,
thus, advance his knowledge of French affairs by correlating modern ruins
and ancient texts. Francis Walsingham's instructions for a nephew preparing to travel to France more explicitly linked travel and history as components of a gentleman's education. Much of his instruction concerned
the reading of histories: "You have principally to mark how matters have
passed in government in those days, so have you to apply them to these
our times and states and see how they may be made serviceable to our age,
or why to be rejected, the reason whereof well considered, shall cause you
in process of time to frame better courses both of action and counsel." All
this he described as the "piece of a traveller to profit himself by."[151] This

---

146. SP 12/42/43, fol. 101. This letter is cited in Adams, *Leicester and the Court*, 353.

147. See BL Lansdowne 229, fol. 73r.

148. Justin Stagl, *Apodemiken: Eine räsonnierte Bibliographie der reisetheoretischen Literatur des 16., 17. und 18. Jahrhunderts* (Paderborn: F. Schöningh, 1983); and works cited in
chapter 4, n. 14, below.

149. PRO SP 12/77/96, fol. 10r. This letter is printed in Sara Warneke, *Images of the Educational Traveller in Early Modern England* (Leiden: Brill, 1995). For Rutland's implementation
of this canon, see Mears, *Queenship and Political Discourse*.

150. PRO SP 12/77/96, fol. 11v.

151. Conyers Read, *Mr. Secretary Walsingham and the Policy of Queen Elizabeth*, 3 vols.
(Oxford: Clarendon, 1925), 1:18.

belief gained currency outside the regime, and from the late 1570s English presses issued a stream of *artes apodemicae*.[152]

While Burghley and Walsingham perceived historical reading as an appropriate activity for a traveler, others suggested that these endeavors required comparable methods. Philip Sidney's two letters to his brother Robert, then traveling in France, best illuminate how Elizabethan counselors conjoined travel and the reading of histories.[153] The first letter equipped Robert with precise categories for observation during his excursion. In particular, he was to take assiduous notes on the topography and military strength of each locale he visited.[154] Philip subsequently sent Robert another letter that suggested familiarity with many facets of the *ars historica*. After recommending reading Bodin and basic chronologies, he instructed Robert to "note the examples of virtue and vice, with their good or evil successes, the establishment or ruins of great estates, with the causes, the time, and circumstances then written of, the enterings and endings of war, and therein, the stratagems against the enemy, and the discipline upon the soldier; and thus much as a very historiographer." Philip thus urged Robert to observe how both moral and material factors controlled the course of terrestrial events. His continuing prescriptions reveal that this method of observation bridged the act of travel and the reading of histories. He directed Robert to read histories with pen and notebook at hand, taking appropriate notes. He ordered that, "when you read any such thing, you straight bring it to his head[ing]" and provided model categories for organizing observations. For example, when Robert encountered an extract useful for developing knowledge of military events, he should "lay it up in the right place of this storehouse, as either military, or more especially defensive military, or more particularly defensive by fortification."[155] Robert was, thus, to record similar notes when viewing French

152. The first of these *artes apodemicae* were translations of the texts of Continental Ramists. Hieronymous Turler's was translated in 1578, Albrecht Meier's in 1579. During the 1580s, English scholars produced original works with a more mathematical focus. See, e.g., William Bourne, *Booke Called the Treasure for Traveilers* (London, 1578), and *Regiment for the Sea* (London, 1580). Later works include Sir John Stradling, *A Direction for Travailers* (London, 1592) (a translation of Justus Lipsius's *Epistola de peregrinatione Italica*), Francis Bacon's 1601 essay "On Travel," and Robert Dallington's 1606 *A Method for Travell*.

153. See, in this vein, Alan Stewart, *Philip Sidney: A Double Life* (London: Chatto & Windus, 2000); and Carlo Ginzburg, *No Island Is an Island: Four Glances at English Literature in a World Perspective* (New York: Columbia University Press, 2000), 31–35.

154. Philip Sidney to Robert Sidney, n.d. [ca. 1579], in *The Correspondence of Sir Philip Sidney and Hubert Languet*, ed. Steuart A. Pears (London: William Pickering, 1845), 196.

155. Philip Sidney to Robert Sidney, London, 18 October 1580, in ibid., 200–201. For similar directions, see also Francis Bacon's advice to Fulke Greville in *The Works of Francis Bacon*,

fortifications or reading accounts of ancient battles. In both cases, the observed phenomena would be methodically reduced to essential, strictly categorized fragments of evidence, which he should analyze to yield technical military expertise.

Like his brother, Robert sought entry into the highest echelons of Continental scholarship, boarding with Johannes Sturm in Strasbourg, and requesting from Joachim Camerarius a copy of Johannes Rosinus's then-unpublished *Corpus Antiquitatum Romanarum* in 1580.[156] He continued to implement his brother's suggestions even as his expertise evolved more toward soldiering than scholarship. In early 1586, he worked through his copy of Lipsius's Tacitus, garnishing the text with annotations reflecting Philip's instructions.[157] Some notes analyzed the motivations of emperors and courtiers, while others stated political apothegms appropriate to treacherous courts, such as: "Thogh a treason be discovered it is not go[od] to make shew 2 se yt: for oftentimes a man is taken in his own practis." And Sidney carefully correlated Tacitus's account with his own experience, bemoaning "a fashion now in our court where a great man wil do one harm 2 cover [hi]s malice with protestations of good[ness] unto him as yf what he did were [for] iustice sake," and describing the mutinous band organized by the Numidian Tacfarinas as Rome's "own Irish rebels."[158] The comparable extracts in his substantial surviving notebooks reveal that Sidney deployed the fundamental tasks prescribed by the *ars historica* throughout his career.[159]

In 1595, the Earl of Essex correlated historical and travel modes of developing experience while preparing the future secretary of state Robert Naunton for a mission to Spain. Essex explained that, to further his political education, Naunton should model his travel observation after his historical reading: "ffor rules and patternes of pollecy are aswell learned out of olde Greeke and Romayne storyes, as out of states which are at thys

ed. James Spedding, Robert Leslie Ellis, and Douglas Denon Heath, 16 vols. (London, 1857–74), 9:9–26. Numerous extant notebooks prove that counselors put these prescriptions into practice.

156. HEH EL 20028.

157. Joel Davis, "Robert Sidney's Marginal Comments on Tacitus and the English Campaigns in the Low Countries," *Sidney Journal* 24 (2006): 1–19.

158. See Tacitus, *Opera*, ed. Justus Lipsius (Antwerp, 1595), 103, 76, 26 (BL shelfmark C.142.E.13).

159. Germaine Warkentin, "Robert Sidney and His Books," *Sidney Journal* 25 (2007): 31–42. Similarly, Ralegh's inveterate enemy Henry Howard, Earl of Northampton, filled many notebook pages with such excerpts. See, e.g., BL Cotton Titus C VI. See, more broadly, Ann Moss, "The Politica of Justus Lipsius and the Commonplace-Book," *JHI* 59 (1998): 421–36; Sharpe, *Reading Revolutions*; and Soll, *Publishing the Prince*.

daye." He considered the collection of intelligence about France and Spain a transfer of Naunton's expertise, explaining that Naunton should "now studye men and accions as yow were wonte to doe bookes." Essex provided an analogy for the desired sort of analysis:

> Thincke it no more advauntage to yow to knowe of twooe Frenche fasshions whether hath the better. If you knowe not the causes of ones ruine and the others rising then it is to fynde in an olde Annalis of suche a daye Alexander over threwe Darius and Caesar obtayned victory of R. for *id demum scimus cuius causam scimus* and take not the pretended cause of the state or the cause of the multitude, but gather out the circumstances of the action it selfe as many causes as yow can and thincke when yow have founde that which is most probable it maye stande for that which is most true.[160]

Naunton was to evaluate causes abroad as he was accustomed to study ancient battles. Historical analysis supplied a method for inculcating political operatives with a rigorous method of observing their own world. This relation proved enduring; in 1607, James Cleland succinctly stated: "*Travelling* in my iudgments is but a livelie Historie."[161] For such men, then, historical observation of causation could be transferred from the past to the present. This method constituted a forceful instrument of analysis that ensured rigorous interrogations of phenomena to yield profitable counsels, and its prescriptions structured the methods that early modern English counselors used to cultivate their experience and deepen their wisdom.

The Elizabethan elite, it should now be clear, aggressively adopted and implemented the methods of the culture of historical counsel. Reading histories or consultation with experts supplied them with precedents that helped shape their advices, while the canons of methical historical observation provided a robust instrument for training clients to accumulate experience and develop prudence. Their clients scoured dusty archives for moldy records, while printing presses issued revised editions of ancient works and new histories. The profit gained by the study of the past was fully ingrained within the political culture. This was the context in which Ralegh reached political maturity, in which he conducted his travels, and the *History* reveals its continuing hold over him. His work

160. Essex quoted in Hammer, "Essex and Europe," 379–80. Note that the quotation (italicized) is from *Posterior Analytics* 1.2.71b9.

161. James Cleland, *Hero-Paideia; or, The Instruction of a yong Noble-man* (Oxford, 1607), 262.

reflects the political culture he had experienced, one that insisted that methodically inspecting every shard of historical evidence generated robust analyses of causation and portrayed historical experts as the natural counselors of kings. Fulfillment of the courtier's role had instigated his rise under Elizabeth, but his time in her government taught him that different tactics were necessary for the effective counselor. The narrative and learned analyses embedded within the *History*, Ralegh hoped, would reverberate with the prudence demanded by James as the king's government faltered.

THE HISTORIAN

Ralegh's work on the *History* reflected his immersion in the culture of historical counsel. His political apprenticeship under Elizabeth had suggested that experience gained through analysis of the past was the most suitable expertise for advising kings. What precisely had occurred during previous ages may have been profoundly uncertain, but the assiduous investigation of all particulars of evidence in a vast range of sources could allow dim insight into the pattern of divine causation. If Ralegh was confident that his mastery of the past would be recognized as a vital political expertise, however, his personal circumstances required him to convey humility in the *History*. His portrayals of the task he assumed accordingly reinforced that it, like any worldly act, was subject to providential judgment.

Many contemporary scholars used the belief that historians not only observed but also participated in the theater of divine creation to shape their self-presentations. Over the sixteenth century, scholars increasingly projected this belief by constructing chronological histories of historians, defining their own labor by its history. Christopher Mylaeus, Bodin, La Popelinière, and others excavated the origins and development of historical writing. Most of these scholars proceeded from the belief that God would not have allowed any moment in history—let alone countless civilizations in bygone millennia—to disappear irretrievably from human memory. Their genealogies therefore assumed the contours of ecclesiastical histories in which historians who accurately represented the past were glorified as illuminators of Providence.[162]

162. Racin treats this to a limited extent in *Sir Walter Raleigh as Historian*. See also Donald Kelley, "History as a Calling: The Case of La Popeliniere," in *Renaissance Studies in Honor of Hans Baron*, ed. Anthony Molho and John A. Tedeschi (Florence: G. C. Sansoni, 1971), 773–89, and "Johann Sleidan and the Origins of History as a Profession."

The Lutheran theologian David Chytraeus gave the most detailed history of histories to date in lectures at the University of Rostock, published in 1563 as *De lectione historiarum recte instituenda*. He identified Moses as the first historian and vividly depicted—in hues Ralegh would later adopt—history as a method of interpreting the divine theater of experience:

> Those things done and acted in this theater of the world by men and God that are worthy of remembrance are conserved from its beginnings until our time in a continuous series, and just as if set before the eyes in a painted table or a lofty mirror, we discern and contemplate what has been done on earth since the first creation. God wanted the memory of the greatest of these things . . . to be conserved amongst men and transmitted to posterity. And clearly the memory of the things that happened before our times in the Church and in Empires would have been extinguished from humanity, if they had not been recorded in the monuments of histories and letters.

Like Ralegh, Chytraeus viewed the role of the historian as bearing the memory of Providence through time, prophetically conjuring knowledge of the past. But, as he proceeded, the Lutheran theologian honored some surprising practitioners of this sacred art. He continued: "Thus God emanated that first and most ancient history through Moses, and then Herodotus succeeded in the footsteps of the Prophets."[163] Chytraeus claimed that the histories of the pagans Herodotus, Thucydides, Xenophon, and beyond were divinely ordered to dovetail neatly with Scripture. He saw the historical works of pre-Christian polytheists as orchestrated to ensure humanity's continuous knowledge of itself.

163. David Chytraeus, "De lectione historiarum recte instituenda," in Wolfius, ed., *Artis Historicae Penus*, 458–49. "Rerum, quae in hoc mundi theatro a Deo & hominibis illius incolis, animadversione & memoria digna ab initio ad nostram usque aetatem, actae & gestae sunt, seriem continuam in Historiae mundi conservavit: in qua, velut in tabula pictum, aut veluti in excelsa specula collocati oculis nostris subiectum cernamus, & contemplemur, quicquid in orbe terrarum, inde usque a prima creatione, memorabile gestum est. Voluit enim Deus harum maximarum rerum memoriam, ut Mundi & Ecclesiae initia, originem, lapsum & reparatione, humani generis, promissionem de Christo, & caeteras patefactione Dei in Ecclesia editas, poenam diluvii, constitutionem & deletionem politiae Iudaicae, seriem quatuor Monarchiarum, & praecipuorum in mundo regnorum res gestas & mutationes, & inprimis Christi Regnum inter homines conservari, & ad posteritatem transmitti. Plane autem extingueretur in genere humano memoria rerum maximarum, quae ante nostram aetatem in Ecclesia & Imperiis acciderunt: nisi literarum & historiae monumentis consignarentur. Itaque Deus ipse primam & antiquissimam Historiam per Mosen edidit: & Herodotus, qui e vestigio Propheticis monumentis succedit." See also Ben-Tov, *Lutheran Humanists and Greek Antiquity*.

To Chytraeus, pagan works also confirmed the historical account in Scripture.[164] He explained: "Herodotus immediately follows the prophetic histories, and because he recited many histories congruent with the Bible, he not only shed light on many places of sacred history, but indeed confirmed the authority and certainty of all doctrine in good minds."[165] Herodotus's work thus constituted evidence of Scripture's literal truth. And Chytraeus's assiduous defense of nonscriptural sources extended, as his opponents delighted in noting, to Annius's forgeries. The appetite for historical knowledge in this second-generation Lutheran pastor trumped *sola scriptura*. Whether they had been produced by orthodox interpreters of Scripture or heterodox witnesses to Scripture's literal truth, all histories were perceived by him as illuminating divine creation.

Many shared Chytraeus's conviction. Above all, it buoyed Annius's adherents, who championed his illumination of aspects of the ancient past otherwise consigned to oblivion as a providential blessing. Ralegh was not in this camp, but his assessment of Annius's forgeries reveals that he shared Chytraeus's conviction that historians were instruments of Providence.

Ralegh knew that Annius's collection consisted of forgeries; as he noted: "*Annius* can make Authors to speake what he list." But that did not proscribe using the Dominican's work. As Ralegh explained: "And sure though his Fragment of *Berosus* with *Annius* his Comment bee very ridiculous in many places (the ancient Copies being corrupted or lost) yet all things in *Berosus* are not to bee reiected. Therefore St. *Hierome* for such Authours gives a good rule. . . . *Let us choose what is good in them, and reiect the rest.*"[166] Annius's forgeries merited consideration, for even rotten texts might yield healthy evidence. Ralegh noted that many respectable authorities willingly relied on Annian evidence despite apprehension about its authenticity, presenting himself as one among many for whom the forged origins of Annius's fragments mitigated, but did not destroy, their usefulness.[167]

Ralegh's position emerges in stark relief when compared to the cel-

164. Chytraeus, "De lectione historiarum," 516. "Deus ipse primam historiam per Mosen scripsit."

165. Ibid. "Has immediate sequitur Herodotus, qui cum aliquot historias cum Biblicis congruentes recitet, non modo lucem multis in locis historiae sacrae adfert: verum etiam autoritatem & certitudinem totius doctrinae in bonis mentib. confirmat."

166. *HW*, 2.21.5.2.533, 1.8.11.5.59. Compare Anthony Grafton, "On the Scholarship of Politian and Its Context," *JWCI* 40 (1977): 150–88.

167. *HW*, 1.10.8.198.

ebrated polymath Joseph Scaliger's blanket dismissal of Annius in his
1583 *De Emendatione Temporum*. As Ralegh explained, Scaliger rejected
any author who cited Annius. Ralegh recoiled against Scaliger's rigidity.
Though Annius's sources lacked sufficient credibility to alone qualify as
unimpeachable, Ralegh professed unwillingness to dismiss any author
simply for mentioning Annius.[168] He instead pronounced: "Where other
Histories are silent, or speake not enough, there may we without shame
borrow of these, as much as agrees with that little which elsewhere we
finde, and serveth to explaine or inlarge it without improbabilities."[169]
Gaps in the historical record, he believed, should be filled by using critical sense to collect available evidence, including Annian forgeries. Ralegh
thought Scaliger's intractable commitment to his textual source base an
impractical stubbornness that compromised the scholar's ability to honor
the divine past.[170]

How Ralegh adjudicated the conflict between Scaliger and Annius was
paradigmatic of his own view of the responsibilities of the historian. He
wrote:

> It is not to be feared, that time should runne backward, and by restor-
> ing the things themselves to knowledge, make our conjectures appeare
> ridiculous: What if some good Copie of an ancient Author could be
> found, shewing (if wee have it not alreadie) the perfect truth of these
> uncertainties? Would it be more shame to have beleeved in the meane
> while, *Annius* or *Torniellus*, than to have beleeved nothing? . . . Let it
> suffice, that in regard of authoritie, I had rather trust *Scaliger* or *Torniel-*
> *lus*, than *Annius*; yet him than them, if his assertion be more probable,
> and more agreeable to approved Histories than their conjecture.[171]

It was more important to tell the history of the world—to bear testimony
to God's creation in all its fullness, complexity, and detail—than to rely
exclusively on credible evidence. Those who hesitated to use conjecture
to magnify thin evidence neglected a critical dimension of the historian's
task.

---

168. He explained: "I beleeve nothing that *Annius* his *Berosus, Metasthenes*, and others
of that stampe affirmes, in respect of their bare authoritie" (*HW*, 2.23.4.570).

169. *HW*, 2.23.4.570.

170. Anthony Grafton, *Joseph Scaliger: A Study in the History of Classical Scholarship*,
2 vols. (Oxford: Clarendon, 1983–93).

171. *HW*, 2.23.4.574.

But Ralegh did not deceive himself that such tenuous evidence could yield unassailable knowledge. As he placed his own historical analyses within the framework of divine Providence, he struggled to ascertain whether they earned divine approval. His clearest exposition of this vexed position—tasked with recording and transmitting human memory, but irreparably limited in what he could know—emerged through an attack on the Jesuit Tommaso Bozio in the *History*. In his anti-Machiavellian 1598 *De ruinis gentium et regnorum*, Bozio advanced the revisionist claim that Abraham, rather than Noah, presided over the postdiluvian settlement of the world and taught orthodox rites to all his progeny.[172] Their adherence to these prescriptions, he claimed, instigated periods of flourishing, while negligence precipitated decline. In Bozio's account, empires traditionally considered pagan such as the Tyrians had honored the religious prescriptions given to Abraham, the ancient Hebrews oversaw a universal empire, and even the polytheistic Romans were little removed from true religion. Bozio argued that virtue was rewarded with temporal happiness and that empires thrived as they approached true theology, an unambiguous defense of the papacy and Spanish universal monarchy.

Ralegh found these claims ludicrous. Bozio's vision, he argued, easily could be turned against Christianity: "Shall we hereupon enforce the lewd and foolish conclusion, which heathen writers used against *Christians* in the *Primitive Church*, that such Idolatrie had caused the Citie of Rome to flourish, and that the decay of those abhominations did also bring with it the decay of the Empire? It might well be thought so, if prosperitie were a signe or effect of true Religion."[173] He pointed to the rapid expansion of polytheistic Rome and its demise shortly after accepting Christianity as unmistakably contravening Bozio's thesis. Most early modern readers would have recognized the tradition evoked by Ralegh's outrage. In the *City of God*, Augustine had made the same point when responding to Eusebius of Caesarea's historical theology, which depicted Rome's growth as divinely ordered to enable the spread of Christianity.[174] For Eusebius and his followers, Rome's embrace of Christianity under Constantine inaugu-

---

172. Tommaso Bozius, *De Ruinis Gentium* (Cologne, 1598). For Bozio, see Robert Birely, *The Counter-Reformation Prince: Anti-Machiavellianism or Catholic Statecraft in Early Modern Europe* (Chapel Hill: University of North Carolina Press, 1990).

173. *HW*, 2.8.3.367.

174. See Theodore Mommsen, "St. Augustine and the Christian Idea of Progress," *JHI* 12 (1951): 361–74; and R. A. Markus, *Saeculum: History and Society in the Theology of Augustine* (Cambridge: Cambridge University Press, 1970).

rated an era of unlimited progress for the human condition and salvation
of human souls. Comparing the disasters that had befallen Rome prior to
its adoption of Christianity to its postconversion glory supplied his proof.

When the Visigoth Alaric sacked Rome in 410, however, opponents of
the church gleefully pointed out that, if prosperity resulted from orthodoxy, Christianity could not be the true religion. Augustine responded to
these critics by devising a powerful new historical theology. He claimed
that, while God staged Providence on the earth, this theater was legible
only to God and that men could not interpret the sacred meaning of terrestrial events without divine illumination. Those so favored could, indeed,
recount prophetically, but God alone selected, in an unknowable fashion,
subjects of revelation. Augustine pronounced humanity's limitations:
"We do not know, therefore, by what judgment God causes or allows these
things to come to pass . . . the just judgments of God are hidden from the
sense and minds of mortals."[175] That Bozio's conclusion rendered divine
judgment so transparently measurable, so easily reducible to material indices, Ralegh implied, was a sure sign of error.

Ralegh's Augustinean vision of humanity's dim ability to know the
divine exemplified his self-presentation in the *History*. Like so many early
modern historians, Ralegh immersed himself in the contemporary itera-
tions of ancient debates, re-creating them to decipher and depict his world.
Here, his oblique reference to a late antique Christian dispute about the
meaning of worldly events undermined a political theory of divine favor
developed by an obscure Jesuit to counter Machiavelli. And, by vocifer-
ously professing his Augustinian allegiances, he preached that it was not
for him to know whether his own work was divinely inspired. Providential illumination remained inscrutable. Despite its political and scholarly
expertise, the *History* presented a commentary of uncertain theological
force, a gesture seeking true piety, a humble plea and tentative hope for
salvation from an unsure prophet.

HISTORICAL CULTURE

Ralegh's decision to construct a massive universal history beginning with
Creation evinced the belief that he belonged to an early modern European
community of learned counselors who deployed historical analysis to produce prophetic advices. Participants in this culture shared many concep-

175. Augustine, *The City of God against the Pagans*, ed. and trans. R. W. Dyson (Cambridge: Cambridge University Press, 1998), 20.2.

tions about their labors. Few historians or statesmen in 1600 would have disparaged those who explored obscure repositories or sought to extract historical knowledge from previously ignored sources—though there were, as we shall see, important exceptions. Most considered histories useful more for their ability to trace causation than for their value as theaters of virtue and vice, and all would have proclaimed that the study of the past constituted a providential laboratory of causation that prepared young men for careers in government. The emphasis on historical training produced a class of individuals throughout Europe who wielded the tools of historical analysis as a potent and pious expertise.

Nevertheless, within this culture there were fissures, for there was no consensus concerning the events or meaning of the past. Participants in this culture by no means shared ideological or theological allegiances. All manner of Catholics and Protestants wielded the tools supplied by the historical culture to glorify their faiths and damn their enemies', while subjects of absolutist monarchs no less than citizens of republican polities could use the past to praise their forms of rule. The culture of historical counsel germinated a bewildering array of historical visions, each seeking to revise and replace its predecessors. The study of the past became a battleground, and scholars refracted their disagreements through an endless array of questions, whether the age of the world, the location of Eden, the trajectory of the Trojan diaspora, or the year of Christ's birth. Ancient history supplied a primary site for dispute, but there were many terrains for the historical polemicist. Some constructed contemporary histories of European states, dynasties, orders, peoples, and wars; others produced reflections on ancient or modern authors; others published fragmentary records of their antiquarian collections; others devised *artes historicae* that consolidated conclusions gleaned from methodical reading. And some never directed their erudition to producing historical narratives, instead applying their expertise in historical analysis only in the formulation of counsels, competing with rival statesmen to control causation in their world.

Ralegh's decision to produce the *History* bespoke his conviction in the value of learned and pious study of the past. His decision to publish it in English reflected a nervous desire to provide illumination to his fellow subjects. Even while he saw the *History* as a petition to Providence, Ralegh implemented the canons and methods of historical culture to advance personal ends. He hoped that the work would persuade readers—including James—of both his prudence and his devotion, convincing the king to install him at the center of the regime. As such, the presentation of the *His-*

tory as a mode of public, historically derived textual counsel constituted an Elizabethan solution to Jacobean problems.

Ralegh's *History*, then, provides a case study illuminating how one member of the culture of historical counsel deployed its scholarly tools to capitalize on a personal opportunity engendered by political crisis. But the work also brings into focus the consequences of the mobilization of the methods of this scholarly community. The culture of historical counsel generated, not an ideological transformation, but a reconfiguration of the methods of making knowledge. Ralegh and virtually every other early modern historian hoped that the disciplined implementation of rigorous historical study would enable scholars to decipher Providence in the world, which would, in turn, stabilize Europe's tottering political and intellectual traditions. But, while those within the culture of historical counsel most often deployed its methods and practices to legitimize entrenched authorities, these scholarly tools exerted a disruptive subterranean influence as the intensifying cycle of revision eroded the foundations of its shared culture. As the following chapters will show, an increased emphasis on culling slivers of evidence from all manner of sources undermined the traditional European sources of power, authority, and truth and generated new ideals of scholarship and statecraft. The compulsion to find ever more sources weakened traditional authorities, as did the generation of innovative methods of processing the expanded evidence yielded from a burgeoning range of sources. When implemented in histories and politics, these methods spurred scholars to overturn received conceptions of the past and generated new instruments of governance. The culture of early modern history transformed Europe through the effects of its practices, and, as the following chapters will demonstrate, Ralegh's *History* shows these processes quietly gripping the early modern world.

CHAPTER TWO

Sources:
From Scripture to the Stars
in Early Modern Chronology

Early modern historians commonly described the sciences of chronology and geography as the "eyes" of history that plotted past events on temporal and spatial axes. This chapter and the next investigate, through the lens of Ralegh's *History*, how these disciplines transformed as early modern scholarly culture altered approaches to sources and methods of reading. Significant background and technical analysis will be required in each chapter to elucidate the goals of Ralegh's project and reveal how he positioned himself within the shifting intellectual landscape of Europe. Both chapters will show how the working habits and questions of early modern scholars reconfigured the tools they had available to make sense of the world around them. This chapter examines how, by expanding their range of credible sources, early modern chronologers weakened the authority of the most revered of all texts. The subsequent chapter, on geography, will investigate how scholarly practices of reading generated new methods of producing secure knowledge.

This chapter begins by demonstrating why the study of chronology was so charged both for European scholarly culture and for Ralegh personally. The plotting of past events was considered a form of scriptural exegesis, and it therefore invoked the same risks as any theological study. Ralegh was only one among many early modern scholars who were alleged to endorse heretical beliefs concerning the first chronological act—Creation. In fact, he adapted a Neoplatonic tradition that ascribed divine knowledge not only to Scripture but also to a small coterie of ancient pagans. But while he produced from these arguments a vision of the past as populated by proto-Christian sages, he presented it to a broader public without embracing the tradition's most radical manifestation, in which the ceaseless expansion of the sources for chronological study challenged the unique sacrality imputed to evidence in Scripture. Situating Ralegh within the context of early modern chronological study therefore illuminates the trajectory he discerned in world history alongside his intellectual and religious allegiances amid a struggle to define the boundaries of credible sources.

THE STATE OF THE DISCIPLINE: SOURCES AND PROBLEMS

There was much at stake in early modern chronology.[1] A traditional component of literal scriptural exegesis in the early sixteenth century, chronology became a modish and innovative scholarly activity during the following half century. The authors of numerous new chronologies devised groundbreaking methods that some readers praised but others excoriated in tones usually reserved for the most virulent of theological polemics.

In 1605, the English Calvinist chronologer Thomas Lydiat illuminated the dangers of misguided chronologies in his *De variis annorum formis*. To Lydiat, the devil himself insinuated chronological errors into histories, for confounding the true order of events furthered his demonic plots. As Lydiat explained: "That chief enemy of mankind, emulating his creator . . . in some cases demolished and obliterated the works of God from the minds and memory of men, in other cases misrepresented them, and in some cases wretchedly perverted chronology." Lydiat proposed that his work would remedy a list of grave theological errors. As he explained: "The first is that the devil propagated among many men the opinion of an eternal world, which insults the glory of God the Creator. And because he

---

1. For secondary literature on historical chronology in the early modern period, see, above all, Grafton, *Joseph Scaliger*, esp. vol. 2, *Historical Chronology*; Anthony Grafton, "From *De die natali* to *De emendatione temporum*: The Origin and Settings of Scaliger's Chronology," *JWCI* 48 (1985): 100–143, and "Some Uses of Eclipses in Early Modern Chronology," *JHI* 64 (2003): 213–29; and Anthony Grafton and Noel M. Swerdlow, "Technical Chronology and Astrological History in Varro, Censorinus and Others," *Classical Quarterly* 35 (1985): 454–65, and "Calendar Dates and Ominous Days in Ancient Historiography," *JWCI* 51 (1988): 14–42. Some of these articles are included in Anthony Grafton, *Defenders of the Text: The Traditions of Scholarship in an Age of Science, 1450–1800* (Cambridge, MA: Harvard University Press, 1991). See also Heinrich Meyer, *The Age of the World: A Chapter in the History of Enlightenment* (Allentown, PA: Muhlenberg College, 1951); James Barr, "Why the World Was Created in 4004 BC: Archbishop Ussher and Biblical Chronology," *BJRL* 67 (1985): 575–608, and "Luther and Biblical Chronology," *BJRL* 72 (1990): 51–67; Robin Bruce Barnes, *Prophecy and Gnosis: Apocalypticism in the Wake of the Lutheran Reformation* (Stanford, CA: Stanford University Press, 1988); William Adler, *Time Immemorial* (Washington, DC: Dumbarton Oaks Research Library and Collection, 1989); Parry, *A Protestant Vision*; and Daniel Rosenberg and Anthony Grafton, *Cartographies of Time: A History of the Timeline* (New York: Princeton Architectural Press, 2010). For Ralegh's chronological practice, see Ernest Strathmann, "Ralegh on the Problems of Chronology," *HLQ* 11 (1948): 129–48.

had kindled in the Egyptians and the Chaldeans a desire to proclaim their own antiquity, they were easily converted to this belief. But if the series of years had been preserved in perfect condition, no question of the world's eternity would ever have risen."[2] Lydiat argued that, when true knowledge of Creation had not been guarded, not only the Egyptians and Chaldeans, but also Aristotle and many others had been inspired by the devil to efface the Creator by belief in an eternal world.

True chronological knowledge distinguished Christians from pagans, but Lydiat also closely identified chronological error with Catholicism. His second error identified the doctrine of free will as a blindness to Providence that stemmed from confused chronology. The devil, he explained had "more easily persuaded many that no providence of God governed the world because, on account of the confusion of times, it could hardly be understood in what just interval of times God laid down the chief events of his and other peoples, and of the entire world. When these are resolved, divine providence and dispensation will clearly shine through."[3] The devil had disordered chronological knowledge to blur the clarity of predestination, thus introducing a conviction that God did not govern the world—and, therefore, insinuating that men could. Catastrophically, sacred history was made illegible, and the past lost its divinely sanctioned function as a demonstrative theater of Providence. The Egyptians and Chaldeans had pridefully bestowed eternity on themselves by accepting diabolic teaching; the Church of Rome's defense of free will was no better.

Lydiat's final criticism precisely enumerated the process by which the confusion of chronologies effected unorthodox beliefs. As he explained: "Sacred history was broken apart by the profane history that [the devil]

2. Thomas Lydiat, *De variis annorum formis* (London, 1605), 1–2. "Verum ille creatoris sui aemulus humani autem generis hostis capitalis, sicut ipsa Dei opera ab initio mundi (permissu nimirum ipsius Dei qui arcano & inscrutabili suo consilio ante iacta mundi fundamenta quomodo haec omnia successura essent iam tum apud se decreverat) partim ex hominum mentibus & memoria delevit atque obliteravit, partim variis modis calumniatus est: ita etiam ordinem ac rationem temporum misere perturbavit. Atque hinc quadruplex malum protulit. Primum enim plurimis hominibus opinionem de mundi aetate (qua opinione quantum decedit gloriae Dei creatoris) hinc propinavit. Cum enim in celeberrimis profanarum gentium Aegyptiis & Chaldaeis aliisque accendisset affectationem antiquitatis: subornavit qui apud ipsas ostentarent innumerorum prope annorum historias atque observationes astronomicas; unde ad mundi aeternitatem facilis fuit transitus. Quod si series annorum mundi ab hominibus sartatecta conservata esset, de eius aeternitate utique nulla quaestio unquam orta esset."

3. Ibid., 2–3. "Secundo multis eo facilius persuasit nulla Dei providentia gubernari mundum, quia propter confusionem temporum vix licet intelligere in qua iusta temporum intervalla Deus praecipuos populi sui & caeterarum gentium totiusque mundi casus coniecerit: quae certe deprehensa apparebunt talia ut in iis divina providentia ac dispensatio clare elucescat."

polluted with innumerable errors regarding the order of times, and likewise sacred interpretations were made contradictory by the inept interpretations of many, and thus he obscured the meaning of sacred history and
shook its authority. Briefly, he nourished the stupidity of Atheists, and the
lies of the Jews, and the apostasy of the Antichristians."[4] The devil had
cultivated chronological pride in many peoples, encouraging them to devise alternative calendars, date time by their own civil institutions rather
than from Creation, and grandly exaggerate their own antiquity. Correlating these mendacious pasts with sacred history had corrupted man's
knowledge. Lydiat reviled the new Gregorian calendar as yet another innovation in timekeeping that abused divine meaning. In his view, Catholic
Rome had revived polytheist Greece. Only Scripture provided a genuine
testimony: all other commentators were anathema to this rigid Calvinist
hermeneutic.

As Lydiat surveyed the existing chronological literature, the monumental scale of his challenge came into focus. The earliest communities
of men had used one single, divinely approved calendar, he claimed, but
the confusion of languages with the fall of the Tower of Babel had frac-
tured chronological as well as linguistic cohesion. For more than three
millennia, civilizations aside from the Israelites had dated events within
increasingly inaccurate calendars. Only by carefully retracing the historical transmission of calendars could any chronologer hope to reconstitute
the true order of events, and only by reimposing the Hebrew calendar as
the instrument of contemporary and historical timekeeping could the full
richness of divine Providence be made evident.

Lydiat, like most chronologers, was more adapter than innovator. Many
contemporaries would have agreed that chronological error had been introduced by mistranslations, exaggeration, and ignorance, whether or not
they saw these as evidence of diabolic machination. Lydiat's goal, in fact,
constituted an idiosyncratically solascripturalist iteration of the calendrical science pioneered by his foremost detractor, the Calvinist polymath
Joseph Scaliger. Scaliger had devised a method to integrate the calendars
of all ancient civilizations two decades earlier, seeking to resolve questions generated by the newly widespread practice of addressing problems of
scriptural chronology by consulting ancient pagan sources. From Lydiat's

---

4. Ibid., 3. "Quarto denique collisa historia sacra cum profana maximam partem a se in-
numeris erroribus inquinata in ratione temporum, adeoque sacrae partibus per ineptas multorum interpretationes inter se collisi, ipsius sententiam obscuravit atque etiam auctoritatem
apud multos vehementer labefactavit. Ac ut verbo dicam, hinc plurimum alit & Atheorum
stultitiam & Iudaeorum pertinaciam & Antichristianorum apostasiam."

perspective, these interventions had cumulatively supplied the grounds to deepen knowledge of the ancient world while imbricating new layers of errors on and presenting intolerable challenges to Scripture.

Though Lydiat viewed himself within a Continental scholarly community, he perceived his endeavors as unique within the British archipelago. Two years later, defending his Hebrew-centric calendrical science from Scaliger's pointed criticism, he noted: "I know nobody in Britain from the number of learned men who performs or performed work in this field; nor is there doubt that very few exist."[5] There were those who would have disagreed. In the 1590s, the chronological publications and lectures of Hugh Broughton and Edward Lively led the queen to appoint a panel of high clerics to arbitrate their dispute publically. The Puritan Hebraicist Broughton, with whom Lydiat would have sided, argued that only scriptural evidence was reliable to determine the murky chronology of the aftermath of the Babylonian Captivity, while Lively, the Regius Professor of Hebrew at Cambridge, solved this problem through a wide range of sources, including pagan authorities.[6]

Ralegh, too, might have disagreed with Lydiat's assessment. As Lydiat composed this denunciation in 1607, Ralegh's work on the *History* led him to chronologies by the Puritan divine John More, Lydiat, and the Scottish minister Robert Pont, and, in the Tower, he may have consulted Thomas Harriot in person about chronological problems.[7] But Ralegh, like Lydiat,

5. Thomas Lydiat, *Defensio tractatus de variis annorum formis* (London, 1607), A4r. ". . . è doctorum autem virorum numero qui insignem eidem studio operam hodie navet aut navaverit in Britannia nostra equidem neminem novi: neque vero dubium est perpaucos existere."

6. Broughton's 1588 *A Concent of Scripture* argued that Scripture alone provided the basis for this chronology. In 1590, he published a translated excerpt of Matthieu Béroalde's 1575 *Chronicum* entitled *A Short view of the* Persian *Monarchie, and of* Daniels weekes. His position was attacked in public lectures by Lively. The conflict culminated in 1591 when Broughton wrote to Elizabeth requesting that ecclesiastical authorities adjudicate the debate. She appointed as arbiters John Whitgift, the archbishop of Canterbury, and John Aylmer, the bishop of London. Though they sided with Broughton, his was a short-lived victory, coinciding with the last moment for several decades in which the Puritans approached control of the Church of England. The eventual publication of Lively's 1597 *True Chronologie of the times of the Persian Monarchy* signaled that the upper echelon of the Church of England, and especially Whitgift, was severing ties with such hot Protestants. For Lively, see Grafton and Weinberg, *"I Have Always Loved the Holy Tongue."*

7. Harriot was a client of Ralegh's fellow Tower inmate Henry Percy, Earl of Northumberland, and, thus, Ralegh's chronologies could have been shaped by interactions with Harriot. But, though Harriot's papers preserve chronological notes digested from Josephus and Sigonio and indicate that he was familiar with the work of Scaliger and Béroalde, his chronologies do not overlap with Ralegh's. See BL Add. MSS 6782–89, esp. MS 6782, fols. 31r–v; MS 6788, fols. 507ff.; and MS 6789, fols. 469ff.

Lively, and Broughton, predominantly looked beyond Britain for chrono-logical experts. As he set out to produce the *History*, he familiarized him-self with the contours of chronological debate by consulting the works of Johannes Funck, Theodor Bibliander, Matthieu Béroalde, David Chytraeus, Scaliger, Lorenz Codomann, Abraham Bucholzer, Gerald Mercator, Dan-iel Angelocrator, Elias Reusner, Paul Eber, Werner Rolevinck, Leonhard Krentzheim, Agostino Torniello, Sethus Calvisius, and Heinrich Bünting while also gleaning chronological opinions from histories, biblical com-mentaries, and other sources. These works constituted vital resources as he constructed the *History*, offering exacting analyses of problems of an-cient chronology and scathing critiques of each other's solutions.

Within these sources, beneath their concern for the dates of epochal events and disputes over chronological minutiae, Ralegh would have rec-ognized that all Christian scholars shared one deeply embedded chrono-logical belief: time began when God created the world. Belief in Creation was a sign of monotheism and distinguished pious men from eternalist polytheists such as Aristotle and the pagan Romans. Nevertheless, the charge of eternalism was common in learned circles, for scholars directed it at their enemies as a conventional means of questioning their orthodoxy. It was especially useful as an oblique attack on the Aristotelians, who contentedly ignored his eternalism while using his philosophical methods in their chairs at European universities.[8] Most conceded that Greek and Roman histories might supply accurate narratives of the classical world, but few disputed that Scripture was always more authoritative than pagan discussions of the deep past. The accusation of eternalism was a power-ful one, and Ralegh, in fact, had been slandered in precisely this fashion. As we will see, his response to this accusation reflected close familiarity with bitter debates concerning Creation and chronology.

RALEGH, CREATION, AND HERESY

In 1594, Ralegh was brought before the Court of High Commission to ad-dress reports that he disparaged belief in Creation and subscribed to anti-Christian chronologies. These allegations reflect the local reception of a wide-reaching confessional polemic, for they largely stemmed from the English Jesuit Robert Parsons's 1592 invective *Elizabethae Angliae reginae*

8. See Stephen Menn, "The Intellectual Context," in *The Cambridge History of Seventeenth-Century Philosophy*, ed. Daniel Garber and Michael Ayers (Cambridge: Cambridge University Press, 1998), 33–86.

haeresim calvinianam propugnantis . . . edictum. This libel initially was inspired by Elizabeth's 1591 proclamation seeking to turn English Catholics against proselytizing priests and Jesuits such as Parsons.[9] Parsons vilified all Elizabeth's ministers, who had, he felt, supported this edict, and he demonized Ralegh for allegedly running a school of atheism that encroached on the queen's authority by forcing anti-Catholic measures through Parliament. The tract was translated into English later that year, with Ralegh's libel condensed as: "Of Sir Walter Rauley's schoole of Atheisme by the waye and of the Coniurer that is M[aster] thereof, and of the diligence used to get young gentlemen to this schoole, where in both Moyses, and our Saviour; the olde, and new Testamente are iested at, and the schollers taught amonge other thinges, to spell God backwarde."[10] This passage softened some of the vitriol of Parsons's original diatribe, which described Ralegh's then client Harriot as a necromancer, further reviling "this Edict written by this Magus and Epicurean teacher of Ralegh, disseminated in the name of the Queen, which lucidly, clearly, succinctly, and without evasion denies all divinity, and all immortality of the soul, and expectation of another life."[11] Parsons thus ascribed the proclamation, implausibly, to Harriot's diabolic pen.

Parsons's libel likely derived from an aggressive misreading of the ac-

---

9. Parsons intended to instill in Catholic Europe outrage at the Calvinist trajectory of Elizabethan England and hoped to inspire another Armada. See Alexandra Walsham, *Church Papists: Catholicism, Conformity and Confessional Polemics in Early Modern England* (Woodbridge: Boydell, 1993); and Michael C. Questier, *Catholicism and Community in Early Modern England: Politics, Aristocratic Patronage, and Religion, c. 1550–1640* (Cambridge: Cambridge University Press, 2006).

10. [Robert Parsons], *An advertisement written to a secretarie of my L. Treasurers of Ingland . . .* ([Antwerp], 1593), 18.

11. Robert Parsons, *Elizabethae, Angliae reginae haeresin Caluinianam propugnantis . . . Responsio* (Leiden, 1592), 28–29. "Et certe si Gualteri quoque Raulaei schola frequens de Atheismo, paulo longius processerit (quam modo ita notam & publicam suis in aedibus habere dicitur, Astronomo quodam Necromanteo praeceptore, ut Iuventutis nobilioris, non exiguae turmae, tam Mosis legem veterem, quam nostram Christi domini ingeniosis quibusdam facetiis, ac dicteriis eludere ac in circulis suis irridere dedicerint) si haec, inquam, schola radices ac robur ceperit, ut ipse Raulaeus in Senatu delectus fuerit, quo reipubl. quoque negotiis praesideat (quod omnes non sine summa ratione expectant, cum primas apud Reginam post Dudlaeum & Hattonum teneat, & ex gregario prope Hiberniae milite, virum principem, ac potentem Reginae sola gratia, nullis praecedentibus meritis effectum videant) quid (inquam) erit expectandum aliud, nisi ut aliquando Edictum aliquod a Mago illo atque Epicureo Raulaeo praeceptore, conscriptum, Reginae nomine evulgatum cernamus, quo plane omnis divinitas, omnis animae immortalitas, & alterius vitae expectatio dilucide, clare, breviter, & citra ambages denegetur, & laesae maiestatis accusentur tanquam reipub. perturbatores, qui contra istiusmodi doctrinam tam placidam, ac in carnis vitiis volutantibus suavem, scrupulos cuiquam aut molestia moveant?"

counts that had emerged from Ralegh's exploration circles, for Harriot and Ralegh encountered ideas of the eternal world, not only in ancient sources, but also in the New World.[12] In 1588, Harriot had written of the beliefs of the natives they encountered in Virginia: "They beleeve that there are many Gods which they call *Mantóac*, but of different sortes and degrees; one onely chiefe and great God, which hath bene from all eternitie. Who as they affirme when hee proposed to make the worlde, made first other goddes of a principal order to bee as meanes and instruments to bee used in the creation and government to follow; and after the Sunne, Moone, and starres, as pettie goddes and the instruments of the other order more principall."[13] Harriot's discussion of the chronological systems of such polytheists may have drawn suspicion on him and his patron, but only after Parsons's insinuation that they subscribed to pagan eternalism did their beliefs face close, hostile scrutiny.

If there was little besides malicious rumor to evince Ralegh's atheism, the number of his detractors allowed the allegation to gain currency. Later in 1592, Archbishop Whitgift's client Thomas Nashe's libelous *Pierce Pennilesse his Supplication to the Devill* was published. Nashe bemoaned "a number that fetch the Articles of their Beleefe out of Aristotle, and thinke of heaven and hell as the Heathen Philosophers." He continued indignantly: "Hence Atheists triumph and reioyce, and talke as prophanely of the Bible, as of Bevis of Hampton. I heare say there be Mathematitions abroad, that will proove men before Adam, and they are harboured in high places, who will maintaine it to the death, that there are no divels."[14] This mathematician was likely Harriot, harbored by Ralegh. Nashe expanded on Parsons by giving a precise explication of Harriot's alleged beliefs.

Ralegh and Harriot's purported atheism crystallized in the delivery of the "Baines Note" to the Privy Council the following spring, in which Richard Baines cataloged Christopher Marlowe's improprieties and explicitly linked his heresies to Harriot and Ralegh.[15] Baines's second item re-

---

12. For the argument that Ralegh subscribed to these views, see M. C. Bradbrook, *The School of Night: A Study in the Literary Relationships of Sir Walter Raleigh* (Cambridge: Cambridge University Press, 1936). Modern scholarship has dismantled Bradbrook's case. See, in particular, Scott Mandelbrote, "The Religion of Thomas Harriot," in Fox, ed., *Thomas Harriot*, 246–79.

13. Thomas Harriot, *A Briefe and True Report of the New Found Land of Virginia* (London, 1588), E2v.

14. Thomas Nashe, *Pierce Pennilesse his Supplication to the Devill* (London, 1592), B3r–v.

15. See Charles Nicholl, *The Reckoning: The Murder of Christopher Marlowe* (London: J. Cape, 1992). For an alternative view, see Constance Brown Kuriyama, *Christopher Marlowe: A Renaissance Life* (Ithaca, NY: Cornell University Press, 2002).

ported Marlowe's belief "That the Indians and many Authors of antiquity have assuredly writen above 16 thousand yeares agone wher as Adam is proved to have lived within 6 thowsand yeares." This linked Marlowe's alleged heterodoxy to the chronological legends of the ancients and the explorations supervised by Ralegh. The third was that "He affirmeth that Moyses was but a Jugler, & that one Heriots being Sir W Raleighs man can do more then he."[16] Marlowe, the note implied, was one member of a seditious, atheist group sympathetic to ancient and contemporary pagans.

Such rumors ultimately led to an official investigation of Ralegh's beliefs. The precipitating event was a dinner late in 1593 hosted by Sir George Trenchard in Dorset, at which Ralegh disputed with Ralph Ironside, the vicar of Winterborne. Ironside complained that Ralegh exhibited suspect beliefs on the nature of the soul, and, in March 1594, the Court of High Commission launched an investigation. Local figures and attendees of the dinner were brought to Cerne and peppered with questions such as, "Who do you know thats an atheist or apostate? Against God? Against providence of the world? In whom doe you know or have harde that hath spoken against god his providence on the worlde? Or of the worldes beginninge? Or ending?" John Davis, the curate of Moscombe, reported that "he knoweth of noe sure parson directlye, but he hath harde Sr Walter Rawleigh by generall reporte hath had some reasoning go against the deitye of god, and his omnipotence." The local man Nicholas Jefferys, who had attended the dinner, stated that "he hard by reporte of divers that Sr Walter Rawleigh and his retenue are generally suspected of Atheisme."[17]

Jefferys's account corroborated the written relation Ironside delivered to the commission. The discussion had begun when Ralegh's half brother Carew Ralegh boasted that he had sinned many times over but never been punished. Ironside replied that, though Carew's body had not been, his soul would be. Walter and Ironside dominated the ensuing conversation. According to Ironside, Ralegh stated: "I have beene (sayeth he [Ralegh]) a scholler some tyme in Oxforde; I have answered under a Bacheler of Arte, & had talke with divers; yet hitherunto in this pointe (to witt what the reasonable soule of man is) have I not by anye beene resolved."[18] Ralegh's expressions of interest in the question—unlike his claim to have received a degree—were likely not exaggerations, for many of the few annotations in his copy of Sebastian Fox Morzillo's syncretist *De naturae philosophia*,

16. BL Harley MS 6848, fol. 185.
17. Ibid., fols. 183r, 184v, 185r.
18. Ibid., 188r.

certainly penned before June 1590, were indexing notes for Morzillo's discussions of the material status of the soul, such as "Whether the soul is
made by a transmission."[19] In response, Ironside "cited the generall definition of Anima out of Aristotle 2 de Anima cap 2. & then a subiecto proprio
deduced the speciall definition of the soule reasonable, that it was Actus
primus corporis organici agentis humani vitam in potentia [the perfection
or first act of an organic human body, having power of life]."[20] Ralegh, he
reported, was not impressed with this display of Aristotelian learning.[21]
Conceding that some at the table might find such technical philosophy
difficult, Ironside restated "that the reasonable soule is a spiritualle & immortal substance breathed into man by God, whereby he lives, & moves &
understandeth, & soe is distinguished from other Creatures." Ralegh was
again dissatisfied, and his response sheds light on the friction between the
two. Ralegh asked: "yea but what is that spirituall & immortall substance
breathed into man?"[22] The substance of the soul interested Ralegh, and
he foregrounded the paradox that an eternal, indivisible, immaterial God
could coexist with a separate immortal substance. But he also indicated
that he did not subscribe to the Aristotelian vision alleged in the Baines
Note. Instead, his criticism highlighted the difficulty of fusing Aristotelian natural philosophy with scriptural Creation.

Ironside was not attuned to Ralegh's implications and, indeed, saw
Ralegh's questioning as undermining Creation rather than his own analytic apparatus. He responded, "the soule quoth I," for which he earned
Ralegh's rebuke for arguing by tautology. Ironside insisted that tautologies
were necessary for argument, before the subject turned to the divine being
itself. According to Ironside, a piqued Ralegh snorted: "Marrye quod Sr
Walter those be like for neither could I lerne hitherto what god is." Ironside reported that a Mr. Fitzjames answered "that Aristotle shoulde saye
he was Ens Encium [thing of things]," invoking the apocryphum that the
philosopher's dying words revealed his recognition of the one true God.
Fitzjames's response, in fact, aimed to support Ironside by legitimizing
the use of Aristotle to articulate Christian doctrine. But Ironside recognized neither that Ralegh highlighted the contradiction of using a pagan
to support Christianity nor that Fitzjames offered a justification. Instead,
Ironside responded: "I answered that whether Aristotle dying in a feaver

19. Sebastian Foxe Morzillo, *De Naturae Philosophia* (Paris, 1560), 161 (Small Special Collections Library, University of Virginia, shelfmark B185.F69 1560). "An Anima fit ex traduce."
    20. BL Harley MS 6849, fol. 188r.
    21. Ibid. "It was misliked of Sr Walter as obscure, & intricate."
    22. Ibid.

shoulde cry ens entium miserere mi, or drowning himselfe in Euripum shoulde say quia ego te non capio tu me capies, it was uncertaine, but that god was ens entium a thinge of thingse having beinge of him selfe, & givinge beinge to all creatures, it was most certaine, and confirmed by god himselfe unto Moyses." He passed over the issue of Aristotle's beliefs as unimportant despite previously having cited his authority on the soul. Ralegh remained dissatisfied and responded: "Yea but what is this ens entium?" When Ironside provided another tautological answer ("I answered it is God"), Ralegh suggested that they cease: "Sr Walter wished that grace might be sayed for that q*uoth* he, is better then this disputation."[23]

Though Ironside related this account, it reveals him as laboring to defend a paradoxical synthesis of Aristotelian philosophy and Christian chronology. Fitzjames hinted at support for Aristotle's applicability to Christianity. And Ralegh suggested that using Aristotelian analysis to define God made the doctrine of Creation incoherent and, accordingly, tried to establish the material and formal statuses of God and the soul. Ralegh did not explicitly articulate his own beliefs, but his inquiry showed sensitivity to the problem of using ancient pagans to affirm a created world. It is, perhaps, with this understanding that the high commission aborted the investigation.

Still, rumors of Ralegh's heterodoxy circulated, and his 1603 treason trial put their power on full display. When Ralegh cited Scripture in his defense, the prosecuting attorney, Edward Coke, swooned: "Oh Damnable Atheist he hath learned some texts of Scripture to force his owne purpose, but falsely alleadged them." Such hysterical invective clearly gained purchase; when delivering his opinion, Chief Justice Sir John Popham upbraided Ralegh:

You have been taxed by the world, with the defense of most heathenish and Blasphemous opinions: which I list not to repeat, because Christian Eares cannot endure to heare them; nor the Authors and maintainours of them suffered to live in a common wealth. You know what men say of Harriot; you should doo well before you goe out of the world to give satisfaction herein. And not to dye with those imputations on you: Let not any Devill perswade you to thinke there is noe eternity in heaven; for if you think thus you shall surely find there is eternity in Hell fire.[24]

23. Ibid., fols. 188r–v.
24. BL Add. MS 73086, fols. 18r, 19r.

Despite his protestations, Ralegh was tarred as an atheist, a heathen, conversant with the devil and the imp Harriot.

CHRONOLOGY AS EXEGESIS

Ralegh's discussions of the proper sources for analyzing the theological significance of time, then, had generated questions concerning his orthodoxy well before he produced the *History*. And, as he well knew, debates about the sources to use in mapping world chronology often precipitated such accusations, for early modern scholars considered chronology after the inaugural event of Creation to reveal similarly God's control over the world.

Chronology and Creation complemented each other as philosophical and historical manifestations of the same monotheist doctrine. That the world had been created endowed it with certain qualities, above all that it was finite and subject to measurable time. The shared goal of chronologers, consequently, was to provide a world chronology that would allow all events to be assigned dates revealing their temporal distance from Creation, the incarnation of Christ, and other events. They faced many obstacles to this task, in particular the question of how to determine the dates of ancient events in the face of scriptural ambiguity and silence. Up until the 1550s, Christian scholars typically relied on philological and literal exegeses of the Bible, seeking to elicit the true chronology of the ancient world by painstakingly inspecting different scriptural traditions and consulting authoritative biblical commentaries. Chronology was, thus, rooted in scriptural explication.

This uniform practice, however, did not yield chronological consensus. The conflicting chronologies of the Hebrew and Greek Bibles had created the bulk of disagreement within Christianity from late antiquity until the early sixteenth century. The lengthier Greek chronology of the Septuagint, to which Eusebius and Augustine subscribed, dated Creation to around 5200 BC; Jerome had integrated the more protracted Hebrew chronology to put it at around 4000 BC in the Latin Vulgate.[25] In 1500, the main issue remained which of these two systems provided a more accurate account of time. The late fifteenth-century chronicler Werner Rolevinck described "the calculation of years, which is contained and diligently noted in scripture." Given the importance of this enterprise for recognizing God's will in the world, he noted, "it seems very surprising that today's commenta-

---

25. The Hebrew Bible placed Creation at 3760 BC. See C. A. Patrides, "Renaissance Estimates of the Year of Creation," *HLQ* 26 (1963): 315–22.

tors on scripture have diverse opinions concerning this material in many places, and that there is not everywhere concordance. But this returns us to the question of whether one must follow the translation of the Greek Septuagint in the calculation of the years, or rather the text of the Hebrew Bible, which was written by Moses."[26] For Rolevinck, chronology was first and foremost a practice of scriptural exegesis requiring close readings of Scripture to fill in its many chronological lacunae and resolve apparent temporal contradictions.

Few commentators a century later would follow Rolevinck in accepting the Septuagint's authority over the Vulgate's; the spreading knowledge of Eastern languages and greater weight of an ideal of scholarship that went *ad fontes* rather than to translations lent Jerome's chronology a considerable advantage. Accepting a Hebrew outline for chronology provided some preliminary yardsticks, and early modern chronologers derived a broad range of possibilities for dates for Creation, generally within one hundred years of 4000 BC. The Flood was almost indisputably at *anno mundi* 1656. The next significant marker was the birth of Abraham either 292 or 352 years after the Flood, though whether the term *birth* referred to his literal birth or to his spiritual covenant with God could add up to seventy-five more years. The Exodus began 430 years later; from this event until the founding of the first Temple was 480 years. The duration of the subsequent era—until the Temple's destruction and the beginning of the Babylonian Captivity—represented an extremely thorny problem. A growing group in the sixteenth century dated the destruction by references within classical authorities. Those who accepted only the authority of Scripture, on the other hand, gave the destruction a date by identifying the moment of Daniel's prophecy of the seventy weeks heralding the birth of Christ and then determining their duration. Most agreed that each week represented a period of seven years and that the prophesized period consisted of 490 years, but others thought that this number rounded off a slightly longer period.

26. Werner Rolevinck, *Fasciculus temporum = Compendio cronológico* (1474; León: Universidad de León, Secretariado de Publicaciones, Cátedra de San Isidoro de la Real Colegiata de León, 1993), 1. "Supputatio annorum: que in sacra historia diligentissime annotata continetur: de qua ut idem augustinus testatur: hoc certissime tenendum est: quod tanta est divina auctoritate roborata: ut omnino falsissimum sit: quicquid ab ea ita discrepat: quod cum ea omnino concordari non possit. Quae cum ita sint: mirum valde miretur: cur sanctae scripturae tractatores de hac matera in tum sunt diversi in pluribus locis usque hodie: ut aut omnino aut vix nequant concordari. Et redit illa antiqua & famosa questio de translatione septuagintae interpretum: an potius ei standum sit in supputatione annorum: an textui hebreorum: quem moyses ille maximus & primus legis promulgator edidit."

Mapping chronology in the latter periods also required sorting through
the morass of dating conventions deployed by ancient peoples. The Hebrews, Persians, and Egyptians often dated events by the year of a king's
reign, the Greeks assigned their dates within the four-year Olympiad cycle, and the Romans either gave dates from the founding of the city or,
later, had simply noted the names of the consuls of the year. Chronologers
struggled to adjudicate between the competing claims among and within
pagan, Hebrew, and Christian accounts, and many adapted elements of the
Greek within outlines that were predominantly taken from the Hebrew.
They captured the challenges of their art by describing it through the metaphor of a labyrinth—an easily entered maze from which one could not be
extricated.[27] There was little agreement between chronologers, and, like
contemporaneous historians, they did not delude themselves that they enjoyed consensus.[28] In attempting to resolve intractable conflicts between
their solutions, early modern scholars devised new methods of evaluating sources that would ultimately challenge the scriptural tradition they
sought to uphold. As we will see, Ralegh's choices in the controversies
illuminate his understanding of ancient world history and his allegiances
on the intellectual battlefields of his own day.

27. Methodical chronology, in this metaphor, was Ariadne's thread. For example, the
Swiss Orientalist Theodor Bibliander wrote: "without [chronology], which is like the thread of
Theseus [Ariadne's thread], history would be an inextricable labyrinth." Theodore Bibliander,
De ratione temporum (Basel, 1551), 2. "Sine qua [chronographia] . . . tanquam Thesei filo, histo-
ria erit Labyrinthus inextricabilis."

28. Consider the debate developed in the second Latin edition (1602) of the Lutheran theologian Lorenz Codomann's 1581 *Annales Sacrae Scripturae*. Included in the updated edition
was a 1581 letter from Frederick Husmann to Louis, Count Palatine, that explained Codomann's interventions. Husmann was critical of Codomann's solutions and, instead, praised
the chronology advocated by Luther in his 1541 *Supputatio annorum*. (For Luther's chronology,
see Barr, "Luther and Biblical Chronology"; Barnes, *Prophecy and Gnosis*; and Headley, *Luther's View of Church History*.) The Lutheran preacher Andreas Pangratius, in another letter to
the Count Palatine included in the edition, defended Codomann. While Husmann had viewed
the discrepancy between the calculations of Codomann and Luther as cause for alarm, Pangratius disarmed this worry with bitter candor. He wrote: "I am not ignorant that more than
40 chronographers exist, none of whom agree on the age of the world. And the one with whom
Husmann agrees is Martin Luther, whose other necessary occupations, even he confessed, prevented him from knowing how to institute an exact calculation." Laurentius Codomann, *Annales Sacrae Scripturae* (Wittenberg, 1602), 18 (second pagination). "Non ignoro plures quam
40 Chronographos extare, quorum nullus cum aliter in annis mundi numerandis congruit.
Cum unico duntaxat illorum D husmannus finaliter convenit, nempe cum D Martino Lu-
thero, qui ut per occupationes maxime necessarias non potuit, ita etiam ingenue fatetur, se
noluisse exactam instituere supputationem." Consensus on the age of the world, and on particular wrangles such as Abraham's birth year, was not found across early modern Europe or
even within Lutheran circles.

NEOPLATONISM AND THE EXPANSION OF SOURCES

Ironically, controversial new sources for ancient chronology were first introduced to refine exegetical analysis of the most unassailable point of consensus: the belief in Creation. Seeking to strengthen the late antique tradition of Neoplatonism revived in the late fifteenth century by Marsilio Ficino and Pico della Mirandola, early sixteenth-century Neoplatonists devised innovative interpretations of pagan creation myths to preserve the theological credibility of their ancient philosophical sources. These efforts to defend their treasured philosophers opened them to accusations of eternalism while precipitating a broad reconsideration of the credibility of all sources containing chronological evidence of God's creation.

The scholar most frequently targeted as an eternalist in Ralegh's sources was Agostino Steuco, the early sixteenth-century papal polemicist, Vatican librarian, and promoter of the *prisca theologia*. Like Ficino and Pico, he drew on late antique Christians such as Eusebius and Lactantius to argue that God's divine truth had always emanated through the world, even before Christ. Though he did not seek to Christianize ancients such as Hermes Trismegistus, Zoroaster, and, above all, Plato, he argued that invaluable, if corrupted, redactions of Mosaic ideas were perceptible in the shards of their writings.[29]

The issue of Creation presented an important problem for Steuco, for demonstrating concordance between Scripture and the ancients would powerfully affirm his claims. In his 1535 *Cosmopoeia*, Steuco boldly pronounced: "That there was an origin of the world, and a certain formation

---

29. For this stance, called the *prisca theologia* or the *perennia philosophia*, see esp. Charles B. Schmitt, "Perennial Philosophy: From Agostino Steuco to Leibniz," *JHI* 27 (1966): 505–32; and D. P. Walker, *The Ancient Theology: Studies in Christian Platonism from the Fifteenth to the Eighteenth Century* (London: Duckworth, 1972). Joseph Levine's "Sir Walter Ralegh and the Ancient Wisdom" considers Ralegh's engagement with this position in the context of the debate between the ancients and the moderns. See also his "Latitudinarians, Neoplatonists, and the Ancient Wisdom," in *Philosophy, Science, and Religion in England, 1640–1700*, ed. Richard Kroll, Richard Ashcroft, and Perez Zagorin (Cambridge: Cambridge University Press, 1992), 85–108, and "Deists and Anglicans: The Ancient Wisdom and the Idea of Progress," in *The Margins of Orthodoxy: Heterodox Writing and Cultural Response, 1660–1750*, ed. Roger Lund (Cambridge: Cambridge University Press, 1995), 219–39. For Steuco, see Ronald K. Delph, "Polishing the Papal Image in the Counter-Reformation: The Case of Agostino Steuco," *SCJ* 23 (1992): 35–47, "From Venetian Visitor to Curial Humanist: The Development of Agostino Steuco's 'Counter'-Reformation Thought," *RQ* 47 (1994): 102–39, "Valla *Grammaticus*, Agostino Steuco, and the Donation of Constantine," *JHI* 57 (1996): 55–77, and "Renovation, *Reformatio* and Humanist Ambition in Rome," in *Heresy, Culture and Religion in Early Modern Italy*, ed. Ronald K. Delph, Michelle M. Fontaine, and John Jeffries Martin (Kirksville, MO: Truman State University Press, 2006), 73–92.

of all things, and that the sky, the land, and man did not exist for eternal time nor for innumerable ages, and that Creation was as sacred books teach, stands not only from [Scripture]—the fidelity of which only a mad and impious man will impugn—but also from the monuments of nearly all peoples, and from continual transmissions of doctrine through the entire world." Many ancient peoples, he insisted, had access to the writings of Moses, and the writings of philosophers such as Orpheus, Hermes, and Plato shone through with evidence that they had read Scripture. He explained that the Chaldeans, the Egyptians, the Phoenicians, and even the Greeks "could have read the books of Moses, who of all writers is most ancient, and from him sucked up those things that are now found in their books."[30] These pagan communities, Steuco proclaimed, revered their copies of the Pentateuch.

For Steuco, the cosmogonic accounts in pagan texts were primary evidence of exposure to Genesis. He explained: "Hesiod, Anaxagoras, Plato and the ancient Greek theologians believed and preached the same thing as Moses." He continued: "When Hesiod said, 'Chaos existed before and after the broad earth, which supports itself by love of things on top of a strengthening weight,' he said two things very much worth knowing, and that concur with Moses in every way. First there was chaos, which is the land and water undifferentiated, as a mass. . . . Then the land existed separately, which Moses called the seclusion of the waters from the land."[31] Steuco conflated the undifferentiated mass that ancient philosophers called *chaos* with the biblical "world without form, and void" (Gen. 1:2).

30. Agostino Steuco, *Opera Omnia* (Venice, 1590), 4r. "Originem mundi, omniumque rerum inventionem quondam fuisse, nec in sempiternum retro tempus, innumerabilibusque saeculis coelum ac terras, hominesque extitisse, ipsam quoque creationem fuisse qualem libri sacri tradiderunt, non his solum oraculis, quibus nemo nisi demens atque impius fidem derogabit, sed & omnium pene gentium monumentis, continuatisque doctrinae per totum orbem terrarum, apud omnes populos, successionibus, constat. Ut tradita per manus a primo genitore, transmissaque ad posteros videatur: Siquidem & apud Aegyptios, & qui priores illis, floruerunt Chaldaeos, atque Phoenices, demum Graecos ipsos, praecipue antiquissimos eorum Poetas ac Theologos, clara atque distincta, eademque non pauca Mosaicae philosophiae, quae sola pura synceraque, caeteris magnis erroribus temeratis, restitit, apparent membra, ut facile sit prudentibus ea recognoscere. . . . Potuerunt quidem librum Mosis, quippe qui omnium scriptorum est antiquissimus, cuncti legisse, & inde hausisse, quae nos in libris eorum reperta, soliti simus admirari."

31. Ibid., 5v. "Haec dixit & monstravit Moses: idem Hesiodum, Anagaxoram, Platonem, veteres Graeciae theologos doceo credidisse ac praedicasse. Atque Hesiodus cum ait *Extitit ante chaos, post haec latissima tellus / Quam super innixum pondus rerum incubat amore.* Duo dixit scitu dignissima, & cum Mose undequaque consentientia. Primum fuisse chaos, id est terram & aquam informia, ac ceu massam. . . . Deinde terram extitisse, quod Moses appelavit seclusionem aquarum a terra."

The heathens, he claimed, understood that a divine disentanglement had given shape to the chaos. But they misunderstood the process itself because of a tangled chronology. They had designated as the first worldly acts the divine separation of land and water that God had performed on the third day instead of the creation of light. This altered chronology had led them to heresy. Once this corruption was identified, Steuco argued, readers could recognize that, despite its errors, the pagan account of Creation constituted a corrupt version of the scriptural account. Not just the Jews, he argued, but many pre-Christian peoples believed in a created world.

As Ralegh's sources testified, Steuco's radical revision of the myths of ancient pagans earned papal support and widespread derision. Calvin and his followers particularly reviled Steuco's scholarship. They pronounced the knowledge of Creation a sign of piety specific to the Jewish and Christian traditions and claimed that Steuco's vision of knowledge of the true God existing since Creation undermined the significance of Christ's Passion. In his 1554 Genesis commentary, Calvin claimed that Steuco's reconciliation of the ancients was tantamount to agreement with their heresies:

> Moses useth not the hebrue worde, which signifieth to fashion or to forme, but to make, or create. Wherefore the sense is, that the worlde was made of nothing. Whereby their vanities are overthrown, which think that the world was matter alwayes without forme, and gather nothing else by the narration of Moses, then that the worlde was newly adorned, and framed with that forme, which it wanted before. This was a common imagination in olde time among heathen men. . . . But it is very absurde and not tollerable for Christian men to labour in defending this filthie errour, as Steuchus does.[32]

Calvin tacitly reversed Steuco's claim. The Vatican librarian had argued that the ancients shared belief in Creation with the Christians, imparting profound credibility to them. Calvin's purposive misreading insisted that Steuco's agreement with the ancients was a sign of his belief in their eternal world.[33]

Some of Calvin's successors were even more vitriolic. The French

32. *A Commentarie of John Calvine, upon the first booke of Moses called Genesis,* trans. Thomas Tymme (London, 1578), 26.

33. See William J. Bouwsma, *John Calvin: A Sixteenth-Century Portrait* (New York: Oxford University Press, 1988), and "The Two Faces of Humanism: Stoicism and Augustinianism in Renaissance Thought," in *Itinerarium Italicum: The Profile of the Italian Renaissance in*

Calvinist Matthieu Béroalde was particularly venomous. He argued that
Scripture was the sole trustworthy instrument of knowledge and that philosophy not drawn wholly from the Holy Books inevitably led to belief in
an eternal world.[34] He insisted that the pagans intended *chaos* to refer to
an object possessing material and form, and he railed against the Aristotelian belief that "there are two principles of all things, which are matter
and form. As if there are two gods, or perhaps more, if indeed first things
[*principia*] consist in two or more things."[35] Béroalde tarred Steuco's erudite syncretism as the abandonment of Scripture and a sure sign of idolatrous paganism.

Calvin and Steuco reflected the two poles of argument that would
emerge concerning the credibility of ancient sources. For Calvin, no source
was reliable but Scripture, and, thus, the study of Creation and all subsequent chronological matters should take the narrow shape of literal and
philological scriptural exegesis. For Steuco, Scripture's truth could be adumbrated by examination of other ancient witnesses and the importation
of multiple authorities. Their conflict molded the dynamic of the study of
early modern chronology, as some authors obsessively transformed their
knowledge of the ancient world by integrating fragments from obscure
sources, while others pronounced more and more caustically that Scripture alone provided credible testimony of the ancient past.

RALEGH'S REFORMING WORLD

When Ralegh dealt with Creation in the *History*, he knowingly addressed
a public aware of his sullied reputation. Accordingly, his treatment sought
to prove his orthodoxy. His approach, however, relied, not on Calvin, but
on Steuco and other Neoplatonists. From their vision of an ancient world
rife with pagan philosophers struggling to decode the Mosaic account of

---

the *Mirror of Its European Transformations*, ed. Heiko A. Oberman and Thomas A. Brady Jr.
(Leiden: Brill, 1975), 3–60.

34. "Those things which we must believe concerning the beginnings of things, the Sacred
prophets teach and set forth much more clearly and certainly than natural philosophers, who
are not skilled enough in those things which they profess." Matthieu Béroalde, *Chronicum*
(Geneva, 1575), 75. "Quae de rerum principiis tenenda sunt nobis, longe certius & clarius Sacra
docent & proferunt oracula, quam Physici: homines earum rerum, quas profitentur, non satis
periti. Quos eius scientiae, quam tractant, non callere principia, ex primo quod modo tractavi-
mus Geneseos capite, nulli obscurum esse potest."

35. Ibid., 75. "Duo scilicet esse rerum omnium principia, quae quidem sint materia &
forma. Quasi vero duo sint dii, vel etiam plures, si quidem duo vel plura statuantur principa."

Creation, Ralegh created a historical theology that took the ancient vicissitudes of true divine knowledge as a mirror for his own world.

Ralegh sought in the treatment of Creation in the *History* to alleviate any residual concern remaining from his trials. In the third chapter, "On the meaning of *In principio,*" he stated: "Before that beginning, there was neither primary matter to bee informed, nor forme to informe, nor any being, but the eternall . . . for if God had but disposed of matter already in being, then as the word *beginning* could not be referred to all things, so must it follow, that the institution of matter proceeded from a greater power, then that of God." God was the only creator; all other things stemmed from his lone initial presence. And Ralegh queried the material and formal dimensions of Creation: "It may be concluded, that matter could not be before this beginning: except we faine a double creation, or allow of two powers, and both infinite, the impossibilitie whereof scorneth defence."[36] He thus evoked Béroalde's criticism of Steuco to supply an orthodox answer to the questions concerning the aspects of Creation he had directed at Ironside two decades earlier.

Similarly, in the preface, Ralegh alluded to the inadvisability of consulting Aristotle on the creation of the world, declaring: "this doctrine of Faith, touching the Creation in time (*for by Faith we understand, that the world was made by the word of God*) be too weighty a work for *Aristotles* rotten ground to beare up." The use of reason alone, Ralegh proclaimed, should have led Aristotle to recognize the necessity of Creation—that it did not severely diminished his credibility. "But for my selfe," Ralegh continued, "I shall never be perswaded, that GOD hath shut up all light of Learning within the lanthorne of *Aristotles* braines."[37] He thus made clear that he still perceived Aristotelian philosophy as inappropriate for discussion of Creation.

Ralegh, however, did not share Béroalde's rigid distaste for all ancients. Following Steuco, he drew heavily on late antique Neoplatonic Christian authors such as Lactantius who had responded to pagan criticisms of Christianity's novelty by appropriating ancient philosophers, demonstrating harmony between philosophy and theology, and arguing that Christianity's longevity was obscured by recent corruptions.[38] He similarly insisted that many ancient authors did possess divine insight. He noted:

36. *HW,* 1.1.3.3.
37. *HW,* D2r–v.
38. Adler, *Time Immemorial,* 234. See also Allen, *Mysteriously Meant;* and Levine, "Sir Walter Ralegh and the Ancient Wisdom."

"*Hermes*, who lived at once with, or soone after, *Moses, Zoroaster, Musaeus, Orpheus, Linus, Anaximenes, Anaxagoras, Empedocles, Melissus, Pherecydes, Thales, Cleanthes, Pythagoras, Plato*, and many others (whose opinions are exquisitely gathered by *Steuchius Eugubinus*) found in the necessitie of invincible reason, *One eternal and infinite Being*, to be the parent of the universall."[39] Ralegh thus culled from Steuco a catalog of ancient monotheists that placed Aristotle in unflattering relief. And, like Steuco, he claimed that the rational monotheism of these ancients had been amplified by exposure to Scripture.

The second chapter of the *History*, "That the wisest of the Heathen, whose authoritie is not to be despised, have acknowledged the world to have beene created by GOD," claimed: "This work and creation of the world, did most of the ancient and learned Philosophers acknowledge, though by divers termes, and in a different maner exprest."[40] Ralegh cited Hermes Trismegistus, Zoroaster, Orpheus, and Pindar as ancient subscribers to a monotheistic, finite universe. Even before addressing the mechanics of Creation, he informed his readers that many pre-Christian learned men subscribed to tenets wholly consistent with Christianity. Like Steuco, he envisioned an ancient world populated by proto-Christian sages. Truly divine teachings and pious belief had existed in an unbroken chain since Creation, preserved, if tenuously, in the teachings of mysterious ancients.

Ralegh criticized ancient figures such as Cham, Alexander, and Nero who, by seeking their own deification, threatened the monotheistic tradition. And, though he acknowledged that their impieties had grown dominant in the ancient world, throughout the *History* he insisted on the existence of a small core of pious scholars whose reverence of Scripture had endured. In a later chapter entitled "That the wiser of the ancient Heathen had farre better opinions of God," he explained: "But that ever *Pythagoras*, or *Plato*, or *Orpheus*, with many other ancient and excellently learned, believed in any of these fooleries, it cannot be suspected, though some of them (overbusily) have mixed their owne inventions with the Scriptures." Homer and Hesiod too exhibited proper knowledge of the divine, and Ralegh impugned those who condemned Homer since "it cannot be doubted, but that Homer had read over all the bookes of Moses, as by places stolne thence, almost word for word, may appear." He cataloged monotheist citations from Plato, Apuleius, and others (again likely drawn from Steuco) and recommended to his readers "those large and learned

39. *HW*, D3r.
40. *HW*, 1.1.2.2.

Collections of *Iustine Martyr, Clemens, Lactantius, Eusebius, [Steuchus] Eugubinus, Peucer, Plessis, Danaeus,* and others."[41] Through this collection of ancient and modern Christian synthesizers, Ralegh integrated his own work within the millennial project of proving the agreement of pious ancient philosophy with Christianity.

His historical narrative emerged from a venerable tradition, but Ralegh also manipulated it effectively. In particular, he audaciously submerged the Calvinist antagonism to Steuco's *prisca theologia* into his own vision of ecclesiastical history in his exegesis "Of the meaning of the words Heaven and Earth." He considered the opinions of Steuco, Pererius, and others but found himself dissatisfied. He declared: "that by the wordes, *Heaven and Earth,* was meant the solid matter and substance, as well of all the Heavens, and Orbes supernall, as of the Globe of the Earth and Waters, which covered it over, (to wit) that very matter of all things, *materia, Chaos, possibilitas, sic posse fieri.* Which matter (saith *Calvin*) was called . . . *the seede of the Universall:* an opinion of ancient Philosophers long before."[42] Ralegh not only lumped the ancient descriptions under one Christian rubric but also used Calvin to certify this position, thus aligning the great reformer with a trajectory of ancient philosophy to which he had been deeply antagonistic. His solution to the question of the material God had used to fashion the earth reconciled not only the ancient pagans with the Christians, but also Calvin with Steuco and Ralegh himself with all. And he performed this sleight of hand with the exegetical maneuver of Steuco's that Calvin had so despised—seeking overlapping elements and moments of concordance within texts at the expense of recognizing clear differences.

The identification of classical philosophers with Calvin was of the utmost significance for Ralegh. He thus characterized Calvin as a recent installment in the periodic reformations of practice, worship, and ecclesiology that had providentially visited the world since the beginning of time. Calvin, Hermes, Steuco, Plato—all were united by their commitment to refine and propagate the worship of the one true divine being. And, if the moderns had come closer to the truth than their Latin, Greek, and Egyptian predecessors, they still were only approaching the wisdom of the ancient Hebrew recipients of Adamic knowledge. Ralegh's vision of the cycles of history consisted of intermittent reformations led by divinely inspired

41. *HW,* 1.6.7.93, 95. Ralegh's modern authors on this list included a Vatican librarian (Steuco), Melanchthon's Lutheran son-in-law (Peucer), and two militant Calvinists (Daneau and the monarchomach Duplessis-Mornay).

42. *HW* 1.1.4.4.

scholars punctuating general degradation among a godless throng. Biblical and modern history meshed to form a narration of constant imminent ruin that was partially broken or momentarily reversed by isolated reformers such as Noah, Hermes, Abraham, Solomon, Lactantius, and Calvin.

Ralegh's world history identified several moments when orthodox devotion had resoundingly triumphed over diabolic influence. Following his assertion of the devout knowledge of heathen wise men, Ralegh detailed the diabolic ceremonies and practices that had eventually been squashed by righteousness. The sacral fire of the Chaldeans had been extinguished, Jove had died, the temples consecrated to Baal and Diana had fallen to ruin, Pan's pipes had broken, Apollo's oracles had been rendered mute. Above all, during Julian the Apostate's reign, two momentous eradications had taken place: the Temple of Apollo at Delphi was finally destroyed, and an earthquake destroyed the effort of Jews, under Julian's license, to rebuild the Temple. If Ralegh was suggesting that the reign of the saints had begun with Julian's death, two generations after Constantine and the Nicene Council, he never made this explicit. Neither did he give any indication that he thought that the medieval church had preserved a core of piety and orthodoxy or that he considered it only recently given to impiety. His post-Christ historical theology remains inscrutable, though it appears to hew closely to that elaborated by John Foxe.[43] But he certainly did not view the devotional state of contemporary Europe as a source of comfort. He portrayed his world as shattering, its cataclysmic decline overwhelming the resolute resistance of learned reformers who, like himself, belonged to an ancient lineage. And, like virtually all his contemporaries, he believed himself to be living through the last days, at a time when the devil scurried among men.[44] He followed the chapter on the confutation of heathens

43. The belief in a small, persistent cohort of believers resembles the historical theology of John Foxe. See Palle J. Olsen, "Was John Foxe a Millenarian?" *Journal of Ecclesiastical History* 45 (1994): 600–624; David Loades, ed., *John Foxe and the English Reformation* (Aldershot: Scolar, 1997); and Christopher Highley and John N. King, eds., *John Foxe and His World* (Aldershot: Ashgate, 2002). See also Catherine Davies, "'Poor Persecuted Little Flock' or 'Commonwealth of Christians': Edwardian Protestant Concepts of the Church," in *Protestantism and the National Church in Sixteenth Century England*, ed. Peter Lake and Maria Dowling (London: Croom Helm, 1987), 78–102.

44. Ralegh's beliefs were permeated with the apocalypticism rife in contemporary European thought. See Paola Zambelli, ed., *"Astrologi hallucinati": Stars and the End of the World in Luther's Time* (Berlin: de Gruyter, 1986); Barnes, *Prophecy and Gnosis*; Ottavia Niccoli, *Prophecy and People in Renaissance Italy*, trans. Lydia G. Cochrane (Princeton, NJ: Princeton University Press, 1990); and Claudia Brosseder, "The Writing in the Wittenberg Sky: Astrology in Sixteenth-Century Germany," *JHI* 66 (2005): 557–76. In the British context, see Paul Christianson, *Reformers and Babylon: English Apocalyptic Visions from the Reformation*

and Jews with the chapter "Of the last refuges of the Devill to maintaine his Kingdome," in which he depicted humanity's great enemy entrepreneurially devising new tactics to deflect souls from righteousness:

> Now the Devill, because hee cannot play upon the open stage of this world (as in those dayes) and being still as industrious as ever, findes it more for his advantage to creepe into the mindes of men; and inhabiting in the Temples of their hearts, workes them to a more effectual adoration of himselfe then ever. For whereas hee first taught them to sacrifice to Monsters, to dead stones, cut into faces of beasts, birds and other mixt Natures; hee now sets before them the high and shining Idoll of glorie, the all-commanding Image of bright Gold. He tells them that Truth is the Goddesse of dangers and oppressions . . . for true wisedome (saith hee) is exercised in nothing else than in the obtaining of power to oppresse, and of riches to maintaine plentifully our worldly delights. And if this *Arch-politician* finde in his Pupils any remorse, any feare or feeling of Gods future iudgement, hee perswades them that God hath so great need of mens soules, that he will accept them at any time, and upon any conditions.[45]

Ralegh's devil, the tempting politician, approached and infiltrated men through different means at different times (with Catholic assurances). Whereas in the early history of the world he had been able to subject whole societies to his worship by perpetuating rituals in his honor, the spread of the true church now forced him to appeal to the greed, avarice, lasciviousness, and ambition of individuals.

---

to the Eve of the Civil War (Toronto: University of Toronto Press, 1978); Richard Bauckham, *Tudor Apocalypse: Sixteenth Century Apocalypticism, Millennarianism, and the English Reformation: From John Bale to John Foxe and Thomas Brightman* (Oxford: Sutton Courtenay, 1978); Katharine Firth, *The Apocalyptic Tradition in Reformation Britain, 1530-1645* (Oxford: Oxford University Press, 1979); Arthur H. Williamson, *Scottish National Consciousness in the Age of James VI: The Apocalypse, the Union and the Shaping of Scotland's Public Culture* (Edinburgh: John Donald, 1979), and "Britain and the Beast: The Apocalypse and the Seventeenth-Century Debate about the Creation of the British State," in *Millenarianism and Modernism in Early Modern European Culture*, vol. 3, *The Millenarian Turn: Millenarian Contexts of Science, Politics, and Everday Anglo-American Life in the Seventeenth and Eighteenth Centuries*, International Archives of the History of Ideas, 175 (Dordrecht: Kluwer Academic, 2001), 15–28; Parry, *A Protestant Vision*; Ute Lotz-Heumann, "'The Spirit of Prophecy Has Not Wholly Left the World': The Stylisation of Archbishop James Ussher as Prophet," in *Religion and Superstition in Reformation Europe*, ed. Helen L. Parish and William G. Naphy (Manchester: Manchester University Press, 2002), 119–32; and Dale A. Johnson, "Serving Two Masters: John Knox, Scripture, and Prophecy," in ibid., 133–53.

45. *HW*, 1.6.9.97.

Though Ralegh portrayed the devil's role in contemporaneous society as diminished from that in ancient pagan culture, he nonetheless saw lingering residue of diabolic societies in his own community, lamenting: "the Trade of Triffles in Oracles, with the Devills telling mens fortunes therein, is taken up by counterfait *Aegyptians*, and coozening *Astrologers*."[46] He saw the street alchemists and magicians of Jacobean London as emanating from a deep Babylonian past no less than he saw Catholics as importing other ancient heresies.[47] In his own time, humanity continued its battle of reform against demonic insinuation. But he did not expect this ongoing struggle to continue much longer. For him, the devil's busy presence in the terrestrial sphere heralded the end of time. As he explained: "And as the Devill our most industrious enemie was ever most diligent: so is he now more laborious then ever: the long day of Mankind drawing fast towards an evening, and the Worlds tragedie and time neere at an end."[48] Ralegh's millennium was drawing to a close, bringing with it time, history, and the fragile terrestrial world, along with its diabolic and hateful, divine and admirable inhabitants.

This, then, was Ralegh's world—divinely created, given to decline, a stage whirling with diabolic intervention and pious resistance, an unremitting series of circular, revolutionary reformations. Its beginning was a sign of God's awesome power, its approaching end a testament to divine judgment. Providence had ensured that devout men had maintained the knowledge of Creation, and Ralegh accepted the historian's task as preserving the memory of this event from the machinations of the devil. By doing so, he established himself within a tradition of prophetic scholars that extended from the beginning of time to his present day, men who functioned as instruments of divine will to stem the tide of the devil's deceits and implore the vulnerable to see God in a hostile, wretched world.

METRICS, CREDIBILITY, AND TIME

Ralegh's approach to his sources remained consistent from his treatment of Creation to his world chronology. In both cases, he ascribed considerable

---

46. *HW*, 1.6.8.96.

47. Ralegh also constructed a genealogy for the art of magic that distinguished between a divine natural philosophy practiced by the progeny of Seth and a debased art polluted by Chaldean and Persian corruptions. See my "'Abraham, Planter of Mathematics': Histories of Mathematics and Astrology in Early Modern Europe," *JHI* 67 (2006): 87–106; Lauren Kassell, "'All This Land Was Full Fill'd of Faerie'"; and my conclusion below.

48. *HW*, 1.6.9.97.

value to the testimonies of ancient pagans. As we will see, his veneration of ancient witnesses provides a point of entry into the debates concerning chronological methods that had exploded throughout Europe's scholarly community in the previous century.

Steuco was not the only scholar whose investigations of ancient history incorporated tendentious pagan testimonies. In the late 1530s, the Dominican Giovanni Maria Tolosani coordinated events by correlating astronomical observations recorded across cultures in his chronological studies of the ancient world, a practice also urged by the German mathematician Peter Apian.[49] But this method did not instigate vitriolic attacks until the Nuremberg Gnesio-Lutheran cleric Johann Funck extended this robust technique for dating events in his 1545 *Chronologia*. Funck's chronology of early world history hinted at this openness to new sources, for it relied heavily on the forged histories of Annius of Viterbo. Ralegh called Funck a *"great Berosian,"* and Scaliger and Sethus Calvisius would demonize him for the same reason.[50] But all these men were heavily indebted to Funck's treatment of world chronology from the Assyrian Empire forward. At the suggestion of Andreas Osiander—Funck's father-in-law and the author of the diluting preface to Copernicus's *De revolutionibus*—Funck had compared ancient historical accounts with Ptolemy's astronomical tables. He had likely learned this technique from Copernicus, who—perhaps following Tolosani, though more likely Apian's recommendations—had noted that Ptolemy began his astronomical observations from 747 BC, when Nabonassar ascended the Babylonian throne. This coincided with the crowning of Salmanassar, the Assyrian king whom Ctesias had identified as a king of the Chaldeans. Copernicus, following Ctesias, conflated the two kings and provided a solid (if inaccurate) joint with which to connect sacred and profane history. Comparing tables of celestial events to the astronomical observations reported by ancient authors—especially eclipses—provided a viable means to precisely date events after 747 BC, including the thorny history of Near Eastern politics in the century before the Babylonian Captivity. Funck applied this method across his sources and, thus, initiated a methodological revolution that transformed the study of ancient chronology from an exegetical to a historical art.

For Funck, the resolution of chronological problems was an act of reformation that strengthened the literal truth of Scripture against diabolic in-

49. This lineage has been fully excavated recently in Rosenberg and Grafton, *Cartographies of Time*, 62–63.

50. *HW*, 1.8.4.139.

tervention. He proclaimed: "What must be desired in such business more than that you might catch the devil in his deceits, and in all his frauds? Which indeed can be done only by the diligent observation of histories and of the times. For if you diligently scrutinize these, you will find that sacred scripture has testimony so firm in the ancient histories, that nothing can be found more certain or more true."[51] Despite his theological differences with Steuco, the two shared a view of how ancient histories might complement Scripture. Once purged of the corruptions inevitably produced by their eternalist authors, Funck claimed, ancient histories demonstrated the perfection of the Holy Books.

Funck's approach quickly became a staple method for many chronological practitioners. They applied the technique to well-known sources to absorb seemingly irreconcilable or indecipherable chronologies into the scriptural framework while rushing to find exotic sources that could similarly be integrated and that might, in turn, illuminate other astronomical arcana. Chytraeus was one of the most enthusiastic, but he recalibrated the balance between ancient histories and Scripture. For Chytraeus, Funck's discovery resonated with the role of Providence at work in the ancient world. In his 1562 *Chronologia*, he explained that God had given regular motions to celestial bodies and the ability to map these motions in time to men. Divine wisdom had foreseen that providing tools to measure time would enable men to recognize the world's finitude and, in turn, God's incomparable greatness. As he explained: "Because of his singular intelligence and immense goodness, God ordered the course of the year, constituted the differences of times, of days, months and years, and conserved the certain and continuous series of years of the world in the Church. He did this because he wanted the difference between eternity and the times of this world to be understood; and he wanted it to be known that nothing was eternal except God the father, the son and the Holy Spirit."[52] The means to measure temporal change were a providen-

---

51. Johann Funck, *Chronologia* (Wittenberg, 1601), 4r. "Quid igitur in tali negocio magis erat exoptandum, quam ut Diabolum in his quoque suis fraudibus, ut in caeteris, mendacem deprehendere queas? Quod equidem sola diligenti Historiarum & temporum observatione fieri potest. Nam si haec diligenter perscrutatus fueris, reperies scripturam sacram tam firma ex Historiis altis habere testimonia, ut aut certius, aut verius inveniri possit nihil."

52. David Chytraeus, *Chronologia historiae Herodoti et Thucydidis* (Helmstadt, 1586), A4v. "Singulari autem consilio & immensa bonitate DEUS, ANNI curriculum ordinavit, & temporum, dierum, mensium, & annorum discrimina constituit, & certam ac continuam annorum mundi seriem in Ecclesia conservavit. Quia vult intelligi discrimen inter aeternitatem & huius mundi tempora: vult sciri nihil aeternum esse nisi Deum patrem, filium & spiritum sanctum."

tially created gift to allow reflection on divine omnipotence. These tools for measuring time became even more essential instruments when the Bible, which should have been the source of incontrovertible chronological knowledge, had been corrupted by ignorant, lazy, or hostile translators. God had mercifully provided ancient pagan witnesses to certify biblical events and enabled the movements of the celestial bodies to track time. Eclipses, in particular, had been assiduously recorded by the ancients, and Chytraeus implored scholars to make use of this providential evidence by comparing their recitations across sources.

Funck and Chytraeus's scholarly acrobatics horrified many of their contemporaries. To their enemies, reliance on sidereal evidence for plotting events evoked Augustine's considerations of time in the *Confessions*. Augustine was convinced that understanding time by the movements of celestial bodies denied its divine origins. He recounted: "I once heard a learned man say that the motions of the sun, moon, and stars constituted time; and I did not agree. For why should not the motions of all bodies constitute time? What if the lights of heaven should cease, and a potter's wheel still turn round: would there be no time by which we might measure those rotations?"[53] There was certainly no divine injunction to root time in the movement of bodies. Though the movements of celestial bodies took place in time and could be justified as metrics, they did not constitute time itself.

Béroalde firmly adopted Augustine's position in his 1575 *Chronicum*. He believed that the only appropriate evidence for ancient chronology lay in Scripture, and he viciously undermined the reliability of astronomical observations. Time, he claimed, was divinely instituted into things, not measured by comparing elements of Creation. Béroalde stated gravely: "Nobody but a fool would attribute the construction of buildings to the time consumed in the work while ignoring the craftsmen; thus, there is nobody unless mad and ignorant of God, who does not confer the cause of those things which are made in time to God the author himself, but to time instead. God is in fact the maker of time, as of other things that are made in time and that vanish daily."[54] Astronomers such as Funck had violated the principles of chronology by insufficiently relying on God's testi-

---

53. Augustine, *Confessions*, trans. F. J. Sheed (Indianapolis: Hackett, 2006), 11.23.29.

54. Béroalde, *Chronicum*, 1–2. "Nam ut nemo nisi mentis inops, structura aedium, artificie praeterito, tempori quod in illud opus consumptum fuit, attribuerit: sic nullus, nisi amens, & Dei ignarum, rerum quae cum tempore fiunt causam non in ipsum autorem Deum, sed in tempus contulerit. Temporis enim, ut caeterorum quae cum tempore fieri & evanescere videmus quotidie, Deus opifex est."

mony revealed in Scripture. By using pre-Christian texts and astronomical knowledge as sources, they gave credibility to the movements of celestial bodies and uncertified authors, subjecting the divine world to the vagaries of created bodies and diabolic styli.

Béroalde's position gained a broad range of adherents. In England, Broughton followed his work closely and published a translation of the work that restricted proper Puritan chronology to the exegesis of Scripture, and Lydiat too embraced his method. But, despite their ravenous anti-Catholicism, their understanding of time emerged from the same font as did that of the Spanish Catholic exegete Benito Arias Montano. In his 1572 *Daniel, sive de Saeculis et Chronologia*, Montano analyzed time without mentioning celestial bodies. He wrote: "The nature, propriety, and efficacy of all those things that are seen in this universe can be demonstrated and known by no more certain index than time. No created thing does not feel and experience the force of this. God indeed imposed this law on all things, that there is nothing but those things that are endowed with this same logic of time."[55] Time had no astronomical basis; it was, rather, a property of being that God instilled within all Creation as testimony of the divine presence. Montano's exclusively scriptural method of measuring time suggested that the Bible provided the only reliable key to chronology.

Montano claimed that one community had strictly maintained a system of timekeeping that reflected its divine origins—that whose deeds and beliefs were memorialized in Scripture. He argued that piety demanded the study and imitation of the ancient Hebrews' unique access to the properly divine mode of timekeeping:

> Sacred letters clearly demonstrate the exact and exquisite reason of times and ages taught by sacred authors, doubtlessly in order that not only might appear the constancy of the divine promise and counsel, but in order that from the observation of times, and series of enacted things, a perpetual demonstration of that divine knowledge—by which such a work appeared—might be made clear to men. And thus far there was never on all earth a nation learned in divine oracles, with the one

---

55. Benedicto Arias Montano, *Antiquitatum Iudaicarum Libri* (Leiden, 1593), 185. "Earum omnium rerum quae in hac universitate conspiciuntur, natura, proprietas, & efficacia nullo certiore indice, quam tempore demonstrari & cognosci potest. Eius quippe vim nulla res creata non sentit & experitur. Deus enim hanc rebus omnibus legem imposuit, ut nihil omnino, cuius tandem generis illud sit, certis quibusdam temporis rationibus distinguatur."

exception of the Israelites, who held the true order of ancient time, and put it forth into the open.[56]

Montano limited the proper resources for establishing a divine calendar to the Bible and claimed that the ancient Hebrews alone had achieved such knowledge. Chronology, in this view, remained strictly a practice of scriptural interpretation.

Montano and Béroalde's Augustinianism constituted the conservative position within a dynamic chronological debate that swept through Europe in the middle of the sixteenth century. The divisions between chronologers did not break down on theological lines, for nearly as little theological harmony existed between Funck and many of his followers as between Béroalde and Montano. Rather, the fault lines concerned the sources that were seen as useful tools for chronological analysis. The latter group increasingly characterized chronology as an exclusively exegetical activity that was debased when subjected to pagan authorities. The Funckians, in turn, insisted that the chronology embedded in Scripture could be understood only with the help of astronomical evidence that had been providentially recorded in the works of ancient authors. Ralegh often consulted and complimented Montano and Béroalde for points of technical scholarship, but his chronological practice leaves no question that he sided with those such as Funck who saw Scripture as the foremost chronological narrative, but one imperfectly understood unless compared to other historical sources.

CHRONOLOGICAL RADICALISM

Funck's methods gained potency in the 1560s with the circulation of an ideal of historical inquiry that prized the compilation and integration of obscure evidence. His successors brought to light an increasing range of sources to correlate with Scripture and, with them, a growing array of solutions and problems. In particular, Joseph Scaliger not only collected an

56. Ibid., 188. "Hac porro de causa tam exactam, & exquisitam temporum ac saeculorum rationem a sacris auctoribus traditam esse, sacrae literae luculenter demonstrant. Nimirum, ut non solum divinae promissionis, & consilii constantia appareret; verum etiam ut ex temporum observatione, & editarum rerum serie, divinae illius sapientiae, a qua tantum opus apparabatur, perpetua hominibus argumenta patefierent. Atque adeo nulla olim in tot terrarum orbe natio fuit, excepta una Israelitica, divinis, nempe oraculis edocta, quae veras antiquorum temporum rationes tenuerit, easque in medium protulerit."

unprecedented corpus of sources; he also created a robust revolutionary tool to facilitate their integration. His works and methods badly compromised the arguments of Béroalde and Montano, but they also challenged Funck's vision of chronological practice by undermining the sacrality of Scripture as the most basic source for ancient chronology.

In his 1583 *De emendatione temporum*, Scaliger recognized that correlating the overload of evidence registered in diverse timekeeping systems demanded a historical calendrical science. Accordingly, he investigated various lunar, solar, civil, and mixed calendars used by a stunning range of ancient communities, including such exotic peoples as Copts and Indians, and determined the beginning and ends of their usages. To integrate all the evidence gleaned from his remarkable collection of sources, he correlated their calendars within a universal matrix for plotting historical events that he called the *Julian Era*. Previously, each chronologer had provided his own zero point, and, thus, scholars might agree that an event occurred in a certain year of the world but disagree on its date with reference to the year of Christ. The Julian Era attacked this problem by providing a fixed point of orientation. It consisted of a temporal cycle of 7,980 years, achieved by multiplying the twenty-eight-year solar cycle, the nineteen-year lunar cycle, and the Roman fifteen-year indiction cycle—metrics that eased the incorporation of different calendars by building their bases into the system. Though beginning prior to Creation, it constituted a scaffold allowing any event to be dated at x year of the Julian Era while also facilitating communication between chronologers.[57] With it, Scaliger was capable of absorbing the dates of events in any history as long as it mentioned dates known either from other traditions or from astronomical evidence.

Scaliger's work culminated the integrative process initiated by Funck. But it also departed from Funck's hierarchy of sources. While Funck had sought to use pagan histories to display Scripture's majestic perfection, with his Julian Era and calendrical science Scaliger gave primary chronological place to celestial motions. The movements of the sun and the moon, rather than Scripture, were the foundations of his chronological system. His followers articulated this symbiotic relation more stridently. In his 1590 *Chronologia*, the Hanover scholar Heinrich Bünting elaborated: "The Chronological doctrine throws the greatest light on mathematical doctrine and is profitable towards the emendation of mathematical reckoning in astronomical troubles. It shows the proportion of the celestial motions, and the progress of the stars both wandering and fixed, and the

---

57. Grafton, *Joseph Scaliger*, 2:249–53.

movements of the sun's eccentric, and the intervals of eclipses of the sun and moon that were seen in different points of history."[58] Astronomy was the predominant way of determining time and, thus, could aid chronology, but secure historical testimony could, in turn, be used to confirm celestial observations. The two fields advanced hand in hand. Those such as Bünting and Scaliger placed intransigent emphasis on the evidence of accounts of ancient eclipses and Erasmus Reinhold's Prutenic tables, whose calculations of celestial positions were based on Copernicus's *De revolutionibus*. Indeed, Sethus Calvisius would be so confident as to write in 1605: "Chronology is the digest of events according to time. Time is a measure of the sky, that is, the motion of a certain star from a given point of the sky to the same point. This motion Astronomers number exactly, in years, months, days, hours, and minutes."[59] Time was an index of celestial movements, no longer an exegetical field only controversially augmented by ancient authorities. Even the chronology of Scripture could be understood only by measuring it against the external key of the heavens.

This astronomical conception of time earned Scaliger and his partisans many enemies, for whom the Julian Era evoked other controversial instruments of early modern scholarship. Noting that the first year of the Julian Era considerably predated the accepted range of dates for Creation, Scaliger's opponents accused him of propagating a chronology that clearly contravened Scripture. He and his followers responded by characterizing the era as a tool or model for calibrating chronology rather than as itself a chronology describing real historical time. Similarly, some defenders of Copernicus such as Osiander—though not Copernicus himself—reassured those worried about the radical possibilities of his claims that constructing a heliocentric model did not demand that the model have real physical existence. Like Copernicus', then, Scaliger's system detailed a revolutionary means of coordinating evidence that was immediately inserted within charged theological debates about the nature of the universe.

Other aspects of Scaliger's methods were still more controversial,

---

58. Heinrich Bünting, *Chronologia Catholica* (Magdeburg, 1608), vir. "Quarto eadem haec doctrina Chronologica, maximam lucem adest doctrinae mathematicae, & prodest ad emendationem calculi mathematici in scrupulis astronomicis, monstrat enim proportionem motuum coelestium, progressum stellarum errantium & fixarum, mutationum excentrotetis Solis, eclipsum intervalla, quae videlicet diversis mundi temporibus deliquia Solis & Lunae visa sunt."

59. Sethus Calvisius, *Chronologia* (Leipzig, 1605), 1. "*Chronologia est rerum gestarum secundum tempus digestio. Tempus autem est mensura Coeli*, hoc est, motus cuiusdam sideris a dato puncto Coeli ad idem punctum. Hunc motum Astronomi exacte, in annis, mensibus, diebus, horis & minutis numerant."

though they relied on traditional tools of philological analysis. By using
scriptural testimony in conjunction with Greek, Roman, Coptic, and Ethiopian evidence, Scaliger set the grounds for a reconsideration of the place
of the Jews within history. Unlike his contemporaries, he did not credit
the Hebrew calendar as superior because intrinsically endowed with divine certification. Rather, he treated it as one of the many calendars deployed by ancient communities and as emerging, like other calendars,
from the soil of history in which all terrestrial events were embedded.
That the ancient Jews used a lunar year was for most an uncontested piece
of received wisdom, and Adam was considered the terrestrial institutor
of this divinely given temporal regime. Scaliger, however, dissected this
claim with penetrating historical and philological criticism:

> If you were to ask a Jew today, what was the form of the ancient He-
> brew year, either he would think you joking, or call you insane, if you
> were to doubt that the Lunar year was instituted by Adam himself.
> Nor would you be better received by a Christian. But in this chapter,
> Moses will speak against this claim. He says the things that ought to
> silence them. The Jews received the Lunar year first when they called
> the months by those names by which they are today known. But those
> appellations are Chaldean. Therefore, that the Lunar year of the Jews
> was received from the Chaldeans is proved by unimpeachable argu-
> ment. When they first received this year, then, is not obscure, if we
> remember that the conquered receive the law of the conqueror. Lunar
> years began to be used by the Jews not before the time when they ac-
> knowledged the Chaldeans as their lord, and were made tributaries to
> them, which happened under Nabopolassar the father of the great Ne-
> buchadnezzar, when he sent his son against Necao king of the Egyp-
> tians with a great army. Ioakim, king of the Jews, owed a stipend to the
> King of Egypt, but his lord changed, and he was made tributary to King
> Nabopollasar.[60]

60. Joseph Scaliger, *De Emendatione Temporum* (Paris, 1583), 79. "Si hodie a Iudaeo quae-
ras, quae forma fuerit anni prisci Hebraici, aut irrideri se putabit, aut insanum dicet, qui dubi-
tes ab ipso Adam Lunarem annum institutum. Neque sane melius accipieris a Christiano. Sed
libro sequenti Moses ipse pro se loquetur. Is ea dicet, per quae illis tacere liceat. Iudaei igitur
tunc primum Lunarem annum acceperunt, cum menses iis nominibus, quibus hodie notati
sunt, appellarunt. Eae autem appellationes Chaldaicae sunt. Ergo annus Lunaris Iudaeorum
Chaldaeis acceptus refertur argumento indubitato. Quando autem primum hunc annum acceperunt, non est obscurum, si scimus, victos a victoribus legem accipere. Ideo non prius a
Iudaeis menses Lunares usurpati caepti, quam Chaldaeos Dominos agnoverunt, & illis stip-
endarii facti sunt. Quod accidit sub Nabopollassaro magni Nabuchodonosori patre, qui filium

As Scaliger continued, he demonstrated that the Jews began using the names of these months in their contracts during the reign of Nebuchadnezzar. The calendar conventionally taken as divine, he proved, was foisted on the Hebrews by the law of the conqueror slightly more than six hundred years before Christ. His use of sources here suggested the radical nature of his approach, for he found in Scripture, not a system of divine timekeeping, but rather philological evidence that enabled a historical analysis of calendars.

Scaliger aggressively pursued the implications of this point. When discussing the calendar used much earlier by Abraham, he wrote: "What form of the year do we think this man used, other than Chaldean, that is, of his country? Or if his long travels outside of his country prohibited this, he could have used which year other than the Syriac in Syria, or the Egyptian in Egypt? Concede that he used one of these three: either Egyptian, or Syriac or Chaldean. Of course these were one and the same."[61] And the calendar they shared charted solar years. Scaliger thus rejected the tradition of a divine Jewish chronology and instead described this nation as adopting the calendars of the communities it inhabited.

Scaliger's diminution of the importance of the ancient Hebrews should be read as a Calvinist emphasis on the transformations engendered by the appearance of Christ rather than as atheism.[62] His method treated the ancient Hebrews as simply one among many communities of timekeepers, no different from the Copts or the Indians or other peoples whose esoteric evidence he sought to control. And this analysis powerfully undermined those chronologists who insisted on the primacy of Scripture. For, if the Hebrew calendar—which was used to date events in Scripture—had been received from communities not blessed with chosen status, then the chronology of Scripture reflected ephemeral calendrical knowledge rather than eternal chronological truth. Scaliger's historical analysis of their calendar thus weakened the belief that the Hebrews possessed purely divine knowledge and challenged the perfection of Scripture. And his hierarchy

---

contra Necao regem Aegypti cum magno exercitu misit. Regi Aegyptio stipendia pendebat Ioakim rex Iudaeorum. Sed mutavit dominum: & regi Nabopollassaro tributarius factus."

61. Ibid., 151. "Qua anni forma unum hominem usum putemus, nisi Chaldaica, hoc est, patria? aut si hoc vetuit longa peregrinatio extra patriam, quo anno uti potuit, quam Syriaco, in Syria? aut Aegyptiaca, in Aegypto? Concede unum ex istis tribus: aut Aegyptiacum, aut Syriacum, aut Chaldaicum. Unus profecto, idemque annus fuit."

62. Similarly, see Debora K. Shuger, *The Renaissance Bible: Scholarship, Sacrifice, and Subjectivity* (Berkeley and Los Angeles: University of California Press, 1994); and David Weil Baker, "The Historical Faith of William Tyndale: Non-Salvific Reading of Scripture at the Outset of the English Reformation," *RQ* 62 (2009): 661–92.

of sources for the study of time clearly enshrined sidereal observations as the primary authority, followed then by their translations into calendar, and only then by Scripture and other historical witnesses.

RALEGH'S METHODS

Early modern chronological scholarship offered many options to its practitioners. Puritans like Lydiat and Broughton sought to protect the inviolability of Scripture by arguing that comparing it to ancient pagan witnesses sullied the Holy Books as historical, transient, immersed in time. Funck and his partisans supplied powerful examples of robust chronologies produced by collating infallible Scripture with ancient pagans. And Scaliger afforded the possibility of radicalism as he tore time from its scriptural bearings and embedded it in the stars, just as he ripped the Hebrew calendar from its Adamic roots and implanted it in Chaldean soil. The *History* reveals Ralegh mixing and matching elements of each tradition to weave together his history of the ancient world. But it also shows that, while he paid greatest respect to Scaliger, he adhered most closely to the practices—and to the vision of the ancient world—professed by Funck.

Throughout the first three books of the *History*, Ralegh addressed the sorts of chronological wrangles that had so captivated sixteenth-century scholars. Like many, he carefully consulted ancient and modern sources, negotiating their evidence to deduce his own unique dates for Creation and ensuing events. His work revealed the inculcation of the norms developed by chronologers in the previous half century, as he ably deployed many of the techniques of his recent predecessors. Above all, Ralegh's guiding chronological principle was concurrence between sources. When similar events were described by two different authorities to have occurred at the same time, he believed that they could be identified as the same event. His model was the conflation—agreed on by Tolosani, Copernicus, Funck, and many others—of Salmanassar and Nabonassar because their coronations were recorded as occurring in the same year. All the events in texts that mentioned this ascension could be correlated using the single coronation as a hinge. Eclipses performed a similar function. Performing this operation—what he called the *account of times*—across many sources revealed world chronology. As he explained: "I thinke it follie to make doubt, whereas Historians and Mathematicall observations doe so thoroughly concurre." Arguing that Salmanassar and Nabonassar were the same person, he proclaimed his method: "I hold a point about which no man will dispute; for it is not likenesse of sound, but agreement of time, and many circumstances else, that must take away the distinction of persons."[63] Once temporal concurrence was established, arithmetic became his primary tool to correlate other events in the text. He thus demonstrated a capable grasp of the methods pioneered by Funck.

Ralegh also showed himself capable of correlating multiple sources in his exploration of questions such as the chronology of the post-Captivity Persian succession. He presented and then quickly dismissed Annius's lineage of Persia's post-Captivity kings. He then listed the generally accepted succession from Cyrus to Darius, citing the Lutheran Caspar Peucer, the Calvinist Polishman Leonhart Krentzheim, the Catholic chronologer Gilbert Genebrard, and Béroalde, while noting minor deviations in Melanchthon. He explained that Eusebius had correlated the dates of these reigns to the Greek Olympiads, such that they corroborated Scripture: "*Eusebius* with the *Latines*, following the *Greekes*, apply the beginnings and ends of every *Persian* King with their Acts, to some certaine Olympiad. . . . Which reference with good agreement betweene severall formes of computation adde the more credit unto both." Finally, he referred to the "Astronomicall computation of *Ptolomie*" to show that the distances between these reigns and the reigns of Nabonassar and Alexander fit his chronology, as did the accounts of Xenophon, Diodorus Siculus, and Josephus. He concluded: "So that whether we follow the accompt of the Olympiads, as doe the *Greeke* Historians, or that of *Nabonassar* with *Ptolomie*, we shall finde every memorable accident to fall out right with each computation." Ralegh integrated evidence found in Scripture, the ancient Greeks, late antique ecclesiastical historians, and modern commentators as well as that derived from astronomical evidence—as he put it "the computation of other Historians, and Astronomers, and likewise with the holy Scriptures."[64] This model clearly aligned him with Funck and distinguished him from Puritan practitioners such as Béroalde.

Similarly, Ralegh ably applied sophisticated analysis to this expanded range of sources in his consideration of the standard problem of how to coordinate the dates found in Scripture with accounts in pagan authors. He wrote two separate accounts addressing this problem. He began book 3 with the chapter "Of the connexion between Sacred and prophane Historie," explaining that, though the records of pagan civilizations prior to the Babylonian Captivity had disappeared, the reign of Nebuchadnezzar marked an era after which reliable pagan histories had survived. These

63. *HW*, 2.25.1.592, 2.23.4.570.
64. *HW*, 3.4.1.43–44.

records contained the names of ancient Assyrian monarchs. Furthermore, the kings mentioned in these histories were also noted in Scripture, thus enabling the correlation of the two: "These later *Assyrian* Kings, and the *Persians*, which followed them, are the first, of whom wee finde mention made both in Prophane and Sacred bookes. These therefore serve most aptly to joyne the times of the old World, (whereof none but the Prophets have written otherwise than fabulously) with the Ages following that were better known, and described in the course of Historie." Still, neither Scripture nor pagan histories offered complete chronologies in themselves. As a result, it was necessary to align firmly established dates within these sources. Ralegh explained:

> Hereby could wee only learne in what age each of them lived, but not in what yeare his raigne beganne or ended, were it not that the raigne of *Nabuchadnezzar* is more precisely applied to the times of *Iehoia-kim* and *Ezekia*. Hence have we the first light whereby to discover the meanes of connecting the sacred and prophane histories. For under *Na-buchadnezzar* was the beginning of the captivitie of *Iuda*, which ended when 70 yeeres were expired; and these 70 yeares tooke end at the first of *Cyrus*, whose time being well knowne affords us meanes of looking back into the ages past, and forwards into the race of men succeeding.

Correlating the translation of empire from the Assyrians to the Persians in sacred and profane traditions allowed a sure joining of the history known only from Scripture to other histories. In particular, Cyrus's reign was dated in many traditions and, as he noted, had been used by Eusebius to connect dates after the Babylonian Captivity.[65]

Ralegh also knew of Copernicus's conflation of Salmanassar and Nabonassar that enabled the dating of events 122 years earlier than Ne-buchadnezzar. He explained that this overlap had gone unnoticed until Copernicus because, while "Cyrus and some other *Persians*" had been referred to by the same names in multiple traditions, in the case of Salmanassar "diversitie of name hath bred question of the persons." Identifying Salmanassar by all his names would enable correlations between more remote ancient histories. Therefore, Ralegh explained, "whereas the Scriptures doe speake of *Salmanassar*, King of *Assur* . . . and wheras *Ptolomie* makes mention of *Nabonassar*, speaking precisely of the time wherein he lived; it is very pertinent to shew, that *Salmonassar* and *Nabonassar*

65. *HW*, 3.1.1.2.

were one and the same man." To unify these two men, it had to be proved
that their descendants were the same, and, thus, "the like reason also re-
quireth, that it bee shewed of *Nebuchadnezzar*, that hee was the same,
whom *Ptolomie* calleth *Nabopolassar*."[66] As evidence, Ralegh referred the
reader to Abraham Bucholzer's proofs, noting that Bucholzer had used Reinhold's Prutenic tables, and he drew from Funck the evidence that the
122-year distance between the ascensions of Nabopolassar and Nabonassar accorded with Scripture. His analysis supplied an exemplary demon-
stration of the arithmetical correlation of evidence drawn from Ptolemy
and Scripture and coordinated by Funck.[67]

Ralegh was deeply committed to mathematically sound positions derived through the Funckian method. And, with this tool in hand, he engaged one skeptic of the identification of Salmanassar and Nabonassar: Joseph Scaliger.[68] Elsewhere, he frequently followed Scaliger's innovations.
Like Calvisius, Ralegh suggested that time was a measure of the stars
rather than a divine attribute, writing: "These observations of the Celes-
tiall bodies, are the surest markes of time: from which he that wilfully
varies, is inexcusable."[69] He thus declared his allegiance to a Scaligerian
depiction of time. And, at the end of the *History*, he appended a series of
chronological tables providing quick reference for his reader coordinated
along the Julian Era (see fig. 2). Eusebius had invented such charts to allow
his readers to compare contemporaneous developments in multiple civilizations, and, by the late sixteenth century, they had become common
appendices to chronologies.[70] Ralegh's explanation of the tables, however,
highlighted both their most practical and their most radical feature: "The
Iulian Period, which I have placed, as the greater number, over the yeares

66. *HW*, 2.25.1.591.

67. "*Functius* doth shew, that whereas from the destruction of *Samaria*, to the devastation of *Ieruslaem*, in the nineteenth of *Nebuchadnessar*, we collect out of the Scriptures, the
distance of one hundred thirtie and three yeares: the selfe-same distance of time is found in
Ptolomie, betweene *Nabonassar* and *Nabopolassar*. For, whereas *Ptolomie* seemes to differ
from this accompt, making *Nebonassar* more ancient by an hundred and fortie yeeres, than
the destruction of *Ierusalem*, wee are to understand that he took *Samaria* in the eighth yeere
of his raigne; so that the seven foregoing yeares added to these one hundred thirty and three,
make the accompts of the Scriptures fall even with that of *Ptolomie*. *Ptolomies* computation
is, that from the first of *Nabonassar*, to the fifth of *Nabopolassar*, there passed one hundred
twentie and seven yeares. Now if we adde to these one hundred twentie seven, the thirteene
ensuing of *Nabuchadnessars* yeares, before the Citie and Temple were destroied, we have the
summe of one hundred and fortie yeeres." *HW*, 2.25.1.592. On the correlation of these two
people, see Grafton, *Joseph Scaliger*, 2:129–31.

68. Grafton, *Joseph Scaliger*, 2:302–4.

69. *HW*, 4.5.7.262.

70. Grafton and Williams, *Christianity and the Transformation of the Book*.

of the World, was devised by that honorable and excellently learned *Ioseph Scaliger*: being accommodated to the *Iulian* yeares, now in use among us. It consisteth of 7980 yeares; which result from the multiplication of 19. 28. and 15, that is, of the Cycle of the Moone, the Cycle of the Sunne, and the yeares of an Indiction. . . . This *Iulian* Period, after the present accompt, alwayes exceedes the yeares of the World by *682*." There was no prior English-language discussion of the "Julian Period" in print; Ralegh was likely explaining for the first time to a vernacular audience the controversial timekeeping system that relied on several centuries of nominal time prior to Creation. He matter-of-factly proclaimed the advantages it offered: "Besides the former uses, and other thence redounding, it is a better Character of a yeare, than anie other *Aera* (as *From the beginning of the World, From the Floud, From* Troy *taken,* or the like) which are of more uncertaine position. More I shall not need to write, as touching the use of explication of these Tables. Neither was thus much requisite to such as are conversant in workes of this kinde: it sufficeth if hereby all be made plaine enough to the vulgar."[71] Ralegh thus sought to transmit to his readers the virtue of Scaliger's chronological instrument, which enabled the more certain mapping of all events on a single matrix while overlooking the controversies and divisions that attended it.

But, despite his admiration of Scaliger, Ralegh was not willing to follow his separation of Salmanassar from Nabonassar. Indeed, Ralegh dismissed Scaliger's rejection of concurrence as a fundamental threat to the historian's ability to correlate Scripture and pagan histories. Scaliger had disentangled Babylonia and Assyria and pronounced that these appellatives referred to two distinct kingdoms. He began by pointing out the intellectual laxity of conflating two historical individuals solely on the basis of their temporal dates if ancient histories offered countervailing evidence. He then demonstrated that *Nabo-* and *Salman-* were, respectively, Chaldean and Assyrian prefixes and noted that, while Salmanassar had ruled from Nineveh, all Chaldean astronomical observations—appropriate to be performed only in the primary royal city—had been taken from Babylon. Scaliger therefore argued that Salmanassar had ruled in Assyria, part of the much greater Babylonian territory under Nabonassar's rule. If Nabonassar and Salmanassar were the same, it would make no sense to speak of Salmanassar "obtaining" these lands during Nabonassar's reign, as Scripture did. And Scaliger referred to historical testimony in Scripture

---

71. *HW*, Tttttt5v. By *character*, Scaliger had meant each year's placement within the solar, lunar, and civil calendrical cycles.

	Iulian. World. Temple.	Rome. Nabon.	Iphit.	Olymp.	Iuda.	Chaldæa.	Egypt.	Rome.	Media	Lydia.
The Expedition of the Scythians. L.2.c.28.§.3.&4.	4054 3372 379	93 88	117	30 1	2	3 1.Nabu-lassar,33	26	12	3	20
	4055 3373 380	94 89	118	30 1	16 1.Iosi-as, 31 2	2	27	13	4	21
L.2.c.28.§.2.	4073 3391 398	112 107	136	34 4	19	20	t.Ne-co, 17	31	22	39
	4075 3393 400	114 109	138	35 2	21	22	3	4 1.Ancus Martius,36	24	41
*	4076 3394 401	115 110	139	35 3	22	23	4	2	7 1.(ardi-res, 40)	42
	4084 3402 409	123 118	147	37 2	30	31	12	10	9	3 1.Sady-attes,12
L.2.c.28.§.1.&2.	4085 3403 410	124 119	148	37 4	31, 17 Iehoahaz, 3.moneths	32	13	11	10	2
Nabuchodonosor had reigned one yeere with his Father, which is to be regarded in Astronomicall observations concerning his time. L.2.c.28.§.6. & C.25.§.1.	4086 3404 411	125 120	149	38 1	18 1.Iehoia-kim, 11	33	14	12	11	3
	4089 3407 414	128 123	152	38 4	4	4 1.Nabucho-nosor the Great, 44	17	15	14	6
	4090 3408 415	129 124	153	39 1	5	2	1.Psam-mis, 12.	16	15	7
	4096 3414 421	135 130	159	40 3	11, 19 Iehoni 3.meneths, 30 zedekia	8	7	22	21	1.Halyat-tes, 57
Zedekia his iourney to Babylon. L.2.c.28.§.6.	4099 3417 424	138 133	162	41 2	zedekia 11.yeeres, 4	11	10	5 1.Tar-quin Pri-scus, 38	24	4
	4102 420 427	141 126	165	42 1	7	14	1.Apries or Hophra, 22	4	27	7
Ierusalem taken by Nabuchodonosor with whose 18.for the more part, and partly with whose 19. this yeere concurres.	4106 3424 421	145 140	169	43 1	11	18	5	8	31	11
	Iulian. World. Nabon.	Rome. Nabon.	Iphit.	Olym-piads.	Capti-uitie.	Chal-dæa.	Egypt.	Rome.	Media	Lydia.
Ierusalem destroyed.	4107 3425	146 141	170	43 2	1	19	6 10	9	32	12
Egypt conquered by Nabuchodonosor. L.3.c.1.§.8.&9.	4111 3429	150 145	174	44 2	5	23	1.Phar.He-phra slein & the king dome of E. Off gouer-ned seuen yeeres by Vicereyes, 6	13	36	16
	4116 3434	155 150	179	45 2	10	28	18	18	8 1.Astya-ges, 35	21
Nabuchodonosor liues wilde; and his Kingdome is gouerned by others for him, during seuen yeeres. L.3.c.1.§.13.	4125 3443	164 159	188	47 4	19	37 1.Euilme-rodach, 3.	25	27	10	30
	4127 3445	166 161	190	48 2	21	39 1.Nigli-far, & Ni lotris, 4	17	29	12	32

Figure 2. Chronological table from the 1614 History of the World, Xxxxxx3v–4r. Special Collections Research Center, Swem Library, College of William and Mary, shelf mark D57. R16 1614.

to disentangle the two: "Mardokempad, who in [2] Kings [17] and Isiah [39] is called Merodac, the first part of his full name Merodac-ken-pad, succeeded Nabonassar. This Merodac is called by Isaiah the son of Baladan, and thus Baladan and Nabonassar are the same, which is true."[72] Having demonstrated that Scripture revealed Baladan and Nabonassar to be the same person, Scaliger noted: "By one solid argument, [the identification of Salmanassar and Nabonassar] can be overturned. Merodac, or Mardokenpad began to rule Babylon in the year of the Julian period 3993, which was the sixth year of Ezechiel, King of Juda. At this time Samaria was captured by Salmanassar. Therefore according to their opinion, Nabonassar's, Salmanassar, and Merodac must be one and the same King. You can see the manifest absurdity [since Scripture said that Merodac was Nabonassar's son]."[73] In other words, credulous correlation of figures based on concurrence resulted in the absurd conclusion that this king had fathered himself. Scaliger, the most masterly manipulator of ancient astronomical records, exposed the limitations of concurrence if used without attention to philological and historical evidence.

Scaliger's confutation of Copernicus's identification, in fact, targeted Annius, whose fabricated lists of Assyrian kings had separated Nabonassar and Merodac by three generations, to Scaliger's exasperation.[74] Scaliger did not intend to disrupt the practice of chronology; all that was necessary was some slight tinkering that he easily performed himself. Ralegh, however, was not willing to relinquish so easily a chronological gain evidenced by concurrence. He did, however, recognize troubling merits in Scaliger's argument. Of all Scaliger's objections, he found the evidence from Isaiah 39 ("At that time Merodach-baladan, the son of Baladan, king of Babylon, sent letters and a present to Hezekiah") the most unnerving. He first brought up this passage when discussing Annius's conflation of kings several generations prior to Nabonassar, but he delayed addressing it, explaining: "I finde matter of more difficultie [for this problem], than can be answered in hast. I will therefore deferre the handling of these objections, until I

---

72. Scaliger, *De Emendatione Temporum*, 214–15. "Nabonassaro successit Mardokempad, qui in libris Regum, & apud Esaiam prophetam dicitur prima tantum parte nominis Merodac, non Merodac-ken-pad. Is Merodac Esaiae dicitur filius Beladan. Itaque Beladan & Nabonassar idem."

73. Ibid., 215. "Sed uno solidissimo argumento illa omnia everti possunt. Merodac, sive Mardokenpad caepit imperare Babylone anni periodi Iulianae 3993, qui erat sextus annus Ezekiae Regis Iuda. quo tempore capta Samaria a Salmanasare. Ergo secundum horum sententiam necesse erat hos tres, Nabonasar, Salmanasar, & Merodac unum, eundemque Regem fuisse. Vides absurditatem manifestam."

74. Annius, *Antiquitatum Italiae ac totius orbis libri*, 244.

meete with their subject in his proper place. . . . Yet that I may not leave too great a scruple in the minde of the Reader, thus farre will I here satisfie him; that how strong soever this argument may seeme, *Scaliger* himself did live to retract it."[75] In fact, Ralegh's source for Scaliger's retraction was Lydiat, who had blatantly misread Scaliger in an attempt to ward off Scaliger's withering criticism.

When Ralegh arrived at his discussion of Merodac, he again returned to Scaliger's identification of Nabonassar with Baladan. But he did not examine Scaliger's scriptural source. Instead, he turned to Ptolemy's tables, noting that, while Nabonassar preceded Merodac, this did not mean that Merodac was his son and, therefore, that the chronologer was not faced with the "manifest absurdity" Scaliger had described. And, to strengthen his argument, he reiterated the falsehood that Scaliger had changed his mind about the correlative conflation of Salmanassar and Nabonassar: "It was enough to satisfie me, in this argument, that *Scaliger* himselfe did afterwards beleeve *Mardocempadus* to have been rather the Nephew, than the Sonne of *Baladan,* or *Nabonassar.* For if he might be either the Nephew, or the Sonne; he might perhaps be neither the one, nor the other." Continuing, Ralegh gestured toward the argument that Scaliger had ostensibly abandoned, proclaiming: "I have taken the paines to search as farre as my leisure and diligence could reach, after any sentence that might prove the Kindred or succession of these two. Yet cannot I finde in the *Almagest* (for the Scriptures are either silent in this point, or adverse to *Scaliger* . . .) any sentence more nearely proving the succession of *Merodach* to *Nabonassar.*"[76] Scaliger's source for this was, as we have seen, Isaiah 39. In this case, Scaliger made use of scriptural testimony that Ralegh had neglected, or conveniently forgotten in his reliance on Ptolemy.

Ralegh here misread Scaliger's attack. He perceived Scaliger's challenge, not as declawing Annius, but as threatening the method that Funck and Copernicus had pioneered to connect sacred and profane histories, thus challenging his own prized chronological method. And this, in turn, drove Ralegh, for this matter at least, into the arms of Annius, Scaliger's target. Concluding his argument that Merodac could have been in the line of Nabonassar without being his son, Ralegh wrote: "This considered, wee may safely goe on with our accompt from *Nabonassar,* taking him for *Salmanassar;* and not fearing, that the Readers will be driven from our booke, when they finde something in it, agreeing with *Annius.*" His mis-

75. *HW,* 2.23.4.571.
76. *HW,* 2.25.1.592.

understanding of Scaliger's objective, and his oversight of a key passage of Scripture, led him to sustain a false identification and to support a genealogy he knew to have been forged. And he reminded his readers that his solution had the virtue of unimpeachable supporting evidence, "no good Historie naming any others, that raigned there in those ages, and all Astronomical observations, fitly concurring, with the yeeres that are attributed to these, or numbred from them."[77] He thus embraced astronomical evidence even when its greatest champion turned to Scripture.

Ralegh's challenge to Scaliger reveals much about his methods and his place in chronological culture. Above all, it suggests that Ralegh had fully absorbed the methods pioneered by Funck in the mid-sixteenth century. Indeed, he appears to have been unwilling to abandon this method, holding to its solutions even when Scaliger developed new ones or undermined its solutions with historical and philological examination. The point here is not that Ralegh was a less agile or innovative chronologer than Scaliger, though he undoubtedly was. It is that, within the set of practices and solutions made available to him by the culture of chronological practice, he adopted some and rejected others. As such, he operated like most other chronologers, whose works resulted from the rigorous application of methods they did not invent. Ralegh thus revealed himself to be an unexceptional member of a broad European community struggling to extricate itself from the chronological labyrinth, in his case by relying predominantly on Funckian methods. His chronology was by itself not innovative, but that that treatment was in English constitutes a significant intervention, for, by rendering these debates and the discussion of the Julian era in the vernacular, he publicized many of the complexities, intricacies, and radical possibilities of early modern chronological practice to a vernacular audience. The *History*, then, introduced to English-reading audiences the mode of European scholarly practice that was aggressively expanding its scope of credible sources for knowledge while developing highly historicized readings of sacred texts.

CONCLUSION

His silences concerning aspects of his chronological culture illuminate as much about his allegiances as about his own methods, for Ralegh overlooked several noticeable dimensions of this community's practice. First, though he discussed the works of Béroalde, Montano, and other strict scrip-

77. Ibid.

turalists and relied closely on the Bible, he never advanced the idea that scriptural exegesis alone yielded sufficient evidence to produce a full chronology of the ancient world. His omission in this regard reflected the direction of chronological scholarship. While in 1500 the main question of credibility for a chronologer was whether to subscribe to the translation of the Vulgate or that of the Septuagint, by Ralegh's time a vastly expanded set of sources could be deemed reliable witnesses. And, while this problem grew even more intractable as the two sides—strict scripturalists and defenders of the ancients, Béroaldes and Scaligers—grew more firmly entrenched and more deeply polarized, the contest between them was slanting more solidly toward the latter. Archbishop James Ussher's 1650 *Annales veteris testamenti*, a masterful interweaving of Scripture, ancient histories, and ancient astronomical information, would, ultimately, provide an authoritative chronology that brought to heel the scholarly community's frantic chronological debate.[78]

Ralegh, however, also overlooked features in Scaliger's work that would drive new scholarship. Scaliger's controversial Julian Era was essential to developing chronological learning, but it would not prove the radical spark that other elements of his work did. In particular, the depiction of the ancient Jewish calendar as merely one among many, without special divine credibility, furnished a powerful model for the radicalisms of Hobbes, La Peyrere, and, above all, Spinoza in the late seventeenth century. These men saw ancient Jews as speaking truths only from within their own community, as reporting a history as susceptible to exaggeration and hyperbole as the eternalist fantasies of the Egyptians or the aboriginal speculations of the Greeks. The ancient Jewish claim to be the chosen lineage of those spared from the Flood was credible only if Scripture was infallible. Subjecting the remnants of ancient Jewish belief to Scaligerian inquiry made more persuasive the ideas that men existed before Adam or that the Flood covered only part of the earth while other areas remained populated, dry, and blithely ignorant of the severe tribulations God imposed on the Israelites.[79]

78. See Barr, "Why the World Was Created in 4004 BC." For British scholars working on an expanded range of sources in the seventeenth century, see, e.g., Alastair Hamilton, *William Bedwell, the Arabist, 1563–1632* (Leiden: Thomas Browne Institute, 1985); Miller, "The 'Antiquarianization' of Biblical Scholarship"; Sheehan, "Temple and Tabernacle"; and Gerald Toomer, *John Selden: A Life in Scholarship* (Oxford: Oxford University Press, 2009).

79. For these developments in seventeenth-century chronology, see Richard H. Popkin, *Isaac La Peyrère (1596–1676): His Life, Work and Influence* (Leiden: Brill, 1987); Grafton, *Defenders of the Text*, 204–15; Alastair Hamilton, *The Apocryphal Apocalypse: The Reception of the Second Book of Esdras (4 Ezra) from the Renaissance to the Enlightenment* (Oxford: Clar-

Ralegh's practices echo resoundingly against these silences, for his mode of chronological analysis firmly aligned him with the traditions articulated by Chytraeus for history, Steuco for Creation, and Funck for chronology. Indeed, they shared a hierarchy of sources that idealized an infallible Scripture but recognized that the failings of its translations and their interpretations could be addressed by consulting ancient sources. This ascription of credibility to pagan witnesses distinguished Ralegh from Puritans such as Lydiat and Broughton, who echoed Béroalde's insistence that Scripture supplied the only trustworthy source for ancient chronology. And viewing his crediting of venerated Egyptians, Persians, Greeks, and Romans through the prism of his Reformation historical theology suggests the significance he ascribed both to these ancient witnesses and to his own endeavors. For, if ancient witnesses provided critical testimony of Creation and chronology, they did so under the guiding hand of Providence. He considered the existence of ancient testimonies and astronomical observations a sacred gift, for the "account of times" from sacred books had become so thoroughly muddled that astronomy constituted the most credible source for post-Captivity chronology. Like most of his contemporaries, Ralegh believed that each epoch received the tools for its own interpretation. The instruments that exegetes, historians, and chronologers used were providentially bequeathed by God, their history a history of man's own loss and gain of sacred knowledge. In Ralegh's hands, they became methods of scholarly reform.

But it is worth concluding with a final reminder of the consequences, unmentioned by Ralegh, of the integration of a broad range of sources to illuminate God's creation. Unalloyed knowledge of Creation and a chronology that reflected the true order of providential events were vital for orthodox learning, but the inconsistencies and contradictions of the foundational texts of Christianity left these uncertain. The Reformation shook the chronological world into feverish activity, stimulating the integration of different sources in an effort to clarify the muddled chronology of the sacred texts. An effort to produce evidence to strengthen scriptural exegesis inspired some of the most original and inventive scholarship that followed, even as Scripture itself descended from its celestial moorings to the realm of the temporal. And the impact of these techniques was not limited to chronological reform. The effects of this revolution extended far beyond

---

endon, 1999); Noel Malcolm, *Aspects of Hobbes* (Oxford: Clarendon, 2002); and Mordechai Feingold, "Oriental Studies," in *The History of the University of Oxford*, ed. Nicholas Tyacke, 4 vols. (Oxford: Oxford University Press, 1997), 4:449–504. See also Nicholas Dew, *Orientalism in Louis XIV's France* (Oxford: Oxford University Press, 2009).

the disciplinary borders of chronology, as ancient history, mathematical sciences such as astronomy and mechanics, and natural philosophy benefited from the new value placed on investigating the temporal regularities and patterns of all celestial and created bodies. And, as we will see in the next chapter, late sixteenth-century scholars deployed disciplined forms of reading in order to cull all the narrowest fragments of evidence from these multiplying sources, a transformation in practice that further challenged the traditional modes of establishing secure knowledge.

CHAPTER THREE

Reading:
Antiquarian Methods
and Geographical Learning

European scholars in the sixteenth century furiously debated the appropriate sources to use when constructing a chronology of the ancient
world. While a dwindling group continued to insist that Scripture alone
provided reliable evidence for the ancient world, most turned increasingly
to ever more esoteric sources for the past. They also developed specific
practices to integrate their new materials with traditional authorities.
Early modern practitioners of geography, like those of its sibling discipline
of chronology, labored to integrate an increasing body of sources. These
scholars did not assume that the influx of contemporary travelers' reports
invalidated received wisdom but instead adapted existing practices of
note taking to synthesize the new missives with the venerable authorities. These techniques, this chapter argues, generated a new economy for
making knowledge in which individual observations and statements were
evaluated primarily by their coherence within a holistic system of explanation, not strictly according to the credibility of their source.

As Ralegh's geographical investigations will show, geographers' application of antiquarian and historical practices of methodical note taking
from a vast array of sources produced a discipline at once arcanely erudite and precisely technical.[1] Their practice emphasized the certainty of

---

1. For early modern geography generally, see, above all, J. B. Harley and David Woodward,
eds., *The History of Cartography*, 3 vols. to date (Chicago: University of Chicago Press, 1987–),
esp. vols. 1 and 3, which contain too many valuable articles to cite individually. See also Numa
Broc, *La géographie de la Renaissance (1420–1620)* (Paris: Bibliothèque nationale, 1980); J. B.
Harley, "Silences and Secrecy: The Hidden Agenda of Cartography in Early Modern Europe,"
Imago Mundi 40 (1988): 57–76; Catherine Delano Smith and Elizabeth Morley Ingram, *Maps
in Bibles, 1500–1600: An Illustrated Catalogue* (Genève: Droz, 1991); Robert W. Karrow Jr.,
*Mapmakers of the 16th Century and Their Maps: Bio-Bibliographies of the Cartographers of
Abraham Ortelius, 1570* (Chicago: Speculum Orbis, for the Newberry Library, 1993); Frank

knowledge gained by the process of extracting, compiling, judging, and synthesizing evidence, rather than by identifying the most authoritative source, and its transformed contours illuminate broader shifts toward the empirical and inductive methodologies increasingly embraced by early modern scholars.[2]

NOTE TAKING AND GEOGRAPHY

During his imprisonment, Ralegh was confined to his rooms, the Tower grounds, and the promenade atop the White Tower's south wall. From here he could look out over the Thames, Tower Bridge, and Southwark or below at the curious crowds who strolled to the southeast corner of the City to observe him. But retreating to his rooms brought him to exotic and distant locales, for his books narrated histories of terrains far from, and far different from, the vistas seen by the captive explorer. His library was stacked full of geographical works. In addition to classics such as Ptolemy, Strabo, and Solinus, his collection of the modern cosmographic masters included Gerald Mercator, Sebastian Münster, Abraham Ortelius, Paulus Merula, Jean Matal, Cornelius Wytfliet, and Petrus Bertius. He also owned local English chorographies by John Leland, John Stow, John Norden, William Lambard, and William Camden and chorographies of the Holy Land by Jacob Ziegler and Christiaan van Adrichem. His library included reports

Lestringant, *Mapping the Renaissance World: The Geographical Imagination in the Age of Discovery*, trans. David Fausett (Cambridge: Polity, 1994); Lesley B. Cormack, *Charting an Empire: Geography at the English Universities, 1580–1620* (Chicago: University of Chicago Press, 1997); Walter Melion, "Ad ductum itineris et dispositionem mansionum ostendendam: Meditation, Vocation, and Sacred History in Abraham Ortelius's Parergon," *Journal of the Walters Art Gallery* 57 (1999): 49–72; Alessandro Scafi, "Mapping Eden: Cartographies of the Earthly Paradise," in *Mappings*, ed. Denis Cosgrove (London: Reaktion, 1999), 50–70, and *Mapping Paradise: A History of Heaven on Earth* (Chicago: University of Chicago Press, 2006); John M. Headley, "Geography and Empire in the Late Renaissance: Botero's Assignment, Western Universalism, and the Civilization Process," *RQ* 53 (2000): 1119–55; and Zur Shalev, "Geographia Sacra: Cartography, Religion, and Scholarship in the Sixteenth and Seventeenth Centuries" (Ph.D. diss., Princeton University, 2004).

2. For information management in early modern Europe, see Wilhelm Schmidt-Biggeman, *Topica Universalis: Eine Modellgeschichte humanistischer und barocker Wissenschaft* (Hamburg: Meiner, 1983); Ann Moss, *Printed Commonplace-Books and the Structuring of Renaissance Thought* (Oxford: Oxford University Press, 1996); Ann Blair, "Reading Strategies for Coping with Information Overload, ca. 1550-1700," *JHI* 64 (2003): 11–28, and *Too Much to Know*; Brian Ogilvie, "The Many Books of Nature: Renaissance Naturalists and Information Overload," *JHI* 64 (2003): 29–40; Jonathan Sheehan, "From Philology to Fossils: The Biblical Encyclopedia in Early Modern Europe," *JHI* 64 (2003): 41–60; and Noel Malcolm, "Thomas Harrison and His 'Ark of Studies': An Episode in the History of the Organization of Knowledge," *Seventeenth Century* 19 (2004): 196–232.

of modern voyages by Simon Grynaeus, Theodor De Bry, Jan Huyghen van
Linschoten, Gerrit de Veer, Richard Hakluyt, André Thevet, and Pierre
Belon alongside accounts of medieval travelers such as Marco Polo, Frere
Haython, and John Plancarpio. These descriptive geographies, modeled after Strabo, depicted the physical features, peoples, customs, rites, cloth-
ing, minerals, weather, foods, flora, and fauna of the Holy Land, the New
World, Africa, and places further afield. They opened new worlds to the
explorer who had marched through Ireland, navigated the Orinoco deep
into South America, and engaged in combat in France and Spain.

Ralegh was not content merely to visit these sites; he also recorded his
journey. As he began work on the *History* in 1607, he deployed a means
of memorializing what he encountered in his narratives of worlds far and
dead, for at this time he compiled a geographical notebook. As he read
of Thevet's journeys to Armenia and Brazil, Ziegler's travels in the Holy
Land, or Ptolemy's and Strabo's accounts of India, he jotted significant passages into this book, preserving the pearls his sources offered. For Ralegh,
restricted to the Tower, thumbing through texts conveyed him to sites he
would never see.

Ralegh's surviving manuscript notebook lays bare his method of note
taking.[3] This manuscript, once in the Phillipps Library but in the possession of the British Museum when identified as Ralegh's in 1953, contains
both his library list and a geographical notebook.[4] Though it is his only
surviving notebook, he likely kept others. The library list was completed
by 1607, but Ralegh continued to return to the notebook, as attested by
two notes that refer to Laelio Bisciola's 1611 *Horarum Subsecivarum tomus*. The layout of the notebook indicates its intended use. Each page fea-
tured a red line splitting an inch-wide margin from the rest of the page
and had a letter as heading, with several pages devoted to each letter. On a
given page, Ralegh would enter the name of an alphabetically appropriate
locale, record the apposite description, and cite the authority in the margin (see fig. 3).

Ralegh's note-taking technique was the same as was used to compile
encyclopedic works he owned such as the Lutheran theologian David Chytraeus's anonymous 1564 *Onomasticon Theologicum*, the Antwerpian antiquarian and geographer Abraham Ortelius's 1587 *Thesaurus Geographi-*

---

3. BL Add. MS 57555 (hereafter cited as *NB*).

4. While the library list has been published and discussed in nearly every work concerning
Ralegh since its discovery, the geographical notebook has not received detailed scrutiny, even
in Skelton's 1965 "Raleigh as Geographer." While Skelton did consider the notebook alongside
Ralegh's Guiana materials and the *History,* he was more interested in the library list.

St: Hiero:

Aram, according to St Hierom, y called Syria or Syria Aram, or charam. of the Hebrews.

Homer

Aramits, ar called by Homer the Syrians or the Syrians Arimits,

Josephus.

Aramei ar called Syrians by Josephus.

Aram named in Ezechiel. 27. Junius calls Syria,

ptolo:
Avia Montanus
in aparatu Bibliæ

Aram=agara, a Cytty in Judea within Ganges.

Aram, the Hebrews call Armenia the greater.

Aram, or charam the septuag: call Mesopotamia, ꝯ in the scriptures (sayth Aurogallus) Syria campestris.

but Aram is teckon for mesopotamia, ꝯ charram or charan for a Cytty therin out of wch Abraham came into Cuna

Aram is also written for Damascus.

Aram padan mesopotamia

Niger f.559.

Scythia ruins universos populos vetustos Arameos appellauit. vulgo Tartaria Syria lingua Dist. id est deserta vocant. Hieronimus et aliter magis.

Arabia petrea.
Nabathei.

Arabia, petrea, Deserta, and foelix. Petrea hath petra for head. wch was somtyme called Rabbath, seated upon the torrent Arnon — it was ome inhabited by the Ammonits, although the cytty of Ar. was of the Moabites, and in Arabia Petrea was the kingdom of Seon, ꝯ of Og: the king of Basan.

Bror:
strabo.

Strabo ꝯ Plini call Ar. Petrea, Nabatea. and the head Cytty Petra is now called Avarb. the scriptures call it petra deserti,

Esaias,

Emitte agnum domine dominatorem terra de petra deserti: ꝯ this petra deserti was somtyme called Mons Regalis. seated up=

Ryorhimius.

pon mare Mortuū, and not uppon the torrent Arnon, for it stand on the top of a hygh hill agaynst the middel pt of the dead sea, it was called of the Hebrews Sela, Avre, Avrem or Areren, Resem, Rereme, but now Crar. mons regalis,ꝯ

petrea
Rabblath,
petrea deserti,
Avarb,
Mons regalis.
Sela, Avre,
Avrem, Areren,
Resem, Rereme
Cras, Mozera.
of ye hebrews teked
saith Hiero: Resem
of ye Syrians,
the Sarazens
Barraab.

Mozera, is an exceeding strong town ꝯ castell, it was the head of the kingdome of Moab and the Cytty ꝯ seat of the kings of Arabia, herein somtyme raigned Rerem, slayn by the Israelites, among ye rest of ye kings of Madian adioyning. This when Sravrus besieged with ye romayn Army ꝯ could not forte it hee was content to take mony by ysuation of Antipater, Amasius k: of Juda tooke it, after he had slayn 10000 men in ye valley salinarū, the mountayn Hor is not far fro it wher Aaron died. It is now the soldans ꝯꝯ therin keepers sixe treasors of Arabia ꝯ Ægypt, it had in tyme of Christianity a Latine Bysshope. The prince of this Cytty commanded all other Jordan.

Adiush:
f.77.

Arabia Petrea, the sarazens call Barraab. contayneth all ye chusty mediauitys au monitys Delautis, Husitos, also the region of Cedar. ꝯ yt ioyning to palestina is Nabathea, wher the whitest Alablaster is found, vide Niger f. 517

cus, and the French Catholic printer Charles Estienne's 1596 *Dictionarium historicum, geographicum, Poeticum.* They, in turn, had modeled their works on Eusebius's *Onomasticon.* These sources served as valuable reference works for readers struggling with the preponderance of provinces, kingdoms, and territories named in ancient sources and Scripture. Chytraeus explained why he began to produce notebooks in his student days: "Often the difficulties of not understanding the proper names delayed my progress and the smoothness with which I read, and I desired to know these things, the etymologies of names drawn from the fonts of their languages, and the sites and distances of places, regions, cities, mountains and rivers." To combat this frustration, he devised a method of reading and extracting passages from Scripture:

> While reading a line from the text of the Bible, at first I would pay attention only to the histories, which naturally delight the soul. Then I would note famous *sententiae,* and afterwards I would compare the German and Greek versions with the Latin. I also adjoined the readings of pious and erudite commentary to each sacred book. I would then excerpt from other sources testimonies concerning individual articles of Christian doctrine, and refutations of heresies, which is indeed the most bountiful fruit of reading the text. At length, I would take pains that I might collect the proper names of people, regions, cities, mountains, rivers, fonts and other things, and I would record the explications of them, which I could then investigate.[5]

Chytraeus produced his *Onomasticon* by reading Scripture, the church fathers, classical sources, scriptural commentaries, and histories according to this final technique.

Chytraeus's method of parsing texts for historical nominatives resem-

---

5. [David Chytraeus], *Onomasticon Theologicum* (Wittenberg, 1564), 5–7. "Saepe tamen remorabantur meum cursum, & suavitati lectionis aliquid molestae aspergebant non intellectae adpellationes propriorum Nominum, in quibus & Hominum illustrium familias, & Nominum etymologias ex Linguarum fontibus sumtas, & Locorum, regionum, urbium, montium, fluminum situs & intervalla cognoscere cupiebam. . . . Hac cupiditate, non inhoneste, ut opinor, incitatus, cum in perlegendo aliquoties ordine Textu Bibliorum, initio historias tantum, quibus natura delectantur animi, attendissem: Deinde sententias aliquas illustres praecipue notassem: Postea versionem Germanicam & Graecam cum Latina contulissem: alias vero unicuique libro sacro, lectionem pii & eruditi commentarii adiungerem: alias Testimonia de singulis doctrinae Christianae articulis & refutationibus haeresium (qui quidem fructus legendi Textum omnium uberrimus est) excerperem: aliquando hanc quoque curam suscepi, ut propria nomina personarum, regionum, urbium, montium, fluminum, fontium, & alia colligerem, & explicationes, quas tunc investigare poteram, adscriberem."

bled his 1564 proposal that students use commonplace books to develop a storehouse of rhetorical treasures.[6] But, while he had required that only the more significant rhetorical passages be transcribed, he demanded that each and every historical and geographical appellative be compiled. The rhetorical commonplace book was, in Chytraeus's formulation, a means to filter out the useless and collect the remarkable, but his historical notebook was designed to amass all testimony from the past.

Ortelius applied the same method to an extensive collection of sources to compile his *Thesaurus*. In his prefatory epistle, he applauded predecessors like Suidas and Callimachus, as well as the contemporary models Robert Etienne and Conrad Gesner, before explaining his method:

> First I scoured all kinds of ancient writings, both sacred and profane (of which some are not yet printed). Then those of the medieval period, then those more recent, including vernacular works. I transcribed from the ancients all names of places (and I did not omit a single one), a great many from the medieval period, and many from recent sources, but only those that sharpen the understanding of classical learning. I added also everything from ancient marbles, engraved tablets, ancient coins, and, in a word, whatever I could draw out that pertained in any way to my project from any kind of ancient inscription in whatever language.[7]

Ortelius approached ancient geography as an exercise in methodical note taking, applied to a more expansive range of objects than just texts. He also studied ancient coins, decaying monuments, submerged fortresses, and any other material remains he could access in person or through correspondence, extending the source base for geographical investigations.[8]

For Ortelius, as for Chytraeus, this process of collecting geographi-

---

6. See Moss, "The Politica of Justus Lipsius and the Commonplace-Book."

7. Abraham Ortelius, *Thesaurus Geographicus* (Antwerp, 1596), †4r–v. "Primum perlustravimus omne genus Scriptorum veterum, tam sacrorum quam prophanorum: (inter quos etiam nonnullos hactenus nondum typis excusos). deinde mediae aetatis: tum multos recentiores, cuiuscunque etiam idiomatis. Ex veteribus omnia locorum nomina, ne uno quidem omiso, in nostrum opus transtulimus. Ex mediae aetatis quoque magnum acervum. Ex recentioribus etiam multa. at ea solummodo quae ad explicationem aciebant doctorum veterum. Adiecimus corollarii loco omnia quae ex antiquis marmoribus, tabulis aeneis, omnisque prisci metalli nummis, & ut uno verbo dicam, quidquid ex omni genere & utriusque linguae inscriptionum vetustarum huic nostro argumento ullo modo servientium, haurire potuimus."

8. Compare Tine Meganck, "Erudite Eyes: Artists and Antiquarians in the Circle of Abraham Ortelius (1527–1598)" (Ph.D. diss., Princeton University, 2003).

cal knowledge was motivated by a desire to understand histories that had
been rendered obscure when toponyms had changed over time or fallen
into obsolescence. Even for Ortelius, the foremost geographer of the sixteenth century, geography remained subordinate to history. In his epistle
to the reader in his famous atlas, the 1570 *Theatrum orbis terrarum*, he
asserted: "Because I believe it to be clear enough how great is the utility of
the cognition of history, kind reader; I have persuaded myself, that there
is almost nobody who has, as they say, tasted history who does not know
how necessary is the knowledge of geography (which is called by certain
men the eye of history) for rightly understanding history."[9] The expeditions of kings and emperors, the migrations of peoples, the borders of past
empires—these could be understood only provided one had a solid grasp of
the spaces in which these events took place. Ortelius thus grounded the
relevance of geographical learning on its role as a handmaiden to historical knowledge and to the analysis of causes.

Assiduous comparison of notes from all manner of sources, Ortelius
believed, would enable scholars to firmly link toponyms with particular
places and to understand how they had changed over time. His methods show how note taking on a microscopic scale and from antiquarian
sources expanded the base of relevant material for geographers much as
chronologers had expanded theirs. Whether traveling, observing ancient
ruins, or reading, Ortelius applied an exacting technique of appellative
note taking. He demanded the isolation of the smallest, most irreducible
fragments in notes recording each evidentiary shard of his objects of observation. This program of distilling every relevant snippet from every
available source—whether textual or material—met the contemporary
ideal of historical practice and generated a deep reservoir of information
about the world's political and physical geography. It differed from that of
encyclopedic predecessors like Vincent of Beauvais and Hugh of St. Victor
both in the range of sources and experiences it demanded and, more importantly, in the minute scale of redaction it prescribed.[10] While medieval
scholars had tended to excerpt or epitomize a few authoritative sources,

9. Abraham Ortelius, *Theatrum Orbis Terrarum* (Antwerp, 1570), Aiiijr. "Cum omnibus
perspectum satis esse credam, quanta sit cognitionis historiarum utilitas, benigne Lector;
equidem mihi persuadeo, neminem poene esse, modo historias primis (quod aiunt) labris gus-
tarit, qui nesciat, quam necessaria sit ad eas recte intelligendas, Geographiae (quae merito a
quibusdam historiae oculus appellata est,) cognitio."

10. For this sort of medieval monastic reading, see C. Stephen Jaeger, *The Envy of Angels:
Cathedral Schools and Social Ideas in Medieval Europe, 950–1200* (Philadelphia: University
of Pennsylvania Press, 1994); Rudolf A. Eliott Lockhart, "Hugh of St. Victor and Twelfth-
Century English Monastic Reading," in *Owners, Annotators and the Signs of Reading*, ed.

the Antwerpian extracted irreducibly small claims and statements from his texts, and, unlike his predecessors, he considered geographical learning insufficient if drawn solely from a small number of canonical authorities. Ortelius's project sought to integrate, harmonize, and explain all available evidence—as Scaliger had for chronology—and, thus, to enable the accurate identification of the geographical phenomena referred to by any toponym throughout history.

If his confinement prevented him from replicating Ortelius's antiquarian fieldwork, Ralegh still mobilized his microscopic method of reading. On many of the pages of his geographical notebook, he carefully entered place-names and citations. For example, the first page for "A" included the different geographical areas referred to by *Aram*. The toponym was identified by Saint Jerome, Homer, Josephus, and the Calvinist exegete Franciscus Junius as Syria, by Ptolemy as India, by Bénito Arias Montano as Mesopotamia, and by the fifteenth-century Italian Dominicus Marius Niger as somewhere in between (see fig. 3 above). Ralegh, then, gleaned information from these authors with the notebook at hand, ready to be inscribed with the information he culled and to serve as a redaction of his sources.

Ralegh did not seek to reproduce the comprehensive scope of Ortelius's study. Instead, the notebook stored a catalog of citations directly relevant to the immediate task of writing the *History*. It was not, however, a perfect or infallible record. Many troubles arose from using the notebook to compress his sources, not the least of which was that he might forget the contexts or misinterpret the meanings of his own notes.[11] The text of the *History* exhibited several slippages possibly attributable to the notebook method. For example, when discussing Japan, Ralegh wrote: "And of the *Isle* of Iapan (now Zipiangari) Venetus [Marco Polo] maketh this report: The Ilanders are exceedingly addicted to religion, letters, and Philosophie, and most diligent searchers out of truth: there is nothing among them more frequent then prayer, which they use in their Churches after the manner of Christians. They acknowledge one King, and worship one God."[12] This was decidedly not what Marco Polo wrote—he described the Japanese as

---

Robin Myers, Michael Harris, and Giles Mandelbrote (New Castle, DE: Oak Knoll, 2005), 1–18; and Blair, *Too Much to Know*.

11. Users of notebooks tended to begin their books according to a predefined structure, but rarely were they evenly meticulous, and many pages of most notebooks are empty. Ralegh's book fits this pattern; the majority of pages lacked annotation aside from their headings, out of alphabetical order, and his library catalog began in the "Z" pages. Compare William Sherman, *Used Books: Marking Readers in Renaissance England* (Philadelphia: University of Pennsylvania Press, 2008).

12. *HW*, 1.7.10.5.116.

idolatrous cannibals. This error was likely due to Ralegh's misreading a citation in a notebook now lost.

Despite these problems, the notebook was a strikingly useful assistant for early modern scholars. While no evidence proves conclusively that Ralegh used the surviving notebook in composing the text of the *History*, his depiction of Egypt clearly derived from its map of Egypt.[13] Even if he did not consult it directly for other matters, the *History* was certainly produced through the mode of reading that structured the notebook itself. Indeed, it seems likely that, in the process of composition, Ralegh often turned to his notebooks rather than to the original sources and that he preferred a thin, clearly organized volume to the dense, magisterial tomes that filled the walls of his cell. The notebook served as a material surrogate for his library. That much of the *History* is cribbed or, as Arnold Williams has demonstrated, translated directly from other sources suggests either that he used many such books or that he transferred passages directly during composition.[14] Ralegh assembled, ordered, and integrated his sources by the note-taking method, and his one surviving notebook offers a point of entry into his working methods.

READING, MAPS, AND MEANING

Ralegh recorded both maps and textual fragments in his notebook, reflecting the profusion of modes of ordering geographical knowledge sparked by the flourishing of this discipline in early modern Europe. Propelled by the vogue for historical analysis, modern explorations, and increasing government demand for resources that would resolve jurisdictional questions, scholars throughout Europe developed sophisticated tools for compiling geographical knowledge. In England, Elizabeth had encouraged scholars such as Christopher Saxton, Richard Hakluyt, William Lambarde, John Norden, and John Dee to map the realm and the world.[15] The formidable erudition of Dee was particularly valued, and, like Hakluyt and Camden, he knew illustrious and innovative Continental scholars, including Ortelius. In fact, Ortelius was widely respected in Britain, where he maintained numerous correspondents, and those embarking on travels were

13. For the two maps, see figs. 5 and 10.

14. Arnold Williams, *The Common Expositor: An Account of the Commentaries on Genesis, 1527–1633* (Chapel Hill: University of North Carolina Press, 1948), 75.

15. Peter Barber, "Was Elizabeth I Interested in Maps—and Did It Matter?" *TRHS*, 6th ser., 14 (2004): 185–98.

often encouraged to use his *Theatrum* as a guidebook.[16] Such Continental connections stimulated innovative geographical work, and scholars such as John Speed and Hugh Broughton drew on Continental predecessors in using visual means to depict sacred geography.[17] And, of course, explorers such as Francis Drake, Thomas Cavendish, and Martin Frobisher presided over voyages that devoted attention to recording observations that were later collected in Hakluyt's 1598–1600 *Principal Navigations*.[18]

Beyond his patronage of Hakluyt, Ralegh was a vital part of the culture of geographical inquiry that had emerged in England under Elizabeth. Geographical expertise had been integral in his role as navigator, pirate, and explorer, and extant maps attributed to his hand date from the Guiana voyages that he oversaw in the 1590s.[19] Ralegh's administrative roles in the Elizabethan regime had given him occasion to use geography in devising position papers concerning the defense of England's southern coast as well as in organizing exploratory missions to Virginia and Guiana. Indeed, his claim to geographical expertise provided one of his main sources of appeal to James, and he would ultimately earn his release when James decided to hazard his prisoner's ability to find El Dorado in the jungles of Guiana.

Throughout Europe, the increased significance attributed to geographical learning prompted scholars to revise modes of encapsulating their knowledge. While Chytraeus, Ortelius, and Henri Etienne produced dictionaries, Grynaeus, Giovanni Battista Ramusio, Linschoten, De Bry, and Hakluyt recorded the expansion of geographical knowledge in collections of travel narratives, and Mercator, Ortelius, and Matal synthesized their hard-earned knowledge in maps of both the minutest provinces and the globe itself. Other authors experimented with nonvisual methods to organize geographical information. Many atlases, such as Sebastian Münster's 1544 *Cosmographia*, consisted predominantly of narrative accounts, and Reiner Reineck's 1583 *Methodus Legendi Cognoscendique Historiam*

16. See the recommendations of Hakluyt in chapter 4 below and of Beale in chapter 5 below as well as the anonymous instructions preparing Lord Zouche for travel to Germany (BL Cotton Nero B IX, fols. 138r–142r).

17. See Hugh Broughton, *A Concent of Scripture* (London, 1588); and John Speed, *The Genealogies Recorded in the Sacred Scriptures* (London, 1611).

18. David Harris Sacks, "Richard Hakluyt's Navigations in Time: History, Epic, and Empire," *Modern Language Quarterly* 67 (2006): 31–62, and "Discourses of Western Planting: Richard Hakluyt and the Making of the Atlantic World," in Mancall, ed., *The Atlantic World and Virginia*, 410–53; and Peter Mancall, *Hakluyt's Promise: An Elizabethan's Obsession for an English America* (New Haven, CT: Yale University Press, 2007).

19. See BL Add. MS 17940A.

provided Ramist diagrams delineating the various genera and particulars of geographical forms. Within these diagrams, Reineck explained the differences between, for example, islands, peninsulas, promontories, isthmi, bridges, and straits and listed examples in order of size.[20] Each mode of presentation assumed a unique approach toward arranging geographical evidence, from reproducing original texts, to processing them through the note-taking method or logical categories, to converting them into images. Maps were, thus, one form among many for organizing geographical knowledge.

Ortelius's publishing career demonstrates the symbiotic relation between mapmaking and note taking. In 1596, the Plantin Press reissued an updated and corrected version of Ortelius's 1587 *Thesaurus*, itself an expanded version of his 1578 *Synonomia Geographica*. Ortelius's exhaustive troll through the books, manuscripts, maps, inscriptions, coins, and antiquities had yielded a massive dictionary of the "ancient names and appellations of all regions, mountains, promontories, hills, forests, deserts, islands, harbors, peoples, cities, towns, provinces, shrines, tribes: and likewise of Oceans, seas, straights, rivers, rapids, gulfs, springs, lakes, and swamps of the entire world." The *Synonomia* preceded by one year the publication of Ortelius's *Parergon*, a supplement to the *Theatrum*, which had been first published in 1570. The *Parergon* was specifically devoted to historical geography.[21] Its first edition consisted of maps of the peregrinations of the apostle Paul through the Hellenic world, the territorial extent of the Roman Empire, and the city-states of ancient Greece, along with a glossary of the toponyms in Ptolemy's *Geographia*. Later editions of the *Theatrum* expanded the *Parergon*, which ultimately included thirty-nine maps and was issued separately from the *Theatrum* in 1624. While some maps represented signal events of sacred history such as the movements of Abraham and Moses and depicted the political geography of the pre-Captivity Promised Land, others traced Alexander the Great's penetration into the East, the peripatetic movements of Jason, Aeneas, and Ulysses, and the political geography of ancient Sicily.

20. For Reineck, see Peter Zeeberg, "Heinrich Rantzau (1526–98) and His Humanist Collaborators: The Example of Reiner Reineccius and Georg Ludwig Froben," in *Germania latina—Latinitas teutonica: Politik, Wissenschaft, humanistische Kultur vom späten Mittelalter bis in unsere Zeit*, ed. Eckhard Keßler and Heinrich C. Kuhn (Munich: Wilhelm Fink, 2003), 539–53; and Grafton, *What Was History?* 142–65.

21. For the history of historical geography, see Jeremy Black, *Maps and History: Constructing Images of the Past* (New Haven, CT: Yale University Press, 1997); and Walter Goffart, *Historical Atlases: The First Three Hundred Years, 1570–1870* (Chicago: University of Chicago Press, 2003).

Ortelius's maps were framed by discussion of his sources and critiques of the inaccuracies of his ancient interlocutors. This apparatus made clear that scholars had been arguing for over a millennium about questions of ancient geography, primarily in the context of sacred history. And the cartographic model of the ancient world that Ortelius produced rested explicitly on the textual investigations he had published the previous year. "Concerning these [locations]," he wrote, "many have written many things, and dissenting opinions exist among learned men. I too will add my opinion, which the reader will be able to judge as he likes, and if he wishes to, he can read what I wrote more extensively in my *Thesaurus.*"[22] While Ortelius augmented the *Parergon* over the next twenty years, he also reedited and reissued the *Thesaurus* twice in the decades after its initial publication. His cartographic innovation rested firmly on his application of the antiquarian methods of extensive collection and microscopic note taking to a tradition of textual, descriptive geography. And the two enterprises continued to proceed hand in hand.

Ortelius's maps were based on the intricate and fragmentary notes gleaned by his antiquarian method. In fact, the conversion of textual information into visual form was conceptualized by early modern scholars as one particular practice of storing and integrating geographical information. The eccentric scholar Sixtus Senensis's 1564 *Bibliotheca Sancta*, a primary source for Ralegh on sacred geography, included among the proper modes of exegesis "sciographia," which he defined as "contemplative and pictorial exposition, which through various figures and the delineations of images more clearly and openly places before the eyes that which cannot properly be expressed in words."[23] The geography of the Holy Land was one of his ideal subjects for sciographical study.

Maps were one system of arranging geographical information that provided insight into history, and they were subject to various economies of emphasis. While Ptolemaic maps and the projections by Mercator and oth-

<hr>

22. Ortelius, *Theatrum*, ir. "Universalis Orbis typum a latere adiecimus: ex qua theologiae candidatus discat conferendo, quantam & quotam huius partem historia Sacra comprehendat. Atque eodem labore hoc quoque, nempe situm duorum locorum in sacris celebrium, Ophyrae utpote regionis & Paradisi terrestris situm. De quibus etsi multi multa scribant, & dissentientes inter doctos opiniones exstent, nos nostram sententiam quoque adiecimus, de qua Lectori pro suo arbitratu diudicare licebit: legatque si lubet, quae fusius de Ophyra scripsimus in nostro dicto Thesauro."

23. Sixtus Senensis, *Bibliotheca Sancta* (Venice, 1566), 264. "Sciographica, hoc est Umbratilis, & picturalis expositio est, quae per varias figurarum & imaginum delineationes clarius & apertius prae oculis ponit ea quae non ad modum aperte verbis exprimi potuerunt, non tam ornamenti ac decoris gratia, quam necessitatis ratione a sacris expositoribus excogitata."

ers struggled to represent the physical form of a round earth on flat sur-
faces, other world images foregrounded elements other than the mimetic.
Bünting produced a T-O map, modified to include the New World and the
Arctic regions, in the shape of a clover—the symbol of his native Hanover.
Ortelius himself produced a world map in the shape of a heart.[24] And, as
we shall see, maps could be annotated as easily as could text and served
just as readily as a space to be inscribed with passages gleaned from other
sources.

Geographical authors thus experimented with a wide variety of alternatives for processing and absorbing geographical knowledge. Maps were
valued because their visual presentation illuminated geographical knowledge only darkly perceptible when presented in text. But, like notebooks,
they were viewed as just one alternative mode of assembling, organizing,
and ordering knowledge of the world, offering both a system with which
to process future notes and insights with which to better investigate
the past.

RALEGH'S GEOGRAPHICAL NOTE TAKING

Ralegh's notebook offers the unusual ability to explore how an early modern geographer made use of his library. The extracts that he recorded in
it reveal that his method of note taking was designed to facilitate his
historical geography and show him experimenting with ways to arrange
extracts gleaned from his reading. The contents and organization of the
notebook represent the product of a precisely structured engagement with
his sources.

Though Ralegh was one of the modern explorers who had opened far-
off lands to prying European eyes, he referred to reports of modern travelers selectively in the *History*. Instead, he primarily relied on older travel
narratives and newer atlases such as those produced by Ortelius and Münster rather than the experiential collections of Linschoten, Hakluyt, and
de Bry. But he did use modern evidence to test received opinions, if not to
undermine ancient authority, thus affording space in his scholarship for
the testimonials of both modern experience and venerable ancient texts.
And his extracts suggest that both modern and ancient accounts were processed in the same fashion, by redaction into brief, fragmentary notes.

In compiling his notebook, Ralegh restricted his focus to the temporal

24. Giorgio Mangani, *Il "mondo" di Abramo Ortelio: Misticismo, geografia e collezionismo nel Rinascimento dei Paesi Bassi* (Modena: Franco Cosimo Panini, 1998).

and spatial purview of the *History*. He was hemmed in by the classical *oecumene*—the world known to the ancients—which had as its Christianized center Jerusalem and the Holy Land. He briefly mentioned England, France, other European states to the north, the Moluccas to the southeast, and Japan to the east. But, aside from in the preface, he rarely discussed a field greater than that bounded by the Himalayas to the northeast and Carthage to the southwest, with only infrequent mentions of non-Egyptian Africa and no systematic attention devoted to the New World. His understanding of East Asia was strikingly landlocked, deriving primarily from the overland explorations undertaken by medieval travelers or the ancient colonists, soldiers, ambassadors, and naturalists who went east through Persia and northern India, rather than from the coastal explorations of contemporary explorers who swung around Africa to Goa and beyond. For the lands and events discussed in the *History*, the overland eastward trade routes of the ancients created geographical knowledge usable in a way that the modern maritime routes did not. Ralegh's methods thus suggest an adherence to the position that each epoch created its own tools for geographical analysis, as with chronology.

These geographical parameters largely structured Ralegh's attention when inscribing his notebook, for his notes primarily addressed the ancient history of the eastern Mediterranean and the Near East. He frequently cited Scripture (especially the Pentateuch and the historical books), Ptolemy, Pliny, and Strabo, while Josephus, Jerome, and Augustine too were noted periodically. But most of his notes refer to modern scholarly discussions of Eastern geography. He drew on Ortelius heavily, using both the *Theatrum* and the *Thesaurus*. For the Holy Land, he excerpted several passages from the 1590 *Theatrum Terrae Sanctae* of the German priest Christiaan van Adrichem. He also took several pages of notes out of the 1595 Latin edition of the Lutheran scholar Heinrich Bünting's *Itinerarium et chronicon . . . sacrae scripturae*. For Syria, he turned to the *Descriptio Terrae Sanctae* of the early thirteenth-century French Dominican Brocard, who, unlike the other authors, had traveled to the area that he studied. He devoted little space in this notebook to Mesopotamia, Persia, Parthia, or Media. Further east, he drew his discussion of ancient Bactria from the French royal historiographer Francois de Belleforest's 1575 *La Cosmographie Universelle*—a French translation and reworking of Münster—and from Wolfgang Wissenberg's 1557 edition of the fifteenth-century Venetian Dominicus Marius Niger's *Geographiae Commentariorum libri*. Throughout the notebook, Ralegh interspersed notes drawn from the French royal cosmographer Andre Thevet's 1575 *Cosmographie Universelle*, Juan Luis

Vives's commentary on Augustine's *De civitate dei*, and Jacob Ziegler's 1536 *Terrae sanctae*.

A closer inspection of these notes will illuminate how the imprisoned explorer drew knowledge of the world from these authors. It will reveal him struggling to devise methods to assemble a coherent system from notes that mined a core of geographical knowledge by excluding other sorts of information. The notebook provided a site for experimenting with modes of arranging his irreducible, narrowly geographical extracts.

The notes from Ortelius and Bünting illustrate the variety of systems Ralegh could use to organize the information gained from interaction with his geographical sources. He cited Ortelius frequently in his notebook, particularly regarding northern Africa. He also copied nine maps and three insets out of the *Theatrum* and two maps of Egypt derived from Ortelius's map of Egypt in the *Parergon*.[25] He divided the functions of Ortelius's image of Egypt into two, devoting one copy to ancient Egyptian geography, emphasizing in the other Egypt as the opening site of Exodus. In the latter, he omitted most of the city names included by Ortelius, instead tracing in bright red inkwash the Israelites sweeping down from Ramses, where they had congregated, through Sucoth, Etham, and Pihatheroth and across the miraculously bifurcated Red Sea to Mara (see fig. 4). His division of Ortelius's image showed that maps could be excerpted as readily as texts.

But these visual representations did not exhaustively convey the information Ralegh wished to store. Ringing the first map of ancient Egypt were notes copied from Ortelius's dictionary, the *Thesaurus* (see fig. 5). The entry adjacent to Babylon (Cairo was sometimes called the Egyptian Babylon, though they were at other times thought to be two different cities) is a clear reduction of Ortelius's text: "Babilon, the Arabians call Mazar. The Chaldeans Alchabyk. Joseph: Leruspolin, the Hebrews Mizraim. Cairo stood on the West Side of it & are now become one Citty, saith

---

25. The first six maps depicted the northern coast of contemporary Africa. Ralegh did not create perfect duplicates; he included only major cities and regions, and he omitted some physical features. Nonetheless, he adhered exactly to the names provided by Ortelius and reproduced carefully the perambulations of the rivers, the tracks of the mountains, and intricate coastlines. Cities were marked by a symbolic palace, and he added chromatic signs of physical geography: fertile or agricultural areas were denoted with a rich olive green, while the barrenness of a terrain was indicated by bright burnt orange, and he added a pale sky blue for coastal areas, rivers, and lakes. The detail of these maps conveyed both complex political and physical geographical information and Ralegh's care in producing them. *NB*, fols. 18v–21r. Not all Ralegh's manuscript maps derived from Ortelius's section on modern Africa; his map of Carthage derives from the *Parergon*'s map of Sicily. Ortelius, *Theatrum*, 20r. He also copied a map of Basan, a province in Canaan, from Adrichem.

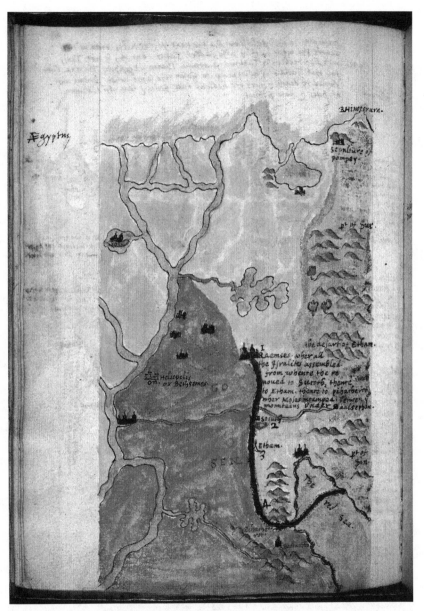

Figure 4. Egypt map from Ralegh's notebook. © The British Library Board.
BL Add. MS 57555, fol. 23v.

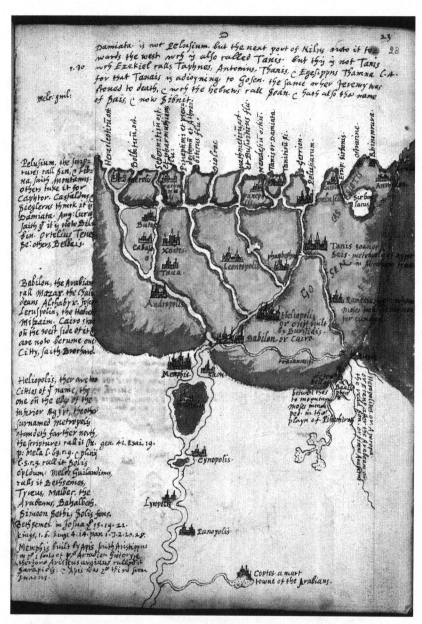

Figure 5. Egypt map from Ralegh's notebook. © The British Library Board.
BL Add. MS 57555, 23r.

Brochard."[26] His note on Pelusium was also cribbed from Ortelius's entry.[27] When Ralegh transcribed the maps from Ortelius's cartographic masterpiece, then, he took Ortelius's advice and consulted the Antwerpian's textual compendium to understand the basis of the maps. He examined the geography of ancient Egypt through both the textual and the visual materials provided by Ortelius, and he relied on Ortelius's summations of the opinions of other commentators.

Ralegh drew considerably more from Ortelius's textual descriptions than from the visual, and, while he infrequently consulted the *Theatrum*, references from the *Thesaurus* heavily dot the notebook. Some of the notes on the map pages drawn from the *Thesaurus* appear almost identically elsewhere. Listed under "B," for example, is the entry: "Babilon in Ægypt, which ye Arabians call Mazar, or Mizar, the Armenians Massar, the Chaldeans Alchabyr, the Hebrews mesraim, now Cairo, & Alcairo, But Brochard says yt Cairo & Babilon were too Cytties ioyned in one."[28] Brochard is given in the margin as the source, although the citation is, again, clearly drawn from Ortelius, illustrating that Ralegh cited works directly that he had accessed at third hand. In these notes, he simulated Ortelius's work of collecting brief extracts to generate his own pool of potent evidence. His method of note taking thus processed Ortelius's text in a variety of ways. He extracted elements of maps as well as texts, fused visual and textual descriptions, recorded similar summaries in multiple contexts, and sim-

---

26. Compare Ortelius, *Thesaurus Geographicus*, M1r. "BABYLON Ptolemaeo etiam Aegypti vetustissima & maxima urbs. Vocatur Arabice *Mazar* aut *Mizir*, Armenice *Massar*, Chaldaice *Alchabyr*, Hebraice *Mesraim*: sic in libello anonymo, sed Postelli, ni fallor. Idem in libello suo historiae Orientalis *Mitzir, Fostat, & Nitzrnlatik* habet. *Misraim* eam quoque Tudelensis nominat. Ab omnibus Europaeis hodie *Cairo*, & *Alcairo* appellatur. Babylonia & Cairus duo esse opida, sed in unum coniuncta, scribit Brocardus."

27. See *NB*, fol. 23r, where Ralegh's note reads: "Pelusium, the Scriptures call Sin & Libna saith Montanus. others take it for Caphtor. Castaldus & Sieglerus think it is Damiata. Ang: Curio saith yt it is now Bilbin. Ortelius Tenesse: others Belbais." Compare Ortelius, *Thesaurus Geographicus*, LL1v: "PELUSIUM πελφσιον, Ptolemaeo Aegypti urbs, ad Nili fluminis ostium, quod ab ea Pelusiacum dicitur, sita. Hunc olum quoque AELIOPOLIM, ab Aelio principe, qui eam triplici muro cinxerat, dictam scribit Sabellicus. Platina in vita Honorii III tradit sic appellatam ab Aelio Pertinace. Sed illum Helvii, non Aelii; praenomen habuisse, numismata antiqua docent, eoque HELVIOPOLIS, & non Aeliopolis diceretur. LIBNA, & SIN in Sacris litteris est, Aria Montano teste. Olim CAPHTOR vocatam, scribit beniamin. Huius mentio fit cap 9. Amos prophetae. Clavem Aegypti cognominat Suidas. & eius incolas Pelusiosas, etiam CASIOS, nominari adit, a Casio monte nimirum, illi vicino. *Belbais* hodie nuncupatur, teste Guil Tyre, Iacobo Vitriaco, & Nigro; *Bilbin* Aug Curioni; *Damiaca* Castaldo, & Zieglero. Nisi tabulae fallunt, Pelusium hodie *Tenesse* dicitur."

28. *NB*, fol. 12r.

ply cribbed the opinions of a selection of the authorities that Ortelius had compiled. His work distilled and reassembled the information he wished to preserve from Ortelius's works.

Ralegh's reading of Bünting's *Itinerarium* demonstrates other approaches to his sources. This work was extremely well-known, going through twenty-seven editions or reprints between 1582 and 1757, including Latin, English, Dutch, and Swedish translations from the German; the English edition alone was issued six times between 1619 and 1682. In it, Bünting traced journeys described in the Bible. Each chapter was devoted to an individual site. Beginning with Adam's expulsion from the Garden and Cain's fugitive steps, Bünting exhaustively detailed the movements of sacred figures from Abraham and his progeny through the Israelites under Moses to Christ and the Apostles, including woodcut maps that traced their paths. Relying mostly on Scripture—though, as with his chronology, he prized the testimony of ancient pagans—he described the travels of individuals in the order of the cities they traversed. He provided accounts of each locale's history and stated its proximity to other places. Any biographical information or exegesis was subsumed under these geographical headings, although further information might be gleaned from his typological expositions of select individuals. Bünting thus reduced the scriptural histories of the ancient world to a spiritual progress.

Ralegh processed and reorganized the extracts gained from Bünting's text even more emphatically than he had Ortelius's. As he read the *Itinerarium*, he jotted down notes of the German's entries for thirty-four holy sites, from Haran, Abraham's point of departure, to the location visited by the Israelites during the Exodus. He did not arrange this information according to one uniform method, likely because he took notes from Bünting's text on separate occasions. He inserted names and notes for each of the five spots visited by Abraham under their alphabetical headings. But he processed the places traversed by Lot, Hagar, Ishmael, Jacob, Esau, and Juda and some of those visited by Joseph and Moses into a tidy digest, encompassing four sides, ordered exactly as he encountered the locations in Bünting. He thus disposed his reading of Bünting in two different ways. For the sites Abraham visited, he ordered his findings alphabetically; for the travels of later Old Testament figures, he distilled his reading into a summary, reproducing Bünting's focus on geographical sequence. His interaction with Bünting's work again demonstrated the ability to create notes according to multiple principles.

The content of Ralegh's entries drawn from Bünting demonstrates how his note-taking method stripped his sources into extracts that were narrowly geographical. For example, for Cadesbarnea, whence Moses sent spies into the Holy Land (Numbers 13–14), Ralegh noted: "Cadesbarne 10 miles from Ierusalem five fro Hebron. a Cytty of Idumea."[29] Recognizing the significance of this anodyne note requires comparison with its source to illuminate what Ralegh judged worth preserving and what merited omission. Bünting had dwelt instead on the significance of Cadesbarnea—his English translator had condensed his entry:

> Cades Barnea a citie of the Idumaeans being derived of *Kadas* and *Barah*, (that is, A holy place) is fortie [English] miles from Ierusalem towards the South: from this place *Moses* sent spies into the land of Canaan, who brought of the fruit of the land, but all of them discouraged the people, onely *Caleb*: wherefore they murmured, and the Lord was angry, and would not suffer them to enter into the land of Promise: So turning their journey, they went to Exeongaber, 148 miles, so that they travelled in the desart 40 yeares, before they could enter into the land of Promise.[30]

Cadesbarnea was where the Israelites' feckless lack of faith finally eroded the patience of God, who, instead of directing them into the Holy Land, sentenced them to forty years of wandering. Ralegh's note thus carefully recorded Bünting's geographical evidence while ignoring Cadesbarnea's role within sacred history.

Though in the notebook Ralegh omitted the divine or historical significance of Cadesbarnea, he treated it carefully in the *History*. "After the returne of the discoverers of *Cades*," he explained, "the wrath of God was turned against *Israel*; whose ingratitude and rebellion after His so many benefits, so many remissions, so many miracles wrought, was such, as

---

29. *NB*, fol. 89r.

30. Heinrich Bünting, *Itinerarium totius sacrae scripturae*, trans. R.B. (London, 1636), 124. For the original, see Heinrich Bünting, *Itinerarium totius sacrae scripturae* (Magdeburg, 1597), 253. "Cades Barnea, Sancta & pura quaedam agitatio, Eine Heilige und reine Bewegung. Cades Barnea Idumaeae civitas est, decem milliaribus a Ierosolymis versus meridiem, ab Hebron autem quinque milliaribus versus austrum sita, habens longitudinem sexaginta quinque graduum & quadraginta scrupulorum, latitudinem autem triginta graduum & unius, cum scrupilis quinquaginta. Hic Moses emisit exploratores terrae Canaan, qui versei, & in concionem introducti, quamvis ostenderent viam magnam, quam secum attulerant, tamen commemorata potentia Cananaeorum, populum consternatum reddiderunt, unde Deus propter murmur & vociferationem populi ad iram provocatus, recusavit eis introitum in terram promissam, versaque nube, triginta septem milliarum intervallo eos reduxit ad Exeongaber maris rubri civitatem, ut ita quadraginta annis obambularent & peregrinarentur in deserto, antequam ingrederentur terram promissam."

they esteemed their deliverance from the *Aegyptian* slaverie, his feeding them, and conducting them through that great and terrible *wildernesse* . . . to be no other then the effects of his hatred." Cadesbarnea thus reemerged as the site of the Israelites' greatest transgression and God's most forceful punishment. God swore that he would smite the lot of the Israelites, and only Moses' meek prayers preserved the nation. The ungrateful tribe was, thus, told that they must return to the Red Sea and that only after having touched its shores again could they turn back to the Promised Land. Ralegh drew from this narrative testimony of God's power and mercy: "Yet as God is no lesse iust than merciful, as God is slow to anger, so is his wrath a consuming fire; the same being once kindled by the violent breath of mans ingratitude: and therefore, as with a hand lesse heavie than hoped for he scourged this iniquitie, so by the measure of his glorie (evermore iealous of neglect and derision) hee suffered not the wicked to passe unpunished; reserving his compassion for the innocent."[31] The narrative significance of Cadesbarnea, stripped down to geographical detail in the notebook, was here restored to its place within a historical narrative and reinvested with sacral meaning.

His response to Bünting's treatment of the mansion of Rephidim too shows Ralegh filling his notebook with neatly geographical entries. Bünting had written:

> Raphadim was a place where the children of Israell pitched their tents in the desert, not far from mount Sinai, 132 miles from Ierusalem towards the Southwest; and signifieth a Grasse bench strewed with sweet herbs and floures: being derived from *Raphad*, which is as much to say in our Language, as To make a bed or place for one to lie down. Here *Moses* strook the rock out of which water issued, *Exod.* 17 which was a type of that spirituall Roch Christ Iesus, 1 *Cor* 10 who being strooke with the staffe of the curse of the Law, out of his pretious wounds and side sent forth that Water of life which runneth into eternall happinesse. In this place the children of Israel fought against the Amalekites, and overcame them, *Ex.* 17.[32]

Ralegh's note eliminated Bünting's typological analyses: "Raphidim in ye desert nere Sinai 33 mile from Jerusalem. Where Moses smote ye rock

---

31. *HW*, 2.5.3.298–99.
32. Bünting, *Itinerarium*, trans. R.B., 118.

& their issewed water. by this place Joshua overthrew the Amaleckits."[33] And, while in the *History* Ralegh again largely ignored Rephidim's geography, he did not turn to Bünting's typological reading. He instead drew continuities between the events that had taken place in Rephidim and the parting of the Red Sea that suggested God's continuing miraculous intervention: "*Moses* with the same rod which heᵹ divided the Sea withall, in the sight of the *Elders* of *Israel*, brought waters out of the Rocke, wherewith the whole multitude was satisfied."[34] Bünting's typology was not explicitly invoked, but the importance of the place was clearly embedded within sacred history.

These examples illuminate how Ralegh used his notebook to distill and reduce texts to their geographical components. He mined his sources' erudition by fragmenting their maps, abbreviating their entries, and reordering the compilations of geographical information they had tirelessly accumulated. The notebook was not intended to encapsulate the whole spectrum of information available regarding its entries. Rather, Ralegh devoted it to considerations of place, distance, and location, omitting other sorts of information—typological, ethnographic, even historical—and organizing it according to a variety of methods, including alphabetical, spatial, and visual. The notebook thus supplied a repository that preserved information about place and location drawn from other texts, reducing their multiform passages into a pointed entry, stripping their narrations to their skeletal information of location and distance.

RALEGH AND OPHIR—THE CERTAINTY OF METHOD, TACIT POLITICS, AND TRADITION

Ralegh's collections of extracts furnished him with a powerful body of evidence that he could use to assess how other scholars had resolved persistent problems of geographical scholarship. As the following treatment of the question of the locations of Ophir will show, his method emphasized the necessity of accounting for every last extract, each of which possessed the ability to reinforce or unsettle previous geographical identifications. And, though the questions he addressed within this method held special resonance for vital political questions, he did not respond to them with polemic but instead deployed an army of snippets quarried from a

33. *NB*, fol. 89r.
34. *HW*, 2.4.1.265.

range of sources to affirm his argument. Within this system, crucial passages could be taken from modern travelers as easily as from venerated ancients, for within this new regime of evaluating arguments the ability to incorporate or explain as many shards of evidence as possible—rather than agreement with recognized authorities—constituted the grounds of persuasion.

Early modern scholars debated the location of Ophir, the distant treasure-filled land to which Solomon had sent triennial convoys, each of which returned home laden with unimaginable burdens of gold. The key scriptural passages were 1 Kings 9:21 (*And they came to Ophir, and fetched from thence gold, four hundred and twenty talents, and brought it to King Solomon*) and 2 Chron. 9:17 ("Moreover the king made a great throne of ivory, and overlaid it with pure gold"). Most commentators followed Josephus in locating Ophir somewhere east of India. But, in 1572, Benedicto Arias Montano's development of Guillaume Postel's insinuation that Ophir lay in the New World stimulated Europeanwide scholarly examination of evidence. Scholars debated Montano's thesis and derived a panoply of locations for this toponym, each betraying assumptions and preferences concerning the location of this exotic trade partner.[35]

Montano's conflation of Peru and Ophir constituted an inventive solution to a variety of intellectual problems and political exigencies. He began with the claim that the New World was known to the ancient world because it had been populated by Noah's great-grandson Ophir, son of Ioctan, grandson of Sem.[36] This identification proved that Native Americans were creations of the same divine being as Europeans—*the New World* was, after all, a fraught appellation. A Noachite genealogy preserved the

35. The following analysis resembles in some respects that in James Romm, "Biblical History and the Americas: The Legend of Solomon's Ophir, 1492–1591," in *The Jews and the Expansion of Europe to the West, 1450–1800*, ed. Paolo Bernardini and Norman Fiering (New York: Bergahn, 2001), 27–46. For Montano, see Zur Shalev, "Sacred Geography, Antiquarianism, and Visual Erudition: Benito Arias Montano and the Maps of the Antwerp Polyglot Bible," *Imago Mundi* 55 (2003): 56–80.

36. For the mapping of the plantation, see Don Cameron Allen, *The Legend of Noah: Renaissance Rationalism in Art, Science, and Letters* (Urbana: University of Illinois Press, 1949); Margaret T. Hodgen, *Early Anthropology in the Sixteenth and Seventeenth Centuries* (Philadelphia: University of Pennsylvania Press, 1964); Giuliano Gliozzi, *Adamo e il Nuovo Mondo: La nascita dell'antropologia come ideologia coloniale: Dalle genealogie bibliche alle teorie razziali (1500–1700)* (Florence: La Nuova Italia, 1977); Benjamin Braude, "The Sons of Noah and the Construction of Ethnic and Geographical Identities in the Medieval and Early Modern Periods," *William and Mary Quarterly* 54 (1997): 103–42; and Shalev, "Geographia Sacra."

monogenetic unity of the human race and of the world and, in turn, the singularity of the divine creator and universality of original sin.[37]

Montano explained that those who had lived in the immediate post-diluvian age had maintained contact with New World brethren and, thus, held more complete cosmological and geographical knowledge than their successors. Scripture, he claimed, contained indications that even in Moses' time the Israelites possessed thorough knowledge of the New World and supplied indisputable philological evidence that Solomon's most treasured trade partner lay in South America. As he explained: "But that land, from which such a copious quantity of the best gold was drawn, and carried to other peoples, [Scripture] openly teaches was then called Parvaim, which word clearly signifies 'two regions formerly known as Peru' to those who read Hebrew: one of which is still known by this name today, and another which is called New Spain by sailors."[38] By claiming that the vicissitudes of time and tongue had transformed the word *Ophir* into *Peru* and that in Hebrew *Parvaim* described Ophir's enlarged empire as "double Peru," Montano argued that sacred writers furnished testimony of knowledge of the entirety of the world.

This knowledge Montano identified as a peculiar ornament of the ancient Israelites that had not been shared by the pagan cultures of antiquity: "None of the Greek or Latin writers whose writings have come down to our own time relates anything that if most diligently examined can be compared with those things that Moses clearly wrote concerning the land of Ophir, or that the Prophet Jonathan, writer of the history of the Kings of Juda, taught copiously and exactly."[39] While Greek and Roman ignorance

37. Montano, *Antiquitatum Iudaicarum Libri*, 5.

38. Ibid., 4. "Verum etiam terram illam, ex qua tanta optimi auri copia eliceretur, & ad alias gentes asportaretur, eam, inquam, terram, tam tum םִיַרְפ Parvaim appellatam esse, aperte docet. quae quidem dictio, iis qui vel tantum Hebraice sunt legere, duas regiones, olim Peru dictas, clare demonstrat: unam quidem, quae eodem vocabulo, hodierno etiam die Peru dicitur: alteram vero, quae nova Hispania a navigantibus est appellata."

39. Ibid., 3–4. "Sed ut haec faciamus, & in aliud tempus differamus, illud non est praetereundeum, amplissimam illam orbis terrarum partem, quae quidem auro, argento, gemmis, aliisque multis, quae ab hominibus maximi fiunt, quaeque ad vitam sunt necessaria, mirandum in modum abundat, quae nuper ab Hispanis navigantibus primum inventa esse creditur, novusque Orbis appellatur, ex ea, quae in sacris traditur libris, terrarum orbis descriptione, apertissime cognosci posse. Quinimo & illud ex sacra scriptura docere possumus, eam terram israelitis fuisse notissimam: illos enim ad eam saepius navigatione contendisse constat. Sane neque Strabo, aut Mela, Stephanus, Solinus, Ptolemaeus, & alii, aut Plato & Aristoteles, qui quidem obscure, ac veluti per aenigmata, de iis, quae sibi ignota erant, disseruerunt; aut poetae illi, qui, ne quid ignorare viderentur, nihil fabulis non aspergebant suis: *nullus denique ex Graecis, Latinisve Scriptoribus, quorum scripta ad nostram usque pervenerunt aetatem, aliquid edidit, quod si, quale tandem id sit, diligenter examinetur, comparari possit cum iis,*

testified to their corruption, the Israelites' knowledge of the New World reflected their more perfect comprehension of God's creation.

The identification of Ophir with Peru served powerful purposes. According to Montano's vision, Solomon's reign had encompassed South America in a worldwide, divinely licensed, and orthodox empire, one in which the Hebraic knowledge of the New World was a sign of divine favor. The Habsburg Empire, ruled by Montano's patron Philip II, had re-created this empire, drawing all the riches of the world into the coffers of a wise and holy king intent on protecting and expanding his nation of chosen subjects. Montano's exegesis, in this case, supplied a powerful scriptural license for Spanish universal monarchy.[40]

Montano's argument sparked controversy throughout Europe, as scholars and polemicists eagerly sought out sources and devised interpretations to support or refute his vision. No scholar examining scriptural or modern history could ignore his work, and Ralegh kept Montano forefront in his mind, even as he initially consulted Ortelius's work concerning Ophir's location. Ortelius, like many others, disagreed with Montano, but, unusually, he had placed Ophir along the east coast of Africa.[41] This alternative identification for Ophir did not directly address the political register of Philip II's ambitions, but the evocation of an ancient, gold-laden, pious kingdom in East Africa, near highly coveted trade routes that the Dutch were beginning to develop, certainly would have resonated politically.

Ortelius, nevertheless, did not explicitly articulate the political significance of his argument. Instead, he began by explaining the problem and cataloging ancient and modern interpretations, before providing the modern evidence that supported his own stance. He explained: "I wish to interpret Ophir as Cephalam, or as some pronounce it Sofalam, in east Africa, as much for the testimony of the great Joannes Barroso that it is goldbearing, as for the voyages of the Portuguese who attest that it gives nothing but gold even now to foreign merchants." The riches brought back from this locale by Portuguese explorers were sufficient to meet Solomon's standard. And, as Ortelius continued, he gave further evidence substantiating his identification: "Also there is that which Thomas Lopes wrote in his Indian navigation, that these Sofalenses have books in their native

---

quae Moses de terra Ophir apertissime scripsit; vel quae Ionathan Propheta, eius, quae est de Regibus iudae, scriptor historiae, copiose & exacte tradidit: aut cum iis, quae ab eo qui Paralipomena, Spiritus sancto dictante scripsit, disertis sunt descripta verbis." (The passage quoted is italicized.)

40. Compare Gliozzi, *Adamo e il Nuovo Mondo*.
41. Shalev, "Geographia Sacra."

tongue which mention Solomon, a king who bore their gold away every third year. Scripture reports that Solomon had ivory from Ophir too."[42] Ortelius here extracted evidence from modern travel accounts that his favored East African community exhibited familiarity with the great Jewish king while also possessing the means to make a throne of ivory.

In his notebook, Ralegh siphoned the Antwerpian's erudition concerning Ophir, as he had for Egyptian Babylon, by excerpting Ortelius's lengthy summation of authorities. However, he also noted carefully what Ortelius believed and why: "Ortelius takes it for Cephala on Africa side; which is indeed exceeding rich in gold, & so might those of the Abisins receive knowledg of the Jewes religion & trew God. & Thomas Lopes in his indian navigation affirmes that the Sephalonses have bookes in their toung of Salomons navigation thither. In Peru there are no Elephants, but in Sephala manie."[43] These notes depart from Ralegh's typical practice of culling lists of previous opinions from Ortelius. And they reveal him as cognizant of the subtle aspects of contemporary debates surrounding the location of Ophir.

When Ralegh noted "so might those of the Abisins receive knowledg of the Jewes religion & trew God," he made clear that he understood that Ortelius was tacitly using this East African location for Ophir to explain the existence of Ethiopian Jews, who some Europeans in the early modern period thought constituted the legendary kingdom of Prester John. Wild

---

42. Ortelius, *Thesaurus Geographicus*, HH1v. "Ego Ophir *Cephalam*, vel ut alii pronunciant *Sofalam*, Africae versus Orientem regionem interpretari malim, tum quod haec teste gravissimo Io. Barroso admodum aurifera sit. adeo ut etiamnum nihil praeter aurum, ut Lusitanorum testantur peregrinationes, exteris mercatoribus communicet. tum quod scribat in sua Indica navigatione Thomas Lopesius, hos Sofalenses habere libros patria lingua scriptos, in quibus legitur Solomonem regem tertio quoque anno hinc aurum tulisse. Ex Ophir etiam ebur habuisse Solomonem sacrae referunt litterae. at hoc Ophyr, ΟΡΗΑΤΗ ὀφατ legit Ioannes Tzetza, & insulam, sive paeninunsulam auream in India esse dicit. De Ophir adde quae habet Iosephus a Costa, lib 1 cap 14. De Natura Novi Orbis. ubi Phir Indiam Orienalem, cum Iosepho Iudaeo, interpretatur. Vide UPHAS."

43. *NB*, fols. 35r–v. "Ophir, 70gint Sopheira, & Souphir. Eupolemus, as in Euseb.1.9.c.4 calls it Urphe, and Iland southe of the redd sea, but not of that red sea bounded by Arabia & Ægypt, but of the East parts of the Persian Sea which was also called red. Epiphanius said it was written Ailon, Marius Niger takes it to be the same which Pto: [Ptolemy] calls auream Chersonesum. Gaspar Varerius is of the same opinion, & hath it the same which wee know to be Malacca. [Franciscus] Vatablus in his bible sett out by Rob[ert] Stevens [Etienne] takes it for Hispaniola. [Guillaume] Postellus, Peru. & so doth Goropius & Montanus & Plessis. but this great area interiacent which Seneca out of Pedo Novarus calls the habitation of the Gods as antiquitie had believed & therfore not navigable by men. neither was it possible before the lodstone found." This abbreviates Ortelius's collection of opinions preceding the quotation in the previous note.

tales had circulated about this far-off kingdom throughout Europe from the medieval period, with various sub-Saharan, Ethiopian, and Indian locations floated as its seat.[44] While some commentators claimed that it had been converted by Saint Thomas the Apostle in the years just after Christ's crucifixion, others such as Ortelius believed that the kingdom was far more ancient and that it had been converted a millennium before Christ. Ortelius applied his Occam's razor to this historical problem as he found in the conflicting testimonies regarding the locations of Ophir and the kingdom of Prester John a single location that explained each historically. And, though Ortelius did not explicitly state this as his technique or purpose, Ralegh capably perceived the implicit significance of his claim.

Similarly, Ralegh recognized that Ortelius's glancing reference to the importation of ivory was a crucial piece of evidence undermining Montano's solution. Since ivory required elephants, Peru's lack of pachyderms put commentators such as Montano in the uncomfortable position of claiming either that Scripture deceived on this point or that its elephants had not yet been discovered. As with the oblique reference to Prester John, Ralegh drew the full implication from Ortelius's subtle reference to ivory.

The opinions Ralegh collected from Ortelius were not the primary ones he mobilized when treating the problem of Ophir during his discussion of the postdiluvian settlement of the world in the *History*, however. Ultimately, he subscribed to Josephus's venerable opinion, returning Ophir to the Far East. His evidence derived primarily from Benedicto Pererius's Genesis commentary rather than from the notes taken from Ortelius in the notebook. He enumerated the opinions of Jerome, Josephus, Montano, Du Plessis Mornay, and Francisco Junius while stating: "*Pererius* takes it rightly for an Island, as St. *Hierome* doth, but he sets it at the head-land of *Malacca*. But *Ophir* is found among the *Moluccas* farther East."[45] This solution's political significance resembled that of Ortelius', for in the mid-1610s English merchants were struggling to gain a foothold in these Indonesian trading zones in the face of Dutch and Portuguese resistance. Like Ortelius, then, Ralegh located Ophir along desired maritime trade routes that his contemporary state sought to tap.[46] Amid a context of frantic competition to acquire valuable trade partners in the East, this identification

44. This is clearly the historical referent behind Bacon's New Atlantis.

45. *HW*, 1.8.15.5.175.

46. Ralegh was connected to these ventures, if in a limited fashion. James's ambassador to the Mughal court, Thomas Roe, had been on a 1610 Guiana voyage heavily advocated by Ralegh. Thanks are due to Rupali Mishra for drawing my attention to Roe.

assumed a significance that it had lacked to Josephus. But, like Ortelius, Ralegh ensconced his argument within a collection of extracts rather than expressing it through transparent polemic.

But his primary aim remained debunking Montano's claim, and Ralegh developed further criticisms by turning to reports from modern scholarly travelers rather than to authoritative ancient sources. He never invoked the strength of antiquity, instead relying on the extracts themselves to persuade. His criticism of Montano, in fact, drew heavily on evidence from the most important sixteenth-century history of the New World, the 1590 *Natural and Moral History of the Indies* of Jose de Acosta, the Spanish Jesuit provincial in Peru.[47] While Acosta too had devoted significant attention to explaining the populated New World without recourse to a second Creation, he did not subscribe to Montano's vision of America's postdiluvian plantation. Citing Montano, he noted: "And there are many others which affirme that our Peru is Ophir . . . grounding it upon that which the holy scripture saith, that they brought from Ophir pure gold, precious stones, and wood which was rare and goodly—which things abound in Peru, as they say." Though Acosta believed that some ancients had known of the New World, he was skeptical of the details of Montano's plantation argument. For one, he explained, "although in this Peru there be good store of gold, yet is there not yet such aboundance as it may be equalled with the fame of the riches that was in auncient time at the East Indies." He confessed that, though Peru had "exquisite Emeralds, and some hard trees of Aromaticall wood, yet I do not finde any thing of so great commendation as the scripture giveth unto Ophir."[48] In his judgment, formed by years spent in the New World, Peru's natural bounties did not compare to those evoked by Scripture. And he noted that Peru lacked elephants, the necessary source of the ivory that Solomon had received from Ophir—a point, as we have seen, that was taken up by Ralegh.

Acosta's observations of the natural history of the New World thus provided Ralegh with evidence contravening Montano's thesis. Acosta's familiarity with South America, furthermore, provided him with an explanation that sapped Montano's philological argument of any strength. As Acosta explained: "the name of Peru is not very auncient, nor com-

47. Jose de Acosta, *The Natural & Moral History of the Indies* (1590), trans. Edward Grimston (New York: B. Franklin, 1970–73), 1. Romm notes that Ortelius initially embraced Montano's position but changed his mind after reading Acosta. See Romm, "Biblical Histories and the Americas," 42–43.

48. Acosta, *The Natural & Moral History of the Indies*, 37.

mon to all that countrie. It hath beene usuall in the discoverie of the new world, to give names to lands and portes of the sea according to the occasions presented at their arivall; and I beleeve that the name of Peru hath bene so found out and put in practice; for we find heere that the name hath bene given to all the countrie of Peru, by reason of a river so called by the inhabitants of the countrie, where the Spaniards arrived upon their first discoverie."[49] The native inhabitants, he elaborated, did not call their land by this name. The appellative *Peru* was so close to the biblical names *Ophir* and *Parvaim* not because it had evolved from them; it was a coincidence borne of misunderstanding, a garbled transmission between two cultures barely capable of communicating.

Ralegh's adaptation of Acosta's criticism reflects his ability to parse fragments of text from lengthier arguments and then invest these extracts with immense significance. It also suggests that he had the ability to discern between advantageous and injurious extracts prudently. For, in the *History*, he did not broach Acosta's argument that Peru did not possess the gold, gems, or woods described in Scripture—perhaps for fear that such an argument would undermine his dreams of being released from the Tower to pursue El Dorado. But he augmented Acosta's explanation of the accidental conflation of *Parvaim* and *Peru*, introducing new details for how the miscommunication had arisen: "When *Francis Pisarro* first discovered those Lands to the South of *Panama*, arriving in that Region which *Atabaliba* commanded (a Prince of magnificence, Riches and Dominion inferior to none) some of the *Spaniards* utterly ignorant of that language, demanding by signes (as they could) the name of the Countrie, and pointing with their hand athwart a river, or torrent, or brooke that rane by, the *Indians* answered *Peru*, which was either the name of that brooke, or of water in generall." This error had been compounded by its hasty circulation to the court of Charles V. As a result: "all that West part of in *America* to the South of *Panama* had the name of *Peru*, which hath continued ever since as divers *Spaniards* in the *Indies* assured me; which also *Acosta* the *Iesuite* in his naturall and moral Historie of the *Indies* confirmeth."[50] Ralegh drew the full implication of Acosta's argument to devastating effect. But he also enhanced it with testimony likely gained during conversation with Spanish sailors and soldiers during his 1595 Guiana expedition. Brief allusions to these discussions strengthened Acosta's

49. Ibid., 38.
50. *HW*, 1.8.15.5.175.

criticism of Montano, and Ralegh culled evidence from this personal experience that reaffirmed his textual extracts.

Indeed, Ralegh was more than willing to cite evidence from his own experience that added to the critical mass of evidence overwhelming Montano's wilting identification. He provided additional testimony of another instance when the first interactions between different language speakers had produced misunderstandings: "The same hapned among the *English*, which I sent under Sir *Richard Greenevile* to inhabite *Virginia*. For when some of my people asked the name of that Countrie, one of the Salvages [sic] answered, *Wingandacon*, which is as much to say, as, *You weare good clothes*, or gay clothes. . . . And in this manner have many places newly discovered beene intituled, of which *Peru* is one."[51] Ralegh's own experience and conversations with subordinates could be extracted to increase the body of evidence challenging Montano's claim. But, more, his extract in this case provided an explanation for why Montano had been misled. Rather than attributing the Jesuit's identification of Peru and Ophir to political pressure or intellectual slackness, he instead turned to evidence coaxed both from his own reading and from his experience to create a tissue of explanation absorbing Montano's conflation.

Ralegh thus directly referred to his own experience, as well as to the oral and textual reports of his contemporaries, in evaluating geographical accounts. But his fellow explorers' intricate knowledge of exotic lands did not lead him to divest himself of ancient geographical knowledge. Rather, the falsity of these instances of serendipitous naming prompted him to recommit to the traditional location for Ophir. He continued: "And therefore we must leave *Ophir* among the *Moluccas*, whereabout such an Island is credibly affirmed to be."[52] Rather than uprooting received wisdom, then, Ralegh's cutting-edge reports from the frontiers of exploration instead confirmed the convictions of the ancients and undermined a novel modern opinion. But at no point did he evaluate claims about the location of Ophir in terms of the author's credibility. Rather, his extracts drew primarily from modern Catholics, and he evaluated them strictly in terms of their capacity for agreement. He framed his dismissal of Montano, not on political grounds, or on the grounds that he was hostile to Montano's brand of philological analysis, but on the basis of a profusion of extracts drawn from text and experience that exposed Montano's conflation as in error.

51. *HW*, 1.8.15.5.175–76.
52. *HW*, 1.8.15.5.176.

Ralegh nowhere addressed the problem of how the New World was inhabited after the Flood. As we will see, Ralegh assessed the distances that groups traveled during the plantation very cautiously. Like Acosta, he likely assumed that the New World had been gradually populated well after the Flood—quite possibly by later descendants of Ophir who had originally settled in East Asia—and that its inhabitants did not maintain contact with the Old World. Like Ortelius, he marshaled available evidence to evaluate and criticize the solutions he encountered. In this case, he used modern reports to confirm an ancient opinion, to undermine tacitly an idealized vision of ancient geography and modern exploration that supported Spanish universal monarchy, and to add appeal to trade routes being developed by British merchants. Though he did not engage in explicit debate with Montano about the nature of the Habsburg Empire, the political and sacred significance of his solution would have been legible to readers acutely sensitive to the undertones lent to scholarship by contemporary European balance-of-power issues.

This process exemplified Ralegh's geographical method. Ralegh turned all texts, ancient or modern, into irreducible, decontextualized extracts. Even his own experience could be fragmented in this fashion. And, in trying to reconstruct the geography of the world, he saw the reports of his contemporary travelers, no less than his firsthand experience, as evidence either affirming or accounting for the range of received scholarly opinions. The collective harmony of the totality of extracts he integrated, rather than the gravity of any definitive text or authority, tacitly swathed a set of political imperatives in a skein of rigorous method, supporting the weight of his persuasive vision of the past. Even when agreeing with the ancients, this method, rather than the credibility of the source, certified the authority of his claim.

RALEGH AND EDEN: GEOGRAPHY AS PROBLEM SOLVER

The snippets of geographical information that Ralegh extracted with the note-taking method were indispensable tools. He correlated and compared them, used them to shed light on each other, and manipulated them to untie perplexing knots in the historical record. Ultimately, the *History* is a pastiche of these extracts, incorporated to create a coordinated textual body in which each component gobbet could be explained by others. The formation of such a coherent textual system constituted Ralegh's claim to geographical and historical expertise and, thus, underwrote his claim to be able to locate El Dorado. Examining his proof for the location of the

Garden of Eden reveals the mechanics of how he expertly integrated interpretations from disaggregated sources. Moreover, it will also reveal how
he wielded his identifications once they had been made, for he directed
his location for paradise to resolve an array of exegetical difficulties in the
History.[53]

Early modern scholars inherited a wide, and often contradictory, range
of evidence about the Garden of Eden. There was little agreement on its
location. The problem went beyond the interpretations of Gen. 2:8, which
read in the King James Version "The Lord God planted a garden Eastward
in Eden" but was translated by Jerome in the Vulgate as "And the Lord
God had planted a paradise of pleasure from the beginning," translations
suggesting entirely different histories and geographies. In addition, Scripture stated that one river went into Eden and four went out: the Tigris, the
Euphrates, the Pison, and the Gehon (Gen. 2:10–14). The first two straight-
forwardly corresponded to the rivers that still bear those names. But the
latter two posed more difficulty. Before the sixteenth century, Josephus's
authority certified the theory that the Pison referred to the Ganges, while
the Gehon was identified as the Nile. These identifications were generally subjected to little critical attention as most commentators found it
appropriate that the four greatest rivers of the world should flow out from
its most divine location. Furthermore, passages within Scripture strongly
supported these identifications. The King James translated Gen. 2:11 as:
"The name of the first [river] is Pison: that is it which compasseth the
whole land of Havilah, where there is gold." *Havilah* was the name of one
of Ioctan's sons who was believed to have accompanied his brother Ophir
in colonizing the farthest eastern portions of the world after the scattering
of the tribes. The Ganges was the most famous river watering these regions, and it was, thus, equated with the Pison. Similarly, Gen. 2:13—"And
the name of the second river is Gehon: the same is it which encompasseth
the whole land of Ethiopia"—was believed to refer to the Nile. Both these
gigantic but little-known rivers watered areas even less known.

The distance between these rivers required explanation, and this led

---

53. For the history of the study of the location of the Garden, see Williams, *The Com-
mon Expositor*; Allen, *Mysteriously Meant*; Joseph Ellis Duncan, *Milton's Earthly Paradise: A
Historical Study of Eden* (Minneapolis: University of Minnesota Press, 1972); Jean Delumeau,
A History of Paradise: The Garden of Eden in Myth and Tradition, trans. Matthew O'Connell
(New York: Continuum, 1995); Jim Bennet and Scott Mandelbrote, eds., *The Garden, the Ark,
the Tower, the Temple: Biblical Metaphors of Knowledge in Early Modern Europe* (Oxford:
Museum of the History of Science, in association with the Bodleian Library, 1998); and Scafi,
Mapping Paradise.

to some exotic and mystical interpretations. Origen, for example, insisted that Eden was to be interpreted allegorically and that paradise had neither geographical nor historical reality. He believed that it should instead be used to direct the mind toward recognition of the boundless power and love of the divine being; indeed, he considered the Garden itself a sacrament. But most Christians argued that paradise possessed a literal location to complement its allegorical meaning. For some, the distance between rivers suggested that paradise had been the entire world before Adam's fall. Others adhered to a mechanical explanation in which Eden was a location above the earth from which waters poured down, clashing cataclysmically to the ground and burrowing deep into the earth before eventually surging to the surface as four far-flung torrents.

Ortelius's catalog collected a staggering range of opinions. Though, as he noted, "the majority situate it in the east and some in Syria," other opinions abounded: Guillaume Postel situated it under the North Pole, some placed it south of the equator, and Joannes Goropius Becanus set it in India. Ortelius's citations included Scripture, late antique fathers, the medieval Syrian bishop Moses Barcephas, and recent scholarly works from such diverse figures as Pererius, Béroalde, the Swiss humanist Joachim Vadian, and the English Orientalist John Hopkinson.[54]

Despite Ortelius's catalog of opinion, a general consensus that located Eden in Mesopotamia had developed gradually over the sixteenth century, finding adherents from across the doctrinal spectrum. The basis for this identification was formulated initially by Steuco in his 1535 *Cosmopoeia*. Steuco had applied to geographical questions the same method he had devised for philosophical and historical problems. Among his geographical insights, he claimed: "I show the location of the region of Paradise, Eden, and I reveal the errors of those of past times, who asserted that the Phison and Gehon were the Nile and Ganges."[55] He was brought to this problem, he claimed, by the implausible geography required by the excessive distance between the rivers identified by Josephus. Instead, he reconsidered the historical Eden by returning to the postdiluvian settlement of the earth described in Scripture. Like Josephus, Steuco worked from the principle that colonizers of lands had named the territories after themselves. Moses and later biblical translators, he claimed, had described places using the names from this postdiluvian political geography. Discerning the

54. Ortelius, *Theatrum*, ir.
55. Steuco, *Opera Omnia*, 50v. "Ostendimusque ubi regio paradisiaca sit Heden, sive Eden, & errorem superioris aetatis patefecimus eorum, qui Phison & Geon, Nilum & Gangem afferuissent."

locations for the rivers described in Genesis, then, required a historicist investigation of postdiluvian settlement.

Steuco easily used this method to rebut the identification of Pison as the Ganges. He explained: "We also find Havilani in Mesopotamia, adjacent to Arabia. Indeed there were two Havilas, although the one, whose region the Phison wandered through, corresponds to the son of Ioctan." In addition to Havila, son of the Semite Ioctan, there was also Havila, the second son of Chush, the eldest son of Ham, the cursed son of Noah. Both these had brothers named Saba or Seba, but, by looking at all their brothers and the territories their families had colonized, one could deduce where each Havila had settled. Though the sons of Chush had, indeed, gone to the Far East, Steuco restricted the travels of the sons of Ioctan to the Near East: "The brothers of Saba, who founded the nation of the Sabeans among the Arabs, included Ophir, who is remembered among the regions or islands at the end of the Red Sea. There was Jobab, from whom Job Arab, the region of Arabia, with the provinces and lands named for the first colonists. It must be believed therefore that his brothers had nearby habitations. The habitation of Havila is placed near Messa, a region in Arabia adjacent to Mesopotamia. Therefore there is a Havila amongst the Arabs."[56] Though derived using the same assumptions as Josephus, this revision recalibrated world history no less radically than Steuco had in proclaiming Egyptian knowledge of true Creation. By claiming that the sons of Ioctan rather than the sons of Chush colonized this swath of land, he suggested that the Arab nations of the Near East derived, not from the line of the cursed Ham, but from the blessed Sem. More importantly, this identification enabled the Pison to water a region that had been settled by the Semite Havila, near where the Euphrates and Tigris converged. Ortelius, in fact, would adapt this reading to locate Ophir on the shores of the Red Sea.

Steuco's historical revision was even more drastic in its analysis of the Gehon. As with the case of Havila, Steuco determined that multiple Gehons had been confused. This still left the problem of Scripture's clear reference to Ethiopia, but he resolved this problem with the same solution. As he explained: "There must be another Gehon, which is a more local

---

56. Ibid., fols. 55r–v. "Chavilani praetera invenimus Mesopotamiae, Arabiaeque adiacere. Siquidem tametsi duo Chavila fuerunt, hunc tamen, cuius regionem peragrat Phison, constat esse filium Iactan. Nam fratres Sabae, qui nationem Sabaeorum Arabum condidit, fuit Ophir, quae memoratur inter regiones aut insulas finis maris rubri: fuit Iobab, unde Iob Arabs, estque regio Arabiae, Nominibus virorum primorum colonorum, terris & provinciis nuncupatis. Credendum igitur fratres propinquas habitationes tenuisse. Habitatio quoque Chavilae ponitur a Messa, regione Arabaiae, Mesopotamiae adiacente. Ergo inter Arabes, Chavila."

tributary of the Euphrates, besides the Nile. I will prove that the Gehon is near Judaea, and that there is an Ethiopia in the books of Moses and among other writers that is not that southern one, but that there is another one to the east."[57] A second Ethiopia as well as a second Gehon would enable him to reduce the geographical area of Eden to literal plausibility.

The ancient source Steuco used to achieve this doubling was not as credible as his source for the previous reidentification; as with his treatment of Creation, he relied on evidence found in the remnants of ancient pagan works. As he explained: "There are two Ethiopias, as the most ancient bard Homer, who chanted things consonant with scripture so often, testified most fully: *The Ethiopians are the outermost men, and a twin colony, for some live to the west, others to the east* [Odyssey 1.24–25]. Homer claimed that some Ethiopians are situated in the east, some in the west." Those in the west were the African Ethiopians, whose lands the Nile watered. But, Steuco continued, "there is another, eastern Ethiopia. And these two areas are split by the Red Sea, which goes between the lands, and extends itself almost to the Mediterranean. One falls to the east, and one to the west, cleaved by the Arabian Gulf. . . . The latter, not the former, is the Ethiopia that the Gehon waters."[58] Scripture was made historically and geographically sensible, and the four rivers all tidily local, only when using an ancient geographical appellation preserved in the texts of the pagan Greek bard. Steuco's synthetic methods allowed him to affix Eden in a convincingly compressed location, demonstrating the historical truth of Scripture.

Steuco's solution rapidly circulated to resounding approval. Genesis commentaries and (Protestant) Bibles began to include maps depicting the region alongside intricate arguments concerning the exact location of

---

57. Steuco, *Opera Omnia*, 55v. "Alius ergo Gehon quam Nilus, particularis eruptio ab Euphrate. Proboque & Gehon esse Iudaeae propinquum, & Aethiopiam in libris Mosis & apud ceteros scriptores esse, non illam solum meridionalem, sed etiam aliam quandam orientalem."
58. Ibid., fols. 55v–56v. "Est igitur duplex Aethiopia, ut Homerus antiquissimus vates, & consentanea divinis litteris saepe canens, locupletissime testatur: *Aethiopes extremi homines, geminique coloni, / Namque sub occasum hi degunt, aliique sub ortu.* Homerus ait alios Aethiopes vergere in occasum, alios in ortum. Qui sunt enim alii occidentales Aethiopes, nisi quos peragrat Nilus, fluvius sub occasu hyemali, fereque ulterius exoriens. Haec Aethiopia Libiae est, maximum latus totius Aphricae. Eaque est Aethiopia in qua degunt Christianissimi hominum, sicut olim optimi omnium ethnicorum, quippe ad quos libenter Deos diverterentur. Alia est Aethiopia orientalis, alterum videlicet latus. Finduntur enim duo latera a mari rubro, introeunte in terras, & pene mari mediterraneo sese associante: alterumque cadit in ortum, alterum in occasum, inter quae labitur, sinus Arabicus, ab aliis mare rubrum appellatus. . . . Hos igitur, non illos circumit Gehon."

the original seat of humankind.[59] By the end of the sixteenth century, few commentators opposed a literal Garden located somewhere in Mesopotamia, and Steuco's method gave impetus to a deeper analysis of ancient geography and the geographical learning of ancient societies.

Ralegh's existing notebook offers little insight into his investigation of paradise, but the text of the *History* illuminates the authors he consulted, for his examination of Eden relied exclusively on Steuco, Béroalde, Sixtus Senensis, Pererius, and Hopkinson. From the latter two he copied passages refuting less credible opinions; his discussion of Bede, Rabanus, and other authorities who made paradise as high as the moon came directly from Pererius; and his criticism of their solutions came directly from Hopkinson.[60] Sixtus similarly offered a catalog of wrongheaded opinions from earlier commentators. These authorities underpinned Ralegh's consideration of the traditions of the location of Eden.

Ralegh, however, did not always draw faithfully from these authors. And, while Hopkinson had made clear that his location for Eden derived from Steuco's analysis, Ralegh constructed a unique intellectual history. He proclaimed: "to give *Beroaldus* his right, I conceive that he ledde the way to *Hopkins*, and to all other later Writers." He granted a dubious priority to Béroalde, whose *Chronicum* was published forty years after Steuco's *Cosmopoeia*. Béroalde's contribution, moreover, was appreciated only at the level of method. Ralegh considered Béroalde's geographical identification suspect because the French Calvinist had placed the Garden in an Eden in Syria, rather than using a Syrian Eden to explain inaccurate references to the Eden of paradise. Furthermore, according to Ralegh, Béroalde "altogether misunderstood two of the foure Rivers (to wit) *Pison* and *Gehon*."[61] If Béroalde's solution impressed Ralegh, it was not for the location it discerned, but for its method.

Like his chronological method, Béroalde's geographical exegesis of the place of Eden was drawn wholly from Scripture. Béroalde lambasted previous authors who, "following foreign errors, which Josephus seems to have spread from a perverse interpretation," suggested the Nile and the Ganges

---

59. Smith and Ingram, *Maps in Bibles*.

60. "These strange fancies and dreames have beene answered by divers learned men long since, and lately by *Hopkins* and *Pererius* writing upon this subiect; of whose arguments I will repeat these few." *HW*, 1.3.7.44. Hopkinson himself had similarly plundered Pererius, transcribing directly several passages, and it is, therefore, difficult to tell from which of the two Ralegh drew. Compare Joannes Hopkinson, *Synopsis Paradis, sive Paradis Descriptio* (Leiden, 1593), 13.

61. *HW*, 1.3.9.47.

as the two rivers.[62] Like Steuco, he used the existence of a second Havila
to move the Pison from India to his Syrian location for Eden. For Béroalde,
the crucial passage was 1 Sam. 15:15: "where Saul is said to have smitten
the Amalekites from Havila to Sur, which borders Egypt."[63] The Amalekites, he observed, inhabited the Sinai Peninsula, between the Holy Land
and Egypt, where the Hebrews had wandered for forty years.

Béroalde also followed Steuco in solving the problem of the two Ethiopias by extending the domain covered by this name east across the Red
Sea. But his crucial source was not Homer. Instead, he deployed a philological iteration of the historicist analysis that Steuco had used to relocate
Havila. As he explained: "The Gehon is a river of that region which is
called Chus, which the Septuagint badly translated as Ethiopia, and the
Latins followed the Greeks." The basis he identified for this mistranslation
was complex. Previous commentators had agreed that Ethiopia had been
settled by Chus, the eldest son of Ham, who was known to be cursed with
a darkened visage for his father's transgressions against Noah. Béroalde
argued that the Greek Septuagint translators had misidentified Chus as
Ethiopia because they knew no darker-skinned people than the Ethiopians
and had, therefore, assumed that *Chus* must refer to this region's original settler. A similar mistranslation had led to the inaccurate reference to
Ethiopia that compounded the error. Béroalde explained that the Greeks
used the term *Ethiopians* to refer to all peoples with "darkened faces,"
including Arabs, and later commentators had mistaken this stereotype for
scholarly rigor.[64] By translating according to the inhabitants' appearance
rather than philological exactitude, the Greek interpreters had introduced

---

62. Béroalde, *Chronicum*, 81. "Neque vero Phison & Gehon, sunt idem quo nonnulli as-
severarunt nimis infulse & insipienter, nempe Nilus & Ganges, quum regiones quas alluunt
Phison & Gehon describat satis aperte Moses, quae nec Aegyptum nec Indiam significant, ut
permultis visum & creditum fuit, sequentibus alienos errores, quos sparsisse videtur Iosephus
ex perversa loci huius interpretatione, qui antiquitatum Iudaicarum libro primo, capite 2, haec
prodidit."

63. Ibid., 83. "Ad haec primi Samuelis 15.15. dicitur Saul percussisse Amalecitas ab Hevila
usque Sur, quae spectat Aegyptum. Ex iis locis, seu regionibus quae Ismaelitae & Amalaecitae
intelliguntur occupasse, quarum termini & limites sunt Sur & Hevila, facile est videre haec
loca longissime abesse ab India."

64. Ibid., 82. "Gehon autem fluvius est eius regionis quae dicitur Chus, pro quae Aethiopiam male reposuerunt interpretes Graeci, deinde etiam Latini Graecos sequuti. Aethiopes
autem Graeci, ab exusta facie nominant eos populos, qui habitantes supra Thebaidem, quae est
superioris Aegypti regio, in Africa morantur, sub zona torrida, & ipsius solis orbita. Atque ita
Geographi omnes sumunt Aethiopes, quos docent esse Africae populos, incolentes regionem
suppositam zonae torridae, quae nihil pertinet omnino ad regionem Chus, quae quidem est
in ea Arabia, a qua sinus Arabicus dicitur Ptolomaeo id mare quo disiungitur ipsa Arabia ab
Aegypto, quod quidem intelligetur mox facilius & apertius."

a significant error, which had, in turn, led to Josephus's wild speculations concerning the location of the rivers.

Ralegh drew heavily on both Steuco and Béroalde to provide an exact location for the physical paradise. He began by commenting on the absurdity of the ancient solution: "Could there be a stranger fancie in the world, then when we finde both these (namely) *Tigris* and *Euphrates* in *Assyria* and *Mesopotamia*, to seeke the other two in *India* and *Aegypt*, making the one *Ganges*, and other *Nilus*? Two Rivers as farre distant, as any of fame knowne or discovered in the world: the Scriptures making it so plaine, that these Rivers were divided into foure branches, and with the Scriptures, Nature, Reason and Experience bearing witnesse."[65] He followed Steuco's innovation by locating the seed of the misreading in a slipshod understanding of the plantation. And he adopted critiques that Hopkinson had leveled at previous authors, pointing out that the several massive rivers intervening between Mesopotamia and the Ganges were difficult to explain according to the accepted identifications. He concluded by referring to the same passage in 2 Samuel that Béroalde had used to prove that a western region had maintained the name *Havila* long after the plantation. Ralegh thus hewed closely to the argument his predecessors had gleaned from Scripture proving the existence of a Near Eastern Havila and, in his account, a Mesopotamian Pison.

Ralegh then moved to his examination of the Gehon, again drawing on Béroalde: "Now, as *Havilah* in the East *India* drew *Pison* so farre out of his way thither, so I say did *Cush* (being by the *Seventie* translated *Aethiopia*) force *Gehon* into *Africa*. For *Cush* being taken for *Aethiopia* by the *Greekes*, whom the *Latines* followed, *Gehon* was long consequentley esteemed for *Nilus*. But *Aethiopians* are, as much, as *blacke or burnte faces* whose proper Countrie is called *Thebaides*, lying to the Southward of all *Aegypt*." He clearly drew this analysis from Béroalde. But the lineage for the solution, and the scrambled way in which he cited authorities, highlights how the note-taking method might muddy intellectual genealogies. Ralegh attributed the solution to Pererius: "This Translation of the *Septuagint*, Pererius doth qualifie in this manner: There are (saith he) two *Aethiopas*, the East, and the West: and this division he findeth in *Strabo*, out of *Homer*. Now because there is no colour to make *Chush Aethiopia* in *Africa*, Pererius will make *Chush* and the land of the *Chusites* . . . to be the East *Aethiopia*." Pererius's solution to the problem of Eden had synthesized the methods of Steuco and Béroalde by using Scripture alone to

65. *HW*, 1.3.13.57.

identify the place of Eden and then turned to Steuco as a corroborating authority. Like Pererius—possibly because he was summarizing the Jesuit's
treatment—Ralegh drew on Steuco to supplement Béroalde's purely scriptural exegesis. But, when he summarized his findings in this section, he
quoted from Steuco, giving as a marginal note "Steuch. Eugub in Gen.c.2."
and quoting: "*There remaineth no doubt* (sayth STEUCHIUS) *but Aethiopia
in the Scriptures, is taken for that Countrie, which ioyneth to Arabia.*"[66]
Ralegh used the purely biblicist analyses advocated by Béroalde, but he
also employed the syncretist tools against which Béroalde had revolted to
confirm his conclusions.

The most noteworthy aspect of the intellectual history Ralegh ascribed
to this solution, however, is the extent to which he ignored issues of authority and, instead, sought to integrate and adapt all relevant accounts.
He drew from an eclectic selection of sources' geographical claims in order to deduce the location of Eden, but what constituted and supported his
analysis was the logical strength of his recombination of the fragments,
rather than the credibility of the works from which they came. His mael-
strom of semiaccurate citations illustrates the dominance of the extract
over the author.

Ralegh did, ultimately, ascribe a precise location to paradise. At the
end of the section, he provided a copperplate "*Chorographicall* description
of this terrestrial paradise," complete with miniature Adam and Eve skip-
ping around a flourishing tree and tributaries of the Tigris and Euphrates
trickling in southern Mesopotamia, unusually far east (see fig. 6). And he
applied his solution to resolve standard problems of scriptural exegesis.
The Septuagint's substitution of Ethiopia for Chus, he explained, had created much confusion. Josephus had suggested that the Midianite daughter
of Jethro whom Moses had married during the Exodus was Ethiopian. This
made no sense, as Ralegh pointed out, unless one recognized that Josephus erroneously assumed that Chusites were Ethiopians, unaware that
they might be Arabs. Similarly, Ralegh turned to 2 Chron. 21:16, which
he translated from the Geneva Bible as: "So the Lord stirred up against
IEHORAM, the spirit of the Philistines, and the Arabians, which confine
the Aethiopians." He pointed out: "Now, how farre it is off betweene the
Philistines, and the *Negro's*, or the *Aethiopians*, every man that look-
eth in a Map, may iudge. For the *Philistines* and *Arabians* doe mixe and
joyne with the Land of the *Chusites*, and are distant from *Aethiopia* about
two and thirtie, or three and thirtie degrees, and therefore not their next

66. *HW*, 1.3.14.60, 62.

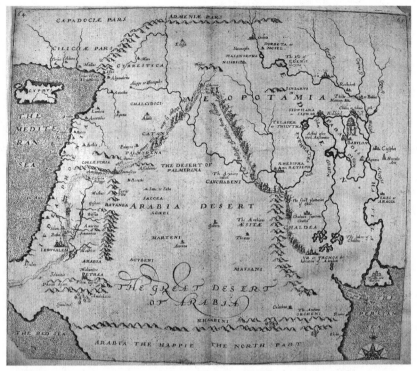

Figure 6. Map of Eden from the 1614 *History of the World*, 64–65.
Special Collections Research Center, Swem Library, College of
William and Mary, shelf mark D57. R16 1614.

Neighbours; but all *Egypt* and the *Desarts* of *Sur* and *Pharan*, are between them."[67] Ralegh here used his own map as an exegetical tool to illuminate the clear corruption of a passage of Scripture. The word translated in this passage as *Aethiopians* should have been *Chusites* to avoid geographical and historical unintelligibility.

Ralegh was able to locate five other places in Scripture where this corruption had rendered the meaning of the text indiscernible. One could fairly assume, he finally claimed, that any scriptural reference to interaction or communication between Israelites and Ethiopians was the product of a polluting Greek redaction. In fact, he used his solution to confute Ortelius's location for Ophir: "And to conclude in a word, the *Hebrewes* had never any acquaintance of fellowship, any warre, treatie of peace, or

67. *HW*, 1.3.14.62.

other intelligence with the *Aethiopian* black *Moores*."[68] The distinction
between African and Arabian Chusites that Steuco had initially drawn
from the ancient Greek bard Homer equipped Ralegh with a tool to correct
later mistakes introduced into Scripture by the ancient Greek translators.

Ralegh constructed his interpretations by synthesizing notes gleaned
from an array of authorities, which he then directed to make sense of difficult or erroneous passages. Each observation that he noted was valued
as a possible piece of the historical puzzle he sought to reassemble. His
scholarly practice was more concerned with weaving a coherent tissue of
extracts than with the traditions, credibility, or authorship undergirding
his sources. This method generated an eclectic approach to evidence and
ascribed truth to geographical identifications on the basis of the method
of their production. Indeed, as Ralegh's confused attributions for Gehon
show, this method sometimes muddied the traditions and lineages of the
ideas they evaluated. Similarly, his geographical work exhibited little explicit engagement with the political dimension implied by Montano and
Ortelius's work or in the methodological dogma determining Béroalde's
reaction to Steuco. His practice of reading and note taking purported to
shear the ideological consequences from their works and bypassed questions of credibility, converting their arguments instead into extracts for
his recombination. His method thus professed to minimize the reliance
on the political or theological credibility of his sources in favor of insisting on its own scholarly rigor.[69]

BACONIAN SCIENCE AS IDEALIZED VISION
OF ANTIQUARIAN READING PRACTICES

If his notebook showed that his reading of geography accorded with standard scholarly practices, his treatment of geography in the *History* reveals
how Ralegh built a delicate web of causal evidence from meaningful clues.
His method for fabricating this tissue stemmed from the initial technique
scholars used to confront any problem: cribbing excerpts, passages, quo-

---

68. *HW*, 1.8.10.4.152.

69. Compare this to the accounts of the construction of the notion of objectivity in Lorraine Daston, "Baconian Facts, Academic Civility, and the Prehistory of Objectivity," *Annals
of Scholarship* 8 (1991): 337–64; Daston and Park, *Wonders and the Order of Nature*; Julie Robin
Solomon, *Objectivity in the Making: Francis Bacon and the Politics of Inquiry* (Baltimore:
Johns Hopkins University Press, 1998); and Perez Zagorin, "Francis Bacon's Concept of Objectivity and the Idols of the Mind," *British Journal for the History of Science* 34 (2001): 379–93.

tations, and extracts from all available sources. In this, he replicated the fundamental note-taking methods deployed by Münster, Mercator, Ortelius, and other innovators of sixteenth-century geography. This absorption of note taking into geographical practice thus had a direct impact on the making of geographical knowledge. Maps and geographical dictionaries presented two of the means devised to make sense of the newly teeming heaps of information from antiquarian research conducted by the early modern geographer. And these enterprises were directed toward the same ultimate goal—deriving a system in which each extract, claim, and textual gobbet could be inserted and explained.[70]

Early modern scholars, far more than their predecessors, performed readings that shredded their sources into minute fragments. But it is important to recognize the justification supporting this enterprise. A 1577 letter from John Dee to Ortelius provides, perhaps, the most transparent insight into the significance of the methodical reconstruction that Ralegh and others performed. The letter effusively praised its recipient, Ortelius, noting that travelers, merchants, and statesmen benefited from his labor whether traveling, contemplating the wider world from home, or conducting public or private business. Dee professed delight at the accumulation of learning about previously unknown lands in the East and the West, agreeing with Ortelius that it was incumbent on the British to find a northeast passage to the Indies. And he described the project he was working on: "I have assembled and examined the monuments of the ancients who have described that route, and digested them into a Nautical manual, from which at last a noble work may be completed, and we may for the first time define the boundaries of that part of the world, which is the largest of all, and the parents of all the best arts, and the site of our human origin and Redemption."[71] Dee, then, sifted through authorities pulling out extracts

70. Note the similarity to the practices in the contemporary communities of natural historians. Compare Paula Findlen, *Possessing Nature: Museums, Collecting, and Scientific Culture in Early Modern Italy* (Berkeley and Los Angeles: University of California Press, 1994), "The Formation of a Scientific Community: Natural History in Sixteenth-Century Italy," in *Natural Particulars: Nature and the Disciplines in Renaissance Europe*, ed. Anthony Grafton and Nancy Siraisi (Cambridge, MA: MIT Press, 1999), 369–400, and "Francis Bacon and the Reform of Natural History in the Seventeenth Century," in Kelley, ed., *History and the Disciplines*, 239–60; Marjorie Swann, *Curiosities and Texts: The Culture of Collecting in Early Modern England* (Philadelphia: University of Pennsylvania Press, 2001); and Adam Fox, "Printed Questionnaires, Research Networks, and the Discovery of the British Isles, 1650–1800," *HJ* 53 (2010): 593–621.

71. John Dee to Abraham Ortelius, Mortlake, 16 January 1577, in *Abrahami Ortelii et virorum eruditorum . . . epistulae*, ed. Jan Hendrik Hessels (Osnäbruck: O. Zeller, 1969), 159.

and citations concerning Eden as Ortelius and Ralegh had, and, like these two, he suggested that modern discoveries and travel narratives should be directed toward knowledge of sacred history.

Dee, however, went further, arguing that each nation should be contacted and integrated into a global project of geographical learning: "But for the purpose of expressing each thing most accurately, each nation (whether Christian or ethnic) must be instructed, counseled and incited to have knowledge of the site of others, for the reason of the incredible utility which will redound to all human kind." And the terminus that Dee ascribed to the restoration of geographical knowledge was not worldly benefit. The effect that he envisioned of this geographical restoration would be far more than the advance of scholarship. He wrote: "Great and certainly unexpected changes and mutations in all states will be made. And hence will seem to loom that end of human things, and most desirable apocalypse."[72] Retracing the steps of the first colonists into the East and the West, observing and recording geographical data, and then compiling and integrating these extracts would allow the restoration of the knowledge that God had instilled in humanity before the Fall and that was dimly known to the Israelites. And this restoration of knowledge would allow time to end. Geography was a divine labor of apocalypse-inducing meditation that could work only when synthesizing the records and monuments of all scholars and travelers to all lands.[73]

"Veterumque aliquot, illud inter, aliqua ratione commemorantium, conquiro monumenta, ac perlustro: indeque nonnulla in Methodum aliquam Nauticam digero: Quo tam praeclarum tandem perficiatur opus. Nimirum ut suis veris terminis illam primum habeamus circumscriptam Orbis terrarum partem, quae, cum omnium maxima, tum humanae Originis et Redemptionis, Campus est unicus et celeberrimus, et omnium praeterea Artium optimarum Parens."

72. Ibid. "Ast ed ad reliquae omnes accuratissime exprimendas, unaqueque Natio (Christiana vel ethnica) ut commodissime ratione vicinitatis potest: ita ut quae universo humano generi inde redundabit, monenda, consulenda, et hortenda: immo praecibus quasi impellenda est. Magnae enim valde et insperatae omnium fient Rerumpublicarum mutationes. Et deinde imminere videtur extrema rerum humanarum, et optabilis Catastrophe."

73. See Stephen Clucas, "Samuel Hartlib's Ephemerides, 1635–59, and the Pursuit of Scientific and Philosophical Manuscripts: The Religious Ethos of an Intelligencer," *Seventeenth Century* 6 (1991): 33–55; Steven Harris, "Networks of Travel, Correspondence, and Exchange," in *The Cambridge History of Science*, vol. 3, ed. Katherine Park and Lorraine Daston (New York: Cambridge University Press, 2006), 341–64; Adam Mosley, *Bearing the Heavens: Tycho Brahe and the Astronomical Community of the Late Sixteenth Century* (Cambridge: Cambridge University Press, 2007); Avner Ben-Zaken, "From Naples to Goa and Back: A Secretive Galilean Messenger and a Radical Hermeneutist," *History of Science* 47 (2009): 147–74; and Markus Friedrich, "Archives as Networks: The Geography of Record-Keeping in the Society

We have seen repeatedly that early modern scholars believed that each age produced and worked with a set of divinely appointed tools. Dee's letter to Ortelius makes clear that, at least to some, the note-taking method and its products were seen as providential gifts for making knowledge. These scholars believed that the integration of inherited texts with knowledge yielded from previously unknown lands was part of a divine plan to bring the world to a close. By shredding texts to irreducible extracts and correlating these with other existing snippets, they were, they felt, performing a sacred labor. As Dee suggests, this work would not be complete until the gobbets were reassembled and all possible knowledge rejoined.

Ralegh's efforts to demonstrate geographical expertise revolved around his disciplined production of knowledge. The meticulous care of his work intended to suggest to his king and his readers that his geographical claims were borne from intensive, methodical labor and, thus, worth crediting. But his approach to producing geographical knowledge illuminates scholarly culture more broadly, for the role his note-taking method played in the composition of the *History* highlights the methodological transformations that gripped early modern Europe. His effort to process texts into irreducible evidence and then reconstitute them within a uniformly coherent system reflected both the diminished power of traditional authorities and the formation of challenging new approaches to making knowledge. The new methodology was exemplified by the inductive philosophy associated with Francis Bacon's New Science and underlay the next century's transformations in natural history, philosophy, medicine, political economy, and diplomacy as well as the continuing rage for antiquarianism.

The practices, techniques, and tools of early modern geographers, then, reflected profound transformations emanating outward from the culture of historical analysis to the scholarly community. As they subjected the authority of revered ancient sources to intense questioning, scholars devised a new system for producing knowledge that emphasized their own methods of parsing, organizing, and synthesizing evidence. This method could be applied to experience as well as to texts, to the natural world as

of Jesus (1540–1773)," *Archival Science* 10 (2010): 285–98. For British imperial programs in this context, see Arthur H. Williamson, "An Empire to End Empire: The Dynamic of Early Modern British Expansion," *HLQ* 68 (2005): 227–56 (reprinted in Kewes, ed., *The Uses of History*, 223–52); Glyn Parry, "John Dee and the Elizabethan British Empire in Its European Context," *HJ* 49 (2006): 643–75; Sacks, "Richard Hakluyt's Navigations in Time," and "Discourses of Western Planting"; and Miles Ogborn, *Indian Ink: Script and Print in the Making of the English East India Company* (Chicago: University of Chicago Press, 2007).

well as to natural histories. The conviction that reconstituting the past required an augmented range of sources to be fragmented into their smallest components of evidence generated a new regime of knowledge production whose impact reverberated throughout scholarly culture, furnishing a methodological emphasis on empiricism and induction to the study of the human past, the present, and the natural world alike. As we will see in the next chapter, however, Ralegh knew that the new histories produced by fusing together these sources resounded with political and theological significance, and he accordingly found evidence in his sources for narratives that emphasized his own expertise.

CHAPTER FOUR

Narration:
Providence and Human Movement

Ralegh extracted passages from a wide range of sources to create a broad pool of geographical and chronological evidence with which he animated his history. Like other early modern historians, he explained change by narrating from these extracts the movements of peoples, customs, and ideas across space and time. His emphasis on historical knowledge reflected a widespread response to contemporary explorations. Few scholars were provoked by Europe's increased traffic with the Asia, Africa, and the Americas to easily discard ancient knowledge. Rather, modern explorations inspired many of them to plumb the significance of ancient voyages and to explain puzzling evidence from the ancient world by attributing earthly transformations to the effects of human movements and migrations. Such historians sought to narrate patterns in these movements that would illuminate the higher workings of Providence.

Ralegh's studies of humans in motion in the ancient world adumbrate how scholars viewed travel as a profound force within the divine theater of particulars. They reveal why Ralegh believed that his expertise supplied a unique mode of analyzing the past. Above all, analysis of them will illuminate the technical process by which he produced historical narrative. Faced with the profusion of extracts derived from his multiplying sources, the early modern historian fulfilled his responsibilities only when constructing a vibrant system that absorbed his evidence. His goal was not just to explain static fragments of text but to mirror in his text a dynamic world pulsating under the vigilant intervention of Providence. As I will conclude, Ralegh's narrative of Alexander the Great's penetration of the East reveals his ability to direct subtle counsel to the king through his reconstructed narratives of historical journeys. This episode, like many others in the *History*, demonstrates how the recombination of narrow fragments of evidence drawn from a wide range of sources produced accounts of the ancient world that layered new significance on or challenged older histories. These narratives of causation constituted the most treasured product of travel, for they were perceived to contain patterns of divine meaning that would shape scholars' evaluations of the world around them.

RALEGH'S EXPERIENCE

Ralegh was an expert in human mobility, for he had closely supervised explorations until late in Elizabeth's reign. After the death of his half brother Humphrey Gilbert in 1583, he and Adrian Gilbert were given custody of the royal patent to pursue North American exploration. In March 1584, Ralegh alone renewed this patent for seven years, and a month later Philip Amadas and Arthur Barlowe led an expedition of North American reconnaissance. The next year, Sir Richard Grenville piloted another voyage from Plymouth that deposited almost one hundred men on Roanoke Island and the mainland. These colonists stayed until 1586, when Francis Drake brought them home. John White was then appointed governor of a second expedition, which departed in 1587. This voyage ultimately proved disastrous; the vagaries of global politics and finance prevented Ralegh from sending supply ships for three years, and, by the time the English returned to Roanoke Island in 1590, they found only mysterious, eroding traces of the "Lost Colony" and none of the colonists. Ralegh, however, remained one of the foremost advocates of exploration, though his focus shifted to South America, and he continued to agitate for voyages to Guiana between his own voyages in 1595 and 1616.[1]

Anti-Spanish policies guided Ralegh's administration of exploratory ventures. His 1596 *Discoverie of Guiana* reflected his agenda of orchestrating voyages to the New World that would erect networks for English trade, found outposts for privateering to disrupt the flow of silver from the New World to Seville, and limit the absorption of native peoples into Spain's Catholic empire. His work was aided by learned advice supported by his-

---

1. See the works of David Beers Quinn, esp., in this context, *Raleigh and the British Empire* (New York: Macmillan, 1949); Mancall, *Hakluyt's Promise*; and Karen Ordahl Kupperman, *The Jamestown Project* (Cambridge: Belknap Press of Harvard University Press, 2007). See also Alden T. Vaughan, "Sir Walter Ralegh's Indian Interpreters, 1584–1618," *William and Mary Quarterly* 59 (2002): 341–76.

torical investigations.[2] Ralegh was the dedicatee of numerous tracts and translations enumerating the fruits of modern travels. The dedicatory epistles introducing these works often praised his role in exploration as foreordained; in the dedication of his 1587 edition of Peter Martyr's *Decades*, Richard Hakluyt the Younger explained that, though Henry VIII had commissioned Sebastian Cabot to explore the Americas, "this task it seems, most honoured Knight, divine Providence has reserved for you." Ralegh consistently consulted Hakluyt for learned advice, and his effort to establish North American settlement was largely justified by Hakluyt's 1584 *Discourse of Western Planting*. There, Hakluyt stated that North American colonization would lead to "thinlargement of the gospell of Christe," augment English trade by supplying desirable commodities to merchants and profitable occupation to the unemployed, and check the growth of the Spanish Empire. He optimistically described Philip II's global dominion as "like the Empire of Alexander the great, wch grewe upp sooddenly and sooddenly upon his death was rente and dissolved for fault of lawfull

2. There is a growing literature on expert travelers and readers of travel accounts in early modern Europe. For Britain, see Eric Ash, "'A Note and a Caveat for the Merchant': Mercantile Advisors in Elizabethan England," *SCJ* 33 (2002): 1–31; Sacks, "Richard Hakluyt's Navigations in Time," and "Discourses of Western Planting"; David S. Shields, "The Genius of Ancient Britain," in Mancall, ed., *The Atlantic World and Virginia*, 489–509; and Alison Games, *The Web of Empire: English Cosmopolitans in an Age of Expansion, 1560–1660* (Oxford: Oxford University Press, 2008). For Continental experts, see Grafton, with Shelford and Siraisi, *New Worlds, Ancient Texts*; Stuart B. Schwartz, *Implicit Understanding: Observing, Reporting, and Reflecting on the Encounters between Europeans and Other Peoples in the Early Modern Era* (Cambridge: Cambridge University Press, 1994); the essays in Karen Ordahl Kupperman, ed., *America in European Consciousness, 1493–1750* (Chapel Hill: University of North Carolina Press, for the Omohundro Institute of Early American History and Culture, 1995), esp. Sabine MacCormack's "Limits of Understanding: Perceptions of Greco-Roman and Amerindian Paganism in Early Modern Europe" (79–129) and John Headley's "Campanella, America, and World Evangelization" (243–71); William Sherman, "John Dee's Columbian Encounter," *International Archives of the History of Ideas* 193 (2006): 131–42; Amanda Wunder, "Western Travelers, Eastern Antiquities, and the Image of the Turk in Early Modern Europe," *JEMH* 7 (2003): 89–119; Eric Ash and Alison Sandman, "Trading Expertise: Sebastian Cabot between Spain and England," *RQ* 57 (2004): 813–46; Nicholas Dew, "Reading Travels in the Culture of Curiosity: Thévenot's Collection of Voyages," *JEMH* 10 (2006): 39–59; Joan-Pau Rubiés, "Travel Writing and Humanistic Culture: A Blunted Impact?" *JEMH* 10 (2006): 131–68; Erik Thomson, "Commerce, Law, and Erudite Culture: The Mechanics of Théodore Godefroy's Service to Cardinal Richelieu," *JHI* 68 (2007): 407–27; Sabine MacCormack, *On the Wings of Time: Rome, the Incas, Spain, and Peru* (Princeton, NJ: Princeton University Press, 2007); Christine R. Johnson, "Buying Stories: Ancient Tales, Renaissance Travelers, and the Market for the Marvelous," *JEMH* 11 (2007): 405–46, and *The German Discovery of the World: Renaissance Encounters with the Strange and Marvelous* (Charlottesville: University of Virginia Press, 2008); and Meserve, *Empires of Islam*.

yssue."[3] He turned also to a conjured past to seek precedents for British colonization, arguing that North America was England's by right since the Welsh prince Madoch had discovered the continent 322 years before Columbus.[4] New World exploration did not mark a modern rupture with history, Hakluyt claimed, since knowledge of the American landmass had been acquired and forgotten periodically throughout history.

Hakluyt's advice aimed to justify English colonization in North America. Other learned advisers devised prescriptions for travelers that derived from *artes apodemicae* resembling those of Essex and Sidney.[5] Dangerous and expensive journeys required careful planning, and details of the expeditions were specified down to the observations to be recorded. Assiduous collection of essential geographical and anthropological minutiae would facilitate the establishment of English settlements among little-known peoples in unforgiving landscapes. Thomas Harriot's *A Briefe and True Reporte*, for example, constituted a polemical encapsulation of the systematic observations Harriot had taken during his voyage to Virginia in 1585, organized to demonstrate the inhabitability of North America.

Harriot's work reflected the endurance of a culture of systematized travel developed before Ralegh inherited control of English exploration in 1583. Under Humphrey Gilbert, the elder Richard Hakluyt had been particularly responsible for producing prescriptions for travel. Hakluyt supplied these in preparation for Gilbert's 1578 North American voyage, and, in 1580, he provided instructions to Arthur Pett and Charles Jackman for their expedition in search of a northeast passage. Hakluyt was only one of several to offer them instructions: William Borough asked that they take astronomical readings to help map the Arctic Circle, while John Dee charted a specific route and suggested that they visit Japan (where he inexplicably thought there might be Englishmen).[6]

Hakluyt enumerated an elaborate series of requests. He suggested that Pett and Jackman map islands that might serve as intermediary harbors and judge whether the Arctic waters were sufficiently dense with fish to attract English fishermen. They should occasionally disembark to evaluate the arability of the land and seek building materials while always observing the defenses of coastal towns. Finally, they should observe local

3. *The Original Writings and Correspondence of the Two Richard Hakluyts* (London: Printed for the Hakluyt Society, 1935), 366 (*Decades* dedication), 211, 264 (*Discourse*).

4. See Gwyn A. Williams, *Madoc: The Making of a Myth* (London: Eyre Methuen, 1979).

5. For a comprehensive list of this literature, see Stagl, *Apodemiken*.

6. Richard Hakluyt, ed., *The Principall Navigations*, 3 vols. (London, 1598–1600), 1: 433–42.

apparel and shops to discern whether any towns might prove a receptive
market for English wool or other commodities. Jackman and Pett were not
only to observe aspects of foreign lands; they were also to import them.
Hakluyt specified: "Bring home with you (if you may) from Cambalu, or
other civil place, one or other yong man, although you leave one for him."
Accompanying this bartered native should be fruits, vegetables, seed,
herbs, and flowers. Other provisions were designed to stimulate trade—
Hakluyt ordered that they show any potential trade partners a map of London in which "the river be drawne fulle of shippes of all sorts, to make
the more shew of your great trade and traffike in trade and merchandize."
Some items were intended to impress their contacts. Hakluyt explained:
"If you take Ortelius booke of mappes with you to marke all these regions,
it were not amisse, and if need were, to present the same to the great Cam,
for it would be to a Prince of marvellous account." Similarly, he suggested
that they bring an herbal and "the booke of the attire of all nations."[7]

But immediate utility—whether mercantile, diplomatic, or military—
alone did not determine the ship's cargo. Hakluyt also suggested that Pett
and Jackman "bring thence some old printed booke, to see whether they
have had print there, before it was devised in Europe, as some write."[8] Hakluyt wished to use the voyage to test the claim that the Chinese had invented printing. This idea circulated out of sixteenth-century Jesuit circles
and received full explication in Juan Gonzalez de Mendoza's 1585 *Historia
. . . del gran reyno del China*, which Robert Parke would translate into
English in 1588 at Hakluyt's suggestion.[9] Gonzalez reported: "The Chinos
doo affirme, that the [printing press'] first beginning was in their countrie,
and the inventour was a man, whome they reverence for a saint . . . it was
brought into Almaine by the way of Ruscia and Moscovia . . . and that
some merchants that came from thence into this kingdome, by the redde
sea, and from Arabia Felix, might bring some books, from whence this
John Cutembergo, whom the histories dooth make author) had his first
foundation." According to Gonzalez de Mendoza, Gutenberg had inherited
the art of printing at the end of a slow circuit in which merchants had

7. *Original Writings . . . of the two Richard Hakluyts*, 150, 155. The book in question may
be the *Theatre de tous les peuples & nations de la terre . . .* produced by the Dutchman Lucas
d'Heere in London between 1567 and 1576, perhaps copied from the manuscript now in the
Ghent library. D'Heere was part of the Ortelius circle; this hints at deeper Dutch roots to the
method of travel and observation adopted by the English. See Meganck, "Erudite Eyes," 168ff.

8. *Original Writings . . . of the two Richard Hakluyts*, 151.

9. Juan Gonzalez de Mendoza, *The Historie of the Great and Mightie Kingdome of China*
(London, 1588), ¶3v.

transmitted this Chinese technology from Russia, down the Urals to the Arab East, and, finally, into Europe. He substantiated this technological lineage with eyewitness experience. As he testified: "for the better credite heereof, at this day there are found amongst them many bookes printed 500 yeares before the invention began in Almanie: of the which I have one, and I have seene others, as well in Spaine and in Italie as in the Indies."[10] Hakluyt did not assume Gonzales de Mendoza's credit but rather wished Pett and Jackman to probe the claim. Amid his diplomatic advice, intricate provisioning, and mercantile plotting, he instructed them to devote precious ship space to transport "some old printed booke" thousands of miles to test inchoate rumors of the Far East origins of the revolutionary— and allegedly divine—technology of printing. As inventions and discovery transformed the European world, scholars used travel to seek the genealogies of its alterations. The system of regularized travel in which Ralegh participated was designed not only to advance the interests of the English state by stimulating trade, spreading the gospel, and checking Spanish expansion. It was also directed to the interrogation of history.

As we will see, Ralegh returned to the question of the Eastern origins of printing, and he used these rumors to prove an even more controversial thesis. His ideas, it should be noted, might have been different had icy Arctic floe not forced Jackman and Pett to return to England long before they reached the Pacific.

HISTORICAL AND THEOLOGICAL TRAVEL

Hakluyt's request that Pett and Jackman test Gonzalez de Mendoza's theories of the origin of the printing press reflected a scholarly culture in which early modern travelers directed their observations to yield information that would benefit historical knowledge. This endeavor extended beyond antiquarian observation to comprehensive explorations of the role of human movement throughout history. Analyses of the significance of past travels and migrations fed arguments concerning the role of Providence on earth, and the interpretation of human movement became a terrain of debate.

Ralegh's library was stocked with reports from recent travelers brimming with historical notes. For example, Ralegh owned the French naturalist Pierre Belon's 1555 *Les Observations de plusieurs singularitez &*

10. Ibid., 101–2.

choses memorables.[11] Belon had traveled to the Near East and Egypt, where he compared the notes he took on flora, fauna, and minerals with ancient accounts, trying to deduce from field experience the precise species to which Latin, Greek, and Hebrew appellatives referred. He also observed the monuments and ruins of past cultures that, battered and spoiled, dotted the landscapes he visited, and he regaled his readers with tales of his visits to the tombs of Adam, Abraham, and Isaac. Belon saw his enterprise as stemming from an ancient tradition of scholarly travelers. In his preface, he wrote of the pre-Socratic philosopher Democritus: "because of the great desire that he had to acquire the practice of knowledge, that is to say the experience as well as the theory . . . he sold his patrimony to his brothers, and used the money to finance long peregrinations through Egypt, India, and Chaldea, to come eventually to the Gymnosophists. Afterwards he returned to Athens with a great reputation and was honored for his knowledge."[12] Democritus was not alone in using travel to accrue honor and renown: "Herodotus, Diodorus [Siculus], Arrian, and many other ancient authors have left to us their written accounts of long voyages, from which men have received an inestimable benefit, considering that all their travels have been preserved through posterity."[13] Beyond the knowledge recorded in their texts, the voyages of these ancients benefited modern scholars by providing evidence that travel facilitated the importation of useful wisdom. Belon's exemplary genealogy of travel thus exalted his own ventures.

Belon's evidence of ancient travelers could have been drawn from any number of world or ancient histories. These examples were given system-

11. Ralegh referred to Belon as "a carefull observer of rarities" when citing him on the grandeur of the Pyramids, which Belon had both entered and measured. *HW*, 1.12.5.216. For Belon, see Ilana Zinguer, "Les stratégies de Belon pour un représentation exotique," *Nouvelle revue du XVIe siècle* 11 (1993): 5–17; and Frédéric Tinguely, *L'écriture du Levant à la Renaissance: Enquête sur les voyageurs français dans l'empire de Soliman le Magnifique* (Geneva: Droz, 2000).

12. Pierre Belon, *Les Observations de plusieurs singularitez & choses memorables* (Antwerp, 1555), *5r–*6v. "Dont Democrite en porte bon tesmoignage, lequel pour le grand desir qu'il avoit d'acquerir la practique de sciences, c'este à dire l'experience aussi bien que le theorique, & principalement d'Astronomie & Geometrie, vendit son patrimoine à ses freres, à fin d'employer l'argent de la vente en loingtaines peregrinations par les pays d'Egypte, Indie & Chaldée, pour parvenir aux Gymnosophistes, & puis apres retourner en Athenes avec grande reputation, & y estre honoré par son scavoir."

13. Ibid., *6v–*7r. "Herodote, Diodore, Strabo, Arrianus, & plusieurs autres anciens, nous ont laissé leurs loingtains voyages par escrit, desquels les hommes ont recue benefice inestimable, attendu que tous leurs travaux tombent au soulagement & repos de la posterité."

atic treatment starting in the 1570s by authors of the *artes apodemicae*.[14] Such authors ascribed to the ancients a level of peregrinatory knowledge that the moderns were only approaching. Hieronymus Turler, for example, vividly depicted the journeys of the ancients in his 1574 *De peregrinatione*, which was translated into English in 1575. Plato in particular earned praised, for he had "traveilled into *Ægypt*, to learne antiquities of the wise men of that lande: from whence there is no doubt, but hee brought all the wisdome and knowledge which hee lefte to posterities, & in which he excelled in such sort, that in respect thereof he was called *Divine*, & Prince of Philosophers."[15] The process by which Plato's philosophy was produced was as meaningful to Turler as the ideas themselves, for he attributed Platonic wisdom less to debate or contemplation than to the antiquarian collection of Egyptian wisdom.

Plato's travels lay in the tradition of an even more esteemed originator whom Turler identified as his own model. Turler claimed to imitate "the example of *Moyses*, who most diligentlye discerned the differences betweene Mountaynes, hilles, Landes, peoples, Townes, fieldes and Forestes, adding moreover what is to bee considered in them all." According to Turler, Moses himself had devised the original *ars apodemica* during the Exodus, and he had wandered through the desert alertly discerning the strengths and weaknesses of surrounding landscapes and peoples. This methodical art of travel he had taught to prepare the spies he dispatched from Cadesbarnea to find a direct route to Canaan: "For thus hee sayte to them whom hee sent to view the lande of *Chanaan*. When yee shall come unto the Hilles, consider the lande what maner one it is, and consyder the people that dwell therein, whether they bee strong or weake: manye or fewe: the Lande good or bad: what Cyties there bee: Walled or not walled: the soyle fertile or barreine: woodie or champion?"[16] This Ramist *ars apodemica* thus had a sacred lineage, and Turler guided travelers toward pious and profitable knowledge by resurrecting Moses' method.

At the height of Europe's first age of discovery and imperial expansion, then, travel theorists sought models in Scripture and in ancient Greek sages

---

14. For this genre, see Justin Stagl, "The Methodising of Travel in the 16th Century: A Tale of Three Cities," *History and Anthropology* 4 (1990): 303–38, *A History of Curiosity: The Theory of Travel, 1550–1800* (Chur: Harwood Academic, 1995), and *Apodemikon*; Joan-Pau Rubiés, "New World and Renaissance Ethnology," *History and Anthropology* 6 (1993): 157–97, and "Instructions for Travellers: Teaching the Eye to See," *History and Anthropology* 9 (1996): 139–90; and my "The English Polydaedali: How Gabriel Harvey Read Late Tudor London," *JHI* 66 (2005): 351–81.

15. *The traueiler of Ierome Turler* (London, 1575), 48, 74.

16. Ibid., 49–50. The questions are Num. 13:18–20.

voyaging to the mysterious East. Increased attention to the influx of new information from parts of the world previously unknown to them did not undermine the strength of European traditions. Instead, scholars like Belon and Turler discerned celebratory precedents for their enterprises, much as had Montano, who saw modern Spanish explorations as re-creating an ancient empire. And, similarly, this emphasis on ancient travel generated detailed new world histories that emphasized the role of travel.

Authors of *artes apodemicae*, furthermore, suffused their interpretations of human movements with their theological convictions.[17] The Swiss Ramist Calvinist Theodor Zwinger, for example, depicted earthly change as enacting the predestined circulation of peoples, ideas, and materials orchestrated by its final cause, God. In his 1577 *Methodus Apodemica*, Zwinger used Aristotelian causal analysis to categorize all species of travel according to their final, efficient, material, and formal causes.[18] Movement, he explained in his introduction, was the category that explained other transformations. Thus, he proclaimed, it "must be assigned an end before all, because from it all remaining causes and species are deduced."[19] In his analysis, Zwinger layered Calvinist predestination over Aristotelian dynamics. In simple terms, Aristotelian dynamics classified all motions into two kinds: natural motion, which was circular and produced by the mobile object seeking its proper habitation, and violent motion, which was conceived of as angular and was produced by the willful intervention of an external force against rest or natural motion. When the object reached its natural habitation, it would cease to move without violent intervention.[20] Synthesizing Aristotelian mechanics with predestination, Zwinger described absolute divine foreknowledge of the movement

17. On the endurance of religious travel through the early modern period, see Thomas F. Noonan, *The Road to Jerusalem: Pilgrimage and Travel in the Age of Discovery* (Philadelphia: University of Pennsylvania Press, 2007)

18. See Ann Blair, "*Historia* in Zwinger's *Theatrum humanae vitae*," in Pomata and Siraisi, eds., *Historia*, 269–96. In this context, see also Jill Bepler, "The Traveller-Author and His Role in Seventeenth-Century German Travel Accounts," in *Travel Fact and Travel Fiction: Studies on Fiction, Literary Tradition, Scholarly Discovery, and Observation in Travel Writing*, ed. Zweder von Martels (Leiden: E. J. Brill, 1994), 183–93; and Jas Elsner, "The *Itinerarium Burdigalense*: Politics and Salvation in the Geography of Constantine's Empire," *Journal of Roman Studies* 90 (2000): 181–95.

19. Theodor Zwinger, *Methodus Apodemica* (Basel, 1577), 1. "Cum motus omnis, tam Voluntatis quam Naturae, ad certum finem dirigatur: peregrinationis profecto, quae motus corporci de loco in locum species existit, Finis ante omnia assignandus erit, ex quo & Causae reliquae & Species insuper deducantur." Ralegh did not own this text, but he did own Zwinger's five-volume *Theatrum humanae naturae*, which also contained this material.

20. Zwinger, *Methodus Apodemica*, a2v.

of souls and bodies through the world until apocalypse, when souls would rest in the heavenly seat: "Although all things are in perpetual motion on account of man, and man is in perpetual motion because of God, nevertheless motion is disposed according to a certain end in rest. But rest cannot occur except through that and with that and in that, which moving all things is moved by nothing. As all the motion of remaining things must be referred to man, thus the quiescence of a moved man must be found in God."[21] Human motion itself constituted one element in the system of created objects seeking their proper providential habitations. Scrutinizing the travels and migrations of peoples showed the mechanics of Providence at work in world history, as a divine hand guiding humanity through time toward one foreordained, though inscrutable, end. The history of human movement constituted kinetic evidence for predestination best explained by sacred mechanics.

Sir Thomas Palmer's 1606 *An essay of the meanes how to make our travailes* drew heavily on Zwinger's work, but his theology of travel modified Zwinger's Calvinist predestination with an Arminian insistence on a limited free will. Palmer was a Kentish nobleman who in 1603 became one of James's gentlemen of the Privy Chamber. His *ars* also relied on Aristotelian causes, but, unlike Zwinger, whose single final mover was a divine being orchestrating all corporeal and spiritual motion, Palmer described "Two lawfull final moovers," one of which was "Prime and principal; the other Congruent and Secondarie." Palmer's God exerted significantly less power over created motion. "The prime [mover]," he wrote, "is divine and spirituall, That afterwards we may leade a more quiet, contented and peacable life, to the honor and glorie of God, with knowledge and understanding. And this no dout ought to bee the first marke, for everie man to shoote at in this life, that by doing the revealed will of God, everie one may seek unto himselfe the assurance of heavenly happinesse, which is incomprehensible and eternall."[22] For Palmer, travel was not subject exclusively to providential design. Travelers were moved by the innate desire to accord with the divine will, rather than by the divine will itself.

Both Palmer and Zwinger described travel as a vital component for understanding the past and Providence, for it both had and was a cause. Their

---

21. Ibid., a3v. "Quandoquidem igitur in perpetuo motu sunt omnia propter hominem, homo propter Deum: motus autem propter finem certum in quiete positum: quies vero non nisi per eum & cum eo & in eo consistere potest, qui omnia movens a nemine movetur: ut reliquorum motus omnis in homine, ita hominis moti quies in Deo reponenda erit."

22. Thomas Palmer, *An essay of the meanes how to make our trauailes, into forraine countries, the more profitable and honourable* (London, 1606), 2, 15.

theological disagreement over the balance of divine and human control nonetheless encased a mutual vision—shared with Belon and Turler—of a past in which fluid exchanges of goods and beliefs inscribed traces of Providence on the surface of the earth. All these authors deemed analysis of ancient travels critical for understanding the plan and pattern of Creation. Their reflections on ancient precedents and contemporary meaning were a means to decipher the system of the world that they inhabited, and the specific forms that their interpretations took reflected their own theological and intellectual allegiances. Ralegh eagerly embraced the significance they granted to travel, for his own experience coordinating and supervising voyages of exploration ascribed him unique expertise with which to analyze, and reanimate, the lessons of the past.

RALEGH, EXPERIENCE, AND ANNIUS

Ralegh's travels and historical investigations were performed in an intellectual culture that viewed travel as a providentially orchestrated method of circulating knowledge, customs, and peoples throughout the divine theater of particulars. This perception had been spurred by the impetus of contemporary explorations, to which historians responded by projecting these processes into the past, using ancient travels to connect historical communities and explain earthly change. As we will see, Ralegh used his travel expertise to legitimize his analyses. In doing so, he both imitated and responded to the decidedly more sedentary originator of this tactic—Annius of Viterbo.[23]

The postdiluvian world was energized for Annius by the constant fluidity of colonists enjoined by God to spread into empty space, and he fabricated their movements to support a world history that accorded with his ecclesiastical politics. One of his favored techniques was the invention of extensive ancient travels to connect individual figures over divergent sets of sources. In his postdiluvian history, for example, he attributed the lapse of myriad communities from the true religion to the travels of Noah's diabolic son Cham, whom he identified as the single figure behind the individuals named as responsible for spreading idolatry to the Egyptians, murderousness to Sicilian giants, and diabolic magic to the Bactrians. Annius's Noah, a learned traveler whose geographical expertise had enabled him to

23. See Allen, *The Legend of Noah*, and *Mysteriously Meant*; Roberto Bizzocchi, *Genealogie incredibili: Scritti di storia nell'Europa moderna* (Bologna: Società editrice il Mulino, 1995); Grafton, "Invention of Traditions and Traditions of Invention in Renaissance Europe"; and Stephens, "When Pope Noah Ruled the Etruscans."

coordinate the postdiluvian settlement of the earth, toured the world in response, reforming those communities infected by Cham's heresies, and enforcing observation of true religion.[24] Noah, Annius claimed, also had been given different names in different communities, and only by recognizing the single figure to whom was attributed all these names could the historian accurately decode world history directly after the Flood. This tactic lent great weight to Annius's ecclesiastical genealogy, for his Noah remained in Etruria after driving Cham from Italy, presiding over the foundation of colonies such as the small city of Rome.[25] Annius thus used ancient travels to explain both the periodical decline of true religion and the Italian Peninsula's divine historical significance.

In Annius's dynamic history, scholars found evidence that they eagerly used to construct genealogies of modern kings and nations, and Annian evidence larded the numerous sixteenth-century histories that examined the ancient origins of the French, German, British, and other peoples. Later scholars devoted serious criticism to identifying the appropriate tools for investigating these origin narratives. In his *Methodus*, Jean Bodin devoted a chapter to establishing "Criteria by which to test the origins of peoples." Most early modern scholars operated with the principles that he proposed.[26] He wrote: "There are three proofs in the light of which origins can be known and evaluated when reported by historians: first, in the proven reliability of the writer; second in traces of language; third, in the situation and character of the region."[27] While Bodin's third category was somewhat idiosyncratic, his first two techniques were based on conventional practice.[28] Evaluating the ancient origins of people was an enterprise primarily requiring philological investigation, either by coordinating the names of regions with the names of their ancient colonizers or by finding authentic ancient texts that reliably described their foundations.

Like Annius and many others, Ralegh's investigations of the origins of peoples began with the postdiluvian plantation. But Ralegh insisted that

---

24. Annius, *Antiquitatum Italiae ac totius orbis libri*, 86.

25. Ibid., 115.

26. For such analyses, see Joan-Pau Rubiés, "Hugo Grotius's Dissertation on the Origin of the American Peoples and the Use of Comparative Methods," *JHI* 52 (1991): 221–44; and Kurt Johannesson, *The Renaissance of the Goths in Sixteenth-Century Sweden: Johannes and Olaus Magnus as Politicians and Historians* (Berkeley and Los Angeles: University of California Press, 1991).

27. Bodin, *Method*, 336.

28. Couzinet, *Histoire et méthode*. Bodin's last criterion derived from his belief that each region was inscribed with a particular character or nature that was also imbued in its inhabitants.

many preceding commentators had allowed enthusiasm to overwhelm their rigor, and, consequently, the history of the plantation had been severely distorted: "But let us goe unto the Worlds plantation after the floud, which being rightly understood, we shall finde that many Nations have supposed or fayned themselves those Ancestors of Fathers, which never saw or approched the bounds of their Countries, and of whom they are by no way or branch descended." For Ralegh, those who had inflated the ancestry of their own peoples had done so despite the existence of unimpeachable evidence, for testimony of Scripture in this regard was so lucid that other sources barely merited consultation. He noted: "If any prophane Author may receive allowance herein, the same must bee with this caution, That they take their beginning where the Scriptures end."[29] When the period a millennium later was studied, Scripture's confused chronology would require its correlation with ancient witnesses, but scholars could delineate the postdiluvian settlement of the earth without recourse to later pagan testimony.

While Ralegh shared elements of Bodin's system of evaluation, he forcefully advocated other bases for criticism. His method of integrating nonscriptural works, he claimed, relied on the application of logic and reason developed through experience. The experience that he referred to in this case was that as a traveler and administrator of exploration under Elizabeth. Ralegh claimed that his method of testing narratives of migration relied first on Scripture and then on his own understanding of the possibilities and limits of human travel. He wrote: "We are to consider that the world after the floud was not planted by imagination, neither had the children of *Noah* wings, to flie from *Shinaar* to the uttermost border of *Europe*, *Africa*, and *Asia* in haste, but that these children were directed by a wise Father, who knew those parts of the world before the floud, to which he disposed his children after it, and sent them not as discouverers,

---

29. *HW*, 1.8.2.130. In fact, Ralegh was generally dismissive of triumphalist national histories and the tales of Trojan origins proclaimed for many contemporary states. He cautioned: "And not to harken to fabulous Authors, who have no other end then to flatter Princes (as *Virgil* did *Augustus* in the fiction of *Aeneas*) or else to glorifie their owne Nations; Let us build herein upon the Scriptures themselves, and after them upon Reason and Nature." *HW*, 1.8.2.131. Elsewhere he wrote: "The like vanitie possessed many other Cities of *Greece*, and many Nations in these parts of the world, which have striven to bring their descent frome some of the Princes, that warred at *Troy*: all difficulties or unlikelihoods in such their Pedigree notwithstanding. But those Nations which indeed, or in most probabilitie came of the *Troians*, were the *Albanes* in *Italy*; and from them the *Romanes*, brought into that Countrey by *Aeneas*: the *Venetians* first seated in *Padua*, and the Countrie adioyning by *Antenor*." *HW*, 2.14.6.458. Geoffrey of Monmouth's Britons were conspicuously absent.

or at all-adventure, but assigned and allotted to every Sonne and their issues, their proper parts."[30] This image of Noah as administrator presented
an idealized version of Ralegh's role under Elizabeth, orchestrating the
extension of a people into little-known parts of the world. Ralegh's own
experience resembled that of the plantation's coordinator.

Indeed, his expertise enabled Ralegh to wield a unique set of tools for
mapping the plantation, for he dismissed improbable national mytholo-
gies with a mode of scriptural exegesis facilitated by this experience. For
Ralegh, the tools of reason and nature took the specific form of an expert
evaluation of the navigability of the land traversed by those performing
the plantation. To illustrate the overgrowth that Noah and his progeny
must have encountered, he drew an analogy between this virgin landscape
and the less fertile English terrain. In England, he explained, "(where the
dead and destroying winter depresseth all vegetative and growing nature,
for one halfe of the yeere in effect) yet in twentie or thirtie yeeres these
our grounds would all overgrow and be covered (according to the nature
thereof) either with woods or with other offensive thickets and bush-
ments." Noah's descendants would have faced a significantly more onerous task in crossing, not just mountains, but "what wonderfull Desarts,
what inpassable fastness of woods, reeds, bryars, and rotten grasse, what
Lakes and standing Pooles, and what Marishes, Fens and Bogs," nourished
by a fertile climate, and unfettered by human intervention for 130 years.[31]
After the confusion of the languages at Babel, Noah's progeny could not
simply have sped into lands designated for them; they must have gradually
trickled into these sites.

Practical consideration led Ralegh to perceive difficulties with the chronology of Annius's account of the plantation. He used Japeth's sons Tubal,
who colonized Spain, and Gomer, who inhabited Italy, as test cases disproving Annius's hyperfluid ancient history. "This *Gomer,*" Ralegh wrote,
"(if we may beleeve *Berosus* and *Annius,* whose authoritie the greatest
number of all our late writers have followed) did in the tenth yeere of *Nim-
rods* raigne depart from *Babylonia,* and planted *Italie.*"[32] Ralegh's practical
experience preparing the erection of settlements in the wilderness revealed
the utter impossibility of such a speedy departure. Since none of the progeny had left Babylon until the confusion of the languages, commentators

30. *HW,* 1.8.2.131.
31. *HW,* 1.8.2.131.
32. *HW,* 1.8.3.132.

needed to determine how long they had engaged in the construction of the
Tower of Babel. Most agreed that there had been significant construction,
and the Byzantine historian Michael Glycas, Ralegh noted, had assumed
that forty years would have been necessary just to build the foundation
for a work of such magnitude.[33] Ralegh continued: "Now to thinke that
this Worke in the newnesse of the World (wanting all instruments and
materials) could be performed in ten yeares; and that *Tubal* and *Gomer* in
the same yeare could creepe through 3000 miles of Desart, with women,
children, and cattell: let those light Beleevers, that neyther tye themselves
to the Scripture, nor to reason, approove it, for I doe not." Annius's chronology exhibited an inattention to Scripture alongside a lack of empirical
knowledge and reason. Once the difficulty of the terrain was recognized,
Ralegh's experience exploring overgrown tropical climes supplied valuable
expertise in evaluating the pace of postdiluvian travel. Ralegh described
the crossing from Babel to Europe as "rather a Worke of 100 yeares then of
10 dayes. For in the West *Indies* of which the *Spaniards* have the experience, in those places where they found neither path nor guide, they have
not entred the Countrie ten miles in tenne yeares."[34] He thus compared
the Spanish plantation of the New World to the postdiluvian plantation to
demonstrate, not typological continuities, but a practical resource for crit-
icizing Annius. The intractability of the South American landscape before
the Spanish machete rendered Annius's accelerated plantation dubious.

Even if one allotted nine years for the construction of the edifice,
Ralegh asserted, it was impossible that Gomer and Tubal had traveled
from deep Assyria to Europe in adequate time with the available technology. He addressed the anticipated objection that they had built boats and
sailed westward: "But we never read of any navigation in those dayes, nor
long after. Surely he that knoweth what it is to imbarque so great a people
as may iustly suppose those Conductors carried with them, will not easily
beleeve, that there were any Vessels in those daies to transport Armies,
and (withall) their Cattle."[35] That Noah had taken his family into an ark
did not mean that he was trained in the art of navigation or that he could
teach it to his posterity.[36] Drawing on a close exegetical reading of Scripture driven by the knowledge of the logistics of travel that his experience
had developed, Ralegh removed the mechanical underpinning of Annius's

33. Ibid.
34. *HW*, 1.8.3.133.
35. *HW*, 1.8.3.134.
36. *HW*, 1.8.3.135.

account. And he reiterated the methods and sources he considered authoritative: "Leaving therefore the fabulous to their Fables, and all men else to their fancies, who have cast Nations into Countries farre off, I know not how, I will follow herein the relation of *Moses* and the Prophets: to which truth there is ioyned both nature, reason, policie, and necessitie: and to the rest, neither probabilitie, nor possibilitie."[37] Ralegh was willing to consider Annius's claims when they accorded with Scripture and the fruits of his experience, but, if they clashed with these intractable criteria, he discarded them quickly.

Ralegh did briefly analyze Gomer and Tubal's migrations. Rather than claiming that the brothers traversed the far reaches of the Mediterranean, he claimed that they had colonized Syria and never traveled further west than Galatea. Still, he ably made use of Annius's conclusions while remaining consistent with his own empirical and rational criteria for human movement. He argued that the progeny of Tubal and Gomer did, eventually, occupy the locations that Annius had assigned them. Of the Tubalines, he wrote: "Without repugnancie of opinions, it may be granted, that in processe of time these people might from their first habitation passe into the Countries neere the *Euxine* Sea, and from thence in after Ages into *Spaine*." Though Tubal could not have brought colonists to Spain in the space of time allotted by Annius, there was no reason to deny that his successors had done so. Following Melanchthon, Ralegh similarly claimed: "Of *Gomer* the like may be said. . . . Hee proceeded further into *Asia* the lesse; and in long tract of time his valiant issue filled all *Germanie*, rested long in *France* and *Brittaine*, and possessed the utmost borders of the earth."[38] This delayed migration explained the philological evidence that supported Annius's arguments. Again, Ralegh objected to Annius's plantation narrative, not for its structure or political impact, but for the impossible pace of human movement its chronology demanded.[39]

Ralegh thus evaluated the historical travels described by Annius according to Scripture, logic, and reason. But, above all, he used his own experience as an Elizabethan administrator to guide his criticism. He did not discard Annius's claims for their spurious origins; rather, it was their challenge to the sources for his own history that prompted his rejection. He clearly had imbibed the Polybian lesson that only experienced men could write truthful histories. And that his experience lay in exploration

---

37. Ibid.
38. *HW*, 1.8.4.138.
39. That Ralegh tied the Britons to Gomer was entirely conventional.

and travel administration both certified his ability to write histories and allowed him to discern the true course of events.[40]

MOTION AND THE MEANING OF EXODUS

Though Ralegh relied on reason and experience to understand human motion, his conception of travel was not secular. He understood human travel and migration within a divine scheme that could be interpreted provided one wielded the proper experience. He revealed his understanding of travel in history in his analyses of the perambulations of scriptural figures.[41] The Exodus in particular maintained consummate significance for analysts of ancient travel, for the duress of the journey anagogically symbolized the difficulty of adhering to orthodoxy; the Israelites' physical wandering itself articulated a disquieting soteriological lesson. Ralegh's analysis drew on an early sixteenth-century tradition that had been adopted by Ortelius and others of tracing the motions of the Israelites in maps of the Exodus. These maps were increasingly included in the sixteenth century in Protestant Bibles, where they functioned as devotional aids. While gazing on the path taken by the Israelites, the viewer reflected on the difficulty of the divine way and the sufferings necessary to lead a life according to sacred prescription.

Like previous authors, Ralegh narrated the Israelites' journey by rearranging dispersed passages from the books of Exodus, Numbers, and Deuteronomy to form a linear historical narrative. He also included an engraved image of the voyage in which he explained: "For all storie without the knowledge of the places, wherin the actions were performed, as it wanteth a great part of the pleasure; so it no way enricheth the knowledge and understanding of the Reader; neither doth any thing serve to retaine, what we reade in our memories, so well as these pictures and descriptions do."[42] Like Ortelius and Sixtus Senensis, he viewed this image as render-

---

40. Note Benjamin Schmidt, "Space, Time, Travel: Hugo de Groot [Grotius], Johannes de Laet, and the 'Advancement' of Geographic Learning," *Lias: The Journal of Early Modern History of Ideas* 25 (1998): 177–99; and Joan-Pau Rubiés, "Travel Writing as a Genre: Facts, Fictions and the Invention of a Scientific Discourse in Early Modern Europe," *Journeys: The International Journal of Travel and Travel Writing* 1 (2000): 5–35.

41. See Smith and Ingram, *Maps in Bibles*; and Melion, "Ad ductum itineris et dispositionem mansionum ostendendam."

42. *HW*, 2.3.2.249. As the authority supporting this claim, Ralegh turned to "that great learned man, *Arias Montanus*." He quoted from the Spanish exegete: "*If narration* (saith he) *be made of those things which are performed, without the observation of the places, wherein they were done: or if Histories be read without Topographicall knowledge, all things will ap-*

Figure 7. Map of the Holy Land from a 1598 Geneva *Bible*.

ing the history more intelligible, imprinting the event and its meaning more clearly on his readers' minds.

Ralegh had the course of the Israelites carefully plotted on a map engraved by William Hole, an early English copperplate engraver who had produced plates for the second edition of Camden's *Brittannia*.[43] Ralegh possessed several comparable Exodus maps in his library. The Geneva Bible contained a woodcut drawn from Calvin's Genesis commentary that traced the path of the Israelites as they plodded toward the Promised Land (see fig. 7). The indiscretions near Cadesbarnea that had prompted God to delay their crossing into Canaan were committed near the twentieth mansion

---

peare so intricate and confused, as wee shall thereby understand nothing but obscurely, nor draw thence any knowledge, but with the greatest difficultie." Ibid.

43. It is impossible to know precisely how closely Ralegh supervised the production of the copperplates, but the close relation between the map of North Africa in his notebook (fig. 5 above) and the relevant section in his map of the Exodus (fig. 11 below) suggests that Hole faithfully engraved the images he received.

Figure 8. "Terrae Israel," Benedicto Arias Montano, from *Biblia Sacra,
Hebraicae, Chaldaice, Graece et Latine,* 6 vols. (Antwerp, 1569–72), vol. 8.
Princeton University Library, Rare Books Division, Department of Rare Books
and Special Collections, (Ex) 5145.1569f.

(or locale where the Israelites had dwelled), and their path was forced into
a loop-de-loop. They eventually reoriented themselves and resumed north-
ward. Cadesbarnea was placed north of the thirty-third mansion, and the
Israelites were shown curving around Zin and Idumaean territory, heading
instead into Moabite regions before eventually entering Judaea. Montano
also traced the path of the Israelites in his map entitled *Caleb* (see fig. 8).[44]
His depiction strikingly differed from the Geneva Bible's; he located the
Red Sea very close to the Mediterranean and compressed the Sinai Peninsula, thus offering the Israelites little wilderness in which to wander.
Montano illustrated the laborious journey by having them twice meander
a lengthy circuit before reaching the Promised Land. Ortelius's map of this
expedition in the *Theatrum* drew from an earlier map by Tilemann Stella
and differed greatly from Calvin's and Montano's (see fig. 9). His Israelites
did not travel in a circle but swept north and south before crossing into Palestine. John Speed's map for his 1611 apparatus to the King James Bible, *The
genealogies recorded in the Sacred Scriptures,* which Ralegh likely owned

44. See Shalev, "Geographica Sacra."

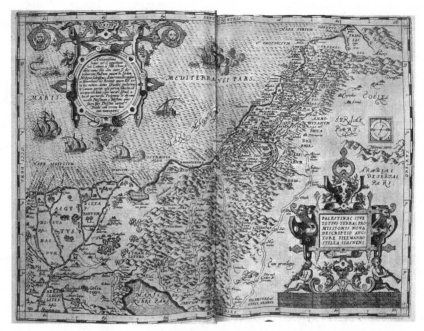

Figure 9. Map of the Holy Land from Abraham Ortelius's *Theatrum Orbis Terrarum*
(Antwerp, 1613), 18–19. Special Collections Research Center, Swem Library,
College of William and Mary, shelf mark 912 Or8 oversize.

as well, closely resembled this depiction (see fig. 10). Speed added an extra
north-south leg to the journey. His path for the Israelites was a series of
lengthy direct movements and abrupt reversals. Ralegh's available sources
illustrated very different paths, varying from largely direct, to circuitous,
to repeated vertical sweeps. Yet they all conveyed the same nongeographi-
cal message—visualizing the trial of the Israelites.

Ralegh's map drew diligently on Speed and Ortelius to depict the trek
of the Israelites in dotted lines (see fig. 11). The figures of the Israelites fled
toward Ramses, northeast of the Red Sea, from a compass of departure
points as they were chased by furious sword-wielding Egyptians. Taber-
nacles at the mansions showed where they encamped on their way, and a
massive train of men split the Red Sea near its northern coast. Hole minutely figured their path between the hills, mountains, and lakes, through
valleys and along foothills, skirting brush and forestry, glimpsing at herds
of cattle and horses. Clustered in pike-wielding phalanxes, miniature warriors battled the Amalekites, Arad the Cananite, and the Amorites. Their
path wound tortuously after they crossed the Red Sea, studded by sudden

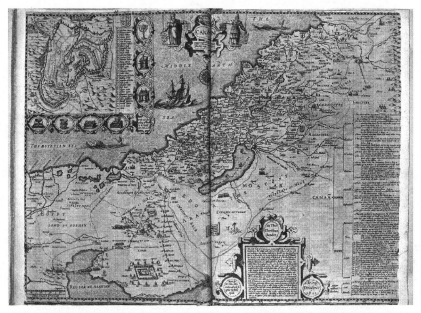

Figure 10. Map of the Holy Land by John Speed from *Holy Bible* (London, 1613).
Special Collections Research Center, Swem Library, College of William and Mary,
shelf mark 220 52 B47 oversize.

deterrents and lurches away from the land of Canaan. Nonetheless, they
persisted north, buffeted between the hills and mountains that dotted the
desert, until they arrived at Rethma. With Cadesbarnea directly to the
north, the Promised Land lay fixed in their path. But the Israelites veered
violently, careening to the east before slaloming wildly among the hills of
the Paran Desert. Finally arriving at the coast town of Esion Gabor, they
turned back to the north. They traced a course east of the Promised Land
until reaching Helmon Ablatham, at which point they broke west and, at
long last, crossed into the Holy Land. Ralegh attributed to the Hebrews an
extremely complex and arduous movement.

Ralegh's map differed in two significant ways from Speed's. While both
gave similar locations to the mansions, the path that Ralegh's Hebrews
took from Cadesbarnea wound between sites more chaotically, lurching
sharply where Speed's had smoothly swept north and south. Ralegh's paths
were less direct, and the route itself appeared choppier and more emphatically flung about. Ralegh thus orchestrated the path of his pilgrims to
show a more violent movement and to portray their ferocious subjection to
divine wrath.

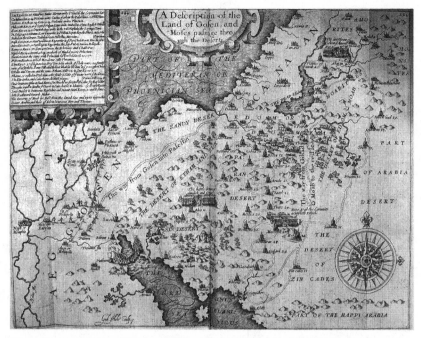

Figure 11. Map of the Exodus from the 1614 *History of the World*, 262–63.
Special Collections Research Center, Swem Library, College of William and Mary,
shelf mark D57. R16 1614.

To illustrate further the trial embedded in the path taken, Ralegh
represented the difficulty of the journey in another way deployed by Ortelius and others. In contrast to the route taken, he traced the direct route
through the desert from Ramses to Gaza, called "The way from Gosen
into Palestin" that Moses had eschewed. At the outset of the journey,
Moses had decided against this straighter trajectory through desert and
mountains "from three respects, the first two naturall; the third divine."
First, when Pharaoh "received intelligence of the way which *Moses* toke,
[he] perswaded himselfe that the numbers which *Moses* led, consisting
of above a Million, if not two Millions of soules . . . could not possibly
passe over those Desart and high Mountaines with so great multitudes of
Women, Children, and Cattell." Moses' feint toward crossing the desert
prompted the complacent Pharaoh to delay his pursuit, earning more time
for the Israelites to separate from Pharoah's troops. The second reason
similarly revealed strategic expertise: "*Moses* by offering to enter *Arabia*
that way, drew *Pharaoh* towardes the East side of the Land of *Gosen*, or
Rameses: from whence (missing *Moses* there) his pursuit after him with

his Chariots was more difficult, by reason of the roughnesse of the way."
Moses, deploying the methodical observation attributed to him by Turler,
prudently led the Hebrews over a terrain that negated the Egyptian advantage in speed and power. But, most importantly, his selection of this
route was an act of faith: "*Moses* confidence in the all-powerfull God was
such, by whose spirit, only wise, he was directed, as he rather made choice
to leave the glorie of his deliverance and victorie to almightie God, than
either by an escape the next way, or by the strength of his multitude, consisting of 600000 men, to cast the successe upone his owne understanding, wise conduction, or valour."[45] Though the path of the Israelites was
approved by strategic analysis, it was directed by God, and Moses' passive
acceptance reflected his supplication to divine will.

The physical movements of the Israelites thus supplied a dynamic alle-
gory of their relationship with God. The path chosen by Moses, but guided
by the divine hand, expressed a moral peregrination illustrating the difficulty of faith. Adhering to a more tortuous route exhibited greater commitment to the benevolent custody of God. Ralegh's map articulated this
relationship by vigorously augmenting the violent tossing of the Israelites.
His choppily careening path for the Hebrews adapted and magnified other
devotional images that equated moral, linear, and peregrinatory difficulty.

HOW RALEGH MADE HISTORY

Ralegh's treatment of the resting place of Noah's Ark represents his most
sophisticated construction of a world historical narrative. His meticulous
and systematic assembly of evidence generated an inventive solution to an
age-old problem that adumbrated the potency of his expertise as a traveler
and a reader. At the same time, Ralegh evoked a providential lesson unmistakable to those familiar with the subtle interpretation demanded of
early modern readers of historical narratives.[46] His analysis of the place of
this relic thus provides an exemplary instance of his methods, techniques,
and expectations.

The Ark was a typological symbol representing both Christ and the
church. Early modern scholars enjoyed unusual near consensus on its location. Scripture stated that the Ark alighted "upon the mountains of Ararat" (Gen. 8:3), and most commentators placed this peak in Armenia. But,

---

45. *HW*, 2.3.7.258.

46. Despite the care Ralegh devoted to this section, no commentator has paid much attention to it. The most careful readings are in Denys Hay, *Europe: The Emergence of an Idea*
(Edinburgh: Edinburgh University Press, 1957); and Allen, *The Legend of Noah*.

although modern travelers to the Near East reported visiting the graves of Abraham, Isaac, and other Old Testament figures, European tourists did not frequent the sepulcher of the Ark.

After his own investigation, however, Ralegh was entirely dissatisfied with the common opinion. He wrote: "For the true place where the *Arke* rested after the floud, and from what part of the world the children of *Noah* trauailed to their first settlement and plantation, I am resolved (without any presumption) that therein the most writers were utterly mistaken." He assured his readers that he had come to this conclusion not "out of my humour or newnesse of opinion, or singularitie; but doe herein ground my selfe on the originall and first truth, which is the word of God, and after that upon reason, and most probable circumstances thereon depending." As he continued, he again restated his commitment to these tools of analysis: "For whereas it is written [Gen. 8:4] *that the Arke stayed upon one of the mountaines of Ararat . . .* I finde neither Scripture nor reason which teacheth any such thing: (to wit) that it rested on that part of *Ararat*, which is in the greater *Armenia*."[47] While Scripture clearly indicated the name of the mountain range where the Ark had come to rest, Ralegh claimed that previous commentators had only mistakenly confined these peaks to Armenia.

Ralegh mustered a bold defense against the standard interpretation, directing reason and conjecture toward scriptural exegesis and modern works. He began by identifying several problems that he perceived with an Armenian landfall. First, it had taken 130 years for Nimrod to migrate with Noah's progeny to Babel. Ralegh may have been cautious about evaluating the speed with which settlers might migrate, but, in this case, he viewed the time allotted as excessive for the task, considering the divine injunction to go forth and multiply. The Ark must have come to rest further from Babel.[48]

Ralegh laid out his next argument in the chapter "That the Easterne people were most ancient in populositie and in all humane glorie." Humanity, he argued, had peopled the Far East before the rest of the world. He noted: "The civilitie, magnificence and multitude of people (wherin the East parts of the world first abounded) hath more waight then any thing which hath beene, or can be said for *Armenia*, and for *Noahs* taking land there."[49] Given that Noah's progeny had gradually spread out from the site

47. *HW*, 1.7.10.2.113–14.
48. *HW*, 1.7.10.3.114–15.
49. *HW*, 1.7.10.4.115.

of the Ark, humanity must have been most populous where it had initially come to rest. An eastern planting explained the massive populations that Semiramis, the Assyrian empress, battled in her colonizing expedition deep into the fertile East only two generations after Nimrod.

Ralegh also found strong supporting evidence in the common opinion that the Chinese were technologically superior to Europeans. He wrote: "And that this is true, the use of Printing and Artillerie (among many other things which the East had) may easily perswade us, that those Sunne-rising Nations were the most ancient." As we have seen, this idea was drawn from Gonzalez de Mendoza's *History of China*. Ralegh explicated this claim (untested by Pett and Jackmann's failed mission) by depicting technical advancement—like population growth—as inherently progressive and produced by years of accumulated wisdom and experience. Like Gonzalez de Mendoza, he claimed that Europeans had not independently discovered printing but instead imported it from the East: "But from the Easterne world it was that *Iohn Cuthenberg* a *Germane*, brought the deuice of Printing. . . . And notwithstanding that this mysterie was then supposed to bee but newly borne, the *Chinaos* had letters long before either the *Aegyptians* or *Phoenicians*; and also the Art of Printing, when as the Greekes had neither any ciuill knowledge, or any letters among them."[50] That the Chinese developed the art of printing thousands of years earlier signaled the antiquity and advancement of their civilization. For Ralegh, Jesuit accounts of the extraordinary technology and population of the Eastern peoples surely signified that East Asian civilizations were more ancient and favored than Armenia and the Near East.

The next argument originated with the postdiluvian story of Noah. Ralegh believed that Noah must have spent the last century of his life quietly cultivating fruit for his winepress, not gallivanting about clearing postdiluvian brush and leveling muddy fields to found new colonies, as Annius had maintained.[51] He found it unlikely that Noah had ever returned as far west as Babylon: "For *Noah*, who was Father of al those Nations, a man reverenced both for his authoritie, knowledge, experience and pietie, would never have permitted his children and issues to have undertaken that unbeleeving presumptuous worke of *Babel*." Nor would his progeny have embarked on the work: "they durst not have disobayed the personall commandement of him, who in the beginning had a kinde of Regal authoritie over his children and people." The disobedience required to construct

50. Ibid.
51. *HW*, 1.7.20.6.119.

the Tower of Babel suggested that Babylon lay a considerable distance from Nimrod's disapproving great-grandfather. This separation accounted for Noah's postdiluvian disappearance from the historical record: "For hee landed in a warme and fertile soile, where hee planted his Vineyard, and drest the earth; after which, and his thanks-giving to God by sacrifice, he is not remembered in the Scriptures, because hee was so farre away from those Nations of which *Moses* wrote."[52] Sacred history focused on lands distant from where Noah had wiled away a wine-addled senectitude.

Ralegh added one more argument to the evidence he had accumulated from experience, scriptural exegesis, and Jesuit travel accounts. Like the point about elephants in Peru, his final argument appeared deceptively simple, but it was undergirded by a thicket of historicized natural knowledge. He explained: "To this if we adde the consideration of this part of the Text, *That* NOAH *planted a Vineyard*, wee shall finde that the fruite of the Vine or Raysin did not grow naturally in that part of *Armenia*, where this resting of the *Arke* was supposed."[53] Noah's lush vines required a landscape far different from barren Armenia. Posing problems that undermined the conventional location of Ararat within Armenia, Ralegh prepared his readers for his revisionist solution.

Ralegh continued to build the case that the "metropolis of all the world's nations" where the Ark alighted was well east of Armenia by absorbing evidence that had seemed to support other locations. Annius had located Mount Ararat in Armenia and, as we have seen, claimed that Noah had spent many years traveling throughout the world before ultimately settling in Viterbo. To substantiate this claim, Annius had forged a lost work by Marcus Porcius Cato, *De originibus*, which gave the Armenians origins among the Scythians, that ill-defined race of militaristic Eurasian barbarians. Ralegh agreed with Annius in one detail of this analysis, but he dismissed the overall picture. He granted: "Herein truly I agree with *Annius*, that those Regions called *Scythia* . . . were among the first peopled." But he argued that a misreading of *De originibus*—one of his own forgeries— had mistakenly led Annius to place Scythia in Armenia. Annius, Ralegh explained, had elsewhere altered a passage from Cato to strengthen his own claim. While the Annian Cato had written "in Scythia Saga renatum mortale genus, in Scythia Saga mankinde was restored," Ralegh noted that Annius "in the *Prooeme* of his Commentaries upon *Berosus*, leaveth out the addition of *Saga* altogether in the repetition of *Cato* his wordes, and

52. *HW*, 1.7.10.6.118.
53. *HW*, 1.7.10.8.121.

writes in *homines Scythia salvatos.*" He argued that eliminating the word
Saga had led Annius to misidentify the site of the Ark, for *Scythia* and
Scythia Saga referred to two different places. The name *Scythia Saga*, he
explained, had metastasized until in Ptolemy's time it was called *Sacara*.[54]
Citing Ptolemy's seventh map, Ralegh argued that this location was "undoubtedly under the mountaines of *Paropanisus*, on which, or neare which
it is most probable that the *Arke* first tooke ground."[55] This region lay
along the Paropanisus, a range within the Caucasus, southeast of the Caspian Sea, where ancient Bactria and Sogdiana abutted a region called Paropanisus and the northern frontiers of India.[56]

Ralegh responded to Annius's inconsistency, then, by turning to Ptolemy. He marshaled further citations from the Venetian Dominicus Marius
Niger's 1557 *Geographiae Commentariorum Libri*, Reinier Reineck's edition of Marco Polo in his 1585 collection *Historia Orientalis*, and then the
account of the early sixteenth-century Polish physician Matthias Michou
in Grynaeus's *Novus Orbis*. These showed that Armenia was distinct from
Scythia while confirming that the ancient Scythians had never reached
Armenia. At the same time, however, Ralegh retained the suggestion of
Annius's Cato that Noah had dismounted in Scythian lands. And he provided his own solution for how these mountains in the Caucasus gained
the name *Ararat* in a virtuoso piece of idiosyncratic historical geographic
argumentation. He explained: "wee must understand, that *Ararat* (named
by *Moses*) is not any one hill, so called, no more then any one hill among
those mountaines which divide *Italie* from *France* is called the *Alpes*: or
any one among those which part *France* from *Spaine* is the *Pyrenian*; but
as these being continuations of many hils keepe one name in divers Countries." The Ararat was a mountain range, not only an individual peak. Indeed, the Ararat conventionally located in Armenia helpfully indicated
which range the term referred to, for "all that long ledge of mountaines,

54. *HW*, 1.7.10.7.119. Annius's omission may have been intentional—Stephens ("Berosus
Chaldaeus") has suggested that Annius included such missteps in imitation of the authentic
historical record. Ralegh's reading here was highly selective; Annius had placed cities with the
word *Saga* all over the world as signs of places where divine priests had once practiced.

55. *HW*, 1.7.10.7.119. Note Ptolemy, *Geographia*, trans. Edward Luther Stevenson (Mineola:
Dover, 1991), 6.12. "The boundary of Sacara on the west is Sogdiana on the side of which . . . is
this country's eastern border. The northern boundary looks toward Scythia, the boundary line
running along the bend of the Jaxartes river."

56. For the medieval and early modern European understandings of this region, see Margaret Meserve, "From Samarkand to Scythia: Reinventions of Asia in Renaissance Geography
and Political Thought," in *Pius II: El piu expeditivo pontifice: Selected Studies on Aeneas
Silvius Piccolomini*, ed. Z. R. W. M. von Martels and A. Vanderjagt (Leiden: Brill, 2003), and
Empires of Islam.

which *Plinie* calleth by one name *Taurus*, and *Ptolomie* both *Taurus*, *Niphates*, *Coatras*, *Coronus*, *Sariphi*, untill they encounter and crosse the mountaines of the great *Imaus*, are of one generall name, and are called the Mountaines of *Ararat* or *Armenia*, because from thence or thereabout they seem to arise." Ptolemy, Ralegh claimed, had given the Ararat's sub-ranges different names "the better to distinguish the great Regions and Kingdomes, which these great mountaines bound and dissever."[57] But, in fact, the Ararat extended from Armenia to India, and Ralegh noted that the Sogdianan branch of the range was called the Paropanisus.

Having established that Ararat could refer to a location in the Caucasus, Ralegh returned to the question of Noah's oenology. The renowned vegetation of the Paropanisus, he argued, evinced a fertile environment perfect for viticulture: "In this part of the World are found the best Vines, so it is as true, that in the same line, and in 34.35 and 36 degrees of Septentrionall latitude are the most delicate Wines of the World . . . and under these Mountaines, *Strabo* affirmeth that the most excellent Vines of the World are found; the clusters of Grapes containing two cubits of length."[58] Once again, natural clues led to historical answers. The vine provided a sign traceable and transmittable throughout history. This was the precise sort of evidence that contemporary travelers collected and that Ortelius and Scaliger prized, here drawn from an ancient authority to confirm Ralegh's novel philological and geographical analysis.

Ralegh thus located the Ark in the Paraponisus Mountains at the intersection of the ancient regions of Sogdiana, Bactria, and Paraponisus (see fig. 12). Humanity was saved high in the icy buttes of the Caucasus. Ralegh, belatedly, acknowledged that this identification followed a dubious predecessor. As he explained: "On these highest mountaines of that part of the World did *Goropius Becanus* conceive that the *Arke* of *Noah* grounded after the Flood: of all his coniectures the most probable, and by best reason approved."[59] Though Ralegh's arguments were entirely his own, his primary precedent for the idea of an eastern landfall for the Ark was the Antwerpian court physician Joannes Becanus Goropius. As noted earlier, in his 1569 *Origines Antwerpianae*, Goropius had argued that the original language spoken by Adam had been Goropius's own native Antwerpian Flemish. Goropius had carved out an intricate history of the

---

57. *HW*, 1.7.10.13.125. Note that Ralegh continued: ". . . as all those Mountaines which cut asunder *America*, even from the new Kingdome of *Granado*, to the streight of *Magellan*, are by one name called *Andes*." Ibid.

58. *HW*, 1.7.10.14.126.

59. Ibid.

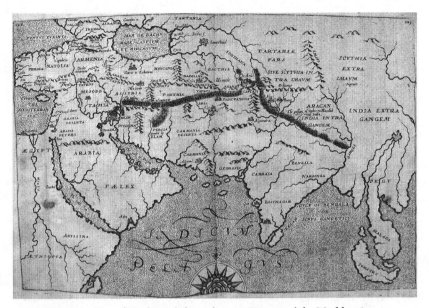

Figure 12. Map of Noah's Ark from the 1614 *History of the World*, 128–29.
Special Collections Research Center, Swem Library, College of William and Mary,
shelf mark D57. R16 1614.

Antwerpian people. By locating the settling of the Ark in the Caucasus
and showing that the ancestors of the Antwerpians had initially migrated
north into Scythia when all other peoples had traveled west toward Babylon, he was able to claim that the Ur-Flems had not been at Babylon, had
not been subject to the confusion of languages, and, therefore, continued
to speak the original Adamic tongue—a sure sign of divine favor. Goropius thus used Annius's tools to invest Antwerp and its denizens with a
potent dignity at a time when the war-ravaged city was in constant need of
aid from Philip II.

Ralegh ridiculed Goropius several times in the *History*, particularly
objecting to the Antwerpian's disbelief in giants. He also chastised Goropius for bragging that he was the first to correctly identify the Tree of the
Knowledge of Good and Evil as a fig tree when the same claim had been
made by the ninth-century exegete Moses Barcephas, "whose very wordes
Goropius useth, both concerning the Tree, and the reasons wherewith
he would induce other men to that beliefe."[60] Ralegh did not tax himself

---

60. *HW*, 1.4.2.67. I have not found such verbatim citation of Barcephas in Goropius's
work.

as severely, although he had hardly been forthcoming in identifying his source for his placement of the Ark. In fact, his strong embrace of Goropius's revisionist account of the Ark reflected a somewhat unusual response to a transparently political Catholic revisionist history. Though Ralegh had been willing to ignore the contemporary implications of Montano's controversial identification of Ophir and Peru, he did not adhere to Montano's proof. And he frequently had been unforgiving to Catholics who had concocted extravagant histories of the ancient world to provide self-serving illustrious genealogies, for example, chastising Bozio, ridiculing Annius's conflation of Janus with Noah, and deriding the learned Spanish Jesuit Juan de Pineda for locating Tharsis (the second source of Solomon's gold) in Spain rather than Carthage.[61] But he overlooked the unabashedly propagandistic basis of Goropius's history and subscribed to his placement of the Ark. Nor did he recalibrate Goropius's history of the postdiluvian plantation to argue that English was the pure Adamic language or that the Britons were peculiarly entrusted with God's favor.

Rather than rebuke Goropius's Flemophiliac world history, in fact, Ralegh adapted his jingoistic version of the deep past for his own personal purposes. How Goropius's Indoscythian Ark aided Ralegh's reconstitution of the past can be understood only by returning to Ralegh's notebook and the history that he attributed to the Caucasus when he commenced work on the *History*. Ralegh devoted five consecutive pages in his notebook—two to maps, three to notes (two of which are reproduced here)—to these Eastern lands far from the beaten track of contemporary European maritime exploration (see figs. 13–16). The maps reworked Ptolemy's seventh map of Asia. The textual extracts did not come from ancient sources; rather, they were taken from the French royal historiographer Francois Belleforest's 1575 edition of Sebastian Münster's *Cosmographia* and from Marius Niger.

Ralegh culled the ancient and modern names of geographical features in Bactria from the work of Belleforest, one of Ralegh's standard sources for Asian geography. He noted that the river known to the ancients as the Ochus was called by the moderns Oboenger and that this river "riseth out of the Paropanisus, now Nochdarizari."[62] The Paropanisus formed Bactria's southern border, and the Ochus flowed north to the Oxus River on its northern border, which, in turn, streamed into the Caspian Sea. Ralegh

---

61. For the attack on Pineda, see *HW*, 2.18.3.499. For that on Annius, see *HW*, 1.8.5.139–40.

62. *NB*, fol. 70v (fig. 13). See Francois Belleforest, ed., *La Cosmographie Universelle* (Paris, 1575), 2.1445. ". . . Ochus, que les modernes appelent *Oboengir*. . . . Il a sa source au mont Paropanise, dit à present *Nochdarizari*."

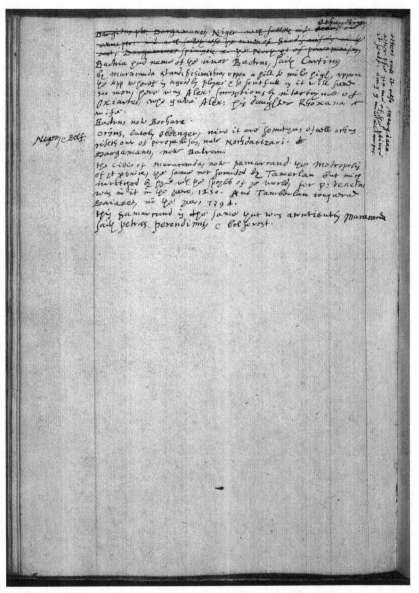

Figure 13. Ralegh's notes on Bactria. © The British Library Board.
BL Add. MS 57555, fol. 70v.

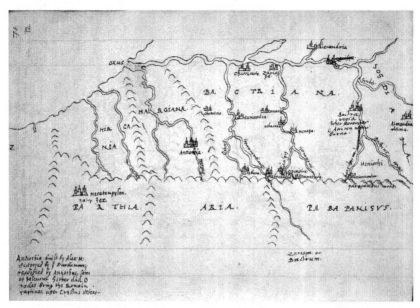

Figure 14. Map of Bactria from Ralegh's notebook. © The British Library Board.
BL Add. MS 57555, fol. 72r.

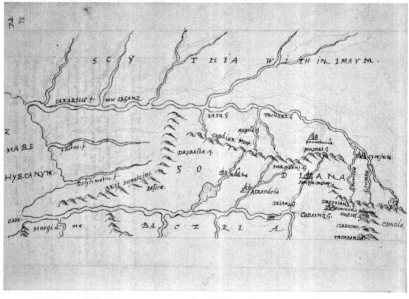

Figure 15. Map of Sogdiana from Ralegh's notebook. © The British Library Board.
BL Add. MS 57555, fol. 73r.

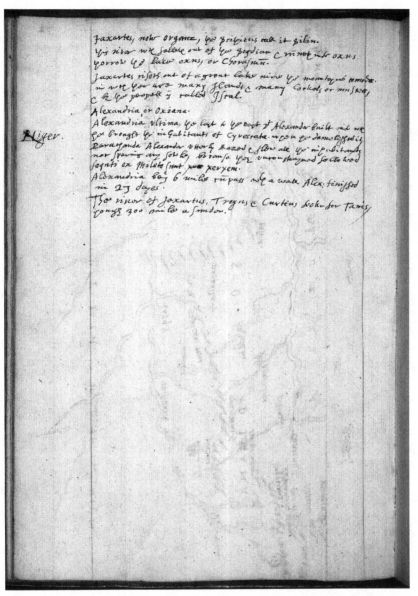

Figure 16. Ralegh's notes on Alexandria Ultima and the Iaxartes.
© The British Library Board. BL Add. MS 57555, fol. 72v.

also relied on Belleforest for the history of this region. He cribbed: "The cittie of Maracanda, now Samarcand, the Metropolis of yt province, the same not founded by Tamerlan but much increased by hym wth the spoyle of ye world, for P: Venetus [Marco Polo] was in it in the yeere 1250. And Tamberlan conquered Baiazet, in the yeare 1394."[63] Ralegh, like Marlowe, used Belleforest as a source for the archetypal Eastern despot Tamburlaine.

Bactria was not only the site of Tamburlaine's savage cruelties but also a possession of the great Khans, the murderous barbarians who dominated the Eastern world with their terror-inspiring rampages. Marco Polo's writings were a main source for these violent Scythians, and their warlike nature was well-known. Tamburlaine and the Khans were only the modern odious people associated with Bactria. The Assyrian Empire had been enlarged massively when Emperor Ninus, the grandson of Nimrod, had defeated Zoroaster, king of Bactria, around the time of Abraham's birth. Of this Zoroaster, Ralegh noted: "*S. Augustine* noteth that *Zoroaster* was said to have laught at his birth, when all other children weepe; which presaged the great knowledge which afterward he attained unto: being taken for the Inventer of naturall *Magicke* and other Arts; for the Corrupter, saith *Plinie* and *Iustine*."[64] While Ralegh did not believe that the Zoroaster who had been defeated by Ninus had invented diabolic magical arts, Belleforest did, with commensurate horror. He described "that King Zoroaster, the first who abused the sciences and perverted true philosophies, calling on malignant spirits. And he instituted that abuse excessively imitated ever since, the belief that men's lives were controlled by these spirits and by celestial bodies."[65] Bactria's history consisted of gruesome violence, the horrific pollution of learning, and devil worship.

---

63. *NB*, fol. 70v (fig. 13). Belleforest, *La Cosmographie Universelle*, 2.1446. "Royaume de Samarcand, ainsi dit la cité capital d'iceluy, que les anciens ont nommee Maracande, & ainsi on se tromperoit, qui disoit que Tamerlan en ayt esté la fondateur, luy suffisant de l'avoir aggrandie, & enrichie (comme dirons) des despouilles de tour l'univers . . . de ceste cité fait mention Marc Pol Venitien lors qu'il dit ainsi: Samarcand est une noble cité, en laquelle il y a de tresbeaux iardins & une campaigne abondante en toute sorte de fruits, que l'homme scauroit desirer: les habitans de laquelle sont in partie Chrestiens, partie Mahometistes, & faicts au grand Cham de Tartare: mais un sien niveu la rendit, qui n'estoit point amy du souverain, ains ont continuellement guerres & inimitié ensemble. Ie vous ay allegué ce venitien qui fut en cette ville environ l'an de nostre Seigneur 1250 pour preuve qu'elle est plus ancienne cite de la faire de la fondation de Tamerlan, lequel à vescu depuis, & n'estoit encore né hors que le susdit Venitien escrivit son histoire: car Tamerlan vainquit Baiazeth Roy Turc (ainsi qu'avons dit) l'an de grace 1394."

64. *HW*, 1.11.1.199–200.

65. Belleforest, *La Cosmographie Universelle*, 2.1445. ". . . les hommes qui iadis sont nez en elle, comme des les premiers siecles elle fut mere de ce Roy Zoroast le premier qui abusa

But there were other historical events associated with the region, and fully understanding why Ralegh located the Ark on its unforgiving borders requires turning to the notes he took while reading the work of Marius Niger. Very little is known about Niger beyond the fact that he also edited a 1518 edition of Ovid's *Amores*, but, after the Petri printing house's 1557 edition of his *Geographiae*, he enjoyed a wide readership in Elizabethan England. Wolfgang Wissenburg, the editor of this edition, explained in his preface that the manuscript version of the work was "tarnished both by neglect and by worms, but it also had been polluted and depraved by a certain corruptor into whose hands it unfortunately had come." Correcting the manuscript had taken significant labor, as Wissenberg explained: "if not for repeated intense reading of the ancients, I would not have been able to understand the genuine sense and mind of the author and restore his places and meanings."[66] Correcting Niger's commentaries against ancient texts might have been a suspect method for a travel narrative, but it ably reconstructed his method of compilation. Niger had constructed the text by synthesizing ancient geographical and historical works into an experiential narrative, and his information on Bactria and Sogdiana was cribbed almost entirely from Ptolemy's material, with periodic additions from Plutarch, Quintus Curtius, and others. Thus, Wissenberg's technique of correction imitated Niger's method of composition.

Ralegh often cited Niger regarding the geography of Asia both in the notebook and in the *History,* and he relied heavily on Niger for Bactria and Sogdiana. Niger's descriptions of these areas appeared both in Ralegh's notes and on the maps themselves. Ralegh originally copied the maps from Ptolemy, but certain crucial differences existed between contemporary printed Ptolemaic maps and Ralegh's manuscript versions (see figs. 15–16 above). On the Bactria map, Ralegh attached a spur named the Bactria Oxus to the most eastern river (south of Bactria Regia) and added an additional river, the Sindis, to its north. Two new cities, Sisimithra and Eu-

---

des sciences, & pervertit la vraie philosophie, appellant les malings esprits: & instituant l'abus trop depius imité, d'astraindre les hommes & aux esprits, & aux corps celestes."

66. Dominicus Marius Niger, *Geographiae Commentariorum libri* (Basel, 1557), †5v. "Caeterum quot, quibusve mendis, nos commentaria haec purgaverimus, aut quas lacunas sustulerimus, dicant qui viderunt, de me enim ipso nihil praedicabo, non enim solum a situ & tineis corrosum fuit exemplar (e quibus Arnoldus Arleninus, vir, ut solertissimus, ita bonis literis iuvandis studiosissimus, illud, felici ut speramus omine eruit nobisque communicavit) verum etiam a Sciolo quodam, in cuius manus satis infeliciter venerat, ita immutatum & depravatum fuit, ut ipsius quoque authoris integritatem & eruditionem saepius mihi fecisset suspectam, si non veterum lectione repetita, non absque magno labore, authoris mentem & genuinum sensum cognovissem, suisque restituissem locis."

crathida, were placed just north of Paropanisus. The city of Bactria Regia was annotated: "where Zoroaster and Avicen were borne." On the map of Sogdiana, finally, he added the city of Parachanda in the northeast.

Each of these differences can be attributed to Ralegh marking his manuscript copy of Ptolemy's map with evidence gleaned from reading Niger. After transcribing the features of Ptolemy's map, then, he opened his copy of Niger, and, carefully poring over the Venetian's narrative, he inscribed new elements on his manuscript map to represent the features seemingly omitted by the ancient. Ralegh read Niger as a source supplementing Ptolemy, whose revisions and improvements he included—precisely as Niger had augmented Ptolemy with Plutarch and Quintus Curtius. Ralegh's addition of an eastern river, in fact, came from an excerpt Niger had drawn from Quintus Curtius. Niger had written: "According to Curtius, there is a fourth river, the Bactrius, more easterly than all the others, flowing out of the said mountain [the Paropanisus], which flows straight into the Oxus, and the region takes its name from this river."[67] Niger had also taken the city of Eucrathida from Quintus Curtius, adding: "And the city of Eucrathida, named for its king, lies near the ridge of the Paropanisus, towards the east."[68] Niger—more sanguine about suspect Eastern arts than Belleforest—had commented on "Bactria . . . where rumor holds that the most learned doctor of medicine, Avicenna, and Zoroaster were born, for we read that here in the times of the ancients the study of good arts did flourish."[69] Reading these passages, Ralegh accordingly inscribed rivers, cities, and the names of these two luminaries on his map.

The final difference in his Bactria map—the addition of the city of Sisimithra—pours crucial light onto the significance that Ralegh attributed to this part of the world. On the following page, he had cribbed from Niger: "by Maracanda stands Sisimithra uppon a hill 2 mile high, uppon the topp wherof is a goodly playne & so frutfulle as it will feed 500 men, here was Alex: [Alexander] sumptiously intertayned of Oxiartes, who gave Alex: his daughter Rhoxana to wife."[70] The addition of Parachanda on the

67. Ibid., 556. "Quartus Bactrius omnibus his orientalior, a dicto iam monte effusus, in Oxam recta influit: a quo fluvio regionem habere nomen Curcius autor est."

68. Ibid. "Et circa Paropanisum iugum prope Zariaspem ad orientem Eucrathida urbs ab imperante cognominata."

69. Ibid. "Bactria . . . ubi medicorum doctissimus Avicenna, & Zoroaster nati fama fert, nam & ibi prisci temporibus bonarum artium studia floruisse legimus."

70. NB, fol. 72v (fig. 17 below). Niger, Geographiae Commentariorum libri, 556. "Iuxta vero Dargamanem Maracanda, Aqua haud procul Sisimithre petra munitissima est, altitudine passuum duorum mil ambitu decem in superiori parte, plana & ferax, ut viros quinquenteos

Sogdiana map also derived from Niger's incorporation of passages from Quintus Curtius. Ralegh excerpted from Niger: "Alexandria ultima, the last in the east yt Alexander built he brought the inhabitants of Cyrescata when he demolisshed it. Parachanda Alexander utterly Razed, & slew all the inhabitants not sparing a sowle, because they unconstrayned followed sequti ex Mileto sunt Xerxem [Xerxes from Miletus]."[71] This reading certainly derived from Niger and not Quintus Curtius because the city Parachanda derived from a corruption or alternate reading of Quintus Curtius 7.5.28: "Perventum erat in parvulum oppidum. Branchidae eius incolae erant. Mileto quondam iussi Xerxis. . . ." Niger had read *Parachanda* for *parvulum* (very small), and Ralegh had echoed his conjuration of a city from a diminutive. Both maps, finally, noted an Alexandria north of Bactria in Sogdiana and, to the southeast, "Alexandria Ultima," the city constructed by Alexander to mark his furthest penetration into the East. Alexander the Great's subjection of this region had, these accounts revealed, exerted a lasting impact on its political geography.

These maps, likely rendered around 1607, contained no mention of the resting place of the Ark. But Ralegh eventually placed this most sacred relic precisely on the Paropanisan Mountains that divided Sogdiana and Bactria. The resting place he gave the Ark thus lay in a famously fertile location near the terminus of Alexander the Great's Eastern expedition. And one passage in the notebook, taken from Niger, suggests Ralegh's first steps toward this conclusion: "The vines about Antiocha [a city noted in Margiana, to the west of Bactria] exceed all others: two men can hardly encircle their trunks, and they have boughs of two cubits."[72] In his early forays into Niger, this note reveals, Ralegh began to accumulate the natural historical evidence that eventually substantiated his Eastern-grounded Ark.[73]

---

alere posset; In ea scribit Strabo Alexander & hospitio sumptuose acceptus est, & Rhoxanam Oxiartis filiam uxorem duxit."

71. *NB*, fol. 72v. Niger, *Geographiae Commentariorum libri*, 558. "Civitates autem in Sogdiana sunt, ad Iaxartem Cyreschata a quibusdam Cyria in montibus a Cyro condita, eius ultimum opus, imperii sui terminus, quod Alexander propter continuas rebelliones evertit. Dein Parachanda oppidulum Branchidarum fuit, quod Alexander ab imis fundamentis moliri iussit, ne quod eius vestigium extaret, oppidanosque ad unum caedere, quoniam huc sponte sequuti ex Mileto sunt Xerxem."

72. *NB*, fol. 71v. The note reads: "the vines about Antiocha exceed all others, quorum truncos duo viri vix complecti quent. Ramum duorum cubitorum [*sic*]." See Niger, *Geographiae Commentariorum libri*, 554. "Est enim locus vites optimas habens, quarum nonnullos truncos duo viri vix complecti queunt, rammum duorum cubitorum."

73. For a different version of this technique, see Nancy Siraisi, "*Historiae*, Natural History, Roman Antiquity, and Some Roman Physicians," in Pomata and Siraisi, eds., *Historia*, 325–54.

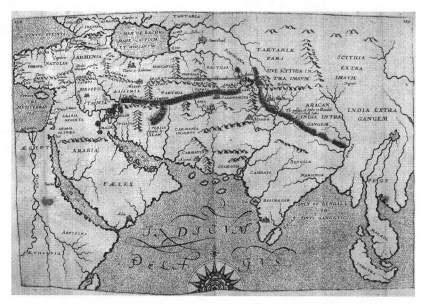

Figure 17. Map of Noah's Ark from the 1614 *History of the World* (fig. 12 above)
with Alexander's path swerving from the Ark superimposed.

When, by 1614, Ralegh had buried the Ark in this craggy sepulcher, it
must have been clear to him that Alexander's Eastern penetration passed
within a short journey of the Ark (fig. 17). Alexander's excursion around
the Caucasus to the Indus skirted the sacred mountain peak. This proximity to the Ark would have conferred a providential charge to the journey as Alexander, returning to the metropolis from which all nations were
spawned to create an empire that dwarfed anything the world had ever
seen, neared a physical object that typologically stood for both the body of
Christ and the church. But Alexander had not recovered the sacred relic.
Indeed, Ralegh was thoroughly unimpressed with the Macedonian's journey.[74] Alexander's march to the east had been accompanied by wanton cruelty, drunkenness, and vice, and Ralegh believed that his success resulted
more from circumstance than from skill. He scoffed at triumphs over effeminate Persians and unwarlike Indians, claiming that Alexander could
never have defeated a well-equipped Roman army. His final analysis aired
his low regard: "If we compare this great Conqueror with other Troublers
of the World, who have bought their glorie with so great destruction, and

74. Anna Beer has discussed Ralegh's dislike of Alexander fully in *Sir Walter Ralegh and
His Readers.*

effusion of bloud, I thinke him farre inferiour to *Caesar*, and many other that lived after him . . . it seemeth, Fortune and Destinies (if we may use those termes) had found out and prepared for him, without any care of his owne, both heapes of Men, that willingly offered their necks to the yoke, and Kingdomes, that invited and called in their owne Conquerours."[75]

Never in the Alexander story did Ralegh mention his proximity to the Ark's resting place, but, as his subsequent narrative made clear, Alexander missed the Ark as a result, not of fortune or serendipity, but of divine judgment on his immorality and iniquity. The features on Ralegh's manuscript maps—both those copied from Ptolemy and those drawn from Niger to which Ralegh attributed entirely conjectural locations—showed Alexander's line of movement. He had founded Antioch, as Ralegh noted below the map in a note taken from Ortelius.[76] Moving eastward, he had been to Maracanda and to the formidable fortress Sisimithres.[77] Were Alexander to have continued east along the foothills of the Paropanisus, his army would have brushed up against the resting place of the Ark. Instead, he deviated north in glory-hungry pursuit of the cowardly Bactrian king Bessus. He founded a city in southern Sogdiana, then swung north to Parachanda. From there he headed south along the tributaries of the Iaxartes but beyond the sepulchre of the Ark, eventually winding back around to found Alexandria Ultima. Deflected by his pursuit of Bessus, Alexander's troops had traversed a crescent around the Ark.

Though the notebook did not continue discussion of Alexander's path, its depiction of Bactria can be correlated with the narrative of the journey and the map of the location of the Ark in the *History*. Just preceding the narrative of Alexander's swerve from Bactria into India is a chapter entitled "How Alexander slew his owne friends." Ralegh recounted Alexander's increasingly drunken acts of murderous revenge and the violence he perpetrated and condoned toward some of his most valuable lieutenants. As Alexander passed north of the Ark into tempestuous northeastern Scythian lands, Ralegh noted, his barbarities toward his followers worsened. In particular, Ralegh criticized the murder of his loyal counselor Callisthenes in a passage worth quoting at length:

In the meane while hee [Alexander] would needes bee honoured as a God . . . *Callisthenes* . . . among many other honest arguments used

75. *HW*, 4.2.23.211.
76. Ralegh's note on *NB*, fol. 71r, derives from Ortelius, *Thesaurus Geographicus*, F3r.
77. *HW*, 4.2.18.202.

to the assembly, he told *Cleo*, That he thought that *Alexander* would
disdaine the gift of God-head from his Vassalls; That the opinion of
Sanctitie, though it did sometime follow the death of those, who in
their life-time had done the greatest thinges, yet it never accompanied
any one as yet living in the World. He further told him, That neither
Hercules nor *Bacchus* were Deified at a banquet, and upon drinke, (for
this matter was propounded by *Cleo* at a carowsing feast) but that, for
the more than manly acts by them performed while they lived, they
were in future and succeeding Ages numbred among the Gods. *Alexander* stood behinde a partition and heard all that was spoken, waiting
but an opportunitie to be revenged on *Callisthenes*, who being a man
of free speech, honest, learned, and a lover of the Kings honour, was
yet soone after tormented to death, not for that hee had betraied the
King to others: but because hee never would condescend to betray the
King to himselfe, as all his detestable flatterers did. For in a conspira-
cie against the King made by one *Hermolaus* and others (which they
confest) he caused *Callisthenees* without confession, accusation, or
triall, to be torne a-sunder upon the racke.[78]

Ralegh concurred with Seneca's assessment that Alexander's execution of
the innocent Callisthenes would be remembered as his "eternal crime."

Ralegh likely read himself as Callisthenes, the truth-telling and loyal
counselor—and, furthermore, another learned traveler—alienated by a
corrupt and drunken court. Like Ralegh, Callisthenes had been persecuted
without recourse to a proper trial despite a reneging accuser; like Callisthenes, Ralegh fretted that kings must guard against the temptations of
self-deification promoted by flatterers.[79] And Ralegh surely saw Alexander's mistreatment of his counselors as being expressed in moral terms by
his swerving from the Ark. Alexander's abuse of power, degradation of his
loyal followers, overextension of his prerogatives, and encroachment on
the realm of the divine were expressed through a dynamic moral geography in which he barely overshot recovery of the typological relic of both
Christ and the church. As the Israelites had been subject to more tortuous wandering in the desert for contravening God's will, so had Alexander been denied knowledge of the Ark. His misgovernment and rejection

---

78. *HW*, 4.2.20.205.

79. Previous scholars have tended to see Ralegh's self-parallels as strongest with Hannibal
(cf. Beer, *Sir Walter Ralegh and His Readers*; and Salas, "Ralegh and the Punic Wars") and De-
metrius (cf. Jack H. Adamson and H. F. Folland, *The Shepherd of the Ocean: An Account of Sir
Walter Ralegh and His Times* (Boston: Gambit, 1969), 398.

of good counsel—transparently comparable to James's initial rejection of Ralegh—deprived him of truly divine knowledge.

Ralegh's rebuke of James, however, was by no means an incitement to rebellion. Instead, it was both personal and political, an expertly delivered censure that characterized Ralegh as a debased prophet whose mistreatment signaled James's corruption. But it also indicated to James how to correct his own errors and, thus, bespoke Ralegh's desire to regain his sovereign's favor. In this case, Ralegh's kinetic providential history revealed his abhorrence of Alexander's bellicosity and exemplified the necessity of his own erudite counsel.

CONCLUSION

Travel inflected all early modern histories, for it provided a profound basis for explaining change. Tracking human movements became a primary task for historians, for skillful manipulation of ancient travels enabled them to restore the broken mirror of the past by correlating sources across traditions and explaining earthly transformations. His personal experience as an explorer and travel administrator gave Ralegh a prized expertise, for it allowed him to deduce whether the conjectures of other scholars were practically feasible and instilled credibility in his interpretations of such motions. But this experience was not something that he could independently have chosen for himself. Rather, his own travel, he believed, had been providentially orchestrated to bestow on him the expertise that qualified him to write the *History*.

Early modern historical practice was a technical art, and Ralegh's relocation of the resting place of Noah's Ark and the *omphalos* of all peoples represented a paradigmatic episode of early modern historical scholarship and analysis. Ralegh began the process by deploying the tools of the antiquarian, combing through wide-ranging sources, and compiling extracts in which were embedded vital clues. In the *History*, he reanimated these fragments of the historical record with judgment, reason, and logic into a coherent narrative that was certified by his experience administering travel. And this deeply revisionist analysis of Alexander's near miss of the Ark itself supplied an exemplary episode illuminating the providential significance of travel. To those readers seeking sacred significance in Ralegh's vibrant world history, the movements of Alexander would have been legible as a morality tale in which a dominating emperor squandered his chance at divine knowledge. In this instance, Ralegh revealed himself as a skilled prophetic historical counselor.

The emphasis placed on the utility of travel as a historical explanation for change, moreover, revealed a shift in the task adopted by the historian. While previous historians had primarily viewed their task as recorders, vessels of revelation, rhetoricians, or polemicists, sixteenth-century historians increasingly viewed themselves as animating evidence to restore the theater of history. As Ralegh's relocation of the Ark shows, these reconsiderations often generated novel theories that challenged firm scholarly consensus. For Ralegh believed himself to have exposed a fundamental mistake deeply embedded within scholarly culture, the revelation of which suggested the need to reassess many elements of the world's history and whose providential and public lessons supplied unmistakable direction for contemporary affairs. Like Goropius, Montano, Ortelius, Bozio, Annius, and so many others, he believed that the present suffered because it inherited a history riddled with error. His solution questioned received truths by formulating a distinct, and disruptive, narrative of the ancient world. These efforts to restore true knowledge instead introduced new ideas, multiplying competing visions without imposing a single, universally held history.

It is clear that Ralegh thoroughly imbibed the perceived value of history that many early modern scholars had described. It is clear as well that he had learned the technical skills that these advocates had recommended. His production of the *History* extended his self-assumed duties of counsel by illuminating causes and effects throughout the past. He saw in the historical method a mode of observation and analysis that would allow him to recognize causes and to reveal the divine significance of all earthly phenomena, from Alexander's travels, to the location of Ophir, to the age of the world. He expertly performed the antiquarian, geographical, and chronological labors necessary to compose a history that contained powerful arguments and examples for conduct and behavior, sustained by his own unique narrative of past events. His mobilization of travel in the *History* reveals an adept participant in a contemporary historical culture, capable of performing the technical labor necessary to interpret causes in the past and to counsel a king in the present. In the following chapter, I will further examine how the didactic lessons he drew from his historical investigations invoked Providence to persuade James to adopt a militaristic, anti-Spanish program with Ralegh at its head, despite the king's long-standing resistance to this policy.

CHAPTER FIVE

Presentation:
Political Practice and the Past

Ralegh's *History* emerged from a culture of learned counsel that inextricably linked historical knowledge and political advice. His methods of constructing his text exhibited his capacity to compile sources, extract evidence, and animate narratives. These meticulous excavations implemented principles of analysis designed to reveal causation and facilitate the formation of prudent counsel favored by reverence for Providence.

The examinations of political problems in the *History* demonstrate that, despite his imprisonment, Ralegh continued to view himself as a royal adviser. In particular, he gave close analyses to the development and reception of military counsel. His experience crusading against the Spanish represented both a potent expertise and a source of conflict with his pacifist king. From the beginning of his reign in England, James had promulgated a pro-Spanish, pacifist policy, propelled by the belief that he held the responsibility of guiding Christendom from rampant confessional warfare toward a settlement accommodating different species of Christianity. Similarly, he had advanced a domestic ecclesiastical policy that proclaimed itself the via media between Puritanism and Catholicism.[1] These policies incurred special hostility from Puritans, who despaired that the king's policies would succor Catholicism at home and abroad. Their concerns were compounded by James's perceived thralldom to counselors such as Cecil and courtier favorites such as Robert Carr. As overlapping crises struck James's faltering government in 1614, Ralegh framed his experience

---

1. Kenneth Fincham and Peter Lake, "The Ecclesiastical Policy of James I," *JBS* 24 (1985): 169–207; Milton, *Catholic and Reformed*; Quantin, *The Church of England and Christian Antiquity*.

to appeal to a king potentially receptive to the hawkish policies he had rejected for the past decade.

Ralegh portrayed himself as able to coordinate an anti-Spanish policy by identifying the past exemplars appropriate for James's situation. He also strove to diminish the significance of his apparent disagreements with the king without deploying excessive flattery, thereby suggesting that he could bridge the differences sundering James and his more intransigent subjects. Finally, he emphasized the risk attendant on ignoring his work by portraying the political lessons it imparted as guided by Providence.

Though modern historians have tended to entangle anti-Spanish and anti-Stuart sentiment in early modern Britain, Ralegh carefully distinguished between the two. Indeed, his political analyses were directed to persuade the Stuarts of the necessity of an anti-Spanish policy. The *History* did not challenge James's right to rule, and the lessons Ralegh perceived in the past do not support the idea, as some have suggested, that a scholarly immersion in classical learning in early modern Europe stimulated radical political theory.[2] As we have seen in his narrative of Alexander's journey, Ralegh's historical examinations deployed conventions of critical counsel to appeal to his monarch. The *History* furnishes little evidence that such scholarship invariably led to either republican ideology or republican practice; instead, Ralegh's efforts were directed toward strengthening a king perceived as weak.

The redefinition of political expertise as rooted in historical observation did not dramatically change the range of political ideologies acceptable in early modern Europe. Nonetheless, Ralegh's work reflected the transformations that historical education wrought in politics. Importing the methods emphasized by historical study to politics reshaped the practices of early modern counselors by producing an unprecedented emphasis on the collection and manipulation of information, exemplified by the intensifying concern for the custody of archives as instruments of power. Use of historical sources, like all methods constitutive of the historical culture, could galvanize radical arguments, and, as James's suspicion of the Society of Antiquaries recognized, those who directed these modes of inquiry toward British history might yield visions of the past that sharply threatened the contemporary order. But such narratives flowed from the

2. Compare Skinner, *The Foundations of Modern Political Thought,* and *Reason and Rhetoric in the Philosophy of Hobbes;* Tuck, *Philosophy and Government;* Peltonen, *Classical Humanism and Republicanism in English Political Thought;* and Andrew Fitzmaurice, *Humanism and America: An Intellectual History of English Colonisation, 1500–1625* (Cambridge: Cambridge University Press, 2003).

methods of historical culture no more readily than those affirming absolutist authority, and the primary political consequence of the absorption
of the dictates of European historical culture into British politics was less
an ideological shift than an alteration in the practices of governance. The
History reveals how Ralegh strove to persuade James of his expertise in
this regard while producing persuasive providential counsel.

POLITICAL MORALITY AND THE
ORIGINS OF GOVERNMENTS

Ralegh believed that the rise and fall of states mirrored God's reward of
virtue and punishment of vice. But governments flourished and declined
according to an inscrutable divine plan, and, while the alterations of states
correlated dimly to adherence to piety and morality, their pasts constituted an opaque theater of divine judgments, darkly legible only to those
endowed with prophetic vision.

Ralegh's task was to illuminate these arcane shadows, and the brac-
ing preface to the *History* provided a compact synopsis of how the transgressions of medieval and early modern kings were avenged on their descendants and subjects. The pattern of history showed that foreordained
misdeeds prompted divine wrath. Ralegh lamented: "Oh by what plots,
by what forswearings, betrayings, oppressions, imprisonments, tortures,
poysonings, and under what reasons of State, and politique subteltie, have
these forenamed Kings, both strangers, and of our owne Nation, pulled
the vengeance of GOD upon them-selves, upon theirs, and upon their prudent ministers!" God punished royal sins by overwhelming kings' plans
and turning their counsels to opposite effect—a punishment felt as much
by their subjects and counselors as by themselves. But this catalog of
royal iniquity was not intended to condemn the institution of kingship;
Ralegh's goal, rather, was "that it may no lesse appeare by evident proofe,
than by asseveration, That ill doing hath alwaies beene attended with ill
successe."[3] His critical history of kings supplied exemplary evidence of
the inescapability of Providence. It was likely the preface that enraged
James, and it is difficult not to interpret it as a tactical error made by an
author who assumed a more sympathetic royal readership than he found.
But, as we will see, Ralegh's account of the providential punishment of
kings merely restated in historical terms James's philosophy of divine-
right kingship.

3. *HW*, C.2.r, A3r.

The preface demonstrated how divine retribution functioned. Punishment generally skipped a generation. For example, Ralegh argued that Edward III's murder of his uncle was avenged on his family first through his grandson Richard II's bloodthirsty tyranny and then through Richard's own deposition and murder at the hands of Henry IV.[4] Henry's tyrannicide itself abrogated the obedience vassals owed their kings, and his grandson Henry VI was, in turn, punished by incompetence and the Wars of the Roses. Similarly, Henry VIII's reign prompted Ralegh to proclaim: "if all the pictures and Patternes of a mercilesse Prince were lost in the World, they might all againe be painted to the life, out of the story of this King."[5] The termination of the Tudor line in Elizabeth punished Henry's mutability, bellicosity, disloyalty, avarice, and, above all, ill-treatment of wives.[6]

Though Ralegh contrasted James's liberality and wisdom with Henry's, James viewed Ralegh's work as a condemnation of kings by a subject, rather than as focusing on the role of Providence that Ralegh had wished to highlight. James's dismissal of "Ralegh's descriptions of the kings that he hates, whomof he speaketh nothing but evil," as well as Chamberlain's account stated earlier suggest that the king felt that Ralegh's criticisms veered too closely toward antimonarchical polemic.[7] Given the chance, however, Ralegh would surely have pointed to the numerous exemplars of royal virtue exalted within the body of the *History*.[8] His history of political institutions, moreover, suggested that James's mode of rule did not violate divine or constitutional laws and, instead, drew on traditions developed in the previous century to support powerful kingship. The genealogy he configured for government supported the model of rule by the king-in-parliament, which was recognized by many early modern Englishmen as licensed by tradition and in no way criminalized tyranny or offered support for subjects to rise up against kings.

Many early modern scholars believed that government itself was of divine institution, and they studied each regime's beginnings for signs of approval or disfavor. Ralegh owned many accounts of the origins of political organization. He knew of Aristotle's theory of aggregating household units and of Cicero's vision of skilled orators persuading their equals to

4. *HW*, A3v.

5. *HW*, B1v.

6. *HW*, B2r.

7. Akrigg, ed., *Letters of King James VI and I*, 388. For the most sensitive analysis of this letter, see Beer, *Sir Walter Ralegh and His Readers*, 37–38.

8. Beer's *Sir Walter Ralegh and His Readers* gives the best sense of the myriad examples of such passages.

rapt obedience.[9] Though neither gave temporal coordinates to the formation of political institutions, later scholars grafted their accounts to the
postlapsarian history of Adam's progeny. The relationship between Adam
and his sons represented different responses to filial obligation—Seth's lineage obedient, Cain's rebellious—that early modern scholars thrust into
contemporary debates. For example, the French Calvinist Lambert Daneau
used the Sethites to naturalize Calvinism as humanity's approved order.
As he explained, in Adamic times, "Their elders ruled over the younger in
their family, and held them subjects to themselves." This model offered
further exemplary lessons for Geneva. Daneau saw the latitude for discord
this society afforded in a world of fallen men, for "there was no magistrate
who spoke the law to the unwilling, who ruled many and diverse families
with the highest authority, who had the right to publicly coerce or punish
those who performed wicked deeds. Therefore crimes remained unpunished, and violence and caprice ruled unbridled in the world."[10] The lack
of a coercive force had enabled the children of Cain to spread evil practices
and subjugate the pious Sethites. This antediluvian order both promoted
a Calvinist ecclesiology and suggested magistracy as the necessary con-
straint against the tyranny of individual whim.

Scholars of all confessions agreed that the Cainites exercised horrific
modes of governance. But they disputed precisely which pollutions the
Cainites had introduced. The key evidence was Gen. 6:4: "There were giants in the earth in those days; and also after that, when the sons of God
came in unto the daughters of men, and they bare children to them, the
same became mighty men which were of old, men of renown."[11] Most concluded that these giants were offspring of unions between Sethites and
Cainites who had assumed undue authority over their contemporaries.
Scholars thus cited this passage to criticize any lawless assumption of
power. Luther wrote in his Genesis commentary: "from that intercourse

9. Compare Aristotle's *Politics* and Cicero's *De inventione*.

10. Lambert Daneau, *Vetustissimarum Primi Mundi Antiquitatum . . . libri* (Geneva,
1596), 248, 391. "Magister proprie tot eo tempore nullus erat, etsi quidam in singulis familiis
aetatis ratione, utpote qui erant maximi natur, praerant: sed qui in invitos ius diceret, pluribus & diversis familiis summa autoritate imperaret, qui eius publicae coercitionis haberet,
qui facinora publice puniret nulla in Orbis regione tunc fuit. Ergo tunc quoque scelera mane-
bant impunita, violentia & libido effraenis in Mundo regnabat."

11. The significance of this passage has been painstakingly analyzed in classic studies. See
Jean Céard, *Le nature et les prodiges: L'insolite au 16e siècle en France* (Geneva: Droz, 1977),
and "La querelle des géants et la jeunesse du monde," *Journal of Medieval and Renaissance
Studies* 8 (1978): 37–76; Antoine Schnapper, "Persistance des géants," *Annales ESC* 41 (1986):
177–200, and *Le géant, la licorne, la tulipe: Collections et collectionneurs dans la France du
XVIIe siècle*, 2 vols. (Paris: Flammarion, 1988–94); and Stephens, *Giants in Those Days*.

of the sons of God with the daughters of men . . . there were not begotten sons of God but giants, that is men who were proud and arrogant, and who assumed to themselves at the same time both the civil government and the priesthood also." He continued: "In this manner the pope assumed to himself the temporal sword and the corporal sword."[12] To Luther, the universalizing papacy replicated the wicked political practice of colossal antediluvians.

Goropius characterized giants quite differently in his 1569 *Origines Antwerpianae*. He sought to attract Philip II's aid by drawing hortatory historical parallels to the Dutch Revolt, and, in the section "Gigantomachia," he correlated the civil war–seared Low Countries with the corrupt society ruled by the Cainites. For Goropius, the term *giant* did not indicate physical enormity. Rather, anyone who preferred the right of arbitrary force to divinely sanctioned authority was a giant: "What are giants but those who strain to shake all things with violently extended hands? Thus they array for battle, in order that they might strive to overthrow the sky itself, that is, the divine action of our mind in which reason dominates . . . by a violent casting of their hands, in which they want all law and all power to be constituted."[13] He equipped the words with etymologies to indicate that "Giants and Tyrants are everywhere the same."[14] And these giants were not necessarily kings.[15] For Goropius, the antediluvian world had devolved into anarchy under the lawlessness of local strongmen. The Flood had been provoked when humanity rejected divine gifts of reason and order and, instead, embraced a politics based on brute savagery.

Goropius redefined giants to create a parallel between the antediluvian world and his own, one in which armies of antipopes terrorized legitimate authority and recognized no greater force than their own power of interpretation. He applied this redefinition to Nimrod, the postdiluvian giant who had overseen the Tower of Babel and the founder of the first mon-

12. Martin Luther, *The Creation: A Commentary on the First Five Chapters of the Book of Genesis* (1544), trans. Henry Cole (London, 1858), 42.

13. Johannes Goropius Becanus, *Origines Antwerpianae* (Antwerp, 1569), 161. "Qui enim alii enim sunt Gigantes, quam qui omnia violentis manibus lateque extensis agere contendunt, atque iis ita considunt, ut & ipsum caelum, id est, divinam mentis nostrae motionem, in qua ratio dominatur, convellere nitantur? Quod igitur Virgilius de Aloidis dixit, id omnibus commune est Gigantibus: qui nihil aliud sunt, quam immania corpora, corporea vi cuncta tentantia; adeo ut caelum velint rescindere, non ratione ulla humana aut divina, sed manibus, id est violenta manuum iniectione, in qua omne ius & omne potestatem volunt esse constitutam."

14. Ibid., 163. "Sunt enim Gigantes & Tyranni iidem omnino, sive definitionem, sive vocum originem examinemus."

15. Ibid., 162.

archy, the Assyrian Empire. Most previous commentators despised Nimrod for building a sacrificial fire and inventing idolatry, and Protestants,
like Luther, depicted him as a precedent for the papacy's unlawful tyranny
over religion.[16] Goropius, similarly, reviled Nimrod for establishing a government based on seized, rather than natural, authority. But, for him, the
Assyrian Empire embodied the unbridled exercise of violent will and the
overweening expansion of temporal authority. He wrote that the project
of the Tower of Babel illustrated two truths: "First, that the people are inclined to follow a stupid and mad Prince; secondly that the demented con-
trivances of insane and proud kings avail nothing against divine will."[17]
Like the reigns of the antediluvian giants, Nimrod's empire demonstrated
humanity's easy acceptance of diabolic tyranny. For Goropius, Nimrod's
deviation from true piety and his self-deification paralleled Lutheran
apostasy.

Ralegh ridiculed Goropius's disbelief in giant men, claiming that the
Antwerpian "thought his owne wit more Giganticall then the bodies of
Nimrod or *Hercules*." But neither did he depict Nimrod as a precedent for
the papacy. His Nimrod was neither gigantic nor tyrannical. His position
had respected predecessors. As he explained: "*Melanchthon* conceived not
amisse hereof: the same exposition being also made by the Authour of that
worke called *Onomasticon Theologicum*, who affirmes that *Nimrod* was
therefore called *Amarus Dominator, A bitter or severe Governour*, because
his forme of rule seemed at first farre more terrible than Paternal authoritie." Nimrod's comparative sternness and effective taxation had generated
complaints that he was a usurping tyrant. But, according to Ralegh, Nimrod had not wielded power unlawfully: "*Nimrod* had the command of all
those, which went with him from the East into *Shinaar*: so, this charge
was rather given him, then by him usurped." Ralegh even diminished
Nimrod's fault in the construction of the Tower. Of the builders, Nimrod
may have been one of "the chiefe Leaders of this presumptuous multitude.
And seeing it is not likely but that some one was by order appointed for
this charge, we may imagine that *Nimrod* rather had it by iust authoritie,

16. Martin Luther, "The Babylonian Captivity of the Church (1520)," in *Works*, vol. 12,
ed. Abdel Ross Wentz (Philadelphia: Fortress, 1959), 12. The Anglican controversialist Andrew
Willet explained: "Even in the presence of God, Nimrod practised tyrannie and crueltie: so
that it grew unto a proverbe, to resemble a cruell tyrant and oppressor to Nimrod." Andrew
Willet, *Hexapla in Genesim* (Cambridge, 1605), 117.

17. Goropius, *Origenes Antwerpianae*, 571. "Nimbrodi insani tyranni, & vasti & efferi
gigantis insanissima cogitatio, duo statim commonstravit, tum quam populus proclivis sit
ad stultitiam & vesaniam Principem sequenda; tum quam nihil valeant superborum insano-
rumque regum dementes contra divinam voluntatem molitiones."

then by violence of usurpation."[18] Ralegh's Nimrod was a legitimate king
who had been unjustly tarred as a tyrant.

Ralegh closely followed the characterization of the two authorities he
cited—Melanchthon and David Chytraeus, the author of the *Onomasticon Theologicum*. In the *Chronica Carionis*, Melanchthon had argued that
Nimrod's ascension restored order to a society degenerating from divine
mores and customs to anarchy:

> Nimrod first dominated Babylon, in order that he might compel his
> neighbors by force into one form of rule. A government constituted by
> force and arms was first made by him. Before this, paternal authority
> had thrived and each was obedient to his elders, but customs and civil-
> ity quickly deteriorated, and rapine and cruelty began to be maliciously
> undertaken. Evil men did not want to be punished or coerced by par-
> ents and neighbors, and they had the support of the united throng of
> the wicked. It was necessary that such men be repressed by military
> strength, and be dragged to justice and punishment.[19]

Nimrod replaced natural, paternal authority with a coercive formal government only when compelled by iniquitous contemporaries. He was, not
an antisocial miscreant, but the protector of order.[20]

Both Chytraeus and Melanchthon were defenders of the four monarchies theory. By defining the Assyrian Empire as a beneficent first monarchy, they provided a transparent lineage substantiating the position
that a Lutheran Holy Roman Empire—the Assyrian Empire's Christian
descendant—was ordained to assert control over fragmented Christendom. The empire, they claimed, should arbitrate disputes in customs and
beliefs, ward off the Ottomans, and eradicate the blighted union of the
Spanish crown and the papacy. Their Nimrod supplied a powerful genealogical sanction for the authority they exalted.

His criticism of Alexander reveals that Ralegh did not endorse their

---

18. *HW*, 1.5.8.81, 1.10.1.185–86.

19. Joannes Carionis, *Chronica Carionis*, ed. Philipp Melanchthon and Caspar Peucer (Geneva, 1581), 22. "Nimrod, id est, amarus dominator. Hic in Babylone primus ita dominatus est,
ut vicinos vi coegerit in unam imperii formam. Ab hoc igitur initium factum est, imperia vi &
armis constituendi, cum antea plus valeret paterna autoritas, & seniori caeteri ultro parerent.
Postea cito, cum mores fierent deteriores, & grassari aliqui rapinis & caedibus coepissent, nec
vellent a parentibus & vicinis coherceri aut puniri, & haberent turbam scelerum sociam &
receptus, necesse fuit tales praesidiis reprimi, & ad iudicia ac poenas pertrahi."

20. Chytraeus's distilled his entry for Nimrod from Melanchthon in the *Onomasticon
Theologicum*. [Chytraeus], *Onomasticon Theologicum*, 476.

four monarchies theory. But he took a clear stance by preferring Melanchthon's Nimrod to the alternative interpretations. Far from using Nimrod
to attack temporal authority's eclipse of ecclesiastical independence—as
contemporary Puritans would have—or suggesting the genealogical equiv-
alence of monarchy to tyranny—as later Parliamentarians and Republi-
cans might—Ralegh strongly defended the original of the form of James's
rule.[21] His blameless Nimrod invented monarchy as a means to defend order from the encroachments of the wicked. Though some subjects might
have been alienated by his stern rule, this in no way undermined the virtuous foundations of necessary kingship; rather, it reflected humanity's
propensity for disorder.

RALEGH AND JAMES I ON THE ISRAELITE KINGS

Comparing James's and Ralegh's treatments of the provision of a king to
the Israelites provides more precise contours to Ralegh's commitment to
monarchy.[22] James erected his 1598 defense of divine-right monarchy, *The
True Law of Free Monarchies*, on a foundation of Scripture, law, and nature.[23] The scriptural justification derived from 1 Sam. 8:9–20.[24] The aging
judge Samuel had been approached by Israelite elders and asked to "make
us a king to judge us like other nations." Samuel prayed for advice: "And
the Lord said unto Samuel, Hearken unto the voice of the people in all that
they say unto thee: for they have not rejected thee, but they have rejected
me, that I should not reign over them." God instructed Samuel to tell the
Israelites that their children would be made the king's servants and that
he would take their grain and olives and wine and animals. Samuel informed the Israelites clamoring for a king: "And ye shall cry out in that
day because of your king which ye shall have chosen you; and the Lord
will not hear you in that day." The Israelites insisted, and God bestowed a
king on them.

21. Christopher Hill, *Intellectual Origins of the English Revolution Revisited*, 136ff.,
briefly mentions Ralegh's treatment of Nimrod.

22. See Larkum, "Providence and Politics in Sir Walter Ralegh's *History of the World*."

23. For the *Trew Law*, see Jenny Wormald, "James VI and I, Basilikon Doron and the Trew
Law of Free Monarchies: The Scottish Context and the English Translations," in Peck, ed., *The
Mental World of the Jacobean Court*, 36–54; Johann P. Somerville, "James I and the Divine
Right of Kings: English Politics and Continental Theory," in ibid., 55–70; and Peter Lake, "The
King (the Queen) and the Jesuit: James Stuart's *True Law of Free Monarchies* in Context/s,"
TRHS, 6th ser., 14 (2004): 243–60.

24. See Eric Nelson, *The Hebrew Republic: Jewish Sources and the Transformation of European Political Thought* (Cambridge, MA: Harvard University Press, 2010).

James detailed precisely how to interpret the passage. He explained: "this speech of *Samuel* to the people, was to prepare their hearts before the hand to the due obedience of that King, which God was to give unto them; and therefore opened up unto them, what might be the intollerable qualities that might fall in some of their kings, thereby preparing them patience, not to resist to Gods ordinance." The Israelites' "errour in shaking off Gods yoke" should not lead them to believe that God would sanction rebellion against the kings they overhastily sought. Rather: "For as ye could not have obtained one without the permission and ordinance of God, so may yee no more, fro hee be once set over you, shake him off without the same warrant." Samuel's catalog of taxes and appropriations simply elaborated what the Israelites should expect from subjection to a rightful monarch. James acknowledged that the obligations were onerous, but subjects could only "arme your selves with patience and humilitie," for their lord and king required absolute obedience.[25]

This divine introduction proved to James that kings were above the law, and he marshaled evidence from Scottish history to show that "kings were the authors and makers of the Lawes, and not the Lawes of the kings." He argued that, though "a good king will frame all his actions to be according the Law; yet is hee not bound thereto but of his good will, and for good example-giving to his subiects." Subjects who believed they were ruled by unjust kings, he noted, did have recourse to modes of resistance: "patience, earnest prayers to God, and amendment of their lives, are the onely lawful meanes to move God to relieve them of that heavie curse." But they were explicitly prohibited by divine injunction from rebellion and bound to accept that kings—even tyrants—would be judged by God alone: "Now in this contract (I say) betwixt the king and his people, God is doubtless the only Iudge, both because to him onely the king must make count of his administration."[26] Absolute obedience remained divinely enjoined on subjects; kings were subject only to God, not to human law.

As Ralegh recognized, James's interpretation did not command universal assent. Ralegh discussed 1 Samuel 8 only briefly, but he devoted most of the space to addressing James's opponents, who believed that the royal confiscations described in this passage contravened the divine edicts of Deuteronomy and Samuel's exposition "to containe the description of

25. James VI and I, *Political Writings*, ed. Johann Somerville (Cambridge: Cambridge University Press, 1994), 67–68.
    26. Ibid., 73, 75, 79–80, 81.

a Tyrant."[27] He likely had in mind James's tutor, the Scottish Calvinist George Buchanan, whose 1579 *De iure regni apud Scotos* attributed limited rights to monarchs and theorized a popular sovereignty in which kings were answerable to their subjects.[28] But Ralegh gave no indication of siding with the monarchomachs. After describing their reading of Samuel, he claimed that ubiquitous familiarity with the *Trew Law* obviated any need to articulate the absolutist position.[29] He presented James's argument as his own, and his decision to forgo elaboration was a gesture of obedient caution. He continued: "Only this much will I say, that if practise doe shew the greatnesse of authoritie, even the best Kings of *Iuda* and *Israel* were not so tied by any lawes, but that they did whatsoever they pleased in the greatest things; and commanded some of their owne Princes, and of their owne brethren to be slaine without any triall of law, being sometime by Prophets reprehended, sometime not."[30] Ralegh emphasized the empirical fact of absolutism even among the most revered of kings, using biblical royal behavior to confirm James's claim that kings were above the law. While amoral machinations sometimes elicited the opprobrium of prophets, other times the wickedest sins were not condemned by the Lord's ambassadors.

In these discussions, Ralegh's opinions appeared to agree closely with James', and, elsewhere in the *History*, Ralegh echoed James's espousal of a monarchy graciously self-limited by law. But his historical narrative subtly recast James's position and hinted at disquiet with the empirical absolutism exercised by kings. In a chapter shortly after his account of Nimrod entitled "Of the beginning and establishing of Governement," he reiterated that the original postdiluvian kings such as Nimrod were positive disciplinary forces. Monarchies, he claimed, had been erected to protect

27. *HW*, 2.16.1.465. In particular, these scholars drew on Deut. 17:14–20, where God prescribed limitations on any king of the Israelites. See Larkum, "Providence and Politics in Sir Walter Ralegh's *History of the World*," chaps. 4, 6, where it is noted that James ignores this problem.

28. See Lake, "The King (the Queen) and the Jesuit," who notes that, in the context in which the *Trew Law* was released to an English audience, the condemnation applied as equally to Parsons as it did to Buchanan. See also Hugh Trevor-Roper, *George Buchanan and the Ancient Scottish Constitution*, *EHR* suppl. 3 (London: Longmans Green, 1966); and Williamson, *Scottish National Consciousness in the Age of James VI*.

29. "The arguments on the contrarie side, as they are many and forcible, so they are well knowne to all; being excellently handled in that Princely discourse of *The true Law of free Monarchies*; which Treatise I may not presume to abridge, much lesse here to insert." *HW*, 2.16.1.465.

30. Ibid.

against corruptors of divine will as humanity multiplied and increasingly inclined to wickedness.[31]

Ralegh's subsequent history, however, slightly modified the history of kingship. Just as the first kings had been instituted to combat iniquity, Ralegh claimed, monarchical abuses had necessitated the development of law as a counterbalance. When kingship was introduced to the postdiluvian world, there had been no constraints on royal prerogative: "For before the invention of Lawes, private affections in supreme Rulers made their owne fancies both their Treasurers and Hangmen: measuring by this yard, and waighing in this balance both good and evill." This potential for monarchical abuse explained the subsequent need to restrain the latitude of kings: "For as the wisedome in Eldership preceded the rule of Kings; so the will of Kings fore-went the inventions of lawes. . . . Hence it came to passe, that after a few yeares (for direction and restraint of Royall power) Lawes were established: and that governement which had this mixture of equalitie (holding in an even balance supreme power and common right) acquired the title of Regall: the other (which had it not) was knowne for Tyrannicall: *the one God established in favour of his people: the other he permitted for their affliction.*"[32] Ralegh thus created his own interpretation of monarchy. Kings may have been installed originally to control wickedness, but they ruled with sacred benevolence when they ruled according to the law. They were not the authors of their own reigns but instruments divinely placed over their own people, and their relation to the law was a matter of Providence and punishment, not of right. Ralegh's account agreed with James that kings were above the law but stressed that violating the law was a sign of punitive tyranny.

Ralegh considered monarchy the most desirable and most just form of government. He acknowledged that no earthly institutions had the right to enforce constitutional limitations on a monarch and did not subject royal prerogative to the law, ignoring Sir John Fortescue's powerful constitutional distinctions between *dominium politicum* and *dominium regale.*[33] He did not claim that James's mode of governance disqualified him from rule, suggest that any constitutional liberties or rights were threatened by his absolutism, or hint that his government justified rebellion or even disobedience on the part of his subjects.

But, while Ralegh did not circumscribe royal authority, the *History*

31. *HW*, 1.9.1.178–80.

32. *HW*, 1.9.1.179 (emphasis added).

33. Sir John Fortescue, *A Learned Commendation of the Politique Lawes of Englande*, trans. Robert Mulcaster (London, 1567).

emphasized that the best kings prudently restrained their own prerogative to measures and methods approved by legal traditions and precedents
such as those produced in Parliament.[34] Institutions of the law, in Ralegh's
view, offered a divine guide toward sustaining sacred governance. This account thus suggested a stance capable of addressing the challenge of ame-
liorating James's relationship with Parliament. His history of monarchies
demonstrated that Ralegh recognized the benevolent origins of kingship,
supported James's reading of the institution of Hebrew kings against the
monarchomachs, and depicted kings as above the law. At the same time,
he attributed a powerful role to Parliament as a body of counsel whose
advice should curb royal excess. Its preservation as a custodian of English
liberties marked the line between tyranny and just kingship. His discussion positioned him as appreciative of both absolutism and Parliament
and, thus, presented him as capable of orchestrating the smooth rule of the
king-in-parliament.

WAR AND HISTORY IN EARLY MODERN EUROPE

Ralegh's history of monarchy characterized him as an obedient subject
whose faith in Parliament derived from the institution's pious enactment
of law rather than from its constitutional superiority to kings. It thus addressed any suspicion James may have retained concerning Ralegh's alleged attempt to overthrow him. In similar fashion, Ralegh's presentation
of his military expertise in the *History* was designed to assuage residual
concerns over the zeal of his bellicosity while also making clear that his
counsels would still appeal to subjects frustrated by James's pro-Spanish,
pacifist policies.

Ralegh at times brazenly appealed to James on military grounds, for
example, by favorably contrasting his comportment toward soldiers with
that of Elizabeth. In fact, Ralegh harshly criticized his queen for her treatment of military men. Though her safety had been ensured by their valor,
he claimed, "I do not remember, that of any of hers . . . were either enriched
or otherwise honoured, for any service by them performed." He enumer-

34. This story thus fits with the postrevisionist narrative of Jacobean political disagreement. For examples of this historiography, see Thomas Cogswell, *The Blessed Revolution:
English Politics and the Coming of War, 1621–1624* (Cambridge: Cambridge University Press,
1989); Richard Cust and Ann Hughes, eds., *Conflict in Early Stuart England: Studies in Religion and Politics, 1603–1642* (London: Longman, 1989); and Thomas Cogswell, Richard Cust,
and Peter Lake, eds., *Politics, Religion, and Popularity in Early Stuart Britain: Essays in Honour of Conrad Russell* (Cambridge: Cambridge University Press, 2002).

ated her many commanders who had died in penury and attributed her lack of appreciation to the destructive lies of ambitious counselors. "But," he noted, "his Majestie hath alreadie payed the greatest part of that debt. For besides the relieving by Pensions all the poorer sort, he hath honored more Martial men, than all the Kings of *England* have done for this hundred yeares."[35] Ralegh thus characterized, if cravenly, the pacific James as wisely charitable to ex-soldiers.

This appeal to James' benevolence was prudent because his extensive military career had made Ralegh a symbol of anti-Spanish war policy. He had been involved in military engagements as a marauding mercenary in the French Wars of Religion, a captain in colonial Ireland, an administrator for expeditions of discovery, a propagandist, an Atlantic privateer, an admiral in a state navy, and the captain of the guard. In all these contexts, he had supported virulently anti-Catholic and anti-Spanish policy. His treatment of warfare in the *History*, however, sought to portray his expertise in tones acceptable to James. These examinations drew on the close interrelation between the study of the past and the conduct of warfare that had emerged in the sixteenth century.[36] The wars that tore through early modern Europe directed scholarly attention to militaria, and scholars and commanders scrutinized histories to find lessons that might offer advantage on their battlefields.[37] Ancient works by Frontinus, Vegetius, and oth-

---

35. *HW*, 5.6.2.717–18. See Rory Rapple, *Martial Power and Elizabethan Political Culture: Military Men in England and Ireland, 1558–1594* (Cambridge: Cambridge University Press, 2009). For Elizabeth's campaigns, see Paul Hammer, *Elizabeth's Wars: War, Government, and Society in Tudor England, 1544–1604* (New York: Palgrave Macmillan, 2003).

36. The literature on warfare in the Renaissance is immense. See, above all, Clifford J. Rodgers, ed., *The Military Revolution Debate: Readings on the Military Transformation of Early Modern Europe* (Boulder, CO: Westview, 1995). See also Geoffrey Parker, *The Army of Flanders and the Spanish Road, 1567–1659: The Logistics of Spanish Victory and Defeat in the Low Countries' Wars* (Cambridge: Cambridge University Press, 1972), and *The Military Revolution: Military Innovation and the Rise of the West, 1500–1800* (Cambridge: Cambridge University Press, 1988); J. R. Hale, *Renaissance War Studies* (London: Hambledon, 1983), and *War and Society in Renaissance Europe, 1450–1620* (New York: St. Martin's, 1985); Christopher Storrs and H. M. Scott, "The Military Revolution and the European Nobility, c. 1600–1800," *War in History* 3 (1996): 1–41; and Philippe Contamine, ed., *War and Competition between States* (Oxford: Clarendon, 2000).

37. See Maurice J. D. Cockle, *A Bibliography of English Military Books Up to 1642 and of Contemporary Foreign Works* (London: Simpkin, Marshall, Hamilton, Kent, 1900); Gunther Rothenberg, "Aventinus and the Defense of the Empire against the Turks," *Studies in the Renaissance* 10 (1963): 60–67; Henry J. Webb, *Elizabethan Military Science: The Books and the Practice* (Madison: University of Wisconsin Press, 1965); Arnaldo Momigliano, "Polybius between the English and the Turks," in *Sesto contributo alla staoria degli studi classici e dei mondo antico* (Roma: Edizioni di storia e letteratura, 1980), 125–41; Gerhard Oestreich,

ers were printed repeatedly, while authors from all over Europe composed new works purporting to reveal the most perfect discipline, weapons, tactics, and fortification.

Authors of these *artes militares* proclaimed a range of sources certifying their expertise. Many English works, including English examples such as Sir Roger Williams's 1590 *A Briefe Discourse of Warre*, were produced by well-heeled soldiers who argued that their accounts were most reliable because they were drawn from experience. Of such works, Ralegh owned the 1582 *Discorsi de Guerra* by the Piacenzan soldier Bernardino Rocca, the Croatian scholar Francesco Patrizi's 1583 *La militia Romana di Polibio*, the Spanish captain Christobal de Roias's 1598 *Teorica y Practica de Fortificacion*, and the 1595 *Commentarius Bellicus* of the Danish noble soldier and scholar Heinrich Rantzau. He also may have consulted such works in the library of his Tower cohabitant, the Duke of Northumberland.[38]

Participation in combat was not the only credible source for military expertise, however, and scholars throughout Europe were considered authorities for expertise gained by reading historical military narratives. In fact, the work that spurred the boom in the publication of military texts was a literary enactment of the *ars historica*, for Machiavelli's 1521 *Arte della guerra* consisted of a set of dialogues in which contemporary commanders discussed ancient military practices.[39] Machiavelli's work gave enduring characterization to Roman military science as profoundly historical, perfected by the analysis of past examples rather than by experience in combat. The Romans, Machiavelli claimed, had mined the examples of their own battles and the wars of the Persians, Greeks, and Egyptians to

---

Neostoicism and the Early Modern State, trans. David McClintock (Cambridge: Cambridge University Press, 1982); Peter Paret and Felix Gilbert, eds., *Makers of Modern Strategy: From Machiavelli to the Nuclear Age* (Princeton, NJ: Princeton University Press, 1986), 11–92; Mark Charles Fissel, "Tradition and Invention in the Early Stuart Art of War," *Journal for the Society of Army Historical Research* 65 (1987): 133–49; Barbara Donagan, "Halcyon Days and the Literature of War: England's Military Education Before 1642," *P&P* 147 (1995): 65–100; Fernando Gonzalez de Leon, "'Doctors of the Military Discipline': Technical Expertise and the Paradigm of the Spanish Soldier in the Early Modern Period," *SCJ* 27 (1996): 61–85; Donald A. Neill, "Ancestral Voices: The Influence of the Ancients on the Military Thought of the Seventeenth and Eighteenth Centuries," *Journal of Military History* 62 (1998): 487–520; and David Lawrence, *The Complete Soldier: Military Books and Military Culture in England, 1603–1645* (Leiden: Brill, 2009).

38. See G. R. Batho, "The Library of the 'Wizard' Earl: Henry Percy Ninth Earl of Northumberland (1564–1632)," *The Library*, 5th ser., 25 (1960): 246–61.

39. See Felix Gilbert, "Machiavelli: The Renaissance Art of War," in Paret and Gilbert, eds., *Makers of Modern Strategy*, 11–31. For Vegetius's use of this method, see Walter Goffart, "The Date and Purpose of Vegetius' *De re militari*," *Traditio* 33 (1977): 65–100.

produce general rules for their art of war, and he claimed to be replicating their methods.

Scholars and military commanders throughout early modern Europe followed Machiavelli's example. Sir Clement Edmondes, the future secretary of state under James, introduced his 1600 commentary on Caesar's *Commentaries* with a section entitled "Reading and Discourse, are requisite to make a souldier perfect in the Arte militarie." He strenuously argued "that a meete practicall knowledge cannot make a perfect soldier."[40] Drawing on the rationale of the *ars historica*, Edmondes explained that personal experience offered too small a pool of evidence to make reliable military knowledge and that aspiring commanders must study past battles as well.

Edmondes reported an exemplary instance of modern warriors deploying military wisdom derived from the ancients at the Battle of Nieuwpoort in 1600.[41] At the outset of this engagement, the Dutch were camped in hills on the Flemish coast, obstructed by Spanish troops who occupied a sandy terrain in the foothills. The Dutch war council initially decided to descend and engage the enemy. But, Edmondes reported, Sir Francis Vere recalled that, when Caesar had been faced with a similar tactical dilemma, he held to the dictum that "the whole scope of the *Romane* discipline . . . did always aim at the advantage of place." Instead of charging into a terrain where footing would be poor, Vere proposed to follow Caesar's example and "rather perswaded his souldiers, disdaining the confrontment of the enemie, to endure their contumely, rather then to buy a victory with the danger of so many worthy men, and patiently to attend some further opportunity." As Vere predicted, the enemy troops impatiently charged, and Edmondes triumphantly noted: "our men had the execution of them for the space of a quarter of a mile or more."[42] He thus offered firsthand testimony of a high council of war reversing its inclination when presented with Caesar's alternative course of action.

Throughout the *History*, Ralegh similarly fused historical reading and firsthand experience to derive abstract principles of martial science. For example, he developed a stratagem from the clever method by which Alexander the Great had taken a well-defended mountain pass. Alexander, he

40. Clement Edmondes, *Observations upon the first five bookes of Caesars* Commentaries (London, 1609), 1.

41. See also Geoffrey Parker, "The Limits to Revolutions in Military Affairs: Maurice of Nassau, the Battle of Nieuwpoort (1600) and the Legacy," *Journal of Military History* 71 (2007): 331–72.

42. Edmondes, *Observations*, 13, 14 (second pagination).

explained, "by setting a great pile of wood on fire with the advantage of a strong winde, wonne a passage over a high and unaccessable Rocke, which was defended against him with thirteene thousand foote. For the extremitie of the flame and smoke, forced them from the place, otherwise invincible." Ralegh noted that he had witnessed a similar tactic: "I saw in the third civill Warre in *France* certain Caves in *Languedoc*, which had but one entrance, and that very narrow, cut out in the mid-way of high Rocks, which we knew not how to enter by any ladder or engine, till at last, by certaine bundells of straw let downe by an yron chaine, and a waightie stone in the middest, those that defended it were so smothered, as they rendred themselves with their plate, monie, and other goods therein hidden." Smoke and fire constituted ideal weapons against entrenched enemies. Similarly, he had heard that natives in Guiana had turned back Spanish explorers using the same maneuver: "three hundred *Spaniards* well mounted, smothered to death, together with their Horses, by the Countriepeople, who did set the long drie grasse on fire to the eastward of them, (the winde in those parts being alwaies East) so as notwithstanding their flying from the smoke, there was not any one that escaped." This annihilation suggested a general principle of New World warfare. He asserted; "to those that shall in times to come invade any part of those Countries, that they alwaies, before they passe into the Land, burne downe the grasse and sedge to the East of them; they may otherwise, without any other enemie than a handfull of straw set on fire, die the death of honnie-Bees, burnt out of the Hive."[43] Ralegh thus used a stratagem employed by Alexander to introduce his own testimony and then prescribe maxims for future colonizers. His own experience bridged past and precept.

Especially in the *History*'s latter books, Ralegh frequently derived military axioms by comparing his own experience with accounts drawn from Polybius and Livy, his primary sources for Roman history. He used such precepts to evaluate ancient generals; most notably, he praised Hannibal effusively and criticized his enemies in Carthage for preventing the great general from capitalizing on his victories.[44] Above all, however, he

43. *HW*, 4.2.16.197–98.

44. Ralegh's description of Carthage during the Punic Wars, e.g., can be read as a cipher of Jacobean policy toward Spain, warning that James's pacifism would, ultimately, result in British ruin. In this typology, Ralegh was represented by Hannibal, an aggressive commander whose battlefield successes were confounded by the machinations of a jealous pacifist party led by Hanno, who resembled Henry Howard. In fact, Ralegh discussed Carthage's strategy in the same language with which he had famously maligned Elizabeth's quavering foreign policy: "It was a great fault in the *Carthaginians*, that embracing so many Enterprises at once, they followed all by halves." *HW*, 5.3.13.491. This echoed his negative appraisal of Elizabeth's mili-

praised the martial wisdom of the Romans. Mastering the minutiae of
advantageous military encounters was, he noted, the "The Occupation of
the *Romans*," and he compared their actions to those of other commanders to demonstrate that they had brought this science to perfection.[45] For
example, Alexander the Great had driven his army into the harsh Persian
winter in pursuit of glory. As Ralegh noted, some commentators had spun
this foolish act to Alexander's honor: "It is said and spoken in his praise:
That when his Souldiers cried out against him, because they could not
indure the extreame frost, and make way, but with extreme difficultie,
through the snow, that *Alexander* forsooke his horse, and led them the
way." Ralegh remained unimpressed: "What can bee more ridiculous than
to bring other men into extremitie, thereby to shew how well himselfe can
indure it? His walking on foote did no otherwise take off their wearinesse
that followed him, than his sometime forbearing to drinke did quench
their thirst." Indeed, he portrayed such acts of bravery as consequences of
poor preparation: "For mine owne little judgement I shall rather commend
that Captaine, that makes carefull provision for those that follow him . . .
than those witlesse arrogant fooles, that make the vaunt of having indured
equally with the common Souldier, as if that were a matter of great glorie
and importance." Alexander's magnanimity did not diminish his defects.
And Ralegh judged Alexander by Caesar, insinuating that the Roman had
perfected military science: "We finde in all the Warres that *Caesar* made,
or the best of the *Roman* Commanders, that the provision of victualls was
their first care."[46] Caesar and Hannibal represented the apex of martial
wisdom, but they were joined by numerous other generals from throughout Rome's republican and imperial history.

His discussions of ancient warfare conveyed that, like the Romans,
Ralegh capably elicited powerful lessons from the interpretation of past
battles. They also revealed how modern generals suffered when ignorant of
precepts offered by these examples and urged the significance of an anti-
Spanish program. In his narrative of Xerxes' invasion of Greece, Ralegh
criticized the recklessness of the Persian offensive. He recited the Persian
counselor Artabanus's unheeded arguments against invading the Greek
peninsula of Athos with a massive army: "because [the sea] had no where
in that part of the world any Port capable of so great a Fleet: insomuch,

---

tary strategy: "Her Majesty did all by halves." *The Works of Sir Walter Ralegh, kt.*, 8 vols. (Oxford: The University Press, 1829), 8:246. See Salas, "Ralegh and the Punic Wars." For Ralegh's
admiration of Hannibal, see also Beer, *Sir Walter Ralegh and His Readers*, 22–59.

45. *HW*, 5.5.5.672.

46. *HW*, 4.2.12.191–92.

as if any tempest should arise, all the Continent of *Greece* could hardly receive them, nor all the Havens thereof affoord them any safetie: and therefore when such shelter shall bee wanting unto them, he prayed him to understand, that in such a case of extremitie, men are left to the will and disposition of Fortune, and not Fortune to the will and disposition of men." Xerxes left his navy vulnerable by ignoring the circumstances of the invasion and the warnings of his counselors. As Ralegh noted: "These Cautions were exceeding weightie, if *Xerxes* his obstinacie had not misprised them. For to invade by Sea upon a perillous Coast, being neither in possession of any Port, nor succoured by any partie, may better fit a Prince presuming on his fortune, than enriched with understanding." And he gave this rule contemporary significance, concluding: "Such was the enterprise of *Philip* the second, upon *England* in the yeere 1588 who had belike never heard of this Counsell of *Artabanus* to *Xerxes*, or had forgotten it."[47] In this interpretation, the Spanish Armada had not been cast adrift by a Protestant wind so much as flung into open waters by historical ignorance.

The defeat of the Armada hovered over his discussions of warfare, Ralegh contrasting English adherence to the rules of the military art with Spanish lack of methodical foresight. In particular, he complimented Charles Howard—the brother of his nemesis Henry—for engineering the small-ship strategy that led to the defeat of the Armada.[48] He explained: "Had the Lord *Charles Howard*, Admirall of *England*, been lost in the yeare 1588 if he had not beene better advised, than a great many malignant fooles were, that found fault with his demeanour. . . . Our Admirall knew his advantage, and held it: which had he not done, he had not beene worthie to have held his head."[49] He again attributed the defeat of the Armada, not to a providential wind, but to the advice that Howard's maritime expertise led him to embrace.

While the threat of the Spanish Armada indicated the necessity of rigorous military thinking, it also exposed England's vulnerable coastlines. Ralegh was pessimistic about the possibility of securely fortifying England against maritime invasion. While discussing the Roman methods of troop transport, he addressed the problem that the speed of ships posed for coastal defense. Because boats moved faster than men, he explained, once soldiers had been positioned opposite an incoming navy, ships could raise

47. *HW*, 3.6.2.61–62.
48. *HW*, 5.1.6.350.
49. *HW*, 5.1.6.350–51.

anchor and arrive at another harbor faster than the land defenses could shift position. Maurice of Nassau often used the ploy of feigning several amphibious assaults before attacking the exasperated Spanish, and Ralegh made clear that England was susceptible to this tactic.[50] He explained: "It is impossible for any maritime Countrie, not having the coasts admirably fortified, to defend it selfe against a powerfull enemie, that is master of the Sea."[51] He recognized that his principle suggested troubling conclusions for English coastal defense. In fact, he frankly admitted that the English troops available in 1588 could not have withstood Parma's troops. This acknowledgment spurred him to caution against accepting a land war: "I hope that this question shall never come to triall; his Majesties many moveable Forts will forbid the experience." A policy of vigorous naval defense constituted the safest measure to prevent amphibious assaults. As he explained: "to entertaine those that shall assaile us, with their owne beef in their bellies, and before they eate of our *Kentish* Capons, I take to be the wisest way. To doe which, his Maiestie, after God, will imploy his good ships on the Sea, and not trust to any intrenchment upon the shore."[52] Ralegh thus fused his discussion of ancient Roman troop transport to his observation of contemporary warfare to formulate an aggressive maritime strategy. Ancient historical exempla, dictates of military science yielded from experience, and knowledge of geography led him to articulate England's need to establish naval superiority as "master of the Sea."

His analyses of ancient warfare clearly indicated that Ralegh considered military expertise to consist of analyzing past examples to derive precepts for action. The enterprises of warriors depended on their enlistment of these tools, and cataclysmic defeats ensued when they were ignored. This expertise was designed to appeal to the king, even one as reluctant to engage in warfare as James, for Ralegh both demonstrated mastery of the abstract principles of warfare and possession of concrete ideas for policy. His discussions of historical battles were intended to persuade James that, under his supervision, the bellicose foreign policy that circumstances demanded would not stoke disaster.

Other elements of the *History* lent an optimistic cast to a war policy. Ralegh perceived factors in addition to the deployment of military science as determining the outcome of battles, and his discussion of these was intended to inspire confidence in English soldiers. Introducing his account

---

50. *HW*, 5.1.9.359.
51. Ibid. Note that Ralegh here refers to Edmondes's commentary on Caesar.
52. *HW*, 5.1.9.362–63.

of the Punic Wars, he asked what would have happened had Alexander marched on Rome. Livy famously had raised this counterfactual to assert that the Romans would have rebuffed the great conqueror, proving them the greatest military force the world had ever seen even three centuries before Caesar.[53] Livy's argument was straightforward. In the East, Alexander had faced effeminate, untrained soldiers and generals addicted to luxury. Against Rome's cadre of well-provisioned, disciplined generals and soldiers who had devoted their lives to honing their martial abilities, his band would have stood little chance.

Ralegh disagreed. Even Rome's expertise would be overwhelmed by the Macedonians' superiority in "Treasure, Horses, Elephants, Engines of batterie," not to mention their superior sea power and alliances with Rome's neighbors.[54] Ralegh then asked whether anything in the Roman disposition might have overcome these disadvantages. Rather than answer directly, he interjected his opinion on the relative quality of the world's soldiers: "If therefore it be demanded, whether the *Macedonian*, or the *Roman*, were the best Warriour? I will answere: The *Englishmen*. For . . . the noble acts of our Nation in warre . . . were performed by no advantage of weapon; against no savage or unmanlie people; the enemie being farre superiour unto us in numbers, and all needfull provisions, yea as well trained as we, or commonly better, in the exercise of warre."[55] While Rome's methodological artifices supplemented the courage of its soldiers, English successes derived solely from martial will.

Ralegh rooted this judgment in a dubious comparative history, examining the results of the armies in Gallic lands over a millennium apart. The ancient Gaul that Caesar's army overran, he noted, was so politically and militarily fragmented that the lowly Germans had reduced it to slavery not long before. This weakness was exacerbated by the ignorance of its inhabitants, whom Caesar described as admiring "*Roman* Towers, and Engines of batterie, raised and planted against their walls, as more than humane workes."[56] Nevertheless, Caesar's army had struggled to overcome this disorganized and untrained enemy.

The English had confronted an entirely different adversary, a sizable

---

53. *Livy*, trans. B. O. Foster (Cambridge, MA: Harvard University Press, 1948), 9.17.

54. *HW*, 5.1.1.310.

55. *HW*, 5.1.1.311. For the beliefs of the English about their own military skill, see Donagan, "Halcyon Days"; and Rosalind Davies, "News from the Fleet: Characterizing the Elizabethan Army in the Narratives of the Action at Cadiz, 1596," in *War: Identities in Conflict, 1300–2000*, ed. Bertrand Taithe and Tim Thornton (Thrupp: Sutton, 1998), 21–36.

56. *HW*, 5.1.1.312.

and well-trained force presided over by a powerful king. The strength of the enemy that the Romans and the English had encountered was crucial for Ralegh's comparison: "The Countrie lying so open to the *Roman*, and being so well-fenced against the *English*; it is note-worthy, not who pre-vailed most . . . but whether of the two gave the greater proofe of milita-rie vertue."[57] Particularly significant were the triumphs at Poissy, Cressy, and Agincourt. Ralegh dismissed those who ascribed these victories to the longbow by emphasizing its inferiority to the French crossbow. Rather, he proudly proclaimed, the miraculous victories could be attributed only to the English soldier's extraordinary valor.[58] And, given this comparison, he exulted "the militarie vertue of the English, prevailing against all manner of difficulties, ought to be preferred before that of Romans, which was as-sisted with all advantages that could be desired."[59]

By ascribing the victories at Agincourt and Poissy to the innate vir-tue of English soldiers rather than to the longbow, Ralegh extended his underlying argument for the viability of an anti-Spanish foreign policy. His explanation attributed these victories, not to transient technological superiority, but to the English constitution. His imitation thus adapted Livy, whose diminution of Alexander astutely highlighted the superior-ity of Roman military education. While Ralegh's interpretation surely ap-pealed to hawkish readers, it may also have provided James with a reason to believe that, despite England's impoverishment, weak army, and infe-rior numbers, a war policy might not result in cataclysmic defeat. English valor and his own ancient expertise, Ralegh insisted, would carry the day against the improvident Spanish.

RALEGH'S FALLEN WARFARE

Though Ralegh wished to suggest the viability of a war-oriented English foreign policy, he recognized the potential danger in its overzealous advo-cacy. Even before James ascended the English throne his commitment to peace had been unwavering, and he was not likely to disown this program without some acknowledgment of its moral basis. Ralegh's paean to En-glish martial virtue was, therefore, tempered by a history of warfare that,

57. Ibid.

58. For the continuing idealization of a noble military ethos, see David J. B. Trim, ed., *The Chivalric Ethos and the Development of Military Professionalism* (Leiden: Brill, 2003); and Roger Manning, *Swordsmen: The Martial Ethos in the Three Kingdoms* (New York: Oxford University Press, 2003).

59. *HW*, 5.1.1.313.

compared to contemporary alternatives, revealed Ralegh as despondent about war's necessity. This approach stressed his agreement with James and presented his desire for a Spanish war as restrained and moderate.

Ralegh's history of warfare constituted an intervention in an ongoing debate about the morality of battlefield engagement. Because Machiavelli advocated a citizen army and criticized the use of mercenaries, modern historians have read the *Art of War* primarily as a republican treatise in line with the *Discorsi*.[60] But Machiavelli's *ars militaris* shared a moral foundation with the practices outlined in *The Prince*. His art of warfare comprised a set of maneuvers intended to shift the trajectory of battle, and, in his account, ancient commanders had confounded their enemies less through tactical deployment of resources than through wit or deceit. On numerous occasions, their stratagems of feigned truces and midnight ambushes clearly contravened Christian knightly ideals, which glorified direct combat between the luminaries of each side. Machiavelli's prescriptions were appropriate for a realpolitik prince intent on enforcing his power. For example, he recommended that the best tactic to subjugate a neighboring people began with consulting them concerning some unrelated venture. Their suspicion having been removed, "thei shal geve thee commoditie, to be able easely to satisfie thy desire."[61] Machiavelli's evidence suggested that ingenuous deceit was the basis of the success of the Roman army, as it was in Roman politics.

If Machiavellian trickery and deception explained the success of Roman arms—if the *ars militaris* rewarded and required diabolic amorality—early modern scholars and commanders feared whether imitation of its military apparatus could be justified theologically. Some responded by giving to military science a genealogy that legitimated its moral basis by putting victory and defeat on theological bases. In his 1602 *The Stratagems of Jerusalem*, the Puritan sergeant-at-arms Lodowick Lloyd argued that the *artes militares* had been a divine gift to the Hebrews.[62] While Machiavelli dissected military encounters with literal and historical interpretive tools, those that Lloyd deployed were purely exegetical. He minutely analyzed the wartime rites of the Hebrews to assert that precise adherence to

---

60. See, e.g., Pocock, *The Machiavellian Moment*, 183–218.

61. Niccolò Machiavelli, *The Arte of Warre* (1520), trans. Peter Withorne (London, 1573), lxxxviiir.

62. See Hale, *Renaissance War Studies*, 488. Hale rightly inserts Lloyd within a thread of Puritan militant divines who conceived of war as a blessing. See also Michael Walzer, *The Revolution of the Saints: A Study in the Origins of Radical Politics* (New York: Atheneum, 1968).

divine injunctions specific to military engagement determined battlefield success. Moses was depicted as the general of a mobile church militant responsible for fulfilling the ceremonial martial requirements God demanded of Israel. As Lloyd explained: "the Lorde set downe certaine martiall lawes to *Moses*, to governe and to rule his people." Foremost of these was orderly array around the Ark of the Covenant, whose tabernacle door was inscribed with these military precepts. Lloyd's *ars militaris*, which sought to revive this sacred discipline, did not address functional material components such as arms and formation; as he explained, the Israelites' victories were gained, "not by devised stratagems out of their owne heads, but by following the commandements of the Lord, which are the onely stratagems of all victories." Pursuit of advantage could not strengthen a divinely blessed people. As Lloyd argued: "The Hebrewes had no such store houses prepared, nor mony laid up, nor provisions readie, but the foode was such from the Lord that they wanted nothing, and yet they conquered more kings, and subdued more countries, then all [other peoples]."[63] And the deceitful stratagems collected by Machiavelli would surely have been taken, by Lloyd, to abrogate this pious science. Lloyd wished to reform an English army on the model of Exodus as a literal church militant, for implementation of this liturgical *ars militaris*, he believed, would endow the English military with the favor of God.

It is unlikely that any English militias or trained bands followed Lloyd's prescriptions. But, across Europe, armies were reorganized according to the Dutch Neostoic humanist Justus Lipsius's 1595 *De Militia Romana*.[64] Lipsius identified the organization and structure of the Roman army as its crucial features. He argued that their successes proved that military fortunes depended on the maintenance of a strict regime of recruitment, order, and discipline, exclaiming: "Look at [Roman] levying of troops: nothing was more precise. Nothing was more suitable than their ordering of troops. Nothing was more severe and divine than their discipline. For if you look only at the minds, numbers, and strength of men, they were often overwhelmed whether in one facet or all of them. But their order and discipline overcame."[65] After Maurice of Nassau implemented

63. Lodowick Lloyd, *The Stratagemes of Jerusalem* (London, 1602), 50–51, 60, 66, 61.

64. For Lipsius, see Oestreich, *Neostoicism and the Early Modern State*. See also Geoffrey Parker, ed., *The Cambridge History of Warfare* (New York: Cambridge University Press, 2005). For reservations, see Peter N. Miller, "Nazis and Neo-Stoics: Otto Brunner and Gerhard Oestreich Before and After the Second World War," *P&P* 176 (2002): 144–86.

65. Justus Lipsius, *Opera Omnia* (Antwerp, 1602), 313. "Quae gens in militia fortior aut felicior? Dilectum vide; nihil accuratius. Ordiné nihil aptius. Disciplina, nihil severius sanc-

the changes Lipsius advocated, the Dutch achieved astounding success in repelling the Habsburgs. Generals across Europe encouraged reform in imitation of the Dutch-Roman model, and English captains who served in the Dutch theater believed that they were participating in a seminary for the Roman *artes militares*. They imported this regimen to England, and Burghley was only one among many who claimed that the English trained bands employed the same regimen as the ancient Romans.[66]

Lipsius also found in classical sources a program of moral philosophy conducive to his model. The decisive elements of military success demanded the values of constancy, resilience, and loyalty prized within Neostoic philosophy.[67] Lipsius had many followers, and their belief that Roman victories resulted from adherence to structural axioms of the *ars militaris* countered the amorality of Machiavelli's deceitful tactics.[68]

Ralegh's efforts to dull his military enthusiasm can be seen in his inflection of the histories of warfare invoked by his predecessors.[69] Like Lloyd, Ralegh recognized the Hebrews as a martial force. In the wake of the revelation on Sinai, he depicted General Moses reforming his people into an organized military unit, explaining: "hee mustered all the Tribes and Families of *Israel*. . . . This great Armie was divided by *Moses* into foure grosse and mightie Battalions, each of which contained the strength of three whole Tribes." He described the size, constitutive tribes, tactical functions, and camp location for each of the battalions.[70]

But, unlike Lloyd, he did not argue that their adherence to divinely given rites constituted a pious military science. Instead of a tabernacle inscribed with military and political lessons, Ralegh's Ark assumed the

---

tiusque. . . . Nam ingenia, numerum, robora hominum si vides; singulis, aut omnibus, saepe vincebantur: superabat Ordo & Disciplina."

66. Burghley claimed: "our discipline of embattailing our army is according to the Roman dizeniers." Quoted in Fissel, "Tradition and Invention," 134.

67. See esp. Oestreich, *Neostoicism and the Early Modern State*, 8, 79; and Mark Morford, *Stoics and Neostoics: Rubens and the Circle of Lipsius* (Princeton, NJ: Princeton University Press, 1991).

68. On Lipsius as a response to Machiavelli, see Oestreich, *Neostoicism and the Early Modern State*, 49. For other similar responses, see Sydney Anglo, *Machiavelli: The First Century: Studies in Enthusiasm, Hostility, and Irreverence* (Oxford: Oxford University Press, 2005), chap. 14.

69. On Ralegh's Machiavellism, see LeFranc, *Sir Walter Raleigh*, passim; and Vincent Luciani, "Ralegh's 'Discourse of War' and Machiavelli's 'Discorsi,'" *Modern Philology* 46 (1948): 122–31. On Ralegh's Neostoicism, see Adriana McCrea, *Constant Minds: Political Virtue and the Lipsian Paradigm in England, 1584–1650* (Toronto: University of Toronto Press, 1997); and Jonathan Gibson, "Civil War in 1614: Lucan, Gorges and Prince Henry," in Clucas and Davies, eds., *The Crisis of 1614 and the Addled Parliament*, 161–66.

70. *HW*, 2.5.1.295.

status of a sacred relic at the center of the Israelite army, a sign of God's power and mercy unrelated to martial endeavors. Those who abandoned its custody committed an exclusively religious, not a military, pollution. Indeed, Ralegh used his discussion of the tabernacle to suggest that he sided with those Anglicans, increasingly favored by James, who resisted Puritan agitation to remove ornamentation from churches by describing church decoration as reflecting the sanctified beauty of a divine gift. Proper caretaking of the Ark, Ralegh explained,

> which all Ages have in some degree imitated, is now so forgotten and cast away in this super-fine Age, by those of the *Familie*, by the *Anabaptist*, *Brownist*, and other *Sectaries*, as all cost and care bestowed and had of the Church, wherein God is to be served and worshipped, is accounted a kinde of *Poperie*, and as proceeding from an idolatrous disposition: insomuch as Time would soone bring to passe (if it were not resisted) that God would be turned out of Churches into Barnes, and from thence againe into the Fields and Mountaines, and under the Hedges; and the Offices of the *Ministerie* (robbed of all dignitie and respect) be as contemptible as these places; all Order, Discipline, and Church-Government, left to newnesse of opinion, and mens fancies: yea, and soone after, as many kindes of Religions would spring up, as there are Parish-Churches within *England*: every contentious and ignorant person clothing his fancie with *the Spirit of God*, and his imagination with *the gift of Revelation*.[71]

Neglect of ceremonial observances of the Ark of the Covenant did not incur battlefield defeat; rather, it heralded the disintegration of religion and the fragmentation of Christian Europe that Ralegh mourned in his own time. Rather than using the rites of the army to focus on Hebrew military exploits, he instead condemned their neglect in the doctrinal sectarians he observed in the world immolating around him and hinted at agreement with the "avant-garde conformity" gaining sway in James's favored ecclesiastical circles.[72]

Ralegh, moreover, described Hebrew warfare as a brutal, artless collision of force. Even on the sole occasion when he commended ancient Hebrew strategizing, he suggested that it was an unusual action: "*Josua*

---

71. *HW*, 2.5.2.296–97.

72. Peter Lake, "Lancelot Andrewes, John Buckeridge, and Avant-Garde Conformity in the Court of James I," in Peck, ed., *The Mental World of the Jacobean Court*, 113–33.

shewed himselfe a skilfull man of Warre, for that in those ancient times he used the stratageme of an ambush . . . he marched all night from his camp at *Gilgal*, and set on them early the next day, when they suspected no enemie at hand."[73] He implied that this simple tactic was unknown in the ancient world. Warfare was not a divinely given art perfectly exercised by God's chosen people, but a human invention gradually advanced by historical study until reaching its Roman zenith.

Further, unlike Lloyd's or Lipsius's genealogy of warfare, Ralegh's did not rehabilitate the status of soldiers by linking military endeavors to piety, morality, or honor. Instead, Ralegh repeatedly decried the tendency of even Christian kings to break oaths in order to gain slight advantage, despite the divine punishments such abrogations surely incurred.[74] And, despite his previous bragging about English valor, he noted the futility of military honor in his discussion of the Roman consul Atilius Regulus. During the First Punic War, Regulus had been captured by the Carthaginians, who had sent him to Rome to convince the Senate to accept terms of peace favorable to Carthage. After swearing an oath to return to Carthage if he could not sway the Senate, Regulus went to Rome, where he convinced the Senate to reject the terms. In a show of principle, he honored his promise and returned to the African city, though he surely anticipated his subsequent execution. Christians such as Augustine joined Roman writers in praising Regulus as an exemplar of Roman integrity.[75] But Ralegh considered his obstinacy foolishly counterproductive. He showed that the course of events rendered such self-sacrifice moot; Regulus had been so intent on preserving Rome's honor that he sacrificed his life to no advantage.[76]

Honor, Ralegh frequently noted, was not always strategically beneficial. Nor was the martial life conducive to the valiant, for Ralegh saw the condition of the soldier as without glory or nobility. Men of arms, he knew from experience, were viewed with suspicion: "From the envie of our equals, and jealosie of our Masters, be they Kings, or Commonweales . . . there is no Profession more unprosperous than that of Men of Warre, and great Captaines, being no Kings." Jealousy constituted only a minor inconvenience compared to the consequences for the iniquities that Ralegh portrayed as unavoidable to the military man. As he explained: "the spoyles, rapes, famine, slaughter of the innocent, vastation, and burning, with a

73. *HW*, 2.6.8.326.

74. *HW*, 2.6.8.327–28, 5.1.4.4.336–37.

75. Erving R. Mix, *Marcus Atilius Regulus: Exemplum historicum* (The Hague: Mouton, 1970).

76. *HW*, 5.1.8.356.

world of miseries layed on the labouring man, are so hatefull to God, as with good reason did *Monluc* the Marshall of *France* confesse, *That were not the mercies of* GOD *infinite, and without restriction, it were in vaine for those of his profession to hope for any portion of them: seeing the cruelties by them permitted and committed, were also infinite.*" Actions that ran contrary to divine injunction were unavoidable to the soldier, adherence to godly behavior impossible. His only hope lay in divine mercy. This disquieting characterization of military men extended even to religious warriors; as Ralegh noted of King David: "The warres which *David* had made were iust, and the bloud therein shed was of the enemies of God, and his Church; yet for this cause it was not permitted that his hands should lay the foundations of that holy Temple."[77] Even David had been subject to divine punishment for his holy wars. Ralegh here subtly complimented the king who had been allowed to build the temple, Solomon, who was one of James's models. But he also appeared motivated to dull the enthusiasm for belligerence arising from Puritans like Lloyd, who saw war with Spain as invested with holy necessity.

Instead of drawing an illustrious genealogy for warfare or attributing desirable moral characteristics to its practitioners, this frank admission of the horrors of military life reveals that, like many of his contemporaries, Ralegh recognized with quiet dread the amorality that Machiavelli had blithely described as part of the soldier's life. Ralegh's military science neither required nor rewarded divinely given moral strictures. Triumphs were won by an amoral military science; soldiers operated in a world in which deceit and cruelty were more important than piety or valor. Ralegh agreed with his sovereign that war was a catastrophe that humans wrought on themselves. But he differed from James by accepting war's inevitability. In his view, humanity's depravity led inexorably to conflict, and it was incumbent on kings and commanders to prepare for war. While James hoped that diplomacy could pacify man's violent nature, Ralegh saw man as so fallen, corrupt, and estranged from God that peace was never possible.[78] And active involvement in the military world required the hope for God's merciful forgiveness. Ralegh's brand of warfare—drawn from reading and

---

77. *HW*, 5.6.2.715, 2.17.4.481.

78. Similarly, in the "Discourse of War" (ca. 1614–16), Ralegh lamented that, because "in human reason there hath no means been found of holding all mankind at peace within itself; it is needful that . . . helping our strength with art and wisdom, [we] strive to excel our enemies in those points wherein man is excellent over other creatures." *The Works of Sir Walter Ralegh*, 8:253–54. In this sense, he represented an older form of Calvinism that more closely adhered to Calvin's thought than did most contemporaneous Calvinists.

personal experience—comprised marauding, pillaging, and massacre, the actions of a scourge rather than a holy warrior. He thus did not disown his military experience or his anti-Spanish strategy. He instead portrayed them to James as the disappointed king's distressing obligation. Ralegh's account, like his history of monarchy, was designed to moderate his apparent conflicts with James and showcase his viability as an elite learned counselor, for it acknowledged his past as a soldier without glorifying it and framed a hawkish foreign policy to both James and the public as an undesirable necessity.

PROVIDENCE AND COUNSEL

Ralegh's depiction of warfare thus sought to defuse tensions between his and James's orientations toward war. Vice and brutality characterized Ralegh's depraved world, and his military expertise constituted a dispiriting testimony of the sins enjoined on its inhabitants. But, for Ralegh, military expertise, though worldly and debased, still constituted a vital element in the enactment of Providence. Warfare was not exclusively a sin against God, for it was also an instrument of divine judgment. Ralegh's treatments of the ancient battles revealed that kings and commanders triumphed when they adhered to advice produced by skilled, loyal counselors, as the examples of Charles Howard and Xerxes alike proved. How advice was received determined the course of wars, and those who ignored or ridiculed sound guidance were punished severely. As Ralegh's history unfolded, his past became a narrative of conflict between virtuous and vicious counsel. As with all events, the decisions of kings were steered by Providence, and their judgments constituted evidence of divine favor or rebuke.

Alexander's defeat of Darius at Issus provided Ralegh with an exemplary episode proving that princes followed or ignored counsels at God's discretion. As he recounted, Darius's obstinate ill judgment had handed Alexander victory. The Persian emperor had marshaled his troops to demonstrate his own magnificence rather than to gain tactical advantage; Ralegh scoffed that he arrayed "rather like a masker than a manne of Warre . . . perswading himselfe, as it seemed, to beat *Alexander* with pompe and sumptuous Pagents."[79] Worse, his tactics displayed a fundamental ignorance of military precepts. His massive army would have held a tremendous advantage over Alexander's smaller forces on an open plane,

79. *HW*, 4.2.4.177.

but Darius prepared to attack while his enemy defended a narrow pass where the numerical advantage was immaterial.

Darius responded horrifically when apprised of these faults—worse, even, in Ralegh's account than in that of his source, Quintus Curtius. When the Athenian exile Charidemus warned that a parade of gold-festooned dignitaries and their wives might terrify bystanders but not hardened Greek soldiers, Darius ordered him executed. Ralegh omitted Quintus Curtius's report that he immediately lamented the decision and funded an honorable burial and, instead, used the episode to invoke the maxim, "That Princes safeties is in a desparate case, whose eares iudge all that is profitable to bee too sharpe, and will entertaine nothing that is unpleasant." Ralegh's Darius continued to maneuver impervious to good advice. Even after Charidemus's execution, Darius's Greek mercenaries suggested that he divide "his huge Armie into parts, not committing the whole to one stroke of Fortune, whereby he might have fought many bat-tailes, and have brought no greater numbers at once then might have beene well marshalled and conducted."[80] This wise proposal dissuaded the haz-arding of the entire army on one tactically unsound assault. But Darius's Persian commanders were unwilling to rely on their own skill in handling smaller units separated from the main force. According to Ralegh, they successfully convinced the emperor that his Greek counselors were trai-tors who too should be executed—though Quintus Curtius had reported only that Darius opted not to heed the mercenary's counsel. In the event, Alexander abruptly vanquished Darius's massive army. For Ralegh, this was both a failure of military science and a sign of Providence. He ex-plained: "The infinite wisedome of God doth not worke alwaies by one and the same way, but very often in the alteration of Kingdomes and Estates, by taking understanding from the Governours, so as they can neither give nor discerne of Counsels."[81] God had deprived Darius of the ability to rec-ognize good counsel, bringing him to adhere to the indulgent counsels of sycophants. By this intervention he transferred the mantle of empire from Persia to Greece.

While reason, experience, and prudence were necessary instruments to produce good counsel, divine will controlled the reception of these aids. Ralegh's treatment of the transformation of empires inflected the impact of military science through providential decisionmaking. In this case, over-

---

80. *HW*, 4.2.4.179–80. Note that Racin (*Sir Walter Raleigh as Historian*, 159–63) discusses this passage as a purely literary amplification.

81. *HW*, 4.2.4.180.

emphasis on magnificent display was the lesser of Darius's two crimes; more important was his arrogant embrace of flattering counsels. This episode admonished James with the consequences of ignoring Ralegh's advices. Warfare may not have been pious, but God rewarded those who followed reasonable counsel drawn from studious examination of the divine theater, punishing those overly committed to their own idols and unwilling to absorb the lessons that had been set out for them. Earthly success was contingent on proper interpretation of the past, and Ralegh warned James of dire consequences if the king ignored Ralegh's masterful history.

HISTORICAL ANALYSIS AND ENGLISH GOVERNANCE

Ralegh's ability to formulate expert counsel was dependent on his adept mobilization of evidence in persuasive narratives. The methods Ralegh deployed reflected the historical analyses, not only of military counselors, but also of secretaries and counselors more broadly. Learned statesmen throughout early modern Europe sought to strengthen their governments by creating the conditions to analyze their own polities as they had been trained to examine histories, collecting vast troves of sources that they scoured for fragments of evidence to recombine.[82] Ralegh's remarkable li-

82. For examples of the expert handling of texts by Elizabethan counselors and administrators, see Paul L. Ward, "William Lambarde's Collections on Chancery," *Harvard Library Bulletin* 7 (1953): 271–98; Andrew Watson, "The Manuscript Collection of Walter Cope (d. 1614)," *Bodleian Library Record* 12 (1987): 262–97; Carlson, "The Writings and Manuscript Collections of Francis Thynne"; Simon Adams, "The Papers of Robert Dudley, Earl of Leicester: 1, The Browne-Evelyn Collection," *Archives* 20 (1992): 63–85, "The Papers of Robert Dudley, Earl of Leicester: 2, The Atye-Cotton Collection," *Archives* 20 (1993): 131–44, and "The Papers of Robert Dudley, Earl of Leicester: 3, The Countess of Leicester's Collection," *Archives* 22 (1996): 1–26; Woudhuysen, *Sir Philip Sidney and the Circulation of Manuscripts*; Pamela Selwyn, "'Such Speciall Bookes of Mr Somersettes as Were Sould to Mr Secretary': The Fate of Robert Glover's Collections," in *Books and Collectors, 1200–1700: Essays Presented to Andrew Watson*, ed. James P. Carley and Colin G. C. Tite (London: BL, 1996), 389–402; Jason Scott-Warren, "Reconstructing Manuscript Networks: The Textual Transactions of Sir Stephen Powle," in *Communities in Early Modern England: Networks, Place, Rhetoric*, ed. Alexandra Shepard and Phil Withington (Manchester: Manchester University Press, 2000), 18–37; Colin Tite, *The Manuscript Library of Sir Robert Cotton* (London: BL, 1994), and *The Early Records of Sir Robert Cotton's Library: Formation, Cataloguing, Use* (London: BL, 2003); Julian Roberts, "Extending the Frontiers: Scholar Collectors," in *The Cambridge History of Libraries in Britain and Ireland*, vol. 1, *To 1640*, 292–321; Pamela Selwyn, "Heralds' Libraries," in ibid., 472–88; Deborah Harkness, *The Jewel House: Elizabethan London and the Scientific Revolution* (New Haven, CT: Yale University Press, 2007), 142–80; Robyn Adams, "'The Service I Am Here For': William Hearle in the Marshalsea Prison, 1571," *HLQ* 72 (2009): 217–38, and "A Most Secret Service: William Herle and the Circulation of Intelligence," in Adams and Cox, eds., *Diplomacy and Early Modern Culture*, 63–81; Neil Younger, "William Lambarde and the

brary, microscopic mode of analysis, and didactic expositions replicated the textual and political practices that increasingly structured government administration in early modern Europe.[83]

The secretariat of Principal Secretary Francis Walsingham best illuminates the importation of practices of historical analysis to politics. Two tracts written by Walsingham's secretaries Nicholas Faunt and Robert Beale reveal the close relation between the methods constitutive of historical analysis and the techniques Elizabethan secretaries devised to mobilize evidence for formulating counsel.[84] The Puritan Beale possessed impeccable credentials as a historically minded adviser.[85] He collected books on the Continent during his Marian exile and then while on diplomatic missions through the 1560s and 1570s. The Frankfurt printer André Wechel printed a collection of rare medieval Spanish chronicles drawn largely from his collection. Wechel praised Beale for "following the custom of most men who value erudition and prudence, he cultivated his mind in those things which are most useful and necessary for those preparing to enter government." In particular, this involved compiling "chiefly those [books] that are not easily found" to "erect a library of the best authors,

---

Politics of Enforcement in Early Modern England," *HR* 83 (2010): 69–82; and Stephen Alford, "Some Elizabethan Spies in the Office of Sir Francis Walsingham," in *Diplomacy and Early Modern Culture*, ed. Robyn Adams and Rosanna Cox (Basingstoke: Palgrave Macmillan, 2011), 46–62 For Tudor administration, see, above all, the works of Geoffrey Elton, esp. *The Tudor Revolution in Government: Administrative Changes in the Reign of Henry VIII* (Cambridge: Cambridge University Press, 1953), and *England, 1200–1640* (Ithaca, NY: Cornell University Press, 1969); Christopher Coleman and David Starkey, eds., *Revolution Reassessed: Revisions in the History of Tudor Government and Administration* (Oxford: Clarendon, 1986); Hoak, *The King's Council in the Reign of Edward VI*; and Alford, *The Early Elizabethan Polity*.

83. For examples of the Elizabethan regime directing these techniques more broadly, see chapter 1, n. 30, above.

84. Examples of this sort of literature include Thomas Wilkes's tract in BL Stowe 296, fols. 7r–19v; Beale's tract in Conyers Read, *Mr. Secretary Walsingham*, 1:423–43; Robert Cecil's *The State and Dignity of a Secretaries of Estates Place* (London, 1642); "Nicholas Faunt's Discourse Touching the Office of Principal Secretary of Estate &c. 1592," ed. Charles Hughes, *EHR* 20 (1905): 499–508; and the document ostensibly by John Herbert in *Select Statutes and Other Constitutional Documents Illustrative of the Reigns of Elizabeth and James I*, ed. G. W. Prothero (Oxford: Clarendon, 1913), 166–68. For secretarial practice, valuable studies include Alan G. R. Smith, "The Secretariats of the Cecils, c. 1580–1612," *EHR* 83 (1968): 481–504; Jonathan Elukin, "Keeping Secrets in Medieval and Early Modern English Government," in *Das Geheimnis am Beginn der europäischen Moderne*, ed. Gisela Engel et al. (Frankfurt: Vittorio Klostermann, 2002), 111–29; Jacqueline Vaughan, "Secretaries, Statesmen, and Spies: The Clerks of the Elizabethan Privy Council" (D.Phil. diss., University of St. Andrews, 2002); and Alford, "Some Elizabethan Spies."

85. For Beale, see Mark Taviner, "Robert Beale and the Elizabethan Polity" (Ph.D. diss., University of St. Andrews, 2000); and Patrick Collinson, "Servants and Citizens: Robert Beale and Other Elizabethans," *HR* 79 (2006): 488–511.

primarily historians."[86] Beale—like his fellow Puritan Daniel Rogers— deployed the practices of Archbishop Parker's circle during his European travels, collecting manuscripts and little-known works.[87]

Beale was appointed clerk of the Council during his brother-in-law Walsingham's secretaryship and assumed the duties of principal secretary when Walsingham was unavailable. His "Treatise of the Office of a Councellor and Principall Secretarie to her Majestie" was written in 1592 for Sir Edward Wotton, who hoped to be appointed principal secretary. Many of his prescriptions concerned the proper textual materials to be collected. In addition to Ortelius's atlas and local maps of England and Ireland, he recommended both "dilligent readinge and observacion of the histories of all Countryes" and "a booke of such Treatyes as have, at the least for the space of one hundred yeares, beene betweene this Realme and other Princes and States abroade." He continued: "By the readinge of histories you may observe the examples of times past, judging of their successe."[88] Like so many of his contemporaries, Beale thus advocated the reading of both histories and records to facilitate the production of future counsel.

The secretary's work was not to read texts passively, and Beale recommended that Wotton produce collections of notes extracted from histories, correspondence, and records according to categories such as *religion*, *Ireland*, *defenses*, and *trade*. Similarly, he explained the utility of this regime of information management: "those remembrances may serve as Notes and heades wherto a Secretarie may referre such thinges as he may gett and be acquainted with in the time of his service. And although there be no present use, yet he shall doe well to inquire and looke after such thinges, to cause some of his Clercks to wright them out and, for avoidinge of confucion, to digest them into such heades to serve his turne wher ther shalbe neede."[89] Beale's clerk read his texts as Flacius and Sid-

---

86. Robert Beale, ed., *Rerum Hispanicarum Scriptores Aliquot* (Frankfurt, 1579), iiir. "Si quid autem hac nostra editione praestititsse videbimur, quod sit iucundum aut utile, iis qui historiarum lectione delectantur, eius rei gratia debebitur clarissimo viro Dn. Roberto Belo . . . indefatigatoque studio & consuetudine multorum virorum qui prudentia & eruditione valebant, animum ita excoluit iis artibus quae accessuro ad rempub. sunt maxima utiles ac etiam necessariae. . . . Nec satis fuit ipsi animum bonis artibus excoluisse, nisi etiam secum domum referret scriptores, quorum lectione perpetuo aliquid ad ingenii cultum adiecerit, quos quocunque pervenit diligenter conquisivit, & praesertim eos qui non ubique sunt obvii, a quibus coemendis nulla precii magnitudine deterreri potuit, & tandem sibi instruxit bibliothecam optimis scriptoribus, & praesertim historiographis, refertissimam."

87. For Rogers in this regard, see BL Add. MS 21088. See also Vine, *In Defiance of Time*, 32–36.

88. Read, *Mr. Secretary Walsingham*, 1:433, 442–43.

89. Ibid., 431.

ney had advised their correspondents to read histories and as Ortelius had read all sources—skillfully excerpting and organizing the materials under specific heads that would facilitate later use. In this case, the implementation of these protocols encouraged the assiduous preservation of textual records for governance.

Faunt, Walsingham's personal secretary, also described a fastidious system of note taking in his 1592 "Discourse touchinge the Office of principall Secretarie of Estate." This work similarly insisted that counselors process their constant influx of textual records according to contemporary practices of engaging histories. One clerk's primary responsibility was to "extract the substance" of incoming missives. Preservation of all these redactions was incumbent, for they might prove useful in future matters; Faunt recommended that they be "well digested into small books, if they bee matteriall, and have anie refference either to thinges past, present, or that bee likely to fall out in accion."[90] And he too ordered that a wide array of collections be created and augmented as appropriate—journals, surveys of England and Scotland, and books archiving documents on foreign negotiations, military matters, coinage, and crown revenues.

His instructions for handling foreign correspondence illuminate the significance of the enormous archive Faunt envisioned. He ordered all commissions preserved, with subsequent communications between the secretary and the correspondent appended, "according to their dates soe neare as canne bee." This assembly of records Faunt explicitly described as creating histories. He recommended: "at ye end of the said negotiacion message Commission treatie etc to sett downe breefly the Causes or occasions whereupon the same was discontinued or howe it end and what effect it brought forth etc. which would serve *instead of an Historie* an apt introduction to other negotiacions that are likely to followe of the same nature."[91] The counselor's collection functioned as a documentary history—differing little from those produced by Flacius and Parker—that would then be used in devising future counsel.

Beale's and Faunt's precepts indicate that learned governors administered the state by analyzing the contemporary polity with techniques learned by analyzing the past. Calendaring and preserving records allowed scholarly counselors to govern effectively by placing tools at their disposal for understanding the condition of the realm and for generating prudent

---

90. "Nicholas Faunt's Discourse," 502. The "Discourse" was addressed to an unknown recipient.

91. Ibid., 505 (emphasis added).

advice. These men conceptualized their collection and preservation of records as the act of producing authoritative collections of case histories of their own time.[92]

Beale's and Faunt's prescriptions, in fact, codified the practices of recording and organization within Walsingham's secretariat. In the mid-1580s, Walsingham recommended that his secretary Thomas Lake compile from his papers "A memorial of collectyons," organized according to categories similar to those described by Beale and Faunt.[93] Lake exceeded Walsingham's request and organized them into compilations by 1588, whose contents he neatly cataloged in Walsingham's "Table Book." This neat octavo volume contained "A state of all the written bookes in the Chests or Abroad."[94] The category "Books of Home Matters," for example, contained collections of records concerning military matters, recusants, ecclesiastical politics, trade, the royal household, Wales, crown lands, the Order of the Garter, and crown finances.[95] Each book was crammed with records; the recusant book, for example, contained page after page of lists of drafts, lists, instructions, reports of sightings of the Jesuit Edmund Campion, abstracts of deputations, copies of commissions, and lists of names of principal recusants and their places of asylum.[96] Lake also provided indices to the contents of the collections, facilitating analysis of the miniature archives constituted by these compilations.[97]

Beale too amassed extensive collections that reveal that implementation of the methods of historical analysis in the ordering of government records applied on a smaller scale the work that Ralegh directed universally to the ancient world.[98] In 1587 or 1588, around the time when Lake was ordering Walsingham's collections, Beale bound in chronological order documents

92. For case histories, see Nancy Siraisi, "Girolamo Cardano and the Art of the Medical Narrative," *JHI* 52 (1991): 581–602, and "Anatomizing the Past."

93. BL Harley 6035, fols. 107r–111r.

94. BL Stowe 162, fol. 1r.

95. Ibid., fols. 3v–4v. The lists within these categories, moreover, were periodically augmented with entries in a different hand and notes indicating when books had been loaned. A marginal note reading "Sr R Cecill hath it of me 1596" has been penned next to "A book of Plotts and discourses" on Scotland, indicating that this "Table Book" was still being consulted six years after Walsingham's death. Ibid., fols. 1v, 2r.

96. Ibid., fols. 32–51r.

97. Note similarities here to the developments described in Adam Fox, "Custom, Memory, and the Authority of Writing," in *The Experience of Authority in Early Modern England*, ed. Paul Griffiths, Adam Fox, and Steve Hindle (Basingstoke: Macmillan, 1996), 89–116; and Paul Slack, "Government and Information in Seventeenth-Century England," *P&P* 184 (2004): 33–68.

98. See *Catalogue of the Additions to the Manuscripts: The Yelverton Manuscripts—Additional Manuscripts 48000–48196*, 2 vols. (London, 1994).

on foreign governments and affairs that he had collected over the previous twenty years. One representative volume consisted primarily of papers acquired while secretary to Ambassador Henry Norris in Paris in 1566, including accounts of the household expenditures of French kings, copies of French treaties, and lists of officeholders. The volume also included materials from Sir John Smythe, ambassador to Spain in 1576–77, creating a compact survey of the two kingdoms.[99] Another representative volume contained a register of medieval treaties involving the English crown that he gathered from rolls and charters alongside extracts concerning the histories and financial operations of Hanse towns.[100] Many of his similar collections include extracts and epitomes of histories and chronicles.[101]

The method by which Beale acquired his sources underscores the significance of these collections. Around 1587, he commissioned a number of friends and correspondents to provide him with copies of the charters of and confirmations from former monastic houses. He noted on many of the papers where the originals were located, who had procured them, and when he had received them. He had been educated at the house of John Hales in Coventry, and he used Hales's sons (or nephews) Charles and John to acquire materials concerning Coventry's Benedictine priory.[102] The Haleses were not Beale's only correspondents. In May 1587, he consulted Sir Henry Fanshawe, the queen's remembrancer in the Exchequer, to make extracts "out of an olde booke written in parchment sometimes apperteyning unto the dissolved Priory of the City of Coventry, conteyning a Register of their charters, deedes and Rentalls."[103] In 1587, a Joseph Wheler obtained records for him on Priors Marston near Coventry, and the same year Beale procured records from a Mr. Sutton of Lincoln's Inn and "old rowles" from a "Mr William Walter of Temple."[104] Beale amassed extracts from records preserved in the Tower, sometimes venturing there to record them himself, other times receiving copies authenticated by the keeper of

---

99. BL Add. MS 48026.

100. BL Add. MS 14029.

101. See, e.g., BL Add. MS 48151.

102. BL Add. MS 32100, fols. 12r, 57r, 80r, 84v, 85v, 87r, 89r, 123r. For the Haleses, see McLaren, "Prophecy and Providentialism in the Reign of Elizabeth I." Note also that the younger John Hales previously had performed scholarly services for Beale by preparing notes to rebut the Scottish bishop John Leslie's defense of Mary's right to succeed Elizabeth. BL Add. MS 48043. This may have happened as early as 1571, though more likely it occurred in the 1580s.

103. BL Add. MS 32100, fol. 20r.

104. For references to Sutton, see ibid., fols. 1–6r, 13r, 34v, 40r. For Walter, see ibid., fols. 17v, 78r, and passim.

the Tower records, Thomas Heneage.[105] He consulted the collections of the antiquarian John Stow and had documents sent to him from the Coventry lawyer Arthur Gregory.[106] He also received documents from Robert Cook, Clarenceux King of Arms, Robert Glover, Somerset Herald, and Burghley's client Walter Cope.[107] Beale thus consulted statesmen, heralds, friends, and antiquaries to compile extracts of charters, rolls, charges, commissions, letters, cartularies, papal bulls, and an Anglo-Saxon gloss. Nor did he omit chronicles; he consulted Stow's copy of Gervase of Canterbury's "Life of Thomas Becket" and Matthew Paris's *Flores Historiarum*.[108]

The significance of Beale's volume emerged from the narrative of church history it supported. The documents illustrated how, under the papal yoke, the medieval church levied outrageous taxes and asserted an economic tyranny that subsumed every English subject.[109] Beale thus adopted Parker's project, using antiquarian methods to produce histories documenting papal intrusion into the English church and English politics.

Beale's techniques of information retrieval and synthesis were his expertise, and, even after his disgrace in the early 1590s, Burghley sent Beale questions to research concerning papal rights and instances of successions to queens in hereditary monarchies. He replied appreciatively to Beale's response that Christianity had been introduced to England in 156 "before the pope were knowne to have any iurisdiction at all," list of restraints on papal jurisdiction in France, Spain, and Germany, and catalog "Of Monarchyes hereditarie by women."[110] At around the same time, Beale also sent Burghley notes from statute books, chronicles, and "ex archivis" on Scottish law and on Edward I's 1291 adjudication of the Scottish succession.[111]

Similar manuscript miscellanies containing catalogs of dispersed repositories or extracts of official records litter English archives.[112] Eliz-

---

105. Ibid., fols. 49r, 73r.

106. For Stow, see ibid., fols. 50r, 52r, 54r, 198r. For Gregory, see ibid., fols. 125r, 126r. For Stow's own use of these same techniques, see Oliver Harris, "Stow and the Contemporary Antiquarian Network," in Gadd and Gillespie, eds., *John Stow (1525–1605) and the Making of the English Past*, 27–36.

107. For Cook, see ibid., fols. 134r, 134v, 135v, 139r. For Glover, see ibid., fols. 77r, 208r, 219r. For Cope, see ibid., fol. 140r.

108. Ibid., fols. 54r, 56r.

109. Compare his note, ibid., fol. 133r: "Charters to shew that the kings and Noblemen did give decimas de dominicis."

110. BL Add. MS 48101, fols. 304ff., 314.

111. See BL Add. MS 48117, fols. 201ff., 206r.

112. For example, a small sample of comparable items in the collection of Lord Chancellor Thomas Egerton, Baron Ellessmere, includes HEH EL 1120, HEH EL 1122, HEH EL 1169, HEH EL 2009, HEH EL 2547, HEH EL 2555, and HEH EL 35 B 60.

abeth's most elite counselors were constantly collecting, circulating, organizing, and interpreting records. To some, statesmen sifting through papers constituted banausic instruments of providential will. Though Burghley was, as his clerk and biographer John Clapham noted, chronically hampered by gout, divine foresight immured his most precious instrument from this malady. Clapham noted: "it was observed by diverse that albeit many weeks together his arms and legs were grievously tormented with that disease, yet his right hand was seldom or never so possessed with it, but that within two or three days he was able to write; God sparing that hand, it should seem, as a special instrument, whereby so much good was wrought for the weal public in his time."[113] He portrayed Burghley's administrative labor as fulfilling divine will, his medical history serving as an exemplary lesson. Ralegh viewed the reconstitution of the past as providential; for Clapham, the means of organizing and interpreting documents for historical analysis was no less imbued with divine oversight.

The consonance between state administration and the production of histories reveals a central feature of Ralegh's petition for favor, for his minute analysis of his astonishing collection of sources exhibited a comparable ability to manage paperwork. His mastery of methods of information management vital to governance—which themselves derived from canons of prophetic historical analysis—was a critical component of his ministerial self-presentation, qualifying him to operate at the center of a reconfigured Jacobean regime as Howard and Cecil had before him and Burghley before them.

Ralegh looked to the theater of ancient histories to discern immutable patterns of causation that would, in turn, allow him to proffer prophetic advice to his king. By no means was his goal to use this past to alter the constitution of England; he rather wished to strengthen Jacobean government by using his expertise to redirect it toward his own desired anti-Spanish policies. The practices of Walsingham and Beale similarly were directed toward firming up the Elizabethan regime. But their methods exerted transformative subterranean effects. Though practitioners of this model did not seek to alter English governance, the application of the methods of historical knowledge transformed political practice. While historians have tended to argue that early modern Europe's political culture transformed when the emphasis on historical study revived classical re-

113. John Clapham, *Elizabeth of England: Certain Observations Concerning the Life and Reign of Queen Elizabeth*, ed. Evelyn Plummer Read and Conyers Read (Philadelphia: University of Pennsylvania Press, 1951), 80–81.

publicanism, investigating the practices of early modern statesmen reveals less an ideological transformation than a dramatic change at the level of quotidian political practice. This shift can be seen in Beale's and Faunt's prescriptions and Walsingham's practices, but it is also suggested by the explosion in the volume of extant sources dating from the late sixteenth century, the increased attention to parish registers and bills of mortality from the 1590s, and the expanding purview of the State Paper Office in the 1610s.[114] It took the shape of an increased concern with the compilation and manipulation of information, and it reflected the concerted intellectual program derived from innovative techniques in the production and evaluation of histories. The consequence of this revision of the modes of political practice was a regime that emphasized the collection, preservation, and deployment of textual records as instruments of counsel and of power, an information state primarily concerned with recording its subjects and enemies as a means to govern them.

HISTORY APPLIED TO ENGLAND

The implementation of historical analysis transformed political practice by emphasizing the compilation and preservation of information. Elizabeth's counselors, always convinced that her regime verged on collapse, frantically collected records with which they could identify her enemies, force intransigent provincials to adhere to her will, and stabilize her regime.[115] But, while historical practices were deployed to strengthen the existing regime, the culture of historical analysis also led some of its participants to construct visions of the past that diverged sharply from received histories justifying traditional authority. The reports of the Society

114. See Ward, "William Lambarde's Collections"; J. C. Robertson, "Reckoning with London: Interpreting the *Bills of Mortality* before John Graunt," *Urban History* 23 (1996): 325–50; Slack, "Government and Information"; and my "From Abbey to Archive: Managing Texts and Records in Early Modern England," *Archival Science* 10 (2010): 249–66.

115. Note that this posits historical analysis as the intellectual response to the problems faced by the regime, problems best elaborated in Steve Hindle, *The State and Social Change in Early Modern England, c. 1550–1640* (Basingstoke: Macmillan, 2000). One might argue that the growth of the news industry represented the expansion of this enterprise beyond the central regime. See Richard Cust, "News and Politics in Early Seventeenth-Century England," *P&P* 112 (1986): 60–90; Adam Fox, "Rumour, News and Popular Political Opinion in Elizabethan and Early Stuart England," *HJ* 40 (1997): 507–620; Joad Raymond, ed., *News, Newspapers and Society in Early Modern Britain* (London: F. Cass, 1999); and D. R. Woolf, "News, History, and the Construction of the Present in Early Modern England," in *The Politics of Information in Early Modern Europe*, ed. Brendan Dooley and Sabrina A. Baron (London: Routledge, 2001), 80–118.

of Antiquaries, a semiformal academy of statesmen, heralds, and scholars who examined local institutions, offices, geographical divisions, customs, and monuments, illustrate how the reanimation of evidence farmed from a broad range of sources might generate alternative pasts that undermined the basis of the contemporary order.

The society began meeting around 1586, with its participants circulating and discussing short tracts until disbanding in 1607.[116] Members—including Beale and several others already mentioned in this chapter—produced histories of English institutions, building them from evidence collected from historical crown proclamations, writs, charters, and chronicles. The society was committed to preserving rare sources for the English past, and, in 1602, Robert Cotton spearheaded a proposal for a national library "to preserve divers old books concerning the matter of history of this realm, original charters, and monuments." This repository, the petition explained, would serve "for the better information of all noblemen and gentlemen studious of antiquity, whereby they may be enabled to do unto her majesty and the realm, such service as shall be requisitie for their place."[117] Past, present, and future records were to be collected in a central location where they could be set to use by skilled analysts of causation.

The tracts that the society produced typically aimed to strengthen the existing political and religious order. Cecil's client Arthur Agarde was the most frequent contributor to the society, and his histories reinforced clear political and religious positions. For example, his 1604 "Antiquity of the Christian Religion in this Island" depicted the English as accepting Christianity in 167 under King Lucius's orders. In Agarde's vision, England then thrived as a Christian nation for 152 years until the Saxons expelled the Britons and turned the nation pagan. At the instigation of the pope, Saint Augustine of Canterbury had reconverted the island in 462, though it again slipped into pagan ruin. Agarde's primary source was "a large booke of St. Augustines of Canterbury, wherein was a full story of our island wrote about Henry the 5 his time," supplemented by an "auncient" catalog of the archbishops of York, registers of Ely and Glastonbury, and Polydore Vergil's

---

116. See Linda Van Norden, "The Elizabethan College of Antiquaries" (Ph.D. diss., University of California, Los Angeles, 1949), and "Sir Henry Spelman on the Chronology of the Elizabethan Society of Antiquaries," *HLQ* 13 (1950): 131–60; Sharpe, *Sir Robert Cotton*; Parry, *The Trophies of Time*; the works of Woolf, esp. *The Idea of History in Early Stuart England*, 191–92; and Vine, *In Defiance of Time*, 51–79.

117. "A Project touching a Petition to be exhibited unto her Majesty [Queen Elizabeth] for the Erecting of a Library and an Academy for the Study of Antiquities and History," in *A Collection of Curious Discourses, Written by Eminent Antiquaries upon Several Heads in our English Antiquities* (2 vols.), ed. Thomas Hearne (London, 1775), 1:324.

Anglica Historia. Agarde, then, scrutinized medieval records and chronicles to solidify an Anglican history in which England had originally converted to Christianity by royal fiat, rather than from papal influence.[118]

Agarde was also one of several members of the society who wrote tracts between 1603 and 1605 on the history of Parliament to counter Polydore Vergil's assignation of the date of the first parliament to 1116.[119] He did not provide a solid date for the foundation of Parliament, but he concluded from his scrutiny of chronicles and records that it was prior to the conversion of the island by Augustine. This chronology refuted the suggestion that papal authority had been exercised in England long before Parliament, with its implication that Parliament had no right to expel the pope. And that Parliament antedated the Norman Conquest presented it—and the common law—as venerable and native rather than a foreign imposition.

Agarde's histories of the English church and Parliament provided firm support for the Reformation. But other histories drawn up by members of the society hinted at more radical pasts in their enthusiastic rebuttals of Vergil. The discussion of Parliament's origins had, in fact, been initiated in 1603 by John Dodderidge, then a sergeant-at-law and a future judge of the King's Bench.[120] Like Agarde, Dodderidge ascribed a deep history to this institution, gleaning from the twelfth-century chronicle *Liber Eliensis*, charters in the eleventh-century abbot Ingulphus of Crowland's dubious chronicle, French historians, Tacitus, Cicero, and Bede evidence that Parliament was a significant component of pre-Roman British governance. Like Daneau and Ralegh, however, Dodderidge harkened to an even earlier past to describe Parliament as the first English political institution necessitated by the faltering of an idyllic freedom. He explained: "Before the time of sovereignty, Nature's law directed men to the love of society, and care to preserve it; and gained free consent even of lawless men, to admit of certain customs as laws, from hence framing matter of form for a com-

118. Arthur Agarde, "Of the Antiquity of the Christian Religion in this Island," in ibid., 2:160–64. See Felicity Heal, "What Can King Lucius Do for You? The Reformation and the Early British Church," *EHR* 120 (2005): 593–614.

119. Arthur Agarde, "Of the Antiquity of Parliaments in England," in Hearne, ed., *Collection of Curious Discourses*, 1:295. This date thus assigned ancient origins to Parliament that easily antedated the Norman Conquest. Compare Christopher Hill, "The Myth of the Norman Yoke," in *Puritanism and Revolution* (London: Secker & Warburg, 1958), 46–111.

120. John Dodderidge, "Of the Antiquity, Power, Order, State, Manner, Persons, and Proceedings of the High Court of Parliament in England," in Hearne, ed., *Collection of Curious Discourses*, 1:281. See Pauline Croft, "Sir John Doddridge, King James I, and the Antiquity of Parliament," *Parliaments, Estates, and Representation* 12 (1992): 95–107; and R. J. Terrill, "Humanism and Rhetoric in Legal Education: The Contribution of Sir John Dodderidge (1555–1628)," *Journal of Legal History* 2 (1981): 30–44.

monwealth. But new springing mischiefs standing remediless by the elder customs, caused, for remedy thereof, the calling of yearly councils, the original no doubt of our after parliaments."[121] He posited an initial, kingless golden age in English history that had collapsed under the weight of unpunished amorality.

While Daneau and Ralegh identified monarchies as the first preventative measures put in place, Dodderidge attributed this role to "great assemblies, then called Counsels, now Parliaments." The members of Parliament in Dodderidge's ancient history were the learned class of ancient Britons. As he explained: "Those sages the Druides . . . had yearly conventions of their nobles and best people, in a middle consecrated plots of this kingdom." This assembly first received the authority to maintain order. And the legal system it devised, Dodderidge insisted, remained in force even in his time: "The ancient laws of the Britaines, which (to the honour of our common laws) have their use to this day, were composed in their common counsels. . . . So before our Britaines learned the laws of their victours, they held their common counsels."[122] Parliament was, thus, the original institution of English governance, protecting the common law that was its original form of justice.

The historical relation between law and king articulated by Dodderidge differed radically from Ralegh's—and even more from James's. The future King's Bench justice envisioned an ancient order in which council preceded king, and law received the consent of the entire community long before monarchy was introduced. His history indicated that the institution of Parliament was indigenous to Britain and had been preserved, if in slightly altered form, since before recorded memory. This vision challenged the royal prerogative with evidence of the historical origins and continuity of the form of government that would later be called the "ancient constitution."[123]

The reports of Agarde and other members of the society likely sought to dilute the potential sharpness of Dodderidge's claims, for his analysis gave full historical exposition to the constitutional vision trumpeted by John Fortescue and later consolidated by Edward Coke. James, in fact, strongly discouraged a prospective reunion of the Society of Antiquaries

---

121. Dodderidge, "Of the Antiquity . . . of Parliament," 282.

122. Ibid., 282–83.

123. J. G. A. Pocock, *The Ancient Constitution and the Feudal Law: A Study of English Historical Thought in the Seventeenth Century* (Cambridge: Cambridge University Press, 1957); Sharpe, *Sir Robert Cotton*; and Glenn Burgess, *The Politics of the Ancient Constitution: An Introduction to English Political Thought, 1600–1642* (Basingstoke: Macmillan, 1992).

in 1614, likely because of the potential danger of this sort of analysis.[124] But Englishmen in later decades who believed that Stuart absolutism violated England's constitution of "time immemorial" clung to this rendition of the British past.[125] It would be misleading to claim that future Parliamentarians uniformly adhered to the historical vision articulated by 1604 among the Society of Antiquaries, or to suggest that civil war inevitably proceeded once Dodderidge fashioned his chronology for the origins of law and kingship in opposition to James's own, or even to insist that Dodderidge recognized his anti-Vergilian analysis as undermining royal authority. Nonetheless, it is significant that the ancient constitution, which is typically described as an insular Stuart artifact, was wrought and honed as an iteration of the culture of historical analysis in late Elizabethan England that itself derived from the flourishing of learned counsel extending throughout Europe.[126] When initially introduced into England, elite counselors directed these practices to furthering the interests of the crown; indeed, Ralegh's *History* represents a species of this form of historical counsel. As the institutional relationship between king and Parliament became contentious in the following decades, those supporting limitations on royal power turned to the history of Parliament.[127] Their concept of the

124. See David Weil Baker, "Jacobean Historiography and the Election of Richard III," *HLQ* 70 (2007): 311–42.

125. For another example, the anonymous compiler of a pre-1617 collection entitled "A Collection of Notes out of the Recordes in the Tower" drew primarily on evidence yielded from medieval Parliament rolls to produce a section entitled "The kinges Aucthourytie limited and restrayned." HEH EL 1169, fols. 16–19.

126. See, in this vein, Alan Cromartie, "The Constitutionalist Revolution: The Transformation of Political Culture in Early Stuart England," *P&P* 163 (1999): 76–120, and *The Constitutionalist Revolution: An Essay on the History of England, 1450–1642* (Cambridge: Cambridge University Press, 2006).

127. Note here the similar sequence of events—though the different chronology—described in Soll's *Publishing the Prince*. For later Jacobean and Caroline historical practice, see works cited in introduction n. 4 above; Pocock, *The Ancient Constitution and the Feudal Law*; Kevin Sharpe, "The Foundation of the Chairs of History at Oxford and Cambridge," *History of Universities* 2 (1982): 127–52; Graham Parry, *The Golden Age Restor'd: The Culture of the Stuart Court, 1603–42* (Manchester: Manchester University Press, 1981); Bradford, "Stuart Absolutism and the Utility of Tacitus"; Salmon, "Seneca and Tacitus in Jacobean England"; R. Malcom Smuts, *Court Culture and the Origins of a Royalist Tradition in Early Stuart England* (Philadelphia: University of Pennsylvania Press, 1987), and "Court-Centered Politics and the Uses of Roman Historians, c. 1590–1630," in *Culture and Politics in Early Stuart England*, ed. Kevin M. Sharpe and Peter Lake (London: Macmillan, 1994), 21–43; Blair Worden, "Ben Jonson among the Historians," in Sharp and Lake, eds., *Culture and Politics in Early Stuart England*, 67–89; Womersley, "Sir Henry Savile's Translation of Tacitus and the Political Interpretation of Elizabethan Texts"; Stenhouse, "Thomas Dempster, Royal Historian to James I"; Mellor, "Tacitus, Academic Politics, and Regicide in the Reign of Charles I"; and Baker, "Jacobean Historiography and the Election of Richard III."

ancient constitution was strengthened by the methods that Continental scholars had developed into a vital technique for acquiring surrogate experience and deriving counsel throughout Europe from the early sixteenth century.[128]

It would be remiss to ignore one lurking influence on this tradition. Dodderidge's vision of a Druidic council prior to the Roman invasion provided an ancient foundation for claims allotting sweeping powers to Parliament. It was, thus, a crucial first incarnation of the later antiquarian investigations of Henry Spelman and Robert Cotton that incited the Parliamentarian cause. But, if Dodderidge's ancient British past resembled theirs, his anti-Roman ancient world, populated by wise savants congregating in parliaments to transmit wisdom orally and create counsel, was precisely the sort of revisionist history stimulated by Annius of Viterbo's forged discoveries. And his methods—seeking out and poring over neglected ancient records and challenging received histories—also derived from an Annian tradition.

Dodderidge's work demonstrates how historical culture enabled, but did not necessitate, powerful ideological transformations in the early modern period. If some readers wished to imitate societies encountered in ancient texts, many others invented the pasts they sought to re-create from the joining of well-known and obscure sources. Scholars combined creative and epistemologically suspect techniques to fuse wildly specious with credible evidence, to concoct inflammatory, shadowy, unclassical visions of the past. And their almost poetic beliefs gave force to the spectacular range of policies and actions that counselors dreamed up to counter the disease, violence, and looming chaos in early modern Europe. Scholarly counselors methodically dreamed the past and transformed the world.

RALEGH IN CONTEXT

Ralegh presented his analysis of historical politics as supporting a clear set of positions. In his discussions of the origins of politics and the genesis of monarchies, he pursued the king's favor. His account suggested that, like James, he considered kings above the law and subject only to divine judgment but that he viewed Parliament as he did Israelite prophets, invested

---

128. Note that this modifies the account in Pocock, *The Ancient Constitution and the Feudal Law*, chap. 1, which saw European influence in this debate only in the "French Prelude" to the legalistic study of medieval societies. My account, by contrast, shows that examinations of both the ancient constitution and the feudal law emerged from the culture of historical counsel.

with the pious responsibility of warning kings against enacting tyrannical abuses. As such, he hoped that his balance of law and absolutism would appeal to all elements of England's fracturing political culture. Similarly, he shaped the historical justification behind his policy of naval superiority to appeal to James's aversion to war. By not celebrating holy war but rather condemning military expertise as necessary to fallen humanity, he sought to dull the aggression latent in the posture he supported and to portray his counsels as both inevitable and regrettable. Nevertheless, the expertise displayed in his analysis of ancient battles demonstrated his ability to spearhead an anti-Spanish policy, which he urged on James by depicting Providence's wrath when wise counsels were eschewed and flattery indulged. Proclaiming accord and minimizing disagreement, he insinuated that he could manage the fractious elements within Jacobean society.

Above all, Ralegh presented himself as suitable for place with the Jacobean regime by implementing the canons of historical practice, proving that he could derive timeless precepts and contingent counsels from meticulous analyses of evidence gleaned from an extensive range of sources. His work replicated the labor demanded of counselors and secretaries within English government, where far-flung materials were brought out of obscurity, excerpts extracted, and the resulting materials laboriously synthesized into a coherent historical system. The universalizing ambitions and focus on the ancient past distinguished Ralegh's tome from many of the more narrow local histories written by other counselors. But it nevertheless emanated from the same constellation of intellectual values and practices. And the culture that developed and disseminated these practices applied them broadly in large-scale narratives encompassing the entirety of the divine theater of particulars as well as in local institutions, geographies, and offices that could be as conservative as they could be provocative. Tracing the adoption of these practices reveals how England discovered and fabricated its own past, administered its state, and struggled to control its future with methods learned from Continental ecclesiastical historians and fabulists.

Reception:
The Afterlife of the *History of the World*

Ralegh's universal history proposed a series of providential truths that supported an aggressive anti-Spanish foreign policy. Ralegh hoped that this program would be implemented by a reformed Jacobean regime in which he would play a major role. Though he produced the *History* over seven years, it was published at a moment when his recommendations might achieve heightened effect, as scandal and corruption magnified James's struggles with Parliament. But James was not swayed by Ralegh's expert manipulation of the canons of historical analysis. Ralegh's argument for his unique suitability vanished behind his criticisms of kings, and the unstable moment for which the *History* presented a solution faded without the captive's release.

The circumstances that structured the *History*, however, never controlled how its readers interpreted it.[1] Hundreds of copies of editions of it are extant.[2] Most contain no markings or only a few inscrutable scrib-

---

1. For readers of histories in England, see Grafton and Jardine, "'Studied for Action'"; Woolf, *Reading History in Early Modern England*, and *The Social Circulation of the Past*; Beer, *Sir Walter Ralegh and His Readers*; and Freyja Cox Jensen, "Reading Florus in Early Modern England," *Renaissance Studies* 23 (2009): 659–77.

2. I have looked at more than two hundred copies of the *History* at the following libraries: the British Library; the Cambridge University Library; the Bodleian Library; the Wellcome Library; the New York Public Library; the Firestone Library, Princeton University; the Marquand Library, Princeton University; the Union Theological Seminary Library; the Alexander Library, Rutgers University; the Franklin Library, University of Pennsylvania; the Columbia University Library; the Houghton Library, Harvard University; the Beinecke Library, Yale University; the Folger Library; Queens College, Oxford; Trinity College, Cambridge; the Swem Library, College of William and Mary; the Walter Ralegh Collection at the University of North Carolina; the Small Special Collections Library, University of Virginia; and the Henry E. Huntington Library. I have also communicated with librarians at the Newberry Library; the John Hay Library, Brown University; New York University; the Victoria and Albert Museum; Wichita

bles and jottings of the owner's name, sums, or geometric designs, and many of their pages give off a dank, malevolent odor borne of centuries of moisture and neglect.[3] But many are festooned with underlinings and marginal annotations revealing readers' responses, and other readers formulated assessments of Ralegh in poems and printed works. In addition, surviving collections of extracts and synopses taken from the *History* show that some readers excerpted or summarized passages as they read, just as Ralegh himself had processed sources from his library into his own notebook. Readers interacted with their copies in various ways that collectively show how Ralegh's work both participated in and helped further a culture encouraging fluid modes of historical reading. His work could be read as a neutral repository of information about the past, as propaedeutic to counsel, or as a transparent reflection of its author's motivations, and, throughout the seventeenth century and beyond, scholars made use of his authority by citing his work in their own writings.

It would be impossible to describe all the methods readers deployed while consuming the *History* or to claim that their notes allow more than suggestive apertures into their responses. As a result, the following studies of reader's interactions are presented as diffuse, episodic analyses rather than as a linear narrative. Nonetheless, a clear pattern will emerge that traces the gradual decline of the political and scholarly culture that brought Ralegh's text into existence. By the end of the eighteenth century, few readers engaged the methodological elements that structured the *History*, and they increasingly evaluated it by standards distinct from the prophetic, antiquarian, and universal mode that Ralegh mobilized. This

---

State University; the William Andrews Clark Memorial Library, University of California, Los Angeles; All Souls College, Oxford; Lady Margaret Hall, Oxford; Merton College, Oxford; New College, Oxford; St. John's College, Oxford; St. Catherine's College, Oxford; Newnham College, Cambridge; Corpus Christi College, Cambridge; St. John's College, Cambridge; St. Catharine's College, Cambridge; Selwyn College, Cambridge; and University College, London. In addition, I have examined extracts from the *History* in the following manuscripts: BL Sloane 3407; BL Harley 1733; BL Harley 4872; BL Harley 1759; BL Add. MS 4985; Wellcome WMS 6880; Cambridge UL MS Gg.2.25; SP 9/14; UNC CSWR 96; HEH HAS 1.2–4 (thanks to digital photographs by Jamie Gianoutsos); and Kendal Record Office, Kendal, Cumbria UK WD RY/Box 36/2 (thanks to digital photographs by Bill Bulman).

3. The most frequent jotting is the name of the owner or owners. Where Ralegh mathematically determined the size of an army or the revenue of a king, many readers checked his sums. Errata are often noted. The majority of annotations are indexing notes—i.e., the names or places treated in the relevant passage—which also constitute most of the separate manuscript notes taken by readers as well. See William Sherman, "What Did Renaissance Readers Write in Their Books?" in *Books and Readers in Early Modern England: Material Studies*, ed. Jennifer Andersen and Elizabeth Sauer (Philadelphia: University of Pennsylvania Press, 2002), 119–37.

shift suggests, not merely the reinvigoration of the classical model that viewed history as a species of rhetoric, but also the erosion of an intellectual economy in which the methodological act of reconstituting the past constituted the foundation of intellectual inquiry.

THE MATERIAL *HISTORY*

Some owners of the *History* viewed the book primarily as a physical object associated with Ralegh. Accordingly, they copied his letters and poems onto its pages. One owner inscribed the poems "Sir Walter Ralegh's Pilgrimage" and "Even such is time" at the front of the book above a transcription of the letter Ralegh wrote to his wife before his scaffold appointment in 1603.[4] Others entered potted biographies of Ralegh into their volumes or bound in printed biographies.[5] Such inscriptions personalized these copies by emphasizing the identity of the author. But there were innumerable ways in which to alter copies. John Bird of Galby in Leicestershire, like many others, underlined passages and inscribed marginal symbols throughout his copy. He repeatedly wrote his name and recorded that he consulted the book at least three times between 1768 and 1780. Most notably, he colored all eight of Ralegh's maps in a range of appropriate colors—painting rivers blue and meadows green—while minutely tracing the outline of individual figures to create his own vibrant, saturated images from Ralegh's maps.[6]

Few readers personalized their copies in this way.[7] More often, they augmented the index included in the back of the *History* with their own entries or created separate lists for their own terms.[8] One Henry Broughton entered numerous additions to Ralegh's index as he read his copy of

4. Trinity College, shelfmark VI.4.4. (Note that in this chapter I will refer to all copies of the *History* by their location and shelfmark. Publication dates for individual copies are noted under "Selected Annotated Books Consulted" in the bibliography.) HEH 69107 also has "Come Be with Me." Copies with biographies bound in include Cambridge University Library Syn.3.61.20; Beinecke Library Vet. A2 c.13; HEH 73406; BL 9005.H.2; and Cambridge Trinity College Munby.a.4.

5. Princeton 29551.745.11q copy 1, like the Victoria and Albert Museum copy, has a potted biography at the beginning.

6. Shelfmark Yale Bg4 035y.

7. The only other example of an illuminated map I have found is New York Public Library shelfmark *KC+ 1617, where the figures in the First Punic War map are colored yellow.

8. See, among other examples of this, Princeton 29551.745.13q, Princeton D17 .xR3 1708 copy 1, Penn Folio D57 .R16 1677 c.1; Trinity College, Cambridge, Wren Library Capell B.1; Yale Bg4 036; and UNC Collection CSWR A12.

the *History* in the Fleet Prison late in 1614, soon after the book was first published. Broughton had purchased it for thirty shillings in November, and he exactingly pored over the book until at least the following February.[9] As he read, he inscribed dozens of notes in the margins. To navigate these, he penned topical indices throughout the book, inscribing at the top or bottom of the page a category such as "fortune" or "pride," followed by long strings of apposite page numbers. The terms Broughton chose as indexing tools were not strictly of one type. While some were moralizing topoi of the sort frequently recommended by early modern commonplace books, others were geographical terms such as "hollanders and netherlands" or antiquarian topics such as "funeral." Broughton's multiplicity of headers did not adhere to one method but rather emerged out of the characteristics of the text that most drew his attention. Only in one place were his terms guided by Ralegh. He converted Jonson's "Mind of the Front" and the *History*'s frontispiece into an index, listing page numbers under "providence," "death," and other elements evoked by the text and illustration. Ralegh's allegorical image became Broughton's memory theater (see fig. 1 above).

Broughton's annotations highlighted aspects of the text he thought merited particular attention while breezing past features he wished to avoid. His treatment processed the *History* into extracts according to his own criteria that he then indexed, thus converting Ralegh's work into his own miscellany. Both Bird and Broughton asserted control over their copies of the *History* through their inscriptions, Bird highlighting the visual intricacy of Ralegh's maps, Broughton ripping the *History* from its narrative genre to create a personalized compendium. Broughton's work, in fact, paralleled Ralegh's method of reading, for, despite his quick purchase of the recently released work, the book appealed to him more for its collection of scholarly evidence than for its author's renown. Other readers of the *History* similarly wrested the text into their own contexts, converting it from Ralegh's providential counsel into any number of other species of historical investigation. Ralegh's remarkable exertion in producing the *History* was repaid by a profusion of interpretations—some overlapping, others incompatible, some focused on the author, others concerned solely with the past, and all, like Bird's and Broughton's, directed to personal ends.

9. UNC Collection CSWR A4. The evidence of dates is at 145 of the first pagination and at the end, 776, of the second.

THE CONVERT'S *HISTORY*

The crowd that congregated to witness Ralegh's execution marveled at his magnanimous comportment in his last moments. Accounts of his scaffold speech were recorded at the time, then copied and circulated, and his execution provoked appraisals of his life from both critics and supporters.[10] One sympathetic witness of Ralegh's last moments versified, "I saw in every standerby / Pale death, life only in thine eye."[11] Ralegh's performance elicited great sympathy, even from many who had previously reviled him.

To some, however, the *History* had already suggested Ralegh's repentance of his sins and embrace of a virtuous life. These accounts proceeded from the assumption that his earlier career had been marked by dissipation. His old friend Stephen Powle possessed a copy of a letter written by "A Stranger" that was "sent to Raleigh not long before he sufferede," preparing the elderly favorite for execution. The writer condemned "brave knowing yett ignorant Rawleigh, knowing too much how to love thy selfe, yett ignorant in bestowing too littel on others," and explained that he had been driven to provide this *ars moriendi* because "thou livest condemn'd and unpittyed." The work comforted the prisoner with the notion that, because he had spent years without "greatnes, Ritches, Liberty, Friends . . . death to thee hath (or should have bin) thine eating supping discoursing companion, yea thy keeper." He assured Ralegh that it was not too late to repent and reminded him that sinners like David, Saint Paul, and Mary Magdalen had not been denied redemption.[12]

But despite his brazen censure, the author also recognized Ralegh's virtues, and he described himself as "one that grieves that soe many of thy perfections by thine imperfections should thus untimely bee extinct." As he continued, this reader praised the *History* as the culmination of Ralegh's virtues, but as a triumph that he would enjoy only from the grave: "Yett thou hast built thee a Monument. Never shall the History of the World (when time hath made thee Dust) but shall speake thee, that thou shalt live untill thy subiect hath ending. Wherefore victoriously weare in

---

10. Manuscript copies of either the speech itself or descriptions of his behavior in the British Library alone include Add. MS 73086, Add. MS 40838, Add. MS 73087, Add. MS 6789 (by Thomas Harriot), Stowe 180, Stowe 141, Harley 1576, and Harley 1327. See Fleck, "'At the Time of His Death.'"

11. BL Cotton Titus C VII, fol. 95r.

12. Bodleian Library Tanner MS 169, fols. 205v.

Death what that didst win in Life, for I shall never see more Rawleigh."[13] To this reader, the *History* was a glorious tombstone that transcended its author's many faults and ensured his everlasting memory in the grateful minds of men.

Many within the Jacobean regime seem to have shared this interpretation. Even while condemning Ralegh to execution, Chief Justice Sir Henry Montague hinted at it, proclaiming: "Your faith hath heretofore been questioned; but I am satisfied that you are a good Christian, for your book, which is an admirable work, doth testify as much."[14] The moderate Calvinist bishop Joseph Hall stated this view more emphatically in his 1646 *The Balme of Gilead*. Hall viewed Ralegh as exemplary evidence of a sinful individual reformed by reflective solitude, stating: "The Court had his youthfull and freer times, the Tower his later age; the Tower reformed the Court in him, and produced those worthy monuments of art & industry, which we should have in vain expected from his freedom & jollity."[15] Ralegh's imprisonment, these men suggested, had harnessed the dynamic powers of a headstrong favorite.

This interpretation of the *History* was expressed most fully in verses inscribed in the manuscript abridgement of the *History*, likely from the 1650s, by Robert Greville, fourth Lord Brooke. Brooke's grandfather had been a Parliamentary commander in the Civil War, and the verses hint that the characterization of the *History* as a sign of Ralegh's devotion would become a Puritan interpretation. The poem began "Whatever Raughlies youth hath been, faire fruites of age may here be seene" and repeatedly distinguished Ralegh's courtly licentiousness from the wisdom he displayed in old age. It continued: "as from Court follie full of blame, to thinke on God his minde to frame: / and for to studie historie, as guided by Divinitie: / rejecting false Antiquetie, which from that truth doth disagree: / yea many doubts he well doth cleare, which in that truth seeme to appeare." Ralegh's debauched life as a courtier had given way to a prophetic examination of the past. And, while the author lamented Ralegh's execution, he also expressed relief that Ralegh had not earned James's favor: "sith new

13. Ibid., fols. 205r–v. More of the letter is printed in Virginia Stern, *Sir Stephen Powle of Court and Country: Memorabilia of a Government Agent for Queen Elizabeth I, Chancery Official and English Country Gentleman* (Selinsgrove, PA: Susquehanna University Press, 1992), 163–64. For Powle, see also Scott-Warren, "Reconstructing Manuscript Networks."

14. David Jardine et al., eds., *The Lives and Criminal Trials of Celebrated Men* (Philadelphia, 1835), 501.

15. Joseph Hall, *The Balme of Gilead* (London, 1646), 216–17.

courting might him foile, as love of life did breed new toile, / his fall-
ing back God did prevent / and stroke of axe to heaven him sent."[16] The
punishments incurred for his courtly sinfulness brought Ralegh to true
religion, while failure to convince James ensured that he could not revert
to his old impieties. The *History*, according to this reading, provided a sign
of exemplary devotion, and its depiction of Providence and the fate of its
author alike supplied demonstrations of divine power. These readers read
the *History* as Ralegh wished, taking the text to mark the moment when
the Stuart prophet eclipsed the Elizabethan favorite.

THE ANTI-STUART *HISTORY*

The anti-Spanish Puritan Thomas Scott also viewed the *History* as evidence of Ralegh's rejection of iniquities and embrace of godliness.[17] On the
publication of the *History*, Scott sent effusive verses to Ralegh. He began:
"Who doubts of Providence, or God denyes; / Let hym thy Booke read, and
thy Life advise." Ralegh's actions had not always resonated with such unalloyed divinity; as Scott explained: "Thy life doth likewise shew, that
as the Devill / Drawes bad from good, God still drawes good from evill."
Ralegh's earlier career was characterized by sin, for Scott explained that
he had been "Treadinge the paths of flattery, falshood, blood / The way to
heaven neglected, thow didst stray." But God had appointed Ralegh's rightful imprisonment to correct his ways. Scott continued: "But now thou'st
found thy selfe: and wee have found / That sicknes taught thee Art to
make men sound. / For hadst thow never fall'ne, th'hadst never writt: / Nor
had'st thow clear'd, but clouded us with witt. / But now thy falshood hath
the truth so showne, / That a true World for a false World is knowne."[18]
Like the poet of Brooke's abridgment, Scott depicted the *History* as replac-
ing a false history with the truth, a divine labor that provided irrefutable
evidence of Ralegh's orthodoxy.

Scott's account of Ralegh's earlier indiscretions did not, however, re-
vile his courtly life as Brooke's poem had. Instead, Scott hinted that he
believed that Ralegh had conspired with the Spanish to overthrow James.

---

16. UNC CSWR A 96, fol. 1. The poem is printed in *The Poems of Sir Walter Ralegh: A
Historical Edition*, ed. Michael Rudick (Tempe: Arizona Center for Medieval and Renaissance
Studies, in conjunction with Renaissance English Text Society, 1999), 203–4.

17. For Scott, see Peter Lake, "Constitutional Consensus and Puritan Opposition in the
1620s: Thomas Scott and the Spanish Match," *HJ* 25 (1982): 802–25.

18. Bodleian MS Rawlinson Poetry 26, fol. 6v (printed in Rudick, ed., *The Poems of Sir
Walter Ralegh*, 188).

This transgression, paradoxically, had created the conditions for him to turn to pious scholarship. Ralegh's career was in itself a lesson of godliness triumphant over sin, but, in this case, the conversion was not only from iniquity to piety but also from collaboration with the Spanish to resistance.

Over the next decade, Scott revised this image of Ralegh. As James declined to provide military support to Continental Protestants in the Thirty Years War and moved toward a Spanish match for Prince Charles, Scott produced a series of publications that projected Ralegh as a symbol of opposition policy. These depictions paid little attention to Scott's conversion narrative and, instead, portrayed Ralegh as an unequivocal icon of anti-Spanish sentiment. In his 1620 *Vox Populi*, for example, Scott attributed Ralegh's demise to the scheming Spanish ambassador, Diego Sarmiento de Acuña, Count of Gondomar.[19] Gondomar had gained considerable influence with James in the mid-1610s and was largely responsible for deepening James's pro-Spanish position, despite the failure of Howard's ministry. Scott depicted Gondomar as a classic evil counselor, consumed by ambition and impiety. Ralegh's execution provided the moment at which Gondomar achieved dominance over the Stuart court. In Scott's account, Gondomar sought to acquire the book and manuscript collections of Isaac Casaubon and Robert Cotton and to dismantle the Bodleian, knowing that "there is no more profitable conversation for Statesmen then amongst schollers & their books."[20] Ralegh's *History* constituted a consummate iteration of the scholarly counsel threatened by the cunning Gondomar.

Scott's depiction of Ralegh as a focus of Stuart grievance was adopted by many commentators over the next two decades. As Anna Beer has shown, those Englishmen disenchanted by the policies of their kings looked to Ralegh's legacy, and the *History* was the only book Oliver Cromwell recommended to his son Richard.[21] In these readings, the critical counsels that Ralegh offered his king occluded his self-proclaimed role as royal adviser, and his efforts to persuade James with compliment were, like his dubious earlier life, ignored. By eliding the context in which the work was

19. Thomas Scott, *Vox Populi* (London, 1620), c1r. Scott was also the author of the 1626 anti-Spanish tract *Sir Walter Rawleighs Ghost*. For an able analysis of radical anti-Stuart readers of Ralegh, see Beer, *Sir Walter Ralegh and His Readers*, 142–54.

20. Scott, *Vox Populi*, D1r–v.

21. Cromwell exclaimed: "Take heed of an unactive vain spirit! Recreate yourself with Sir Walter Raleigh's History; it's a Body of History; and will add much more to your understanding than fragments of Story." Oliver Cromwell to Richard Cromwell, Carrick, 2 April 1650, in *Oliver Cromwell's Letters and Speeches*, ed. Thomas Carlyle (1897; reprint, New York: AMS, 1980), 162.

produced, they created a Ralegh who symbolized Stuart injustice and a *History* that sanctioned rebellion against tyrants.

THE FLATTERER'S *HISTORY*

Other readers were not nearly so impressed with the *History*. One anonymous reader expressed unambiguous hatred of Ralegh in annotations likely produced in the late 1630s or early 1640s. All aspects of Ralegh's life and work elicited hostile responses. Next to his discussion of Henry VIII as a "merciless prince," this reader inscribed: "You might have beene somewhat more sparing for your mrs's sake."[22] From this reader's perspective, Ralegh's harsh criticism of James's grandfather had angered the king, who had repaid the insult by showing little charity toward his widow.[23]

Though in this one instance Ralegh had displayed a lack of cunning, this reader perceived him as nastily deceitful. Where Ralegh lamented the sad fates of military men brought down by the envy of courtiers, the reader protested: "you had a hand in the noble Earle of Essex's death." Three decades after this event, Ralegh's rumored insouciance at the earl's execution supplied ammunition for those who despised him. The reader, in fact, felt that Ralegh cravenly misrepresented his Elizabethan experience in order to praise James. In the preface, Ralegh had barely discussed Elizabeth beyond claiming that Henry's sins had been divinely avenged by her lack of heir. For the reader, this revealed Ralegh's heartlessness. Where Ralegh referred to Elizabeth as "that renowned lady," the reader penned: "And is this all? O base ingratitude." Similarly, where Ralegh claimed that Elizabeth had not rewarded soldiers sufficiently, the reader scoffed: "This is a lie. Witness yr selfe." But the malice this annotator felt toward Ralegh was best encapsulated in a note responding to his complimentary words for James's treatment of ex-soldiers. Here, this reader crowed: "All ye world knoweth ye king never loved a souldier. This king tooke off your head in cold bloud."[24] Ralegh's attempts to ally himself with James's military policy foundered against the king's impervious pacifism, and his demise

22. UNC Collection CSWR A8, fol. A4v.
23. Beer, *Bess: The Life of Lady Ralegh.*
24. UNC Collection CSWR A8, 5.6.2.617, A5v, 5.6.2.618, 619. Note also that twice this reader rebutted Ralegh's criticisms of Aristotle. Where Ralegh criticizes Aristotle and Aristotelians, the reader wrote: "I believe you light your small candle at his Torch" (B6r). When Ralegh wrote of the "brabblings of the Aristotelians" (*HW*, 1.11.2.172), this reader wrote: "You were not soe wise as Aristotle."

inspired callous delight. To this observer, Ralegh was an ambitious and di-abolic man whose single-minded pursuit of favor compromised his wife's security and insulted the queen to whom he owed his prominence. This *History* was suffused with disingenuous flattery and deceits motivated only by the goal of restoring its author to favor, where he would again ma-neuver only in pursuit of his own aggrandizement.

THE SOCRATIC *HISTORY*

The poet and newswriter Samuel Sheppard complimented the *History* ef-fusively in his 1651 *Epigrams Theological, Philosophical, and Romantick*. In Ralegh he saw a modern Socrates, for the brilliant insights of both had alienated powerful but small-minded men and led to their hasty execu-tions. As the Athenians had belatedly discerned the virtue of Socrates' ad-vice, so the English appreciated the *History* only after its author's death. As Sheppard explained: "So we, while thou on earth with us didst live, / Slighted thy worth, not having hearts to give, / Thee thanks, and honour for that gift of thine, / The lovely Issue of thy braines divine." Sheppard tes-tified that Ralegh's contemporaries had been ungenerous readers, brought by their own malice—as Ralegh had anticipated—to impugn the work. He assured the deceased that the *History* had at last gained appropriate appre-ciation: "Rest sacred spirit, while thy work shall be / Devoutly honoured by Posteritie."[25] Sheppard's *History* resounded with sure evidence of God's favor and had, thus, forced the approval of later generations.

Sheppard's political stance, however, did not resemble Scott's or Brooke's. While he had supported Parliamentary forces early in the 1640s, by 1647 Sheppard became alarmed at the radicalism spreading through the army and outraged at the imprisonment of Charles I. For the next two years, he wrote for royalist newsbooks and was imprisoned after the king's execution. Though after his release he managed to avoid further conflict with Commonwealth authorities, his *Epigrams* reflected deep royalist af-finities. His politics suggest that the *History* could be seen as furnishing support for partisans of monarchy no less than its enemies.

In this case, Ralegh was embraced by a figure whose religious radical-ism gave way, when confronted by its more extreme forms, to a conserva-tive reaction. Sheppard likely believed that Ralegh would have followed

---

25. Samuel Sheppard, *Epigrams Theological, Philosophical, and Romantick* (London, 1651), F3r–v (also printed in Rudick, ed., *The Poems of Sir Walter Ralegh*, 203–4).

this same path, one in which the right to critical counsel did not extend to rebellion and in which monarchical preservation of order far outweighed constitutional niceties. To those of this position no less than to Scott, Ralegh could be taken as a debased prophet whose forewarnings of dangers to divinely approved government were met with mocking and punishment. If Scott and Sheppard disagreed concerning the nature of these threats, they nevertheless shared the conviction that Ralegh had diagnosed the fissures gashing England. Sheppard's work thus shows that the *History* could be embraced as a tragic, pious precedent by early modern Englishmen of all orientations, including those bereaved by the fall of the Stuarts.

THE ROYALIST *HISTORY*

Sheppard was hardly the first pro-Stuart figure to assess the *History* positively. The absolutist polemicist Peter Heylyn, for example, added Ralegh to his canon of writers of universal history in the second edition of his *Mikrokosmos*. Heylyn placed Ralegh in the tradition of Moses, Berosus, Sleidan, and Münster, but he quoted Martial's assessment of Sallust that Ralegh was "Primus in Historia."[26] Readers who shared Heylyn's political orientation readily perceived the *History* as offering supporting evidence, and the absolutist theorist Robert Filmer consulted Ralegh's work repeatedly while writing his *Patriarcha*.[27] Filmer viewed Ralegh as a fundamental source for a world history in which absolute monarchy always signaled divine preference. He cited Ralegh to avow that Nimrod had legitimately inherited his title to kingship, and he quoted him to prove that the Israelites had been ruled by absolute monarchs. He even used Ralegh rather than James for his absolutist interpretation of 1 Samuel 8: "Sir W. *Raleigh* confesses, all those Inconveniences and Miseries which are reckoned by *Samuel* as belonging to Kingly Government were not Intollerable, but such as have been born, and are still born, by free Consent of Subjects towards their Princes."[28] Ralegh's entrenched belief in monarchy made the *History*

---

26. Peter Heylyn, *Mikrokosmos: A Little Description of a Great World* (Oxford, 1627), 20. For Heylyn, see Anthony Milton, *Laudian and Royalist Polemic in Seventeenth-Century England: The Career and Writings of Peter Heylyn* (Manchester: Manchester University Press, 1997).

27. Note that this counters Beer's claim in *Sir Walter Ralegh and His Readers* that readings that occluded Ralegh's political stance emerged only in the 1650s.

28. Robert Filmer, *Patriarcha; or, The Natural Power of Kings* (London, 1680), 80–81. For Filmer, see Gordon Schochet, *The Authoritarian Family and Political Attitudes in 17th-Century England: Patriarchialism in Political Thought* (New Brunswick, NJ: Transaction, 1988).

as credible a source for Cavaliers as its preference for kings who subjected themselves to law made it useful to Roundheads.[29]

Annotations produced by royalists suggest that they valued the *History* as a theater of Providence in which divine patterns could be discerned. As one disgruntled royalist read the *History* in the late 1650s and early 1660s, he noted in the margins correlations between a sundered England and past societies disintegrating under evil regimes. This anonymous annotator carefully recorded instances when the English governments of the previous two decades had followed the example of earlier illegitimate usurpers. The processes by which Cromwell had assumed dictatorial control, he believed, corresponded to the events that had led to past tyrannies. For example, where Ralegh discussed Dionyius's establishment of tyranny in Syracuse after the expulsion of "those of judgment," the reader noted: "The new Government of England." He furthered the parallel: "Cromwell another Dionysius." Similarly, where Ralegh began the story of Agathocles—the Sicilian who ruled so cruelly that he earned even Machiavelli's condemnation—the reader noted: "Many Agathoclesses in these times, & Tyrants like him."[30]

Deep historical continuities extended to the minute processes by which the calamities of his time unfolded. Next to Ralegh's examination of how, in the aftermath of the Peloponnesian War, "thirtie Tyrants got their Dominion in Athens," the reader drew precise correspondences between the rise of this cabal and "the parlaments first election & indowinge of them wth supreame priveledge."[31] His orderly notes demonstrated how events had proceeded in the exact same sequence. Of the tyrants' condemnation of their enemies, he wrote, "The case of Strafort," referring to the whirlwind of condemnation amid straining relations that led Charles to capitulate to Parliament and endorse the Earl of Strafford's execution in 1641. Where Ralegh had noted that the tyrants had justified their murders with slanderous lies, the reader noted: "The very proceeding of the parlament after Strafords death." Like Parliament, the Thirty Tyrants had raised an army and slaughtered the nobility. They had then disarmed the

29. Similarly, that Ralegh's "Dialogue between a Royal Counselor and a Justice of the Peace" (later slightly edited when published as *The Prerogative of Parliaments*) was a dialogue allowed Filmer to draw evidence for absolutism from the words Ralegh placed in the mouth of the royal counselor. Note that Filmer attributed these sentiments to Ralegh when claiming that the Magna Carta did not bind royal prerogative. See Filmer, *Patriarcha*, 121.

30. BL 1311.I.I., 5.1.4.3.327, 5.1.4.4.335, 341.

31. Ibid., 3.9.2.108. Note that, in 1658, George Thomason too made a manuscript pamphlet consisting of extracts from this section that listed English tyrants alongside the Athenians.

rest of the nation and levied outrageous taxes to provision the soldiers. The reader finally observed that Charles II offered amnesty to the surviving tyrants after their rule was broken, as the Athenians had.[32]

This reader did not view Charles's clemency favorably, nor did he praise the curtailed reign of his father. Where Ralegh recounted that God had signaled his anger at the Israelites by allowing the Ark of the Covenant to fall into the possession of heathens, the he noted: "The sinnes of the pristes & people causeth Gods presence to fall into the hands of the wicked." He viewed the overturning of authority as punishment for the errors of the Caroline church.[33] And, where Ralegh noted that Agesilaus, the king of Sparta, "was a Prince very temperate, and valiant, and a good leader in warre, free from covetousnesse, and not reproched with any blemish of lust," the annotator penned: "Nothing similar to Kings Charles I and II."[34] Nonetheless, he expressed hope that Charles II would violently rid the church and state of the tyrannical heathen. Next to Ralegh's treatment of the end of the Babylonian Captivity, he wrote: "I hope our K Charles the second will do the like here in England, clense our Church from the filth of Haeresy & error, restore our orthodox cleargy to their places & reestablish the sacrifice of the liturgy now longe neglected and breake downe that Brasenface serpent of Genevan discipline."[35] This royalist reader, then, found in the *History* historical precedents to help resolve the perturbations destroying Britain. And he also discerned models by which the latter Charles might reassert order, pronouncing his clear preference for the more robust, Israelite restoration.

Whether Charles chose to rule with the heavy hand that he desired, this reader expected providential judgment to exact retribution eventually, for the enemies of monarchy had violated divine law. Where Ralegh discussed the Eighth Commandment, the reader inscribed: "Tyrannous parlaments Robbinge Sequestrating Murhthering & plundering Souldiers who by these lawlesse acts from a beggerly condicion attaine to honorable tytles & make themselves able to live in all luxury." The actions of the Interregnum governments were sure to elicit God's most terrible wrath, as the *History* furnished evidence that an unforgiving God was willing to smite even zealous followers if they deviated from his will. Ezekias, Ralegh had noted, had incurred divine disapproval because he "rejoyced too much at

---

32. BL 1311.1.1, 3.9.3.110. "By such an acte of oblivion K C.2 goes about to secure the peace of England."
33. Ibid., 2.15.2.460.
34. Ibid., 1.12.8.154. "Similis Carlo 1 et 2 Regibus nihil."
35. Ibid., 2.25.1.591.

the destruction and lamentable end of his enemie." In response, this reader cautioned: "Take heede of Thanksgivinges for murther though it be doone against the professed enimies of God." Similarly, that David had been denied the right to build the Temple was taken by this reader to prophecy terrible punishments for his Interregnum enemies. He asked: "If God will not permit those that slaye the enimies of God to builde holy places what will he do wth those that murther the Saints & destroye the houses built to the honor of his name."[36] Ralegh's work demonstrated God's overawing punishment of seditious rebels. The Restoration, this reader expected, would witness swift and ineffable revenge.

Ralegh's divine theater, then, was not intelligible and usable only to the godly. Though Scott's Ralegh represented a symbol of anti-Stuart agitation, royalists too confirmed their convictions with his work. From its narratives, readers of all political inclinations culled providential counsels and derived evidence that suggested the divine approval of their own pieties. The shared belief that a truthful depiction of the past would adumbrate God's will and pattern of Creation led them all to credit the *History* as an instrument disseminating divine knowledge.

THE PROPHETIC *HISTORY*

While this same anonymous reader perceived Ralegh's reconstitution of the past as a mirror that could be used to reflect his present, he also perceived moments in the *History* when Ralegh personally offered prophetic insight into the course of events. Ralegh had lamented the death of Prince Henry, writing of "the losse of that brave Prince; of which, like an Eclypse of the Sunne; wee shall finde the effects hereafter." Next to this passage, the anonymous annotator wrote: "Rawleyes too true prophesye."[37] Ralegh here was credited with discerning the catastrophic consequences of Henry's death and the failed rule of Charles I. Whether from illumination or expertise, his intensive examination of the providential theater had enabled him to perceive England's approaching devastation.

In fact, this reader was one of several mid-seventeenth-century Britons who saw Ralegh's analysis of the riotous past as prophetically anticipating their tumultuous present. In his 1659 *Eyaggeloigrapha*, the godly Welsh lawyer John Lewis pressed for continuing reformation in Wales. In support, he quoted Ralegh's description of overenthusiastic iconoclasm evacuating

36. Ibid., 2.4.13.285, 2.25.3.595, 2.17.4.481.
37. Ibid., 5.1.7.351.

God from the church.[38] He marveled that "he so long before should fore-
tell the humour, and as it were, the fortune, of Religion in these dayes."
Though Lewis claimed not be to certain "whether it was the foresight of
a great Brain, or Prophesie," other readers expressed less ambivalence.[39]
The royalist antiquary William Dugdale included the same passage in the
dedicatory epistle to his 1658 *The History of St Pauls Cathedral,* observing: "How far forth these prophetick words of his are now fulfilled, I need
not give instance."[40] John Bird noted it as well a century later, writing:
"So true a prophesie [of] the wreched times."[41] Ralegh's mourning for the
decline of the church continued to earn him the status of prophet into the
eighteenth century.

The royalist diarist and founding member of the Royal Society John
Evelyn was similarly struck by Ralegh's evocation. Next to this same passage in his copy of the *History* he wrote: "This prophecy I have my selfe
seene come to passe literaly, I saw St Paules Cathedral made a stable of
Horses & the Altar and decent decoration the Brass Inscription of Tombs
and Sepulcher ript off & violated by the Rebells & Paricides of St Pawles
1648 till 1660."[42] These readers—despite doctrinal differences—saw in Ralegh's lamentation a prognostication of the calamities of the Interregnum.
They shared Ralegh's view of the past as a divine theater that anticipated
the course and meaning of future events, and they interpreted the *History*
as a prophetic lament for their own desolation.

Rather than ascribe such parallels solely to patterns divinely implanted
in the theater of Creation, these readings attributed prophetic insight to
Ralegh, suggesting that Providence worked through him rather than simply through the unfolding of events that he narrated. As such, they encapsulated his idealized goal of the historian, for they portrayed his reconstitution of the past as prophetically revealing Providence, enabling readers
to genuflect before divine judgment in their own world.

THE COUNSELOR'S *HISTORY*

To Evelyn, James's treatment of Ralegh had irreparably damaged the king's
reputation. While discussing Antipater's execution of Demosthenes, Ra-

---

38. The lengthy passage quoted in chapter 5 above at n. 71.

39. John Lewis, Esq., *Eyaggeloigrapha* (London, 1659), 17.

40. William Dugdale, *The History of St Pauls Cathedral in London* (London, 1658), A3v. I
thank Jan Broadway for this reference.

41. Yale Bg4 035y, 2.5.1.296.

42. Evelyn's copy is BL Eve.b.36; the passage lies on 249 of this 1628 edition.

legh had explained that sentencing a learned man to death could reverberate through posterity. Had Demosthenes been allowed to live, he explained, "the rest of [Antipater's] proceeding in this action might well
have passed for very milde: whereas now all such, as either are delighted
with Orations of *Demosthenes*, or have sur-rendred their iudgments to Authors iustly admiring him . . . condemne him utterly, calling him a bloudy
tyrant." Next to this passage, Evelyn penned: "the same may be thought of
K *James* putting to death that excellent Historian S W. Raleigh."[43] Ralegh's
warnings concerning the execution of learned counselors—in this passage
as well as his discussion of Callisthenes and Charidemus—had not been
heeded by his stubborn king. For Evelyn, this judicial murder left a lasting
stain on the Stuart dynasty, for it had cast a sinister glow over the relative
tranquility of James's reign.

Evelyn found other material in the *History* that should have provided
surrogate experience warning its readers of English vulnerability. Next to
the passage in which Ralegh advocated the aggressive defense of English
coasts lest the enemy feast on "Kentish capons," Evelyn noted: "which
document had we taken in the late Dutch Warr, we had escaped the re-
proof & insult at Chaltham [*sic*]."[44] By overlooking counsel squarely apparent in the *History*, the British had enabled the Dutch to sail into the
Medway in 1667 and destroy much of the laid-up British fleet.

Some of his contemporaries did examine the *History* in the way Evelyn recommended. Joseph Williamson carefully read through his copy of
the *History* sometime after 1668. Williamson was likely undersecretary
of state at the time, though he would gain increasingly significant posts
before his appointment as secretary of state in 1674.[45] Williamson was an
expert administrator, and he advanced through the Restoration regime on
the strength of his management of several crown offices and his skilled
coordination of domestic intelligence networks. He displayed his expertise in information management as he turned his copy of the *History* into
a usable source for prudent counsel and polished oratory. His notes from
the *History* were compiled into a large commonplace book, along with
snippets taken from sources including James's *Works* (1616), Paolo Sarpi's
History of the Council of Trent (1620), John Spottiswoode's *History of the
Church of Scotland* (1655), Famiano Strada's *History of the Low Countries*

43. BL Eve.b.36, 4.3.6.185.

44. Ibid., 5.1.10.408. Ralegh's passage is quoted in chapter 5 above at n. 51.

45. For Williamson, see Alan Marshall, *Intelligence and Espionage in the Reign of
Charles II* (Cambridge: Cambridge University Press, 1994), and "Joseph Williamson and the
Conduct of Administration in Restoration England," *HR* 69 (1996): 18–41.

(1657), Rushworth's *Historical Collections* (1659–70), and Paul Rycaut's *Present State of the Ottoman Empire* (1668). He equipped this volume with an alphabetical table in front including headings such as "Ambition," "Popery," "History," "Navy," and "Trade." His commonplace book, like others from the early modern period, thus served as a miscellany to order his readings, processed according to a range of moral, geographical, disciplinary, and historical categories.

Rather than resting on his reading table waiting to be inscribed as Williamson read his sources, the notebook marked the end of a complex circuit of reading and writing. Williamson first annotated the margins of his copy of the text with posies, *NB's*, and other marks.[46] He then copied synopses of these apposite passages onto a separate piece of paper. These collections of notes he then cut into thin strips, each bearing one or several excerpts. He then distributed these scraps of paper into their appropriate headings before ordering all the fragments within each category. Each strip was then labeled with a number in the upper-right-hand corner to serialize the proper organization. Finally, he pasted each slip in order onto the page of the commonplace book to ensure the preservation of his notes. His book thus consisted of scraps of paper pasted to its pages, each marked with scrawled distillations of his sources.

Ralegh's work served Williamson as a particular authority for the headings of "war" and "rhetoric," though he also gleaned evidence from the *History* for "Heraldry," "Trade," and other categories. Most of his notes from Ralegh addressed naval matters during the Punic Wars. These extracts infrequently transcribed whole passages, more often loosely summarizing several sentences. They were oriented toward devising policy and tactics to aid Britain's effort to gain control of the seas. For example, where Ralegh discussed the necessity of guarding England's coast, Williamson extracted careful notes showing how Maurice of Nassau had moved his fleet around to frustrate the Spanish while recording the other instances of modern warfare that Ralegh had cited to prove his point. Williamson also noted, "On Invasion, why a Fleet of Sea can prevent it," followed by brief jottings of Roman examples. He also recorded virtually all Ralegh's references to the Dutch, suggesting that this reading may have taken place during the Third Anglo-Dutch War (1672–74). Williamson, it appears, looked to Ralegh for justificatory exemplars of an aggressive maritime policy as Britain strove to dominate the seas.[47]

---

46. Williamson's copy of Ralegh is in Queen's College, Oxford, shelfmark Upper Lib 3.E.15 d.
47. PRO SP 9/14, passim.

Williamson also harvested brief rhetorical turns from Ralegh in the form of pithy turns of phrase. In the "rhetoric" section, he pasted numerous scraps from Ralegh inscribed with axioms such as "Flatterers betray a man to himself" and "He that feigneth himself a sheepe, may chance to be eaten by a wolfe."[48] Even two word phrases such as "barbarous outrages" merited recording. For Williamson, then, the *History* provided, not only a set of episodes from the past from which strong maritime policy could be formulated, but also a repository of oratorical flourishes that could be used to magnify the force of his counsels.

Williamson shared Evelyn's conviction that the considerable wisdom underlying Ralegh's work aided the production of prudent advice. Both Williamson and Evelyn subjected Ralegh's historical learning to minute observation, and the resulting fragments were given new significance when reinserted in their contemporary contexts. They thus turned Ralegh's own methods of disaggregation on his own work. But Williamson also ascribed to Ralegh an oratorical sophistication that few other seventeenth-century readers sought to glean. His work reflected the application of two modes of reading history, both the rhetorically oriented classical model prized by Livy, Cicero, and earlier humanists and the causation-oriented antiquarian models developed and disseminated over the sixteenth century. By applying these methods to modern histories as well as to Ralegh's work, Williamson sought to cultivate persuasiveness and formulate secure counsel. And his skill in amassing and manipulating minute fragments supported his administrative expertise, for such management of textual records and informants' letters spurred his ascent through the Restoration regime.

THE SCHOLARLY *HISTORY*

Many readers did not elicit counsel from Ralegh, focusing instead purely on his scholarship, devoid of political significance. They were not always complimentary—for example, one anonymous eighteenth-century reader cross-referenced passages in which Ralegh contradicted himself.[49] Others turned Ralegh's critical methods on his work, comparing the *History* to

48. Ibid., fol. 162v.

49. This reader, who owned a copy of the 1617 edition (BL 799.m.23), inscribed "x see p 236" at the passage "For it is no where found, that *Noah* himselfe, or any of the Sonnes of his owne bodie came with this troupe into Babylonia." *HW*, 1.10.2.86. At this citation, he inscribed "x see page 186" next to the passage "Soone after the confusion at *Babel* (as it seemes) *Cham* with many of his issue and followers . . . came thither and tooke possession of the Countrie." *HW*, 2.2.1.236. It should be noted that "S. I Newton" is inscribed on p. 9 of this copy.

other works and applying experience and reason to resolve their disagreements. One anonymous reader included evaluations of Ralegh's geographical and genealogical claims amid his transcriptions of passages from the *History*. He devoted particular energy to disproving Ralegh's argument that scriptural translators had mistakenly identified Cush as Ethiopia. This reader stiffly resisted the philological ingenuity deployed by Ralegh, Béroalde, and Steuco, insisting instead that the approved translations of the Septuagint and the Latin Vulgate as well as the works of Josephus should not be overturned by "base coniectures or uncerten report of some few late travellers & that uncontrouledlie may tell us what they please."[50]

This reader, however, did not simply invoke ancient authority to substantiate his position. Instead, his criticism of Ralegh's argument mobilized Ralegh's methods. As he pointed out, the Septuagint may have been a Greek translation, but the translation process had been performed in Alexandria under Ptolemy II Philadelphus. That the translation occurred in a kingdom neighboring Ethiopia weakened the idea that the distance between Greece and Ethiopia had enabled Hellenophones unfamiliar with Africans to mistranslate the passage. Either Ptolemy or Egyptian scholars would have reproved the translators "had they let slip any such growse errour or mistaking in their translation, as to place Chush in Ethiopia, <u>and</u> their next neighbour country, if no such Nation had ever been there <u>but in Arabia</u> knowne to abide." Egyptian learned men, this reader argued, would have scoffed at the error of "translating Chush Aethiopia (if it were otherwise) as we Brittans should doe at them that shold tell us Hibernia were France, or Galia Scotland, or Albania, Ireland."[51] Citing Bellarmine in the margin, he acknowledged that the Septuagint had introduced mistranslations, but he nevertheless could not accept the geographical credulity that he saw in Ralegh, Steuco, and Béroalde's innovative relocation of Cush.

Such readers directed their readings toward scrutinizing the coherence of Ralegh's vision. Though they did not follow their source in plumbing the providential politics Ralegh had perceived as emerging from the subsequent narrative, their modes of reading assessed his scholarship and the coherence of the fabric of history he wove together from the extracts he disjoined from his sources. They shared his desire to direct personal experience and textual savvy toward testing the pasts they encountered as they read.

50. BL Harley 4872. The notes extend from fol. 35r to fol. 51v. The quotation given in the text appears on fols. 47v–48r.

51. BL Harley MS 4872, fol. 48r.

THE REFERENCE *HISTORY*

Far more often, readers turned to the *History* as a reference work for the ancient world. The book served this function for a wide range of individuals, and scholars on both sides of the Civil War like John Milton and Sir Thomas Browne culled from Ralegh detailed analysis of the location of paradise, the resting place of the Noah's Ark, and other age-old exegetical problems.[52] Similarly, the Puritan iconoclast William Dowsing (1596–1668) used the *History* as a master narrative of the ancient world. He purchased his copy in late 1629, fourteen years before he received an appointment to remove "Monuments of Superstition and Idolatry" from the churches in Cambridge and surrounding counties (see fig. 18).[53] Throughout this period, Dowsing amassed an impressive collection of scriptural commentaries, confessional polemics, sermons, and histories, the margins of which he splattered with endorsements or challenges and vitriolic condemnations of the state of the church. The fragmentation of the Parliamentary cause appears to have muted his enthusiasm for reformation, and his notes became increasingly restrained after 1646. But, though he owned the *History* throughout his most passionate period, none of his copious notes in it assumed this adversarial stance. Many assiduously entered scriptural citations where Ralegh had omitted them, while others were traditional indexing notes, often reentered in Ralegh's index or on the title page. A few of these hint at his religious fervor—such as his indexing of passages on "Ye Destruction of blody kings"—but most reflect a more neutral stance, and the above note was shortly followed by a reference to "K James his Liberality to captayns."[54] Most of his annotations, however, dispassionately cross-reference passages from the *History* to one of around one hundred other books in his library, including many whose margins he had filled with copious invective. These notes reveal that, until at least 1662, he read

52. Robert R. Cawley, "Sir Thomas Browne and His Reading," *PMLA* 48 (1933): 426–70; Duncan, *Milton's Earthly Paradise;* and Helena Maragou, "The Portrait of Alexander the Great in Anne Bradstreet's 'The Third Monarchy,'" *Early American Literature* 23 (1988): 70–81.

53. Dowsing's copy is at Swem Library, College of William and Mary, shelfmark D57. R16 1617. He wrote his name and the date of purchase on the frontispiece. For Dowsing, see John Morrill, "William Dowsing: The Bureaucratic Puritan," in *Public Duty and Private Conscience in Seventeenth-Century England: Essays Presented to G. E. Aylmer,* ed. John Morrill, Paul Slack, and Daniel Woolf (Oxford: Clarendon, Oxford, 1993), 173–204, revised as "William Dowsing and the Administration of Iconoclasm," in *The Journal of William Dowsing: Iconoclasm in East Anglia during the English Civil War,* ed. Trevor Cooper (Woodbridge: Ecclesiological Society/Boydell, 2001), 1–28.

54. Dowsing's *History,* on the "Mind of the Front."

Figure 18. Detail of the frontispiece of the 1614 *History of the World*, with annotations by William Dowsing. Special Collections Research Center, Swem Library, College of William and Mary, shelf mark D57. R16 1614.

Ralegh alongside histories ancient and modern such as those of Livy and Camden, travel narratives such as Bünting's *Itinerarium* and *Purchas his Pilgrimage*, natural histories by Pliny and Edward Topsell, and, above all, modern theological works such as Foxe's *Acts of Monuments* and sermons and scriptural commentaries by Hugh Latimer, Andrew Willett, George Abbot, Joseph Caryl, William Greenhill, and many more.[55] These notes never challenged Ralegh's authority or conclusions, instead gesturing to instances where other authors had found polemical significance in the issues Ralegh discussed. Dowsing, it seems, did not read Ralegh as a controversial author; instead, he referred to the *History* when seeking an authoritative narrative of the ancient world that could deepen his understanding of the theological interpretations he encountered elsewhere.

This function may explain some of the many instances in which the *History* was circulated as a gift.[56] Similarly, copies were often donated to college libraries throughout the seventeenth and eighteenth centuries, and Degory Wheare, the first holder of a chair in history at Oxford, gave it principal place among modern works of universal history.[57] The work could be seen as providing for university students a single English overview of the complexities of ancient history.[58] Some students took notes that followed Ralegh's text closely, recording topical headers as they worked through his

55. The latest publication date of any of these works is Thomas Fuller's 1662 *Worthies of England*.

56. Copies of the *History* that have notes indicating that they were gifts during this period include BL c.115.h.5, BL 581.k.13, BL 9006.i.9, BL 9005.q.1, UL RCS.Case.a.94, UL Syn.7.63.246, Bodleian Library Vet. A3 c.88, Princeton D57.xR155q copy 2, Folger STC 20638, UNC CSWR A1, UNC CSWR A4, John Hay 2-Size D57.R25 1634, and Wellcome 42872/D.

57. Degory Wheare, *Relectiones Hyemales* (Oxford, 1637). For Wheare, see J. H. M. Salmon, "Precept: Example, and Truth: Degory Wheare and the *ars historica*," in *The Historical Imagination in Early Modern Britain: History, Rhetoric, and Fiction, 1500–1800*, ed. Donald R. Kelley and David Harris Sacks (Cambridge: Cambridge University Press, 1997), 11–36.

58. Too many copies of the *History* were in college libraries by the eighteenth century to list. Special attention should be drawn to the copy given to Jeremiah Dummer for the Yale College Library (shelfmark 1742 Yale Library 10.2.7). The donor likened Dummer to Bodley and Sheldon and compared his collection to the libraries at Alexandria, Pergamon, and the Vatican, before writing: "I pray you accept this book, written by an author / than whom there is no other more worthy in the entire world to be read / Between the manuscripts of the Trogus bookcase and the sacred works on Vergil / Let the image of Ralegh protect your bookshelves." "Hunc, precor, accipias librum, quem scripserat auctor/ Quo non est alius dignior orbe legi; / Archetypos interque TROGOS, sanctosque MARONES. / RALEGHI pluteos servet imago tuos." Below, he inscribed "That Ralegh himself wrote this History of the World / who first uncovered to us these western shores." "Hanc Mundi Historiam scripsit Raleghius ille, / Qui primum occiduas nobis detexerat oras."

text.[59] Many notes from the *History*, however, indicate that students often did not seek to absorb the whole narrative of ancient history, instead gravitating to specific passages according to their own preferences. As a student in Oxford in 1650, the Lancashire antiquary and future member of Parliament Daniel Fleming recorded copious extracts from the *History* in a notebook.[60] Fleming's notes summarized everything from Ralegh's exemplary descriptions of ancient Romans to criticisms of Annian conjectures, but above all they reveal an interest in references to natural historical phenomena such as giants and mountains. Andrew Melville, similarly, filled a notebook with notes from the *History* while studying divinity at Glasgow in 1699–1700. Melville was most concerned with Ralegh's scriptural history and issues of world chronology, and he inscribed similar notes in the volume from the Abbé de Vallemont's 1698 *Ductor Historicus* and Laurence Echard's 1695 *The Roman History*.[61] In this capacity, the *History* remained useful long after its readers left university. John Jackson—a Presbyterian minister who was ejected from Cambridge in 1650 for refusing to recognize the Commonwealth—similarly entered extracts from Ralegh's discussions of divine intervention in the world into a notebook in 1663, primarily focusing on Ralegh's analyses of Creation, the location of paradise, and the course of biblical history. The rest of the notebook contained extracts drawn from William Burton's 1658 commentary on the Antonine Itinerary, Alexander Ross's 1653 *Pansebeia*, Dugdale's 1656 *Antiquities of Warwickshire*, and John Speed's 1611 biblical genealogies.[62] This collection thus provided him with a reference book adumbrating providential aspects of world history. All these collections filtered the *History* and other sources through the note taker's specific interests, but these directed readings were enabled by the *History*'s role as reference work, authoritative on specific moments of history as well as its general progress.

While these readers used the *History* as one of a number of historical reference works, less scholarly readers used it as their primary guide to the past. A copy owned by the Comberbach family of Nantwich, Cheshire, contains hundreds of annotations from the late seventeenth century and the early eighteenth.[63] Most were terse indexing terms or just the word

59. Note, e.g., that one Mr. Nevis filled a volume with topical indexing terms and names from the *History* and from Ussher's *Annales*. BL Sloane 3407, fols. 1r–25r.

60. Fleming's notes are in Kendal Record Office, Kendal, Cumbria UK WD RY/Box 36/2. (Thanks are due to Bill Bulman for digital photographs.)

61. Melville's notes are Wellcome WMS 6880, fols. 29r–42r.

62. Cambridge University Library, MS Gg.2.25.

63. Bodleian Library K 3.6 Art.

note, highlighting the focus of the text; representative examples include "note for education," "note that in the first age men were of more excellency then ever since," and "note Themistocles pollicy."[64] Such phrases generally identified historical figures, geographical terms, or providential judgments as the central features of Ralegh's passages. These notes were oriented less toward helping the Comberbachs order their reading than enabling them to scan the text quickly.

The Comberbachs seem to have treasured their copy of the *History,* as the book was signed and annotated in at least three hands by at least two generations of the family. While the tanner John Comberbach was likely responsible for most of the notes, some may have been written by his youngest daughter, Diana, who also signed the copy.[65] She would be by no means the only woman to sign her name inside a copy of the *History,* and an increasing number of women left marks in copies of the *History* in the nineteenth century.[66] Of course many women may have read the *History* without inscribing their names or have heard it read aloud by their male or female relatives, but the Comberbach copy notably provides an extensive set of notes derived from repeated family reading. And these notes suggest that, for an ordinary family in late seventeenth-century Nantwich, Ralegh's work could serve as an authoritative reference work to be closely examined in learning about all aspects of the world. As such, this specific mode of interaction with Ralegh's work extended over a broad social spec-

64. There are glimmers that the Comberbachs viewed Ralegh within a tradition of anti-Spanish martyrdom. One of the Comberbachs wrote "Sweet Raleigh" in the margins next to his discussion of "when our spirits immortall shall be once separate from our mortall bodies" (ibid., C3v) and "note this for the king of Spain I think" where Ralegh had written "I doe not much doubt, but that some of those Kings, with whom we are now in peace . . . as soone as their coffers shall be full, they shall declare themselves enemies to the people of England" (ibid., 5.6.1.426). If they did not share Ralegh's anti-Spanish policies, they were, nevertheless, capable of discerning his transparent hints of it.

65. John Comberbach (1670–1727) and all his children were born in Nantwich. Diana was born in 1706. She signed the top of A1r. This genealogical information comes from John's diary at cumberbatch.org (accessed August 18, 2010).

66. An Elizabeth Finch signed her 1652 copy (Folger R163). A Margaret Weld signed a 1700 abridgement (UNC CSWR A98). Another copy has notes reading both "Mary William our book" and "Meary Clark her book 1715." (UNC CSWR A17). Sometime after 1736, Ann Kilborn signed her copy (HEH 79046). In 1833, a Mary Cameron inscribed her name in her copy (BL fc/249 DSC). Susanna Malshaw wrote her name in a copy in 1846 (Princeton [EX] n29551.745q [copy 1] 26 [103]). In May 1881, a Margaret Jarret Elmsley sent her copy of the *History* to her brother Robert Keith Pringle, explaining: "This old Book from my husband's Library he liked to dip into it—The Piety of it is a striking contrast to *History* in the present day!! 'The Bible, the Whole Bible' was true History in every word to our Fathers! may it be to all our generations" (Bodleian Library Vet. A2 c.13). Note also the copy of Ross's continuation (BL 9005.q.1) that contains the note "Sarah Mitford 1701 given her by her grandmother."

trum, from learned elites such as Milton and Browne to provincial tanners and their daughters. For all these readers, Ralegh's *History* supplied a comprehensive and reliable description of the entire ancient world rather than a historical polemic.

THE TRAVELING *HISTORY*

Charles I's chaplain, Alexander Ross, engaged closely with Ralegh's use of sources in his 1653 *Som Animadversions and Observations Upon Sir Walter Raleigh's History of the World.*[67] He disagreed in particular with Ralegh's location of the sepulcher of Noah's Ark, and he punctured his arguments one by one. For example, he noted: "Wee know by relation of Travellers, Historians, and Geographers, that in *Armenia* are plentie of verie good Wines, and contrarie in *India* there are no wines, or verie scarce." Indeed, Ross disputed Ralegh's entire characterization of the Far East as a civilized site of ancient and pious knowledge, instead trumpeting a humanist veneration of Greek antiquity. As he wrote: "For civilite and learning wee finde that the Western Greeks did civilize and instruct the Eastern Asiaticks." Nor did he accept China's proclaimed technological superiority: "as for the stories of *China* I give little credit to them, nor do I believe that Printing and Artillerie, with other Arts, were so manie years among them, before wee knew the use of them, no more, then that the World was created so manie thousand years before *Moyses* his computation which is the belief of the *Chinois.*"[68] Ross conflated Ralegh's praise of ancient Chinese civilization with the exaggerated heathen chronologies that Ralegh had so strongly criticized. Accepting the claims of Gonzalez de Mendoza, according to Ross, reflected a dangerous credulity.

But other readers embraced Ralegh's conclusions about the East. The Puritan clergyman Nathanael Carpenter faithfully reiterated Ralegh's proof for the location of Noah's Ark in his 1625 *Geographie Delineated.* Carpenter subscribed to the position that "The People of the *Easterne* Hemispheare in Science, Religion, Civility, Magnificence, and almost every thing else, are farre superiour to the Inhabitants of the *Westerne.*" Like Ralegh, he developed the idea that an ancient devotion persisted in lands that Europeans faintly knew, and he encouraged Englishmen to explore the East seeking to rediscover ancient wisdom. He enjoined his readers: "Let

67. For Ross, see Adrian Johns, "Prudence and Pedantry in Early Modern Cosmology: The Trade of Al Ross," *History of Science* 35 (1997): 23–59.

68. Alexander Ross, *Som Animadversions and Observations upon Sir Walter Raleigh's History of the World* (London, 1653), 10, 12.

every man by beholding the *nationall* vices of other men, praise Almighty
God for his owne happinesse: and by seeing their vertue, learne to correct
his owne vice. So should travaile in this Terrestriall Globe bee our direct
way to Heaven."[69] Carpenter thus explicitly articulated the pious urgency
of global exploration that Ralegh's geography implicitly suggested.

Most Britons, of course, would not undertake the travel that Carpenter's plea entailed, but some used the *History* to discover exotic marvels.
Many of Daniel Fleming's notes concerned awe-inspiring Eastern mountains that allegedly dwarfed the hills he knew. Of famed Grecian peaks,
he quoted from Ralegh that the "mountains of Olympus, Atho, and Atlas
over-reach & surmount all windes and cloudes . . . ye pagan priests, sacri-
ficing on these mountaine tops, doe not find ye ashes (remaining of their
sacrifices) blown thence, or washt away with rains, when they turne."
Fleming omitted a crucial passage, however. After recounting these tales
of ashes unmoved, Ralegh had written: "yet experience hath resolved us,
that these reports are fabulous, and *Plinie* himselfe (who was not sparing in the report of wonders) avoweth the contrarie."[70] Fleming excised
Ralegh's opinion to record solely the tale of ethereal Olympian crests.

Other readers learned about the East through readings of the *History*.
These included Thomas Browne, who followed Ralegh's arguments closely
concerning the resting place of Noah's Ark. More strikingly, the Comberbachs gleaned from the *History* advice about foreign lands that they were
unlikely ever to use. For example, next to Ralegh's recommendation that
explorers in the New World "burne downe the grasse and sedge to the East
of them," one of the Comberbachs wrote: "A good observation & woorthy
noting for Travellers."[71] They were particularly attentive to Ralegh's reports about the wisdom of the East. Where Ralegh described ancient Chinese printing and firearms, they noted in the margins "note the Chinians
had ordinance powder & printing tyme out of minde" and "note Sr Walter
his opinion touching China Japan the East Indies & of their Citties Civil-
lity Antiquity & Religion." Next to Ralegh's argument that Ophir lay in
the Moluccas rather than in Peru, one of the family dutifully wrote, "note
the east India Islandes more abounding in gould to the Spaniardes America."[72] The Comberbachs extracted a vision of the East as wise, technologically savvy, and bursting with gold.

69. Nathanael Carpenter, *Geographie Delineated* (Oxford, 1625), 250, 286.

70. Kendal Record Office, Kendal, Cumbria UK WD RY/Box 36/2, fol. 68v. Moreover,
Ralegh noted of Augustine, "whom herein I mistrust." The passage is *HW*, 1.3.8.45.

71. Bodleian Library K 3.6 Art. Ralegh's passage is quoted in chapter 5 above at n. 43.

72. Ibid., 1.7.10.4.115–16, 1.8.15.5.176.

This view of the East as suffused with remarkable ancient wisdom was embraced by British Orientalists for at least two centuries. The belief that divine knowledge had been disseminated throughout India in the dawn of the postdiluvian world allowed later scholars to proclaim that their own sophisticated learning merely restored ancient Eastern wisdom. The Orientalist and jurist William Jones, for example, proclaimed to the Asiatick Society in 1794: "I can venture to affirm, without meaning to pluck a leaf from the neverfading laurels of our immortal Newton, that the whole of his theology and part of his philosophy may be found in the *Védas* and even in the works of the *Súfis*."[73] Indeed, men associated with the East India Company in the late eighteenth century like Jones and Nathaniel Halhed put into action the older, universalizing scholarly vision advocated by Ralegh and Dee, in which travelers and correspondents across the globe conveyed observations to construct complete knowledge of the earth. The techniques of knowledge creation and information retrieval that early modern scholars inherited from the practices of ecclesiastical history would, thus, provide both the intellectual justification for mining the wisdom of the East and the methods that scholars such as Jones would employ.[74] Ralegh, Dee, and Jones shared a desire to restore ancient wisdom and reveal the significance of the divine theater of particulars. Whether in 1600 or in 1800, it could be harnessed by studied techniques of observation, methodical reading, and incessant correspondence with travelers.

THE TORY *HISTORY*

Readers of all political positions, as we have seen, perceived parallels between their contemporaries and the litany of figures Ralegh described in the ancient world. One Whiggish reader around 1678 correlated the Tory ministry of Thomas Osborne, Earl of Danby, with the ascendancy of Philip of Macedon's evil counselor Apelles. Ralegh had described how Apelles had inserted himself as a buffer between the king and his other advisers and then visited financial ruin on Macedonia through his damaging policies. Apelles' baseless confidence, according to Ralegh, led him "to resolve these and all other difficulties, by only saying, *Sir, be ruled wholly by me,*

---

73. William Jones, *Works*, 6 vols. (London, 1799), 1:170.

74. See Thomas R. Trautmann, *Aryans and British India* (Berkeley and Los Angeles: University of California Press, 1997); and Simon Schaffer, "The Asiatic Enlightenments of British Astronomy," in *The Brokered World: Go-Betweens and Global Intelligence, 1770–1820*, ed. Simon Schaffer, Lissa Roberts, Kapil Raj, and James Delbourgo (Sagamore Beach, MA: Science History, 2009), 151–91.

and all shall be as you would wish." He thus exemplified the destructive
sycophant, and the Whig reader inscribed next to this passage: "Ld Trea-
surer Denby his verry design."[75] As with so many others, Ralegh's work
furnished to this reader parallels with which to analyze his own times.

This reader, however, did not attribute special insight to Ralegh; still
less did he follow "Philanax Misopapas," who gave the title of *Raleigh
Redivivus* to his eulogizing 1683 biography of the early Whig leader the
Earl of Shaftesbury. Instead, he criticized aspects of Ralegh's work that
provided support for absolutism. When discussing the domain and jurisdiction of laws in a chapter entitled "That only the Prince is exempt from
humane law, and in what sort," Ralegh had proclaimed that King David's
confession to God, "against thee onely have I sinned," indicated that "the
Prince cannot be said to be subject to the law." The reader bristled at this
statement. He wrote: "in this the Author mistake in not makinge a difference between Monarchy Absolute and Monarchy mixt: for England being
a Compound governmt the legislative power is not in ye king but in ye
3 Estates (vixt ye King ye Lord & ye Comons)." Rather than seeking the
ideal form of government by scrutinizing Providence's signals to humanity, this reader indignantly outlined England's historical constitution. By
contrast: "David & other absolute Princes who pretend their eleccon &
title from God either by imediat call or by Conquest have no equalls in
their legislative power as kings & their descendants coming to their power
by Eleccon & Compact have."[76] David had ruled absolutely, but, for this
reader, doing so marked his rule as arbitrary, licentious, and unworthy of
imitation.

Rather than turn to the past to find support for his own convictions,
this reader assessed Ralegh according to Whig principles. In his view, England possessed a legitimate species of government independent of Adamic
or Israelite forms of government. The reader concluded: "For from whom-
soever the trust arises, to them the trusted is Accountable."[77] He thus
contradicted Ralegh's claim that David answered only to God. Even the
most revered of biblical kings, in this reader's view, constituted a usurping
tyrant rather than a pious model. The reader thus accepted Ralegh's narrative but rejected its counsels. Though the *History* supplied individual
past parallels for the present, Ralegh's admiration of ancient tyrants and
commendation of absolutism reinforced the exegetical error of divine-

75. Shelfmark UNC CSWR A12, 5.4.2.997.
76. Ibid., 2.4.16.229.
77. Ibid.

right monarchy to which this Whig reader would have attributed the Civil Wars.

THE MORALIST'S *HISTORY*

One anonymous reader entered extracts from the *History* into his manuscript "Moral Commonplace Book" in the early eighteenth century. Most of these notes condemned the corrupt reigns of Judaic kings that culminated in the destruction of the Temple. For example, the reader summarized Ralegh's condemnation of the malicious Judaic king Jehoram, noting how "the *Corrupted* affections of Men; *impugning the reveald* will of God; accomplishe neverthelesse; *his hidden purpose* & without Miraculous *means*, counfound themselves in the seeming Devices *of their own* folly."[78] Jehoram's reign illustrated humanity's impotence in the face of Providence. Indeed, the author conceived the task of the historian as conveying such divine judgments, noting: "Wherefore, it being the End & Scope of all History to teach by *Example* of times past, such wisdom, as may guide, our desires & actions, the Chronicles being writ by Men *Inspired by God*, instruct men yt wch is most requisite; for *us to* know both here; & hereafter preparing Examp wch illustrate this *rule*. Yt the fear *of the Lord is beginning* of wisdom."[79] Like so many other readers, he understood Ralegh's work as presenting exemplary moral lessons.

Though this reader attributed conventional significance to Ralegh's work, the other sources he used to populate his commonplace book did not resemble Ralegh's work. Erasmus's *Adagia* supplied his main source, followed by Matthew Hale's 1676 *Contemplations, Moral and Divine*, Bishop Jeremy Taylor's 1650 *Holy Living* and 1651 *Holy Dying*, and biblical commentaries by Hugo Grotius. These pious works held similar moralizing purposes, and they stimulated edification by mobilizing scriptural exegesis, sermonizing, and philological analysis. But change and causation played little role in their writings. Rather, they sought to pronounce eternal theological wisdom that, when internalized, would bring their readers closer to God.

For this reader, the *History* was most valuable for its expositions of the power of Providence. But that Ralegh used historical analysis to achieve this goal was of little significance, for the family of texts with which he associated the *History* did not share Ralegh's conviction that the theater

---

78. BL Add. MS 4985, fol. 4. The passage is *HW*, 2.19.5.447.
79. Ibid., fol. 6v, quoting from *HW*, 2.21.451.

of the past best illuminated sacred Providence. To their authors, piety was not produced by exposing God's oversight of causation or by tracing Providence's dynamic elevation of men in order to bring them low. Histories rather constituted one particular mode within a larger genre of improving literature. This reader, then, recognized that the *History* was intended to help cultivate wisdom. But his reading occluded Ralegh's certainty that an understanding of Providence required knowledge of causation and, instead, converted Ralegh's text into a series of static moralizations.

THE REVOLUTIONARY WAR *HISTORY*

In November 1779, the Chathamite Charles Pratt, first Earl Camden, wrote a letter to his daughter Elizabeth concerning her reading. Camden was one of the eighteenth century's most prominent defenders of the liberties of British subjects; his brief tenure as lord chancellor was the high point of a career marked by momentous judicial rulings and principled opposition. Like other Chathamites, Camden saw George III's treatment of his colonies as violating subjects' rights, and he viewed the outbreak of war with despondent resignation, supporting neither American independence nor imperial aggression.

The letter to Lady Elizabeth seemed far removed from these concerns. Camden was delighted to learn that his daughter had tired of "that trash the press sends forth every month under the name of Novels." He had little patience for such works, to say the least. He wrote: "Silly Love is the perpetual subject: The Stile is ordinary, & the Language scarce Grammar. They are all written for Bread by low-bred females & have a vent only in circulating librarys for the amusement of ignorant Girls & Macaronis while their Hair is dressing, the only time they read at all." Given Elizabeth's good judgment, he was unsurprised that she preferred "intertaining history," but he worried that tedious modern histories would not meet with her approval. Accordingly, he had sent her Herodotus and Xenophon, and he eagerly awaited her response. To further discern her tastes, he also sent "a great favourite of mine, Sr W Ralegh's History of the World." Camden tried to ensure her enjoyment of Ralegh's work by managing her reading. He wrote: "I wd advise you to begin in the middle, where I have marked the place wch treats of the Greek & after that of ye Roman transactions. When you find a part dull pass over to something else, & don't upon any Account strain your attention to any reading that is not perfectly agreeable." In a slip attached to the letter, he noted: "The part of the book where I *would* advise you to begin is in the third Book of the first part page 44

Section 7. I have doubled down the leaves in that place." If Ralegh's work did not strike her fancy, he offered to send collections of travel narratives, the Decameron, or de Scudery's *Le Grand Cyrus*.[80]

Camden's recommendations directed his daughter to skip the meticulous scholarly treatments analyzing Creation and the location of paradise along with nearly the entire narrative of the biblical past. Overlooked too was the universal scope of history that Ralegh had crafted to inspire piety and virtue in his reader. Instead, Camden's prescription seemingly recommended that his daughter view the *History* as an edifying narrative of Greek and Latin antiquity. Ralegh's motivations were sheared away, leaving only an English adaptation of classical sources with the recognition that even this might prove too tedious for her.

Where Camden instructed Elizabeth to begin reading, however, suggests that he viewed the *History* as somewhat more. The section to which he directed her lay in the middle of Ralegh's treatment of the Persian Empire, directly after his discussion of the early history of Athens. Here, Ralegh narrated the Ionian Revolt during the reign of Darius, which inaugurated the Persian Wars and the eventual downfall of the Persian Empire. Darius, he had noted, had ruled his Greek colonies by establishing tyrants over them. But, he observed, "as it is the custome of Nations halfe conquered (witnesse *Ireland*) to rebell againe upon every advantage and opportunitie: so did the *Ionians*, and other *Graecians* . . . seeke by all meanes possible to free themselves."[81]

At the outset of the uprising, Ionian representatives had gone from city to city throughout Greece, convincing the Athenians and others to join their makeshift revolt against the empire. For six years the alliance held out against the Persians, winning occasional battles, destroying Sardis, and infuriating Darius. But their victories did not endure. Darius's unrelenting attacks and promises of clemency gradually stripped Ionia of its allies, and eventually "the Towne it self . . . was taken by force, the Citizens slaine, their wives and children made slaves, and their goods a bootie to the *Persians*."[82] Once the Ionians were vanquished, a distrustful Darius practiced a cruel domination over Hellas that, in turn, provoked a successful uprising a decade later, inaugurating the Golden Age of Athens.

Camden instructed his daughter to begin reading at a moment when Ralegh's narrative possessed unmistakable contemporary overtones. The

---

80. Centre for Kentish Studies, U840 C7/5. Camden's copy was in the 1621 family of editions.
81. *HW*, 3.5.7.54.
82. *HW*, 3.5.7.56.

Ionian Revolt clearly mirrored the rebellion faced by George III, when another collective of small colonial states arose against a mighty empire. Camden's directions tacitly suggest that, for him, the past still furnished a mirror of causation whose proper absorption enabled readers to properly anticipate the looming course of events. That he concealed this function of histories as augmenting experience, on the other hand, suggests that he may have been uncertain whether his daughter would have embraced the study of the past for such parallels. Perhaps he thought better of earnestly insisting on this role for historical reading, privately expecting that such powerful applications of the study of the past would appeal to her once she discerned in Ralegh's narrative the ephemerality of George III's inevitable victory.

THE LITERARY RALEGH

Though the *History* continued to elicit approval throughout the eighteenth century, readers increasingly imported systems of evaluation that did not reflect Ralegh's own priorities. In his 1713 *A Dissertation on Reading the Classics*, Henry Felton praised Ralegh's work, exclaiming: "Sir Walter Raleigh's History of the World is a work of so vast Compass, such endless Variety, that no Genius, but one Adventuruos as his own durst have undertaken that great Design." But, for Felton, the exacting labor demanded of compiling, evaluating, and synthesizing Ralegh's monumental collection of sources did not inspire admiration. He wrote: "I do not apprehend any great Difficulty in collecting & Common-placing an universal History from the whole Body of Historians; that is nothing but mechanic labour." Ralegh's erudition, his voracious acquisition of texts, and his skill in parsing them were of little interest, more menial craft than exalted knowledge. His rhetorical expertise in synthesizing them, however, constituted a marvelous achievement: "But to digest the several Authors in his mind, to take in all their Majesty, Strength and Beauty, to raise the spirit of meaner Historians, and to equall all the Excellencies of the best, is Sir *Walter's* peculiar praise." Felton continued: "His Style is the most perfect, the happiest, and most beautiful of the age he wrote in; majestic, clear, and manly, and he appears everywhere so superior rather than unequal to his Subject, that the Spirit of *Rome* and *Athens* seems to be breathed into his work." In fact, Ralegh's marvelous Attic prose would have been better turned to different subject matter: "[In] my opinion his admirable performance in such a prodigious Undertaking, sheweth, that if he had attempted the History of his own Country or his own time, he would have excelled even

Livy and *Thucydides* . . . and would have transmitted his History as the
Standard of our Language even to the present age."[83] Universal history offered little enticement to this reader, who did not share Ralegh's interest
in world chronology, postdiluvian colonization, and scriptural exegesis.
Ralegh's historical culture flickered only dimly for Felton, obscured by a
classical preference for rhetorical and literary verve.

Ralegh continued to be a potent symbol into the eighteenth century,
at times recast—as in Thomas Freeman's pirated world history attributed
to Ralegh—as a contemporaneous man of letters (see fig. 19). Nonetheless, the criteria used to judge Ralegh's work were shifting. In 1765, Joseph Bromshead, a student at Queen's College, Oxford, wrote a letter about
the *History* to a Mrs. White of Norwich consisting of a long excerpt from
Felton.[84] Bromshead's decision to focus on Felton's literary assessment,
rather than Ralegh's biography or erudite features of the work, reflected
the emerging view of the *History*. While the most prominent mid-eighteenth-century critics complimented Ralegh's style, they felt that his
discussions of erudite sources and arcane evidence prevented him from
fully realizing the literary potential of historical writing. In 1751, Samuel
Johnson complained in the *Rambler* that, though Ralegh was "deservedly
celebrated for the labour of his researches, and the elegance of his style; . . .
he has endeavoured to exert his judgment more than his genius, to select
facts, rather than adorn them; and has produced an historical dissertation,
but seldom risen to the majesty of history."[85] David Hume, most famously,
cautioned: "if the reader can have the patience to wade through the Jewish
and Rabbinical learning which compose the half of the volume, he will
find, when he comes to the Greek and Roman story, that his pains are not
unrewarded. Raleigh is the best model of that antient style, which some
writers would revive at present."[86] These works reflect the emerging status
of literary criticism, assessing the rhetorical potency and style of the *History* while ignoring its foundation of antiquarian research, Continental
erudition, and analysis of providential causation.

Such mid-eighteenth-century criticisms resonated with the transformations in English learned culture of the previous 150 years. Continental
scholarship was no longer envied. The Bible seemingly was supplanted as

---

83. Henry Felton, *A Dissertation on Reading the Classics, and forming a Just Style* (London, 1713), 199–201.

84. Joseph Bromshead to Mrs. White, Queen's College, Oxford, 1765. The letter is pasted
into the front binding of Firestone Library, Princeton University (EX) 29551.745q (copy 2).

85. *The Rambler*, no. 122 (18 May 1751): 141.

86. David Hume, *The History of England*, vol. 6 (Dublin, 1769), 134.

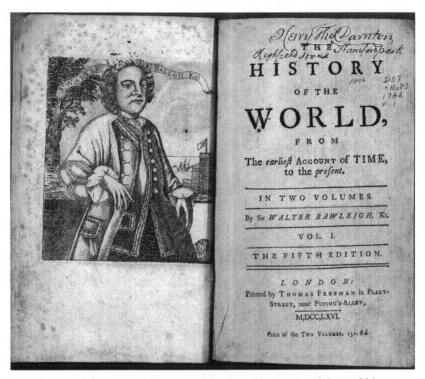

Figure 19. Frontispiece and facing portrait from *The History of the World from the Earliest Account of Time to the Present* (London: Thomas Freeman, 1766). Sir Walter Raleigh Collection, North Carolina Collection at the University of North Carolina at Chapel Hill, UNC CSWR D22.1.

ideal history by the Roman and Greek historians beloved by a profoundly neoclassical age, their witty apothegms and well-ordered periods providing fodder for recitation and imitation, if not the foundation of virtue. Ralegh's intricate techniques of compiling, correlating, and adjudicating evidence from different authors were figured as luridly banausic, for eloquence and rhetoric had replaced the analysis of causation as the ideal fruit of reading histories. Pleasure and moral rectitude, but not experience, were to be gained by imbibing such literary marvels.

CONCLUSION

The *History* embodied a movement in scholarly practice that would, Ralegh hoped, transform England and the world. Like many of his contemporaries, Ralegh intended his discussions of Continental scholarship to refine the erudition and piety of his countrymen. He sought to inspire scholarly counselors to dissect the past, generating knowledge of Providence with which they would formulate divinely approved counsels. And he hoped that readers would admire his devotion, directing toward him the appreciation and respect he little expected from the greater public.

Some readers would interpret the *History* in this fashion; those like Scott and Sheppard were convinced by its counsels and saw it as a product of a man worthy of imitation. For Evelyn and Williamson too, Ralegh's past supplied vivid parallels for contemporary events, and his artful restoration of the theater of Providence constituted a valuable source for developing counsel. Those who scrutinized his arguments imitated his project, subjecting the work to the methodological analysis that Ralegh had directed at his own sources. For the Comberbachs and others, his work supplied a satisfying compendium of the ancient world, an edifying source that brought into their home the richness of God's creation. And, most powerfully, his skillful discernment of future events marked him to Evelyn, Carpenter, and others as a prophet. These readings reflected striations and permutations within the historical culture that had produced Ralegh's work and that he wished to disseminate to his countrymen.

But readers of the *History* were by no means restricted by the canons of historical culture, and they subjected it to a diffuse and unpredictable array of interpretations. Ralegh could not control the *History*'s meaning for its readers, and in many of their hands it accrued significance independent of his goals. James's hostile reading was only the first of many revisions. At least one reader, as we have seen, saw it as a monument of obsequiousness, a sure sign of Ralegh's ingrained Machiavellianism. Others ignored his fine-grained analyses of scriptural history, rejecting his exegetical arguments and antiquarian digressions as meandering and tedious. Over the seventeenth century, this last criticism gradually gained ascendancy, and, while Ralegh's style continued to elicit respect, observers increasingly ignored the scriptural history that had so captivated his attention and derided the focused erudition that had yielded his most striking insights.

Above all, the very methodology that rooted the production of the *History* declined in readers' evaluations. Early modern historians presumed that attention to the most minute particulars of obscure sources would be divinely rewarded, forcing humanity to recognize how God had effected earthly change. The practices Ralegh employed had been geared toward deciphering causation by directing his attention to the potential impact of the slightest of factors. His extensive compilations of contemporary commentators, painstaking subjection of his sources to exacting analysis, and reanimation of their extracts into a vibrant history constituted a process of producing experiential wisdom that shaped how he governed and interpreted the world and his own life.

But these practices increasingly went unnoticed or unappreciated by readers. Neither did they continue to perceive in his narratives the lessons of causation that Ralegh had wished his analyses to unmask or the reservoir of experience that he strove to bequeath to his countrymen. His passionate commitment to reconstituting the past as a guide to the present, the very heart of his prophetic labor, faded behind an emphasis on persuasion and presentation. History was, again, increasingly seen as a species of rhetoric, valued more for its artful elocutions and pithy sayings than for its exposure of past workings of providential causation. Histories were no longer supplicatory labors to restore quiescent harmony to the fallen and splintered theater of the divine.

Conclusion

R alegh's *History* emerged from an intellectual culture that valued historical training as the optimal preparation for public life. Throughout
early modern Europe, scholars and statesmen turned to the past to provide
providential justifications for their political and scholarly visions. Their
investigations did not unearth the single, universally shared narrative they
hoped to find but instead generated discordant histories marred by periods
of haunting oblivion, chronological entanglements, forgotten toponyms,
and hopelessly prejudiced testimony. In response, they adapted tools from
their existing scholarly culture to furnish methods with which a shared
and indisputable history might be generated. They hoped that these techniques would yield narratives reflecting the true course of events under
God's creation whose didactic lessons would inspire contemporary kings
and statesmen to pursue political programs invested with divine favor.

As we have seen, the methods constitutive of historical analysis exerted their own impact throughout scholarly culture. The emphasis on
collecting a vast trove of sources to be parsed into minute extracts and recombined into charged narratives transformed how European scholars revered their authoritative texts while altering the scholarly processes they
deemed productive of true knowledge. New narratives that challenged
the old increasingly emerged from these methods, and political practice
was configured to facilitate the application of historical modes of analysis
to governance in the present. The methods disseminated as the analytic
practices of historical culture inexorably transformed what they had been
designed to preserve.

But the emphasis on historical culture contained the seeds of its own
unraveling as well. As the recitation of the past again became classified
as a field of rhetoric, a new form of learning crystallized from the meth-

ods and ambitions of the culture of historical analysis. Over the seventeenth century, the intellectual regime now associated with the scientific revolution gradually challenged the preeminence of humanistic learning. The philosophical method pioneered by Francis Bacon that was essential to this movement prized an empirical approach to knowledge requiring the compilation of vast troves of natural and textual particulars, inductive reasoning, and the rejection of traditional accounts of causation on grounds of experience. It thus gave abstract, systematic form to the methods of historical analysis while preferring the unchanging natural world to the mutable past as the object of analysis. In Bacon's hands, the practices of historians were concatenated into a natural philosophy whose appeal lay in its power to produce unassailable knowledge by elevating correlated observations of natural historical particulars into universal truths.[1]

The discussion of the history of natural knowledge in the *History* offers a final instance illuminating how the primary consequence of the historical turn lay in its methods rather than in the contours of the past it uncovered. Toward the end of book 1 of the *History*, Ralegh included an extensive treatment of the ancient knowledge of natural magic.[2] His discussion broached a dangerous subject. He had faced recurrent allega-

1. See Charles Webster, *The Great Instauration: Science, Medicine, and Reform, 1626–1660* (London: Duckworth, 1975); Barbara Shapiro, "History and Natural History in Sixteenth- and Seventeenth-Century England: An Essay on the Relationship between Humanism and Science," in *English Scientific Virtuosi in the 16th and 17th Centuries*, by Barbara Shapiro and Robert G. Frank Jr. (Los Angeles: William Andrews Clark Memorial Library, University of California, Los Angeles, 1979), 1–55; Stephen Pumfrey, "The History of Science and the Renaissance Science of History," in *Science, Culture, and Popular Belief in Renaissance Europe*, ed. Stephen Pumfrey, Paolo L. Rossi, and Maurice Slawinski (Manchester: Manchester University Press, 1991), 48–70; Findlen, "Francis Bacon and the Reform of Natural History"; and my "Ocean of Lies."

2. For Renaissance magic and the occult arts, see Don Cameron Allen, *The Star-Crossed Renaissance: The Quarrel about Astrology and Its Influence in England* (Durham, NC: Duke University Press, 1941); D. P. Walker, *Spiritual and Demonic Magic from Ficino to Campanella* (London: Warburg Institute, 1958); Frances Yates, *Giordano Bruno and the Hermetic Tradition* (London: Routledge & Kegan Paul, 1964); Margaret Aston, "The Fiery Trigon Conjunction: An Elizabethan Astrological Prediction," *Isis* 61 (1970): 159–87; Charles Webster, *From Paracelsus to Newton: Natural Magic in the Making of Modern Science* (Cambridge: Cambridge University Press, 1982); Nicholas Clulee, *John Dee's Natural Philosophy: Between Magic and Religion* (London: Routledge, 1988); Brian Copenhaver, "Natural Magic, Hermetism, and Occultism in Early Modern Science," in *Reappraisals of the Scientific Revolution*, ed. David Lindberg and Robert Westman (Cambridge: Cambridge University Press, 1990), 261–302, and "The Occultist Tradition and Its Critics in Seventeenth Century Philosophy," in Garber and Ayers, eds., *The Cambridge History of Seventeenth-Century Philosophy*, 454–512; Deborah Harkness, *John Dee's Conversations with Angels: Cabala, Alchemy, and the End of Nature* (Cambridge: Cambridge University Press, 1999); and Lauren Kassell, *Medicine and Magic in Elizabethan London: Simon Forman, Astrologer, Alchemist, and Physician* (Oxford: Clarendon, 2005).

tions of heterodoxy and harboring practitioners of suspect magic—most notably Thomas Harriot—and he surely wished to avoid stoking further suspicion.[3] Especially concerning was that James I's 1597 *Daemonologie* had condemned a broad range of magical arts as ancient pagan pollutions of legitimate intellectual practices.[4] Ralegh thus proceeded cautiously when he discussed magic. Nonetheless, he developed a history that defended the knowledge that had been accused of signaling his and Harriot's godlessness.

James had claimed that the category of magic had been created by an ancient Chaldean corruption of invaluable knowledge of the heavens. The king praised knowledge of the "course and ordinary motions" of the planets as a venerable study, for farmers and physicians operated by correlating sidereal configurations with seasons and sicknesses. But this approved form of astrology, he lamented, had led those of impure faith "to truste so much to their [the stars'] influence."[5] The Chaldeans had attributed causal agency to the celestial bodies rather than recognizing them as signs of a divine pattern of Creation, and their Persian and Egyptian inheritors magnified this error by sacralizing everything from the flights of birds to reflections in fingernails. Ralegh's contrasting treatment began with the study of the four known Zoroasters from the ancient world. Ralegh conflated two of these figures into an ancient Persian magus contemporary with Abraham whom Augustine and Pliny had blamed for inventing diabolic magic. Following the Florentine nobleman Pico della Mirandola, he claimed that all ancient magi had inherited Chaldean learning, and therefore argued that Zoroaster could not have invented the arts he practiced.[6]

3. For Ralegh's patronage of these arts, see Stephen Pumfrey and Frances Dawbarn, "Science and Patronage in England, 1570–1625: A Preliminary Study," *History of Science* 42 (2004): 137–88.

4. See Stuart Clark, "King James's Daemonologie: Witchcraft and Kingship," in *The Damned Art: Essays in the Literature of Witchcraft*, ed. Sydney Anglo (London: Routledge & Kegan Paul, 1977), 156–81.

5. James I, *Daemonologie* (Edinburgh, 1597), 12–13.

6. *HW*, 1.11.1.200. For Ralegh on Zoroaster, see Kassell, "'All Was This Land Full Fill'd of Faerie.'" For Pico, see S. A. Farmer, *Syncretism in the West: Pico's 900 Theses (1486): The Evolution of Traditional, Religious, and Philosophical Systems: With Text, Translation, and Commentary* (Phoenix: Medieval and Renaissance Texts and Studies, 1998); H. Darrel Rutkin, "Astrology, Natural Philosophy and the History of Science, c. 1250–1700: Studies toward an Interpretation of Giovanni Pico della Mirandola's *Disputationes adversus astrologiam divinatricem*" (Ph.D. diss., Indiana University, 2002), esp. 230–467; and Steven Vanden Broecke, *The Limits of Influence: Pico, Louvain, and the Crisis of Renaissance Astrology* (Leiden: Brill, 2003), 55–81. For Pico's later opinions, see Anthony Grafton, *Commerce with the Classics: Ancient Books and Renaissance Readers* (Ann Arbor: University of Michigan Press, 1997), 93–134.

In so doing, he also enumerated the species of learning—astrology and medical alchemy—that he assigned to natural magic: "I doe not thinke that *Zoroaster* invented the doctrine of the Horoscopes or Nativities; or first found out the nature of hearbs, stones, and minerals, or their Sympatheticall or Antipatheticall workings." As he continued, Ralegh linked the study of these arts to a people far more pious than Persian magi or their Chaldean predecessors. He explained: "I rather thinke that these knowledges were farre more ancient, and left by *Noah* to his sonnes." Humanity's appointed savior had practiced the magical arts later adopted by the Chaldeans. But he too had not created these arts, and Ralegh continued to trace the genealogy of natural knowledge back from Noah nearly to Creation: "*Iosephus* and *Cedrenus* affirme, that *Seth* first found out the Planets, or wandring Starres, and other Motions of the Heavens: for if this art had been invented by *Zoroaster*, hee could not have attained to any such excellencie therein, in his owne life time; but being a man (as it seemeth) of singular iudgement, hee might adde somewhat to this kinde of knowledge, and leave it by writing to posteritie."[7] His Zoroaster worked within the intellectual traditions of the Chosen People, advancing astronomical and natural historical learning that had been cultivated by the divinely approved first generations of humanity.

Despite his and James's different characterizations of Chaldean wisdom, Ralegh insisted that his position agreed with that of his king since both he and James recognized that the term *magic* encompassed certain legitimate arts along with their corruptions. He explained: "For the *Magicke* which His Maiestie condemneth, is of that kinde whereof the Devill is a partie." He too cataloged illicit sorts such as sorcery, witchcraft, and enchantment, describing them as "the corruptions, which have made odious the very name of *Magicke*, having chiefly sought (as in the manner of all impostures) to counterfeit the highest and most noble part of it."[8] Like James, he attributed demonic arts to ungodly pollutions of vital learning.

Ralegh detailed three forms of legitimate knowledge degraded by diabolic magic. The first two were again astrology and medical alchemy.[9] The last, however, stridently departed from James's view. Ralegh described the highest component of true magic by turning to the theological beliefs of Zoroaster. This ancient magus, he explained, "was exceedingly learned: especially in the first and highest" type of magic. "In his *Oracles*," Ralegh

7. *HW*, 1.11.1.200.
8. *HW*, 1.11.2.201–2.
9. *HW*, 1.11.2.202.

continued, "[Zoroaster] confesseth God to be the Creatour of the Universal: he beleeveth of the *Trinitie*, which hee could not investigate by any naturall knowledge: hee speaketh of Angels, and of *Paradise*: approveth the immortalitie of the soule: teacheth Truth, Faith, Hope, and Love, discoursing of the Abstinence and Charitie of the *Magi*." As evidence he cited a quotation from Zoroaster drawn from Francesco Patrizi's 1593 *Magia Philosophica*, that demonstrated, he believed, a belief in a single trinitarian deity.[10] Zoroaster's theology thus constituted Ralegh's highest form of magic.

For support, Ralegh turned to Pico's claim that knowledge of magic allowed scholars to distinguish between causes effected naturally or by divine intervention: "*Mirandula* . . . might with good reason avow, that the uttermost of natures workes being knowne, the workes which *Christ* did, and which (as himselfe witnesseth) no man could doe, doe manifestly testifie of themselves, that they were performed by that hand which held Nature therein but as a pencill, and by a power infinitely supreme and divine; and thereby those that were faithlesse, were eyther converted or put to silence." Since magic established the limits of natural power, its experts could distinguish supernatural influence from the ordinary course of nature. Only those truly versed in the powers of nature could recognize miracles. And Ralegh again recommended the magical arts by noting that the danger of corruption had not deterred its most exalted practitioners: "Neither did the abuse of *Astrologie* terrifie *Abraham* (if we may beleeve the most ancient and religious Historians) from observing the motions and natures of heavenly bodies; neyther can it dehort wise and learned men in these daies from attributing those vertues, influences, and inclinations to the Starres and other lights of Heaven, which God hath given to those his glorious creatures."[11] Uncorrupted magic had been viewed since the deep past as a requisite of pious learning, for its active engagement with natural knowledge facilitated a sacred means of appreciating the divine.

Ralegh's account of magic followed a tradition inaugurated by Pico and expanded by Annius, Reinier Reineck, and others.[12] The construction

---

10. *HW*, 1.11.2.202–3.

11. *HW*, 1.11.2.204–5, 1.11.4.207.

12. For the histories of the mathematical and astrological arts, see Nicholas Jardine, *The Birth of History and Philosophy of Science: Kepler's A Defence of Tycho against Ursus, with Essays on Its Provenance and Significance* (Cambridge: Cambridge University Press, 1984); Anthony Grafton, "From Apotheosis to Analysis: Some Late Renaissance Histories of Classical Astronomy," in Kelley, ed., *History and the Disciplines*, 261–76; Harkness, *John Dee's Conversations with Angels*, chap. 6; Polydore Vergil, *On Discovery* (1499), ed. and trans. Brian P. Copenhaver (Cambridge, MA: Harvard University Press, 2002), vi–xxx; several articles in *JHI*

of this account, however, exemplified the methods and goals of his work. To understand the distant past, Ralegh extracted fragments of evidence from revered ancients like Pliny, Josephus, and Augustine and placed them alongside evidence from modern scholars like Pico and Patrizi (as well as Scaliger, Bünting, Pererius, Caspar Peucer, and Aeneas Syvlius Piccolomini). He manipulated them all to produce a revisionist genealogy linking Zoroaster to the Hebrew patriarchs through the Chaldeans. This attribution of divine wisdom to a reviled figure justified his chronological speculations and Harriot's eccentric mathematical scribbles plucked from observation of the sky. Ralegh inventively examined the past to characterize learning in his present. And he smoothed this narrative over to fit within contemporary England, dulling his controversial claims to project obedience and proclaim agreement with his sovereign.

Ralegh's history of magic further illuminates how his work intervened in his broader intellectual culture. Ralegh considered the natural knowledge that he and Harriot had gained from empirical observation to constitute a significant component of the first proper worship practiced by Adam, Seth, and their posterity. Some later figures like Newton saw themselves in such a genealogy, conceiving their investigations of the natural world as reviving those of the ancient Persian sages and antediluvian Hebrews.[13] Ralegh thus legitimized the emergent natural sciences by their ancient lineage. But the genealogical license for new practices embedded in the *History* was not the primary debt that the scientific revolution owed to early modern historical culture. Future generations of scholars would trace the motions of bodies through the celestial sphere, scour the earth to catalog obscure plants, minerals, and animals, and correspond incessantly about the knowledge that they gleaned from the investigation of nature. They would correlate and recombine these findings, seeking signs of divine truth or use them to test certainties derived from rationalist pieties. As such, they invested natural philosophy with the tools derived pursuing prudence from historical investigation. But they would decreasingly depict

---

67, no. 1 (2006), including Robert Goulding's "Histories of Science in Early Modern Europe: Introduction" (33–40) and "Method and Mathematics: Peter Ramus' Histories of the Sciences" (63–85), James Steven Byrne's "A Humanist History of Mathematics? Regiomontanus' Padua Oration in Context" (41–61), my "'Abraham, Planter of Mathematics,'" and Kassell's "'All Was This Land Full Fill'd of Faerie'"; and Goulding, *Defending Hypatia: Ramus, Savile, and the Renaissance Rediscovery of Mathematical History* (Dordrecht: Springer, 2010).

13. In this context, see the essays included in James E. Force and Richard H. Popkin, eds., *Newton and Religion: Context, Nature, and Influence* (Dordrecht: Kluwer, 1999), esp. Robert Markley's "Newton, Corruption, and the Tradition of Universal History" (121–44) and Ben-Zaken's "From Naples to Goa."

such enterprises as reviving a divine knowledge of the ancients. The ascendancy of history as the master discipline of the early modern period transformed how contemporaries imagined the past, but its primary impact emanated from the novel practices forged and disseminated by the culture of historical analysis. The emphasis on empirical compilation of sources, antiquarian parsing of evidence, and experiential and inductive animation of narratives structured the methodological changes that struck all fields of knowledge. This set of practices encouraged investigation of a broader range of sources that ultimately compromised the autonomy of Scripture as testimony of God's will. They stressed the collection of minute scraps of evidence that gradually diminished the role of authorial credibility in evaluating evidence and elevated the place of experience, they generated precise new histories that fundamentally reconceptualized the past, and they encouraged a configuration of political practice that prioritized information management over virtue. In Ralegh's treatment of ancient magic too, we can see how the practices embedded in the culture of historical counsel stimulated the innovative new intellectual economy that replaced it, for his method of instilling natural magic with sanctity relied on the empirical and inductive approach to evidence that undergirded many of the innovations of the scientific revolution. The historical turn transformed early modern Europe not primarily by promoting imitation of past societies or by generating a historicist self-consciousness. Rather, as its practitioners introduced and circulated historical methodologies of making knowledge in all fields, they overturned long-established political and intellectual sureties, even as the discipline of history was again reconfigured as a species of rhetoric.

Few practitioners saw their methods as challenging the traditions they inherited, and Ralegh was not among those who did. Like erudite Christian statesmen and courtiers of all confessions, Ralegh believed that Providence had dispersed fragments of true knowledge amongst individuals throughout history and across the globe, and he envisioned his attempts to reconstitute the past as a species of prophecy. And if his *History* claimed for himself the mantle of godly counselor, his insights were produced by scholarly tools of illumination rather than by divine revelation. Along with the vast majority of early modern scholars, he believed that consulting a broader range of sources would enhance the authority of Scripture, and that modern travelers' accounts would reveal which ancient authors were most credible. He believed that producing prophetic historical narratives would enable the reconstitution of one single vision of the past and that orienting political practice around the manipulation of texts would fortify counselors' virtue. His employment of the tools of historical analysis strove to strengthen the political and intellectual order he saw buckling under the exploitation of depraved humanity by dishonest counselors and demonic machination. The *History* fashioned him as a humble learned counselor and prophet of causation, imbued with wisdom, and favored by Providence. It clarified his expertise by conjuring a past that insisted on the imperative of geographical, apodemic, and military knowledge while asserting that Providence operated through counsels driven by expertise in these fields. He was the ideal statesman for the world he made, and, thus, he hoped to earn release from the Tower and appreciative reintroduction to public life.

It was not inevitable that Ralegh should fail. In fact, in the aftermath of Northampton's death, the king granted greater influence to Francis Bacon, whose 1605 *Advancement of Learning* had dedicated to the king a methodological treatise recommending the same empirical and inductive practices that Ralegh implemented in the *History*, and who repeatedly used historical analyses to formulate counsel and advance his career.[14] Ralegh's mobilization of the techniques of learned counsel foundered on James's indignation at the *History*'s inclusive catalog of royal indiscretion. But the king, in fact, did see value in the expertise elaborated by Ralegh. Two years after the publication of the *History*, he paroled the captive scholar, pressed by penury to assay the old explorer's knowledge of the Guianan interior. Ralegh failed to find the promised gold mine, and the revelation of his geographical ignorance was compounded when his inability to prevent his crew from raiding a Spanish fort belied his purported expertise in command. Though Ralegh ably implemented the canons of historical analysis, his final expedition revealed him as incapable of exercising the virtues the *History* sought to evince.

The continuing life of the *History* only sometimes reflected its author's demise. There were readers who saw the work in the pattern of Ralegh's life, a sign of his depravity or martyrdom. But many others disassociated his work from his biography and, instead, viewed the text as an invaluable quarry for their own experiential wisdom. And, while Britons from all walks of life consulted it as an authoritative source, their governments continued to elevate learned counselors steeped in knowledge of the past and in historical modes of information management to preside over their administrations. Even as the work failed to achieve Ralegh's personal

---

14. Julian Martin, *Francis Bacon, the State and the Reform of Natural Philosophy* (Cambridge: Cambridge University Press, 1992).

goals, the efflorescence and transformation of historical culture within England's political and intellectual spheres enabled his work to exercise renewed impact as new readers ineluctably generated fresh interpretations of the *History* to meet their ceaselessly altered contexts.

But let us end with the aging explorer in his Tower quarters, amid the occasional friends and relentless swirl of ink and papers with which he tried to organize his bulging library. Perpetually condemned to Tower Hill, he nonetheless struggled to salvage his own life, to earn his liberty in the role of scholarly prophet to his king. For seven years, dim hopes pressed him to refract the shadows of the past into vivid illumination, to restore the withered memory of men by revivifying God's glorious Providence in his majestic, miserable Creation. He exactingly pored over the mysteries of long-dead civilizations and struggled with the arcana of modern erudition, piecing together a past that would, he hoped, ameliorate his king and critics. Ordained by his ordeals, his books and scholarly apparatus constituted his liturgy. In the desperate labor he grasped at as his calling, he faintly drew the tattered past around him, hoping that in history he would find his salvation.

BIBLIOGRAPHY

SELECTED MANUSCRIPTS CONSULTED

British Library

Add. MS 4985	Seventeenth-Century Commonplace Book
Add. MSS 6782–89	Thomas Harriot's Papers
Add. MS 14029	Historical Notes and Collections by Robert Beale
Add. MS 17940	A Map of Guiana
Add. MS 21088	Daniel Rodgers' Historical Notes
Add. MS 21579	Thomas Danett's Translation of Commynes
Add. MS 21923	William Bowyer's Genealogy for Paulet
Add. MS 32100	Robert Beale's Extracts from Monastic Records
Add. MS 39177	Historical Extracts of Sylvanis Morgan
Add. MS 40838	Ralegh's Letters
Add. MS 48026	Papers of Beale
Add. MS 48101	Political Tracts and Papers of Beale
Add. MS 48043	Papers of Beale
Add. MS 48117	Papers of Beale
Add. MS 48151	Medieval Materials Collected by Beale
Add. MS 48162	Naval and Military Papers
Add. MS 57555	Ralegh's notebook
Add. MS 73085	Documents Related to Second Guiana Trip
Add. MS 73086	Documents Related to Ralegh's Execution
Cotton Nero B IX	Instructions to Lord Zouche
Cotton Titus B VIII	Ralegh's Outline for Discourse on Naval Warfare
Cotton Titus C VI	Collections of Henry Howard
Cotton Titus C VII	Miscellaneous Materials Including Trial Documents
Cotton Titus D X	Collections of John Bale
Egerton 3790	Matthias Flacius Illyricus's Compilation for Matthew Parker
Harley 1327	Miscellaneous Papers concerning Ralegh

Harley 1576   Miscellaneous Notes from Histories
Harley 1733   Commonplace Book
Harley 1759   Notes from the *History*
Harley 4872   Notes from the *History*
Harley 6035   Rough copy of Council Ledger
Harley 6849   Records of Investigation by the Court of High Commission
Lansdowne 48   Burghley's Precedents from the Tower
Lansdowne 94   Burghley's Historical Notes
Lansdowne 103   Burghley's Instructions to Beale
Lansdowne 229   Robert Glover's Miscellany
Lansdowne 350   Evaluation of Ralegh's Life
Sloane 3407   Late Seventeenth-Century Journal
Stowe 141   Official Papers, Including Scaffold Speech
Stowe 162   Francis Walsingham's Table Book
Stowe 180   Collection of Papers, Including Trial Records
Stowe 296   Thomas Wilkes' Discourse on Counsel

Bodleian Library

MS Tanner 169   Collections of Stephen Powle
MS Rawlinson Poetry 26   Poetry Miscellany

Wellcome Library

WMS 6880   Manuscript Notebook of Andrew Melville

Cambridge University Library

MS Gg.2.25   Manuscript Notebook of John Jackson

Kendal Record Office, Kendal, Cumbria, UK

K WD RY/Box 36/2   Manuscript Notebook of Daniel Fleming

Public Record Office, Kew

SP 9/14   Commonplace Book of Joseph Williamson
SP 12   State Papers, Domestic—Elizabeth I
SP 70   State Papers, Foreign—Elizabeth I

Henry E. Huntington Library, San Marino, CA

EL 1120   Thomas Egerton's Notes from Patent and Close Rolls
EL 1122   Egerton's Copies of Statutes

EL 1169	Notes from Tower Records
EL 2009	Arthur Agarde's Extract from Parliament Rolls
EL 2547	Egerton's Notes from Rolls in Tower
EL 2555	Collections out of Tower Records
EL 35 B 60	Egerton's Index to State Records
EL 62136	William Lambarde's Black Book of the Exchequer
HAS 1.2–4	Henry Hastings' School Exercises
HM 160	Bowyer's Genealogy for Leicester
HM 26341	Collections of Lawrence Nowell
HM 2649 A–B	John Jewel's copy of *Archaionomia*

Walter Raleigh Collection, University of North Carolina, Chapel Hill

UNC CSWR 96	MS Abridgment of the *History*

Centre for Kentish Studies, Canterbury

U840 C7/5	Letter from First Earl Camden to His Daughter

Cecil Papers, Hatfield House

MS 102/84	Robert Cecil to George Harvey
MS 140	Burghley Genealogies
MS 162	Thomas Tresham to Robert Cecil
MS 165	Burghley's Notes from Tower Records
MS 171	Burghley's Historical Polemic on Papacy
MS 203/6	David Chytraeus to Burghley
MS 230	Historical Notes
MS 333	Burghley Almanac
MS 334	Burghley Almanac

SELECTED ANNOTATED BOOKS CONSULTED

Foxe Morzillo, Sebastian. *De Naturae Philosophia.* Paris, 1560. Small Special Collections Library, University of Virginia, B185.F69 1560.

Ralegh, Walter. *History of the World.* London, 1614. BL C.38.i.10.

———. *History of the World.* London, 1614. Cambridge University Library Syn.3.61.20.

———. *History of the World.* London, 1614. Bodleian Library K 3.6 Art.

———. *History of the World.* London, 1614. Firestone Library, Princeton University 29551.745q [copy 2].

———. *History of the World.* London, 1614. Wichita State University Library SC 1231.

———. *History of the World.* London, 1614. Beinecke Library, Yale University Bg4 035y.

———. *History of the World.* London, 1614. Huntington Library HEH 69107

———. *History of the World.* London, 1614. UNC CSWR A4.

——. *History of the World*. London, 1617. Swem Library, College of William and Mary, D57.R16 1617

——. *History of the World*. London, 1617. BL 1311.1.1.

——. *History of the World*. London, 1617. BL 799.m.23.

——. *History of the World*. London, 1617. Bodleian Library Vet. A2 c.13.

——. *History of the World*. London, 1617. Beinecke Library, Yale University Bg4 036.

——. *History of the World*. London, 1617. New York Public Library *KC+ 1617.

——. *History of the World*. London, 1621. Trinity College, Cambridge VI.4.4.

——. *History of the World*. London, 1621 UNC CSWR A6.

——. *History of the World*. London, 1628. BL Eve.b.36.

——. *History of the World*. London, 1634. UNC CSWR A8.

——. *History of the World*. London, 1634. Beinecke Library, Yale University, 1742 Yale Library 10.2.7.

——. *History of the World*. London, 1652. Wellcome Library 42872/D.

——. *History of the World*. London, 1666. Firestone Library, Princeton University 29551.745.11a copy 1.

——. *History of the World*. London, 1666. Queen's College, Oxford Upper Lib 3.E.15 d.

——. *History of the World*. London, 1666. UNC CSWR A12.

——. *History of the World*. London, 1677. Firestone Library, Princeton University, 29551.745.13q.

Tacitus. *Opera*. Edited by Justus Lipsius. Antwerp, 1595. BL shelfmark C.142.E.13. Robert Sidney's copy.

SELECTED PRIMARY SOURCES

An asterisk (*) indicates either that Ralegh owned the work or that his references to it in the *History* suggest firsthand consultation.

*Acosta, Jose de. *The Natural & Moral History of the Indies* (1590). Translated by Edward Grimston. New York: B. Franklin, 1970–73.

*Adrichem, Christian. *Theatrum terrae sanctae*. Cologne, 1590.

*Alfragani. *Chronologica et Astronomica Elementa*. Edited by Jacob Christmann. Frankfurt, 1590.

*Angelocrator, Daniel. *Chronologiae . . . Prodromus*. Hamburg, 1597.

*——. *Rationis Temporum . . . Libri*. Frankfurt, 1611.

*Annius of Viterbo [Giovanni Nanni]. *Berosi Sacerdotis Chaldaici, Antiquitatum Italiae ac totius orbis libri*. 1498. Antwerp, 1552.

Antient Kalendars and Inventories of the Treasury of His Majesty's Exchequer. Edited by Francis Palgrave. London, 1836.

*Antoninus of Florence, St. *Chronicorum Opus*. Lyon, 1586.

*Apollonius, Levinus. *De Peruviae . . . Inventione*. Antwerp, 1566.

Aubrey, John. *Brief Lives*. Edited by Richard Barber. Woodbridge: Boydell, 1982.

*Augustine. *The City of God against the Pagans*. Edited and translated by R. W. Dyson. Cambridge: Cambridge University Press, 1998.

——. *Confessions*. Translated by F. J. Sheed. Indianapolis: Hackett, 2006.

Bacon, Francis. *The Works of Francis Bacon.* Edited by James Spedding, Robert Leslie Ellis, and Douglas Denon Heath. 16 vols. London, 1857–74.

Bale, John. *Illustrium Maioris Britanniae Scriptorum . . . Summarium.* Wesel, 1548.

*———. *Scriptorum Illustrium Maioris Britanniae . . . Catalogus.* Basel, 1557–59.

———. "New Year's Gift" (1549). In *John Leland's Itinerary,* ed. John Chandler, 1–17. Thrupp: Sutton, 1993.

*Banosius, Theophilus. *De Politia Civitatis Dei et Hierarchia Romana.* Frankfurt, 1592.

*Bar-Cephas, Moses. *Commentarius de Paradiso.* Edited by Andreas Masius. Antwerp, 1569.

*Barlandus, Hadrian. *Comitum Historia et Icones.* Leiden, 1584.

*Barozzi, Francisco. *Cosmographia.* Venice, 1585.

*Barreiras, Gaspar. *Historia Antiqua.* Edited by Jonas Bonutius. N.p., 1599.

Baudouin, Francois. "De institutione historiae universae, et eius cum iurisprudentia coniunctione." In *Artis Historicae Penus,* ed. Joannes Wolfius. Basel, 1579.

Beale, Robert, ed. *Rerum Hispanicarum Scriptores Aliquot.* Frankfurt, 1579.

*Bellarmine, Robert. *Opera Omnia.* Frankfurt a.M.: Minerva, 1965.

*Belleforest, Francois, ed. *La Cosmographie Universelle.* Paris, 1575.

*Belon, Pierre. *Les Observations de plusieurs singularitez & choses memorables.* Antwerp, 1555.

*Benzoni, Girolamo. *Novae novi orbis historiae.* Geneva, 1578.

*Bernard, Jean. *Discours de plus Memorables Faicts des Roys & Grands Seigneurs d'Angleterre.* Paris, 1579.

*Béroalde, Matthieu. *Chronicum.* Geneva, 1575.

*Bertius, Petrus. *Tabularum geographicarum contractarum libri.* Amsterdam, 1616.

*Beuther, Michael. *Animadversionum sive Disceptationum tàm historicarum quàm chronographicarum liber.* Strasbourg, 1593.

*Bibliander, Theodore. *De ratione temporum.* Basel, 1551.

*Bilson, Thomas. *The Survey of Christs Sufferings for Mans Redemption.* London, 1604.

Birch, Thomas. *Memoirs of the Reign of Queen Elizabeth, from the year 1581 till her Death.* London, 1754.

*Bisciola, Laelio. *Horarum Subsecivarum Tomus.* Ingolstadt, 1611.

Blundeville, Thomas. *A very breife and profitable Treatise declaringe howe many counsels, and what maner of Counselers a Prince that will governe well ought to have.* London, 1570.

———. *The True Order and Methode of Wryting and Reading Hystories.* London, 1574.

Bodin, Jean. *Method for the Easy Comprehension of History* (1566). Translated by Beatrice Reynolds. New York: Norton, 1969.

*Boemus, Joannes. *The Manners, Lawes, and Customes of all Nations.* Translated by Edward Aston. London, 1611.

Bolton, Edmund. "Hypercritica; or, A Rule of Judgment for Writing or Reading Our History's." In *Annalium Continuatio.* Edited by Nicolaus Triveth. Oxford, 1722.

*Bongarsius, Jacques, ed. *Rerum Hungaricarum Scriptores.* Frankfurt, 1600.

Botero, Giovanni. *Relations, of the Most Famous Kingdoms and Common-Weales throughout the World.* London, 1608.

——. *The Reason of State* (1589). Translated by P. J. Waley and D. P. Waley. London: Routledge & Kegan Paul, 1956.

Bourne, William. *Booke Called the Treasure for Traveilers.* London, 1578.

——. *Regiment for the Sea.* London, 1580.

*Bozius, Tomasso. *De Ruinis Gentium.* Cologne, 1598.

*Brisson, Barnabé. *De Regio Persarum Principatu.* Heidelberg, 1595.

*Brocard of Mt. Sion. *Descriptio Terrae Sanctae Exactissima.* Antwerp, 1536.

*Broughton, Hugh. *A Concent of Scripture.* London, 1588.

——. *A Short view of the* Persian *Monarchie, and of* Daniels weekes: *Beeing a peece of Beroaldus works.* London, 1590.

*Bucholtzer, Abraham. *Index Chronologicus.* Frankfurt, 1616.

*Bünting, Heinrich. *Itinerarium totius sacrae scripturae.* Magdeburg, 1597.

*——. *Chronologia Catholica.* Magdeburg, 1608.

*——. *Itinerarium totius sacrae scripturae.* Translated by R.B. London, 1636.

*Buxeda de Leyva. *Historia del reyno de Iapon.* Zaragoza, 1591.

*Calvin, John. *A Commentarie of John Calvine, upon the first booke of Moses called Genesis.* Translated by Thomas Tymme. London, 1578.

*Calvisius, Sethus. *Chronologia.* Leipzig, 1605.

*Camden, William. *Britannia.* London, 1586.

——. *Anglica, Normanica, Hibernica, Cambrica a veteribus Scripta.* Frankfurt, 1605.

*——. *Remaines of a Greater Work.* London, 1605.

*——. *Annales Rerum Anglicarum, et Hibernicarum, Regnante Elizabetha.* London, 1615.

*Camerarius, Philipp. *Operae Horarum Subcisivarum.* Frankfurt, 1602–9.

Cardano, Girolamo. *Proxenata, seu, De Prudentia Civili Liber.* Leiden, 1627.

*Carionis, Joannes. *Chronica Carionis.* Edited by Philip Melanchthon and Caspar Peucer. Geneva, 1581.

Carpenter, Nathanael. *Geographie Delineated.* Oxford, 1635.

*Casmannus, Otto. *Marinarum Quaestionum Tractatio.* Frankfurt, 1596.

Castiglione, Baldassare. *The Courtyer of Count Baldessar Castilio.* Translated by Thomas Hoby. London, 1561.

Cecil, Robert. *The State and Dignity of a Secretaries of Estates Place.* London, 1642.

*Cedrenus, Georgius. *Annales.* Basel, 1566.

Chamberlain, John. *The Letters of John Chamberlain.* Edited by Norman Egbert Mc-Clure. 2 vols. Philadelphia: American Philosophical Society, 1939.

*Charpentier, Jean. *Platonis cum Aristotele in Universa Philosophia, Comparatio.* Paris, 1573.

*Chassanion, Jean. *De Gigantibus.* Basel, 1580.

*Chaumeau, Jean. *Histoire du Berry.* Lyon, 1566.

Clapham, John. *Elizabeth of England: Certain Observations Concerning the Life and Reign of Queen Elizabeth.* Edited by Evelyn Plummer Read and Conyers Read. Philadelphia: University of Pennsylvania Press, 1951.

*[Chytraeus, David]. *Onomasticon Theologicum.* Wittenberg, 1564.

*——. *Chronologia historiae Herodoti et Thucydidis.* Rostock, 1567.

*————. "De lectione historiarum recte instituenda." In *Artis Historicae Penus*, ed. Joannes Wolfius. Basel, 1579.

Cleland, James. *Hero-Paideia; or, The Instruction of a yong Noble-man*. Oxford, 1612.

*Codomann, Lorenz. *Annales Sacrae Scripturae* (1581). 2nd Latin ed. Wittenberg, 1602.

*Coenalis, Robert. *Gallica Historia*. Paris, 1557.

*Conti, Natale. *Mythologiae*. Frankfurt, 1596.

The Correspondence of Sir Philip Sidney and Hubert Languet. Edited by Steuart A. Pears. London: William Pickering, 1845.

*Crusius, Paulus. *Liber de Epochis seu aeris temporum et imperiorum*. Basel, 1578.

Curio, Caelius Secundus. "De Historia Legendi Sententia." In *Artis Historicae Penus*, ed. Joannes Wolfius. Basel, 1579.

*Curtius Rufus, Quintus. *History of Alexander*. Translated by John C. Rolfe. 2 vols. Cambridge: Harvard University Press, 1946.

Dallington, Robert. *A Method for Travell*. London, 1605.

*Daneau, Lambert. *Vetustissimarum Primi Mundi Antiquitatum . . . libri*. Geneva, 1596.

Day, Angel. *The English Secretorie*. London, 1586.

*De Bry, Theodor. *India Orientalis*. Frankfurt, 1598.

*————. *Indiae Orientalis Pars Octava*. Frankfurt, 1607.

*De Busbeq Ghislain, Ogier. *The Four Epistles of A. G. Busbequius Concerning his Embassy into Turkey*. London, 1694.

Dee, John. *John Dee's Library Catalogue*. Edited by Julian Roberts and Andrew G. Watson. London: Bibliographical Society, 1990.

*De Escalante, Bernadino. *A Discourse of the Navigation which the Portugales doe Make to the Realmes and Provinces of the East Partes of the World*. Translated by John Frampton. London, 1579.

*de Indagine, Johannes. *Introductiones Apotelesmaticae*.

*de Lucinge, René. *De la Naissance, Durée, et Chute des Estats* (1588). Geneva: Droz, 1984.

————. *La Maniere de Lire L'Histoire* (1614). Geneva: Droz, 1993.

*de Monluc, Blaise. *Commentaires et Lettres de Blaise de Monluc, Maréchal de France* (1592). 5 vols. Paris: Mme Ve J. Renouard, 1864–72.

*de Pineda, Joannes. *In Salomonem Commentarios Salomon Praevius*. Mainz, 1613.

*De Roa, Martin. *Singularium Locorum ac Rerum Libri*. Cordoba, 1600.

*De Roias, Christoval. *Teorica y Practica de Fortificacion*. Madrid, 1598.

*De Sainct Julien, Pierre. *De L'Origine des Bourgongnons*. Paris, 1581.

*de Serres, Jean. *Inventaire general de l'histoire de France*. Paris, 1600.

*De Torres, Diego. *Relacion del Origen y Successo de los Xarifes*. Seville, 1586.

*De Villamont, Jacques. *Les Voyages du Seigneur du Villamont*. Lyon, 1607.

*De Vio, Thomas. *Commentarii Illustres*. Paris, 1539.

*Dinoth, Richard. *De Bello Civili Belgico*. Basel, 1586.

*Dresserus, Matthaeus. *Isagoges Historicae Pars Prima*. Leipzig, 1598.

Drummond, William. *The Works of William Drummond*. Edinburgh, 1711.

Ducci, Lorenzo. *Ars Historica*. Ferrara, 1604.

————. *Ars Aulica; or, The Courtiers Art*. London, 1607.

Dugdale, William. *The History of St Pauls Cathedral in London*. London, 1658.

*Eber, Paul. *Calendarium Historicum*. Wittenberg, 1579.

*Edmondes, Clement. *Observations upon the first five bookes of Caesars* Commentaries. London, 1609.

Elyot, Thomas. *The Boke Named the Governour*. London, 1580.

*Emmius, Ubbo. *Rerum Frisicarum Historia*. Leiden, 1606.

*Etienne, Charles. *Dictionarium historicum ac poeticum*. Paris, 1553.

*Eusebius of Caesarea. *Thesaurus Temporum*. Edited by Joseph Scaliger. Leiden, 1606.

*Eytzinger, Michael. *Pentaplus Regnorum Mundi*. Antwerp, 1579.

*Fabricius, George. *In Primum Librum Mosis, sive Genesin Commentarius*. Strassbourg, 1584.

Felton, Henry. *A Dissertation on Reading the Classics, and forming a Just Style*. London, 1713.

Filmer, Robert. *Patriarcha; or, The Natural Power of Kings*. London, 1680.

Flacius Illyricus, Matthias. *Catalogus Testium Veritatis*. Strassbourg, 1562.

———. *Ecclesiastica Historia*. 13 vols. Basel, 1562–74.

Foglietto, Uberto. "De Ratione Scribendae Historiae." In *Artis Historicae Penus*, ed. Joannes Wolfius. Basel, 1579.

Foreign Intelligence and Information in Elizabethan England: Two English Treatises on the State of France, 1580–1584. Edited by David Potter. Cambridge: Cambridge University Press for the Royal Historical Society, 2004.

Fortescue, Sir John. *A Learned Commendation of the Politique Lawes of Englande*. Translated by Robert Mulcaster. London, 1567.

Foxe, John. *Acts and Monuments*. London, 1563.

Foxe Morcillo, Sebastian. "De Historiae Institutione." In *Artis Historicae Penus*, ed. Joannes Wolfius. Basel, 1579.

*Freigius, Johannes Thomas. *Quaestiones Physicae*. Basel, 1579.

———. *Historiae Synopsis*. Basel, 1580.

*———. *Mosaicus: Continens Historiam Ecclesiasticam*. Basel, 1583.

*Froissart, Jean. *Historiarum Opus Omne*. Edited by Johannes Sleidanus. Paris, 1537.

*Funck, Johann. *Chronologia*. Wittenberg, 1601.

*Galatinus, Petrus. *Opus de Arcanis Catholicae Veritatis*. Basel, 1550.

Garrard, William. *The Art of Warre*. London, 1591.

*Genebrard, Gilbert. *Hebraeorum breve Chronicon*. Paris, 1572.

———. *Divinarum Hebraicarumque Literarum . . . Chronographiae Libri*. Paris, 1580.

*Gentillet, Innocent. *A Discourse Upon the Meanes of Wel Governing and Maintaining in Good Peace, A Kingdome, or Other Principalitie*. Translated by Simon Patericke. London, 1602.

*Geoffrey of Monmouth. *Historia regum Britanniae*. Cambridge: D. S. Brewer, 1985.

*Glycas, Michael. *Annales*. Basel, 1572.

*Godefroy, Denis. *Antiquae Historiae*. Strassbourg, 1604.

*Godwin, Francis. *Catalog of Bishops*. London, 1601.

*Gonzalez de Mendoza, Juan. *The Historie of the Great and Mightie Kingdome of China*. Translated by Robert Parke. London, 1588.

*Goropius Becanus, Johannes. *Origines Antwerpianae*. Antwerp, 1569.

*Goulart, Simon. *Morum Philosophia Historica.* Geneva, 1594.

*Gramaye, Jean-Baptiste. *Asia.* Antwerp, 1604.

*Gregorius de Valentia. *Commentariorum Theologicorum Tomi.* 4 vols. Ingolstadt, 1591–97.

*Grynaeus, Simon, ed. *Novus Orbis.* Basel, 1555.

*Guagninus, Alexander. *Sarmatiae Europeae Descriptio.* Cracow, 1578.

Guicciardini, Francesco. *The History of Italy.* Translated by Sidney Alexander. New York: Macmillan, 1968.

*Guicciardini, Lodovico. *Description de tout le Pays-Bas.* Antwerp, 1567.

Hall, Joseph. *The Balme of Gilead.* London, 1646.

*Hakluyt, Richard, ed. *The Principall Navigations.* 3 vols. London, 1598–1600.

———. *The Original Writings and Correspondence of the Two Richard Hakluyts.* London: Printed for the Hakluyt Society, 1935.

*Harriot, Thomas. *A Briefe and True Report of the New Found Land of Virginia.* London, 1588.

Harry, George Owen. *The Genealogy of the High and Mighty Monarch, James.* London, 1604.

Hearne, Thomas, ed. *A Collection of Curious Discourses, Written by Eminent Antiquaries upon Several Heads in our English Antiquities.* 2 vols. London, 1775.

*Heuterus, Pontus. *Rerum Burgundicarum Libri.* Antwerp, 1584.

Heylyn, Peter. *Mikrokosmos: A Little Description of a Great World.* Oxford, 1627.

Hickes, Michael. *The "Anonymous Life" of William Cecil, Lord Burghley.* Edited by Alan G. R. Smith. Lewiston: Mellen, 1990.

*Hoeschelius, David, ed. *Geographica Marciani Herocleotae, Scylacis Caryandensis, Artemidori Ephesii, Diceaearchi, Messenii, Isidori Characeni.* Augsburg, 1600.

*Hopkinson, Joannes. *Synopsis Paradis, sive Paradis Descriptio.* Leiden, 1593.

Hume, David. *The History of England.* Vol. 6. Dublin, 1769.

*Irenicus, Franz. *Exegesis Historiae Germaniae.* Hanover, 1518.

*James I. *Daemonologie.* Edinburgh, 1597.

———. *Letters of King James VI and I.* Edited by G. P. V. Akrigg. Berkeley and Los Angeles: University of California Press, 1984.

———. *Political Writings.* Edited by Johann Somerville. Cambridge: Cambridge University Press, 1994. Note that Ralegh had read the *Trew Law of Free Monarchies.*

John Leland's Itinerary. Edited by John Chandler. Thrupp: Sutton, 1993.

Johnson, Samuel. *The Rambler,* no. 122 (May 18, 1751).

Jones, William. *Works.* 6 vols. London, 1799.

*Jornandes. *De Getarum, sive Gothorum Origine.* Leiden, 1597.

*Josephus, Flavius. *The Famous and Memorable Workes of Iosephus.* Edited by Thomas Lodge. London, 1602.

"Journal of Francis Walsingham, from Dec. 1570 to April 1583." Edited by Charles Trice Martin. *The Camden Miscellany,* vol. 6. London: Camdem Society, 1870.

*Lazius, Wolfgang. *De Gentium Aliquot Migrationibus.* Frankfurt, 1600.

*Knolles, Richard. *The Generall Historie of the Turkes.* London, 1603.

*Krentzheim, Leonhart. *Observationum Chronologicarum Libri.* Legnica, 1606.

*Lambarde, William. *A Perambulation of Kent.* London, 1576.

*La Popeliniére, Lancelot Voisin. *L'Histoire des Histoires*. Paris, 1599.

*———. *L'Histoire de la Conqueste des Pais de Bresse & de Savoye*. Lyon, 1601.

*Leland, John. *Assertio Inclytissimi Arturii Regis Britanniae*. London, 1544.

*Le Maire de Belges, Jean. *Oeuvres*. 3 vols. Geneva: Slatkine Reprints, 1969.

Lewis, John, Esq. *Eyaggeloigrapha*. London, 1659.

Leyser, Polycarp. *Adamus*. Leipzig, 1604.

*———. *Noachus*. Leipzig, 1605.

*Lily, George. *Chronicon*. Frankfurt, 1565.

Lipsius, Justus. *Opera Omnia*. Antwerp, 1602.

Liveley, Edward. *True Chronologie of the times of the Persian Monarchy*. London, 1597.

*Livy. *Ab Urbe Condita*. Translated by B. O. Foster, Frank Gardner Moore, Evan T. Sage, and Alfred C. Schlesinger. 14 vols. Cambridge, MA: Harvard University Press, 1919.

Lloyd, Lodowick. *The Stratagemes of Jerusalem*. London, 1602.

Llwyd, Humphrey. *A Breviary of Britayne*. Translated by Thomas Twyne. London, 1573.

*Luis of Granada. *Sylva Locorum Communium*. Leiden, 1586.

Luther, Martin. *The Creation: A Commentary on the First Five Chapters of the Book of Genesis* (1544). Translated by Henry Cole. London, 1858.

———. *Works*. Vol. 12. Edited by Abdel Ross Wentz. Philadelphia: Fortress, 1959.

*Lydiat, Thomas. *De variis annorum formis*. London, 1605.

———. *Defensio tractatus de variis annorum formis*. London, 1607.

Lynche, Richard. *An Historical Treatise of the Travels of Noah into Europe*. London, 1601.

*Machiavelli, Niccolò. *The Arte of Warre* (1520). Translated by Peter Withorne. London, 1573.

*———. *The Discourses* (1531). Edited by Bernard Crick. Translated by Leslie J. Walker. Harmondsworth: Penguin, 1970.

———. *The Prince* (1531). Translated by George Bull. New York: Penguin, 1981.

*Manlius, Joannes. *Locorum Communium Collectanea . . . ex lectionibus D. P. Melanchthonis*. Basel, 1563.

*Marloratus, Augustinus. *Thesaurus Sacrae Scripturae*. London, 1574.

*———. *Genesis cum Catholica Expositione Ecclesiastica*. Morges, 1585.

*Matal, Jean. *Asia Tabulis Aeneis*. Oberursel, 1600.

*———. *Europa Tabulis Aeneis*. Cologne, 1600.

*Mercator, Gerardus. *Chronologia, hoc est, Temporum Demonstratio*. Cologne, 1569.

*———. *Atlas*. Dusseldorf, 1596.

*Mercier, Jean. *In Genesin*. Geneva, 1598.

Mercurii Gallobelgici. Cologne, 1596.

*Montano, Benedicto Arius. *Antiquitatum Iudaicarum Libri*. Leiden, 1593.

*———. *Naturae Historia*. Antwerp, 1601.

*Montius, Petrus. *De Unius Legis Veritate*. Milan, 1522.

*Münster, Sebastian. *Cosmographia Universalis*. Basel, 1554.

*Musset, Louis. *Discours sur les Remonstrances et Reformationes de Chacun Estat*. Paris, 1582.

*Mylaeus, Christophorus. *De Scribenda Universitatis Rerum Historia*. Paris, 1551.

Nashe, Thomas. *Pierce Pennilesse his Supplication to the Devill*. London, 1592.

*Naucler, Johannes. *Chronica*. Cologne, 1614.

*Nestor, Jean. *Histoire des Hommes Illustres de la Maison de Medici*. Paris, 1564.

"Nicholas Faunt's Discourse Touching the Office of Principal Secretary of Estate &c. 1592." Edited by Charles Hughes. *EHR* 20 (1905): 499–508.

*Niger, Dominicus Marius. *Geographiae Commentariorum libri*. Basel, 1557.

*Noguier, Antoine. *Histoire Tolsaine*. Toulouse, 1556.

*Norden, John. *Speculum Brittaniae*. London, 1593.

Oldys, William. *The Life of Sir Walter Ralegh from his Birth to his Death on the Scaffold*. London, 1740.

Oliver Cromwell's Letters and Speeches. Edited by Thomas Carlyle. 1897. Reprint, New York: AMS, 1980.

*Ortelius, Abraham. *Theatrum Orbis Terrarum*. Antwerp, 1570.

*———. *Thesaurus Geographicus*. Antwerp, 1596.

*———. *Theatrum Orbis Terrarum*. Antwerp, 1601.

———. *Abrahami Ortelii et virorum eruditorum . . . epistulae*. Edited by Jan Hendrik Hessels. Osnäbruck: O. Zeller, 1969.

Palmer, Thomas. *An essay of the meanes how to make our trauailes, into forraine countries, the more profitable and honourable*. London, 1606.

*Paradin, Guillaume. *Histoire de Nostre Temps*. Lyon, 1550.

Parker, Matthew. *De Antiquitate Brittanicae Ecclesiae*. London, 1572.

———. *Correspondence of Matthew Parker*. Edited by John Bruce and the Reverend Thomas Thomason Perowne. New York: Johnson Reprint, 1968.

Parsons, Robert. *Elizabethae, Angliae reginae haeresin Caluinianam propugnantis . . . Responsio*. Leiden, 1592.

[———]. *An aduertisement written to a secretarie of my L. Treasurers of Ingland. . . .* [Antwerp], 1593.

Patrizi, Francesco, of Cherso. "De Legendae Scribendaeque Historiae Ratione Dialogi." In *Artis Historicae Penus*, ed. Joannes Wolfius. Basel, 1579.

———. *De Militia Romana*. Ferrara, 1583.

*———. *Magia Philosophica*. Hamburg, 1593.

*———. *Nova de Universis Philosophia*. Venice, 1593.

*Patrizi, Francesco, of Siena. *Compendiosa Epitome Commentariorum*. Cologne, 1591.

———. *De regno et regis insititutione*. Strasbourg, 1608.

*Pelargus, Christophorus. *In Secundum Librum Mosaicum, Exodum Sacram, Commentarius*. Leipzig, 1604.

———. *In Numeros Sacros Quartum Librum Mosaicum Commentarius*. Leipzig, 1606.

*Pererius, Benedicto. *Commentariorum . . . et Disputationem in Genesim*. Cologne, 1601.

*Peucer, Caspar. *Commentarius de Praecipuis Divinationum Generibus*. Wittenberg, 1560.

Pezel, Christoph. "Oratio de Historia." In *Artis Historicae Penus*, ed. Joannes Wolfius. Basel, 1579.

*Pico della Mirandola, Giovanni. *Opera Omnia*. Basel, 1601.

*Plutarch. *The Lives of the Noble Grecians and Romanes*. Translated by Thomas North. London, 1579.

*Polybius. *The Histories*. Translated by Robin Waterfield. Oxford: Oxford University Press, 2010.

*Pont, Robert. *A Newe Treatise of the Right Reckoning of Yeares*. Edinburgh, 1599.

Pontano, Giovanni Gioviano. "Actius Dialogus." In *Artis Historicae Penus*, ed. Joannes Wolfius. Basel, 1579.

———. *De Principe* (1493). Roma: Salerno, 2003.

Possevino, Antonio. *Apparatus ad omnium gentium historiam*. Venice, 1597.

*Prise, John. *Historiae Brytannicae Defensio*. London, 1573.

Ptolemy. *Geographia*. Translated by Edward Luther Stevenson. Mineola, NY: Dover, 1991.

Ralegh, Walter. *The Discouerie of the Large, Rich, and Bevvtiful Empyre of Guiana*. London, 1596.

———. *The History of the World*. London, 1614.

———. *An Abridgment of Sir Walter Raleigh's History of the World*. Edited by Lawrence Echard. London, 1698.

———. *An Abridgment of Sir Walter Raleigh's History of the World*. Edited by Lawrence Echard. London, 1700.

———. *An Abridgment of Sir Walter Raleigh's History of the World*. Edited by Lawrence Echard. London, 1702.

———. *The Works of Sir Walter Ralegh, kt*. 8 vols. Oxford: The University Press, 1829.

———. *The Letters of Sir Walter Raleigh*. Edited by Agnes Latham and Joyce Youings. Exeter: University of Exeter Press, 1999.

———. *The Poems of Sir Walter Ralegh: A Historical Edition*. Edited by Michael Rudick. Tempe: Arizona Center for Medieval and Renaissance Studies, in conjunction with the Renaissance English Text Society, 1999.

———. *Sir Walter Ralegh's* Discoverie of Guiana. Edited by Joyce Lorimer. Aldershot: Ashgate, for the Hakluyt Society of London, 2006.

———. *Tubus Historicus*. London, 1636. Authorship is unknown but traditionally attributed to Ralegh.

*Ramelli, Agostino. *Le Diverse et Artificiose Machine*. Paris, 1570.

*Rantzau, Heinrich. *Commentarius Bellicus*. Frankfurt, 1595.

Reineck, Reiner. *Methodus Legendi Cognoscendique Historiam*. Helmstadt, 1583.

*———. *Historia Orientalis*. Helmstadt, 1585.

*———. *Historia Julia*. 3 vols. Helmstadt, 1594–97.

*Reuchlin, Johann. *De Verbo Mirifico, 1494. De Arte Cabalisticai, 1517. Faksimile-Neudruck in einem Band*. Stuttgart–Bad Canstatt: F. Frommann Verlag (G. Holzboog), 1964.

*Reusner, Elias. *Ephemeris, sive Diarium Historicum*. Frankfurt, 1590.

*Rhodoginus, Lodovicus Caelius. *Lectionum Antiquarum Libri*. Leiden, 1562.

The Roanoke Voyages, 1584–1590: Documents to Illustrate the English Voyages to North America under the Patent Granted to Walter Raleigh in 1584. Edited by David B. Quinn. London: Hakluyt Society, 1955.

Robortello, Francesco. "De Historiae Facultate Disputatio." In *Artis Historicae Penus*, ed. Joannes Wolfius. Basel, 1579.

*Rocca, Bernardino. *Discorsi di Guerra*. Venice, 1582.

*Rolevinck, Werner. *Fasciculus temporum* = *Compendio cronológico* (1474). León: Universidad de León, Secretariado de Publicaciones, Cátedra de San Isidoro de la Real Colegiata de León, 1993.

*Rosa, Joannes. *Virtus Romana*. Frankfurt, 1604.

Ross, Alexander. *The History of the World: the Second part in Six books*. London, 1652.

———. *Som Animadversions and Observations upon Sir Walter Raleigh's History of the World*. London, 1653.

———. *The Marrow of History*. London, 1662.

*Sardus, Alexander. *De Moribus et Ritibus Gentium*. Hamburg, 1599.

Savile, Henry. *Commentarius De Militia Romana*. Amsterdam, 1649.

*Scaliger, Joseph. *De Emendatione Temporum*. Paris, 1583.

*Schmidel, Ulrich. *Vera Historia, Admiranda cuiusdam navigationis quam . . . confecit*. Nuremberg, 1599.

Scott, Thomas. *Vox Populi*. London, 1620.

*Senensis, Sixtus. *Bibliotheca Sancta*. Venice, 1566.

*Serarius, Nicolaus. *Trihaeresium*. Mainz, 1604.

*Severtus, Jacques. *De Orbis Catoptrici seu Mapparum Mundi Principiis*. Paris, 1590.

Sheppard, Samuel. *Epigrams Theological, Philosophical, and Romantick*. London, 1651.

Shirley, John. *The Life of the Valiant & Learned Sir Walter Raleigh, Knight*. London, 1677.

*Sigonius, Carlo. *De Republica Hebraeorum*. Leiden, 1701.

*Sleidanus, Johannes. *De Quatuor Summis Imperiis*. Geneva, 1559.

*———. *De Statu Religionis et Reipublicae, Carolo Quinto Caesare, Commentarii*. Paris, 1559.

———. *Sleidans Breifwechsel*. Edited by Hermann Baumgarten. Strassburg: Trübner, 1881.

Smith, Thomas. *De Republica Anglorum*. London, 1583.

Smythe, Sir John. *Certain Discourses Military* (1590). Ithaca, N.Y.: Cornell University Press, 1964.

*Snecanus, Gellius. *Methodica Descriptio, et fundamentum trium locorum communium sacrae Scripturae*. Leiden, 1584.

Speed, John. *The Genealogies Recorded in the Sacred Scriptures*. London, 1611.

*Steuco, Agostino. *Opera Omnia*. Venice, 1590.

*Stow, John. *A Survay of London*. London, 1590.

Stradling, Sir John. *A Direction for Travailers*. London, 1592. A translation of Justus Lipsius's *Epistola de peregrinatione Italica*.

*Stucki, Johann Wilhelm. *Antiquitatum Convivialium Libri*. Zurich, 1597.

*———. *Sacrorum Sacrificiorumque Gentilium Brevis et Accurata Descriptio*. Zurich, 1598.

*Thevet, André. *La Cosmographie Universelle*. Paris, 1575.

*Thucydides. *History of the Peloponnesian War*. 4 vols. Translated by C. Forster Smith. New York: Putnam's, 1920.

*Thuroczy, Janos. *Chronica Hungarorum* (1473). Edited by Elisabeth Galántai and Julius Kristó. Budapest: Akadémiai Kiadó, 1985.

*Tornielli, Agostino. *Annales Sacri*. Lucca, 1756–57.

*Torquemada, Antonio. *Hexameron; ou, Six Journées*. Translated by Gabriel Chappuys. Lyon, 1582.

Turler, Jerome. *The traueiler of Ierome Turler*. London, 1575.

*Twyne, John. *De Rebus Albionicis, Britannicis atque Anglicis, commentariorum libri*. London, 1590.

*Valles, Francisco. *De Sacra Philosophia*. Lyon, 1622.

*Van Linschoten, Jan Huygen. *Voyages into ye Easte and West Indies*. Translated by William Phillip. London, 1598.

*Vergil, Polydore. *On Discovery* (1499). Translated by Brian Copenhaver. Cambridge: Harvard University Press, 2002.

———. *Historiae Anglicae Libri*. Leiden, 1604.

*Verstegan, Richard. *A restitution of decayed intelligence: In antiquities*. Antwerp, 1605.

*Vignier, Nicholas. *Rerum Burgundiorum Chronicon*. Basel, 1575.

*———. *De la Noblesse, Ancienneté, Remarques, & Merites d'honneur de la troisiesme maison de France*. Paris, 1587.

*Vipera, Mercurius. *Opus de Prisco; τ Sacro Instituto*. Rome, 1517.

Viperano, Giovanni Antonio. "De scribenda historia." In *Artis Historicae Penus*, ed. Joannes Wolfius. Basel, 1579.

Vives, Juan Luis. *On Education: A Translation of the De tradendis disciplinis of Juan Luis Vives*. Translated by Foster Watson. Cambridge: University Press, 1913.

*Vorst, Conrad. *Tractatus Theologicus de Deo*. Steinfurt, 1610.

The Walsingham Letter-Book or Register of Ireland, May 1578 to December 1579. Edited by James Hogan and N. McNeill O'Farrell. Dublin: Stationery Office, for the Irish Manuscripts Commission, 1959.

Wheare, Degory. *De Ratione et Methodo Legendi Historias Dissertatio*. Oxford, 1625.

———. *Relectiones Hyemales*. Oxford, 1637.

*Willet, Andrew. *Hexapla in Genesim*. Cambridge, 1605.

*William of Tyre. *A History of Deeds Done Beyond the Sea*. New York: Columbia University Press, 1943.

Williams, Roger. *The Works of Sir Roger Williams*. Edited by John Evans. Oxford: Clarendon, 1972.

Wilson, Thomas. "The State of England (1600)." Edited by F. J. Fisher. *The Camden Miscellany*, 3rd. ser., vol. 52. London: Camden Society, 1936.

Wolfius, Joannes, ed. *Artis Historicae Penus*. Basel, 1579.

*Ziegler, Jacob. *Terrae Sanctae*. Strassbourg, 1536.

Zwinger, Theodor. *Methodus Apodemica*. Basel, 1577.

*———. *Theatrum Humanae Vitae*. 5 vols. Basel, 1586–87.

SECONDARY SOURCES

Adams, Robyn. "'The Service I Am Here For': William Hearle in the Marshalsea Prison, 1571." *HLQ* 72 (2009): 217–38.

———. "A Spy on the Payroll? William Hearle and the Mid Elizabethan Polity." *HR* 83 (2010): 1–15.

———. "A Most Secret Service: William Herle and the Circulation of Intelligence." In *Diplomacy and Early Modern Culture*, ed. Robyn Adams and Rosanna Cox, 63–81. Basingstoke: Palgrave Macmillan, 2011.

Adams, Simon. "The Papers of Robert Dudley, Earl of Leicester: 1, The Browne-Evelyn Collection." *Archives* 20 (1992): 63–85.

———. "The Papers of Robert Dudley, Earl of Leicester: 2, The Atye-Cotton Collection." *Archives* 20 (1993): 131–44.

———. "The Papers of Robert Dudley, Earl of Leicester: 3, The Countess of Leicester's Collection." *Archives* 22 (1996): 1–26.

———. *Leicester and the Court: Essays on Elizabethan Politics*. Manchester: Manchester University Press, 2002.

Adamson, Jack H., and H. F. Folland. *The Shepherd of the Ocean: An Account of Sir Walter Ralegh and His Times*. Boston: Gambit, 1969.

Adler, William. *Time Immemorial*. Washington, DC: Dumbarton Oaks Research Library and Collection, 1989.

Alford, Stephen. *The Early Elizabethan Polity: William Cecil and the British Succession Crisis, 1558–1569*. Cambridge: Cambridge University Press, 1998.

———. "Some Elizabethan Spies in the Office of Sir Francis Walsingham." In *Diplomacy and Early Modern Culture*, ed. Robyn Adams and Rosanna Cox, 46–62. Basingstoke: Palgrave Macmillan, 2011.

Allen, Don Cameron. *The Star-Crossed Renaissance: The Quarrel about Astrology and Its Influence in England*. Durham, NC: Duke University Press, 1941.

———. *The Legend of Noah: Renaissance Rationalism in Art, Science, and Letters*. Urbana: University of Illinois Press, 1949.

———. *Mysteriously Meant: The Rediscovery of Pagan Symbolism and Allegorical Interpretation in the Renaissance*. Baltimore: Johns Hopkins University Press, 1970.

Alsop, J. D. "William Fleetwood and Elizabethan Historical Scholarship." *SCJ* 25 (1995): 155–76.

Anglo, Sydney. *Machiavelli: The First Century: Studies in Enthusiasm, Hostility, and Irreverence*. Oxford: Oxford University Press, 2005.

"Archival Knowledge Cultures in Europe, 1400–1900." Edited by Randolph Head. Special issue, *Archival Science* 10 (2010).

Ash, Eric. "'A Note and a Caveat for the Merchant': Mercantile Advisors in Elizabethan England." *SCJ* 33 (2002): 1–31.

———. *Power, Knowledge and Expertise in Elizabethan England*. Baltimore: Johns Hopkins University Press, 2004.

———, ed. *Expertise: Practical Knowledge and the Early Modern State*. Osiris 25. Chicago: University of Chicago Press, 2010.

Ash, Eric, and Alison Sandman. "Trading Expertise: Sebastian Cabot between Spain and England." *RQ* 57 (2004): 813–46.

Asher, R. E. *National Myths in Renaissance France: Francus, Samothes and the Druids*. Edinburgh: Edinburgh University Press, 1993.

Aston, Margaret. "The Fiery Trigon Conjunction: An Elizabethan Astrological Prediction." *Isis* 61 (1970): 159–87.

Backus, Irena. *Historical Method and Confessional Identity in the Era of the Reformation (1378–1615)*. Leiden: Brill, 2003.

Baker, David Weil. "Jacobean Historiography and the Election of Richard III." *HLQ* 70 (2007): 311–42.

———. "The Historical Faith of William Tyndale: Non-Salvific Reading of Scripture at the Outset of the English Reformation." *RQ* 62 (2009): 661–92.

Barber, Peter. "Was Elizabeth I Interested in Maps—and Did It Matter?" *TRHS*, 6th ser., 14 (2004): 185–98.

Barkan, Leonard. *Unearthing the Past: Archaeology and Aesthetics in the Making of Renaissance Culture*. New Haven, CT: Yale University Press, 1999.

Barnes, Robin. *Prophecy and Gnosis: Apocalypticism in the Wake of the Lutheran Reformation*. Stanford, CA: Stanford University Press, 1988.

Barr, James. "Why the World Was Created in 4004 BC: Archbishop Ussher and Biblical Chronology." *BJRL* 67 (1985): 575–608.

———. "Luther and Biblical Chronology." *BJRL* 72 (1990): 51–67.

Barrera-Osorio, Antonio. *Experiencing Nature: The Spanish American Empire and the Early Scientific Revolution*. Austin: University of Texas Press, 2006.

Batho, G. R. "The Library of the 'Wizard' Earl: Henry Percy Ninth Earl of Northumberland (1564–1632)." *The Library*, 5th ser., 15 (1960): 246–61.

———. "Thomas Harriot and the Northumberland Household." In *Thomas Harriot: An Elizabethan Man of Science*, ed. Robert Fox, 28–47. Aldershot: Ashgate, 2000.

Bauckham, Richard. *Tudor Apocalypse: Sixteenth Century Apocalypticism, Millennarianism, and the English Reformation: From John Bale to John Foxe and Thomas Brightman*. Oxford: Sutton Courtenay, 1978.

Bautier, Robert-Henri. "La phase cruciale de l'histoire des archives: La constitution des dépôts d'archives et la naissance de l'archivistique." *Archivum* 18 (1968): 139–49.

Beal, Peter, and Grace Ioppolo, eds. *Elizabeth I and the Culture of Writing*. London: BL, 2007.

Becker, Peter, and William Clark, eds. *Little Tools of Knowledge: Historical Essays on Academic and Bureaucratic Practices*. Ann Arbor: University of Michigan Press, 2000.

Beer, Anna. "'Left to the World without a Maister': Sir Walter Ralegh's *The History of the World* as a Public Text." *Studies in Philology* 91 (1994): 432–63.

———. *Sir Walter Ralegh and His Readers in the Seventeenth Century: Speaking to the People*. New York: St. Martin's, 1997.

———. "Sir Walter Ralegh's Dialogue betweene a Counsellor of State and Justice of Peace." In *The Crisis of 1614 and the Addled Parliament*, ed. Stephen Clucas and Rosalind Davies, 127–41. Burlington, VT: Ashgate, 2002.

———. *Bess: The Life of Lady Ralegh, Wife to Sir Walter*. London: Constable, 2004.

Bellany, Alastair. *The Politics of Court Scandal in Early Modern England: News Culture and the Overbury Affair, 1603–1660*. Cambridge: Cambridge University Press, 2002.

Bennet, Jim, and Scott Mandelbrote. *The Garden, the Ark, the Tower, the Temple: Biblical Metaphors of Knowledge in Early Modern Europe*. Oxford: Museum of the History of Science, in association with the Bodleian Library, 1998.

Bentley, Jerry. *Politics and Culture in Renaissance Naples.* Princeton, NJ: Princeton University Press, 1987.

Ben-Tov, Asaph. *Lutheran Humanists and Greek Antiquity: Melanchthonian Scholarship between Universal History and Pedagogy.* Leiden: Brill, 2009.

Ben-Zaken, Avner. "From Naples to Goa and Back: A Secretive Galilean Messenger and a Radical Hermeneutist." *History of Science* 47 (2009): 147–74.

Bepler, Jill. "The Traveller-Author and His Role in Seventeenth-Century German Travel Accounts." In *Travel Fact and Travel Fiction: Studies on Fiction, Literary Tradition, Scholarly Discovery, and Observation in Travel Writing*, ed. Zweder von Martels, 183–93. Leiden: E. J. Brill, 1994.

Betteridge, Thomas. *Tudor Histories of the English Reformations, 1530–83.* Aldershot: Ashgate, 1999.

Birely, Robert. *The Counter-Reformation Prince: Anti-Machiavellianism or Catholic Statecraft in Early Modern Europe.* Chapel Hill: University of North Carolina Press, 1990.

Bizzocchi, Roberto. *Genealogie incredibili: Scritti di storia nell'Europa moderna.* Bologna: Società editrice il Mulino, 1995.

Black, Jeremy. *Maps and History: Constructing Images of the Past.* New Haven, CT: Yale University Press, 1997.

Black, P. M. "Matthew Parker's Search for Cranmer's 'Great Notable Written Books.'" *The Library*, 5th ser., 29 (1974): 312–22.

———. "Laurence Nowell's 'Disappearance' in Germany and Its Bearing on the Whereabouts of His Collectanea, 1568–1572." *EHR* 92 (1977): 345–53.

Black, Robert. "The New Laws of History." *Renaissance Studies* 1 (1987): 126–56.

Blair, Ann. *The Theater of Nature: Jean Bodin and Renaissance Science.* Princeton, NJ: Princeton University Press, 1997.

———. "Mosaic Physics and the Search for a Pious Natural Philosophy in the Late Renaissance." *Isis* 91 (2000): 32–58.

———. "Reading Strategies for Coping with Information Overload, ca. 1550–1700." *JHI* 64 (2003): 11–28.

———. "*Historia* in Zwinger's *Theatrum humanae vitae*." In *Historia: Empiricism and Erudition in Early Modern Europe*, ed. Gianna Pomata and Nancy G. Siraisi, 269–96. Cambridge: MIT Press, 2005.

———. *Too Much to Know: Managing Scholarly Information before the Modern Age.* New Haven, CT: Yale University Press, 2010.

Borchardt, Frank L. *German Antiquity in Renaissance Myth.* Baltimore: Johns Hopkins University Press, 1971.

Boutcher, Warren. "Humanism and Literature in Late Tudor England: Translation, the Continental Book, and the Case of Montaigne's *Essais*." In *Reassessing Tudor Humanism*, ed. Jonathan Woolfson, 243–68. Basingstoke: Palgrave Macmillan, 2002.

Bouwsma, William J. "The Two Faces of Humanism: Stoicism and Augustinianism in Renaissance Thought." In *Itinerarium Italicum: The Profile of the Italian Renaissance in the Mirror of Its European Transformations*, ed. Heiko A. Oberman and Thomas A. Brady Jr., 3–60. Leiden: Brill, 1975.

———. *John Calvin: A Sixteenth-Century Portrait*. New York: Oxford University Press, 1988.

———. *The Waning of the Renaissance, ca. 1550–1640*. New Haven, CT: Yale University Press, 2000.

Bradbrook, M. C. *The School of Night: A Study in the Literary Relationships of Sir Walter Raleigh*. Cambridge: Cambridge University Press, 1936.

Bradford, A. T. "Stuart Absolutism and the Utility of Tacitus." *HLQ* 46 (1983): 127–55.

Braude, Benjamin. "The Sons of Noah and the Construction of Ethnic and Geographical Identities in the Medieval and Early Modern Periods." *William and Mary Quarterly* 54 (1997): 103–42.

Broadway, Jan. *"No Historie So Meete": Gentry Culture and the Development of Local History in Elizabethan and Early Stuart England*. Manchester: Manchester University Press, 2006.

———. "Political Appropriation: Reading Sir Walter Ralegh's 'Dialogue between a Counsellor of State and a Justice of Peace.'" Centre for Editing Lives and Letters, 2006. http://www.livesandletters.ac.uk/papers/SOTC_2006_01_001.pdf.

Broc, Numa. *La géographie de la Renaissance (1420–1620)*. Paris: Bibliothèque nationale, 1980.

Brooks, Christopher, and Kevin Sharpe, with rejoinder by D. R. Kelley. "History, English Law and the Renaissance." *P&P* 72 (1976): 133–46.

Brosseder, Claudia. "The Writing in the Wittenberg Sky: Astrology in Sixteenth-Century Germany." *JHI* 66 (2005): 557–76.

Brown, Elizabeth A. R. "Jean du Tillet et les Archives de France." *Histoire et archives* 2 (1997): 29–63.

Brushfield, T. N. "Sir Walter Ralegh and His 'History of the World.'" *Report and Transactions of the Devonshire Association* 19 (1887): 398–418. Seen in an independent reprinting held by the Princeton University Library that has been repaginated as 1–30.

Burgess, Glenn. *The Politics of the Ancient Constitution: An Introduction to English Political Thought, 1600–1642*. Basingstoke: Macmillan, 1992.

Burke, Peter. "A Survey of the Popularity of Ancient Historians, 1450–1700." *History and Theory* 5 (1966): 135–52.

———. *The Renaissance Sense of the Past*. New York: St. Martin's, 1970.

———. "Tacitism: Scepticism and Reason of State." In *The Cambridge History of Political Thought, 1450–1700*, ed. J. H. Burns and Mark Goldie, 479–98. Cambridge: Cambridge University Press, 1996.

———. "Early Modern Venice as a Center of Information and Communication." In *Venice Reconsidered: The History and Civilization of an Italian City State, 1297–1797*, ed. John Martin and Dennis Romano, 389–419. Baltimore: Johns Hopkins University Press, 2000.

Byrne, James Steven. "A Humanist History of Mathematics? Regiomontanus' Padua Oration in Context." *JHI* 67 (2006): 41–61.

Carley, James Patrick. "John Leland in Paris: The Evidence of His Poetry." *Studies in Philology* 83 (1986): 1–50.

———. "Monastic Collections and Their Disposal." In *The Cambridge History of the*

Book in Britain, vol. 4, *1557–1695*, ed. John Barnard and Donald F. McKenzie, with the assistance of Maureen Bell, 339–47. Cambridge: Cambridge University Press, 2002.

———. "The Dispersal of the Monastic Libraries and the Salvaging of the Spoils." In *The Cambridge History of Libraries in Britain and Ireland*, vol. 1, *To 1640*, ed. Elizabeth Leedham-Green and Teresa Webber, 265–91. Cambridge: Cambridge University Press, 2006.

Carlson, David. "The Writings and Manuscript Collections of the Elizabethan Alchemist, Antiquary, and Herald Francis Thynne." *HLQ* 52 (1989): 203–72.

Catalogue of the Additions to the Manuscripts: The Yelverton Manuscripts—Additional Manuscripts 48000–48196. 2 vols. London, 1994.

Cawley, Robert R. "Sir Thomas Browne and His Reading." *PMLA* 48 (1933): 426–70.

Céard, Jean. *Le nature et les prodiges: L'insolite au 16e siècle en France*. Geneva: Droz, 1977.

———. "La querelle des géants et la jeunesse du monde." *Journal of Medieval and Renaissance Studies* 8 (1978): 37–76.

Christianson, J. R. *On Tycho's Island: Tycho Brahe and His Assistants, 1570–1601*. Cambridge: Cambridge University Press, 2000.

Christianson, Paul. *Reformers and Babylon: English Apocalyptic Visions from the Reformation to the Eve of the Civil War*. Toronto: University of Toronto Press, 1978.

Clanchy, M. T. *From Memory to Written Record: England, 1066–1307*. London: Blackwell, 1993.

Clark, Stuart. "King James's Daemonologie: Witchcraft and Kingship." In *The Damned Art: Essays in the Literature of Witchcraft*, ed. Sydney Anglo, 156–81. London: Routledge & Kegan Paul, 1977.

Clarke, Katherine. *Between Geography and History: Hellenic Constructions of the Roman World*. Oxford: Clarendon, 1999.

Clucas, Stephen. "Samuel Hartlib's Ephemerides, 1635–59, and the Pursuit of Scientific and Philosophical Manuscripts: The Religious Ethos of an Intelligencer." *Seventeenth Century* 6 (1991): 33–55.

Clucas, Stephen, and Rosalind Davies, eds. *The Crisis of 1614 and the Addled Parliament*. Burlington, VT: Ashgate, 2002.

Clulee, Nicholas. *John Dee's Natural Philosophy: Between Magic and Religion*. London: Routledge, 1988.

Cochrane, Eric. *Historians and Historiography in the Italian Renaissance*. Chicago: University of Chicago Press, 1981.

Cockle, Maurice J. D. *A Bibliography of English Military Books Up to 1642 and of Contemporary Foreign Works*. London: Simpkin, Marshall, Hamilton, Kent, 1900.

Cogswell, Thomas. *The Blessed Revolution: English Politics and the Coming of War, 1621–1624*. Cambridge: Cambridge University Press, 1989.

Cogswell, Thomas, Richard Cust, and Peter Lake, eds. *Politics, Religion, and Popularity in Early Stuart Britain: Essays in Honour of Conrad Russell*. Cambridge: Cambridge University Press, 2002.

Coleman, Christopher, and David Starkey, eds. *Revolution Reassessed: Revisions in the History of Tudor Government and Administration*. Oxford: Clarendon, 1986.

Collinson, Patrick. "The Monarchical Republic of Queen Elizabeth I." *BJRL* 69 (1987): 394–424.

———. "Puritans, Men of Business and Elizabethan Parliaments." *Parliamentary History* 7 (1988): 187–211.

———. "The Elizabethan Exclusion Crisis and the Elizabethan Polity." *Proceedings of the British Academy* 84 (1994): 51–92.

———. "One of Us? William Camden and the Making of History." *TRHS*, 6th ser., 8 (1998): 139–63.

———. "Servants and Citizens: Robert Beale and other Elizabethans." *HR* 79 (2006): 488–511.

Conrad, F. W. "The Problem of Counsel Reconsidered: The Case of Sir Thomas Elyot." In *Political Thought and the Tudor Commonwealth: Deep Structure, Discourse and Disguise*, ed. Paul A. Fideler and T. F. Mayer, 75–107. London: Routledge, 1992.

Contamine, Philippe, ed. *War and Competition between States*. Oxford: Clarendon, 2000.

Copenhaver, Brian. "Natural Magic, Hermetism, and Occultism in Early Modern Science." In *Reappraisals of the Scientific Revolution*, ed. David Lindberg and Robert Westman, 261–302. Cambridge: Cambridge University Press, 1990.

———. "The Occultist Tradition and Its Critics in Seventeenth Century Philosophy." In *The Cambridge History of Seventeenth Century Philosophy*, ed. Michael Ayers and Daniel Garber, 454–512. Cambridge: Cambridge University Press, 1998.

Cormack, Lesley B. *Charting an Empire: Geography at the English Universities, 1580–1620*. Chicago: University of Chicago Press, 1997.

Couzinet, Marie-Dominique. *Histoire et méthode à la Renaissance*. Paris: J. Vrin, 1996.

Crawford, M. H., and C. R. Ligota, eds. *Ancient History and the Antiquarian: Essays in Memory of Arnaldo Momigliano*. London: Warburg Institute, 1995.

Crick, Julia. "Geoffrey of Monmouth: Prophecy and History." *Journal of Medieval History* 18 (1992): 357–71.

Croft, Pauline. "The Reputation of Robert Cecil: Libels, Political Opinion and Popular Awareness in the Early Seventeenth Century." *TRHS*, 6th ser., 1 (1991): 43–69.

———. "Sir John Doddridge, King James I, and the Antiquity of Parliament." *Parliaments, Estates, and Representation* 12 (1992): 95–107.

Cromartie, Alan. "The Constitutionalist Revolution: The Transformation of Political Culture in Early Stuart England." *P&P* 163 (1999): 76–120.

———. *The Constitutionalist Revolution: An Essay on the History of England, 1450–1642*. Cambridge: Cambridge University Press, 2006.

Curran, Brian. *The Egyptian Renaissance: The Afterlife of Ancient Egypt in Early Modern Italy*. Chicago: University of Chicago Press, 2007.

Cust, Richard. "News and Politics in Early Seventeenth-Century England." *P&P* 112 (1986): 60–90.

———. "Catholicism, Antiquarianism, and Gentry Honour: The Writings of Thomas Shirley." *Midland History* 23 (1998): 40–70.

Cust, Richard, and Ann Hughes, eds. *Conflict in Early Stuart England: Studies in Religion and Politics, 1603–1642*. London: Longman, 1989.

Daston, Lorraine. "Baconian Facts, Academic Civility, and the Prehistory of Objectivity." *Annals of Scholarship* 8 (1991): 337–64.

Daston, Lorraine, and Katharine Park. *Wonders and the Order of Nature, 1150–1750.* New York: Zone, 1998.

Davies, Catherine. "'Poor Persecuted Little Flock' or 'Commonwealth of Christians': Edwardian Protestant Concepts of the Church." In *Protestantism and the National Church in Sixteenth Century England*, ed. Peter Lake and Maria Dowling, 78–102. London: Croom Helm, 1987.

Davies, Rosalind. "News from the Fleet: Characterizing the Elizabethan Army in the Narratives of the Action at Cadiz, 1596." In *War: Identities in Conflict, 1300–2000*, ed. Bertrand Taithe and Tim Thornton, 21–36. Thrupp: Sutton, 1998.

———. "'The Great Day of Mart': Returning to Texts at the Trial of Sir Walter Ralegh in 1603." *Renaissance Forum* 4, no. 1 (1999). Available at http://www.hull.ac.uk/renforum/v4no1/davies.htm.

Davis, Joel. "Robert Sidney's Marginal Comments on Tacitus and the English Campaigns in the Low Countries." *Sidney Journal* 24 (2006): 1–19.

Dean, L. F. "Bodin's 'Methodus' in England before 1625." *Studies in Philology* 39 (1942): 160–66.

———. *Tudor Theories of History Writing.* University of Michigan Contributions in Modern Philology. Ann Arbor: University of Michigan Press, 1947.

Delph, Ronald K. "Polishing the Papal Image in the Counter-Reformation: The Case of Agostino Steuco." *SCJ* 23 (1992): 35–47.

———. "From Venetian Visitor to Curial Humanist: The Development of Agostino Steuco's 'Counter'-Reformation Thought." *RQ* 47 (1994): 102–39.

———. "Valla *Grammaticus*, Agostino Steuco, and the Donation of Constantine." *JHI* 57 (1996): 55–77.

———. "Renovation, *Reformatio* and Humanist Ambition in Rome." In *Heresy, Culture and Religion in Early Modern Italy*, ed. Ronald K. Delph, Michelle M. Fontaine, and John Jeffries Martin, 73–92. Kirksville, MO: Truman State University Press, 2006.

Delumeau, Jean. *A History of Paradise: The Garden of Eden in Myth and Tradition.* Translated by Matthew O'Connell. New York: Continuum, 1995.

de Vivo, Filippo. *Information and Communication in Venice: Rethinking Early Modern Politics.* Cambridge: Cambridge University Press, 2007.

DeVun, Leah. *Prophecy, Alchemy, and the End of Time: John of Rupescissa in the Late Middle Ages.* New York: Columbia University Press, 2009.

Dew, Nicholas. "Reading Travels in the Culture of Curiosity: Thévenot's Collection of Voyages." *JEMH* 10 (2006): 39–59.

———. *Orientalism in Louis XIV's France.* Oxford: Oxford University Press, 2009.

Diener, Ronald. "The Magdeburg Centuries: A Bibliothecal and Historiographical Analysis." Ph.D. diss., Harvard University Divinity School, 1978.

Ditchfield, Simon. *Liturgy, Sanctity and History in Tridentine Italy: Pietro Maria Campi and the Preservation of the Particular.* Cambridge: Cambridge University Press, 1995.

Donagan, Barbara. "Halcyon Days and the Literature of War: England's Military Education Before 1642." *P&P* 147 (1995): 65–100.

Dover, Paul. "Deciphering the Diplomatic Archives of Fifteenth-Century Italy." *Archival Science* 7 (2007): 297–316.

Dubois, Claude-Gilbert. *Celtes et Gaulois au XVIe siècle: Le développement littéraire d'un mythe nationaliste.* Paris: J. Vrin, 1972.

———. *La conception de l'histoire en France au XVIe siècle.* Paris: A.-G. Nizet, 1977.

Duncan, Joseph Ellis. *Milton's Earthly Paradise: A Historical Study of Eden.* Minneapolis: University of Minnesota Press, 1972.

Earle, Peter. *The Last Fight of the Revenge.* London: Collins & Brown, 1992.

Edwards, Edward. *The Life of Sir Walter Ralegh.* 2 vols. London: Macmillan, 1868.

Elsner, Jas. "The *Itinerarium Burdigalense*: Politics and Salvation in the Geography of Constantine's Empire." *Journal of Roman Studies* 90 (2000): 181–95.

Elton, G. R. *The Tudor Revolution in Government: Administrative Changes in the Reign of Henry VIII.* Cambridge: Cambridge University Press, 1953.

———. *England, 1200–1640.* Ithaca, NY: Cornell University Press, 1969.

Elukin, Jonathan. "Keeping Secrets in Medieval and Early Modern English Government." In *Das Geheimnis am Beginn der europäischen Moderne,* ed. Gisela Engel et al., 111–29. Frankfurt: Vittorio Klostermann, 2002.

Erasmus, Hendrik Johannes. *The Origins of Rome in Historiography from Petrarch to Perizonius.* Assen: Van Gorcum, 1962.

Farmer, S. A. *Syncretism in the West: Pico's 900 Theses (1486): The Evolution of Traditional, Religious, and Philosophical Systems: With Text, Translation, and Commentary.* Phoenix: Medieval and Renaissance Texts and Studies, 1998.

Feingold, Mordechai. "Oriental Studies." In *The History of the University of Oxford* (4 vols.), ed. Nicholas Tyacke, 4:449–504. Oxford: Oxford University Press, 1997.

Ferguson, Arthur B. *Clio Unbound: The Perception of the Social and Cultural Past in Renaissance England.* Durham, NC: Duke University Press, 1979.

———. *Utter Antiquity: The Perception of Prehistory in Renaissance England.* Durham, NC: Duke University Press, 1993.

Ferrary, Jean-Louis. *Onofrio Panvinio et les antiquités romaines.* Rome: École française de Rome, Palais Farnèse, 1996.

Fincham, Kenneth, and Peter Lake. "The Ecclesiastical Policy of James I." *JBS* 24 (1985): 169–207.

Findlen, Paula. *Possessing Nature: Museums, Collecting, and Scientific Culture in Early Modern Italy.* Berkeley and Los Angeles: University of California Press, 1994.

———. "Francis Bacon and the Reform of Natural History in the Seventeenth Century." In *History and the Disciplines: The Reclassification of Knowledge in Early Modern Europe,* ed. Donald Kelley, 239–60. Rochester, NY: University of Rochester Press, 1997.

———. "The Formation of a Scientific Community: Natural History in Sixteenth-Century Italy." In *Natural Particulars: Nature and the Disciplines in Renaissance Europe,* ed. Anthony Grafton and Nancy Siraisi, 369–400. Cambridge: MIT Press, 1999.

Firth, Charles. "Sir Walter Raleigh's *History of the World*." In *Proceedings of the British Academy,* 427–46. London, 1917–18.

Firth, Katharine. *The Apocalyptic Tradition in Reformation Britain, 1530–1645.* Oxford: Oxford University Press, 1979.

Fissel, Mark Charles. "Tradition and Invention in the Early Stuart Art of War." *Journal for the Society of Army Historical Research* 65 (1987): 133–49.

Fitzmaurice, Andrew. *Humanism and America: An Intellectual History of English Colonisation, 1500–1625.* Cambridge: Cambridge University Press, 2003.

Fleck, Andrew. "'At the Time of His Death': Manuscript Instability and Walter Ralegh's Performance on the Scaffold." *JBS* 48 (2009): 4–28.

Flower, Robin. "Lawrence Nowell and the Discovery of England in Tudor Times." *Proceedings of the British Academy* 21 (1937 for 1935): 48–73.

Force, James E., and Richard H. Popkin, eds. *Newton and Religion: Context, Nature, and Influence.* Dordrecht: Kluwer, 1999.

Fox, Adam. "Custom, Memory, and the Authority of Writing." In *The Experience of Authority in Early Modern England*, ed. Paul Griffiths, Adam Fox, and Steve Hindle, 89–116. Basingstoke: Macmillan, 1996.

———. "Rumour, News and Popular Political Opinion in Elizabethan and Early Stuart England." *HJ* 40 (1997): 507–620.

———. *Oral and Literate Culture in England, 1500–1700.* Oxford: Clarendon, 2000.

———. "Printed Questionnaires, Research Networks, and the Discovery of the British Isles, 1650–1800." *HJ* 53 (2010): 593–621.

Fox, Levi, ed. *English Historical Scholarship in the Sixteenth and Seventeenth Centuries.* London: Dugdale Society, for the Oxford University Press, 1956.

Fox, Robert, ed. *Thomas Harriot: An Elizabethan Man of Science.* Aldershot: Ashgate, 2000.

Franklin, Julian H. *Jean Bodin and the Sixteenth-Century Revolution in the Methodology of Law and History.* Westport, CT: Greenwood, 1977.

Frazier, Alison Knowles. *Possible Lives: Authors and Saints in Renaissance Italy.* New York: Columbia University Press, 2005.

Freeman, Thomas S. "Providence and Prescription: The Account of Elizabeth in Foxe's *Book of Martyrs*." In *The Myth of Elizabeth*, ed. Susan Doran and Thomas S. Freeman, 27–55. Basingstoke: Palgrave, 2003.

Friedrich, Markus. "Archives as Networks: The Geography of Record-Keeping in the Society of Jesus (1540–1773)." *Archival Science* 10 (2010): 285–98.

Fubini, Riccardo. "Osservazioni sugli *Historiarum florentini populi libri xii di* Leonardo Bruni." In *Studi di storia medievale e moderna per Ernesto Sestan* (2 vols.), 1:429–32. Florence: Leo S. Olschki, 1980.

Fussner, F. Smith. *The Historical Revolution: English Historical Writing and Thought, 1580–1640.* London: Routledge & Kegan Paul, 1962.

Gadd, Ian, and Alexandra Gillespie, eds. *John Stow (1525–1605) and the Making of the English Past: Studies in Early Modern Culture and the History of the Book.* London: BL, 2004.

Gajda, Alexandra. "The State of Christendom: History, Political Thought and the Essex Circle." *HR* 81 (2008): 423–46.

Games, Alison. *The Web of Empire: English Cosmopolitans in an Age of Expansion, 1560–1660.* Oxford: Oxford University Press, 2008.

Gibson, Jonathan. "Civil War in 1614: Lucan, Gorges and Prince Henry." In *The Crisis of 1614 and the Addled Parliament: Literary and Historical Perspectives*, ed. Stephen Clucas and Rosalind Davies, 161–76. Aldershot: Ashgate, 2003.

Gilbert, Felix. *Machiavelli and Guicciardini: Politics and History in Sixteenth-Century Florence*. Princeton, NJ: Princeton University Press, 1965.

———. "Machiavelli: The Renaissance Art of War." In *Makers of Modern Strategy: From Machiavelli to the Nuclear Age*, ed. Peter Paret and Felix Gilbert, 11–31. Princeton, NJ: Princeton University Press, 1986.

Ginzburg, Carlo. *No Island Is an Island: Four Glances at English Literature in a World Perspective*. New York: Columbia University Press, 2000.

Given-Wilson, Chris. *Chronicles: The Writing of History in Medieval England*. London: Hambledon Continuum, 2004.

Gliozzi, Giuliano. *Adamo e il Nuovo Mondo: La nascita dell'antropologia come ideologia coloniale: Dalle genealogie bibliche alle teorie razziali (1500–1700)*. Florence: La Nuova Italia, 1977.

Goffart, Walter. "The Date and Purpose of Vegetius' *De re militari*." *Traditio* 33 (1977): 65–100.

———. *Historical Atlases: The First Three Hundred Years, 1570–1870*. Chicago: University of Chicago Press, 2003.

Gonzalez de Leon, Fernando. "'Doctors of the Military Discipline': Technical Expertise and the Paradigm of the Spanish Soldier in the Early Modern Period." *SCJ* 27 (1996): 61–85.

Goulding, Robert. "Histories of Science in Early Modern Europe: Introduction." *JHI* 67 (2006): 33–40.

———. "Method and Mathematics: Peter Ramus' Histories of the Sciences." *JHI* 67 (2006): 63–85.

———. *Defending Hypatia: Ramus, Savile, and the Renaissance Rediscovery of Mathematical History*. Dordrecht: Springer, 2010.

Grafton, Anthony. "On the Scholarship of Politian and Its Context." *JWCI* 40 (1977): 150–88.

———. *Joseph Scaliger: A Study in the History of Classical Scholarship*. 2 vols. Oxford: Clarendon, 1983–93.

———. "From *De die natali* to *De emendatione temporum*: The Origin and Settings of Scaliger's Chronology." *JWCI* 48 (1985): 100–143.

———. *Forgers and Critics: Creativity and Duplicity in Western Scholarship*. Princeton, NJ: Princeton University Press, 1990.

———. "Invention of Traditions and Traditions of Invention in Renaissance Europe: The Strange Case of Annius of Viterbo." In *The Transmission of Culture in Early Modern Europe*, ed. Anthony Grafton and Ann Blair, 8–38. Philadelphia: University of Pennsylvania Press, 1990.

———. *Defenders of the Text: The Traditions of Scholarship in an Age of Science, 1450–1800*. Cambridge, MA: Harvard University Press, 1991.

———. "The Ancient City Restored: Archaeology, Ecclesiastical History, and Egyptology." In *Rome Reborn: The Vatican Library and Renaissance Culture*, ed. Anthony Grafton, 87–124. Washington, DC: Library of Congress, 1993.

——. *Commerce with the Classics: Ancient Books and Renaissance Readers.* Ann Arbor: University of Michigan Press, 1997.

——. *The Footnote: A Curious History.* Cambridge, MA: Harvard University Press, 1997.

——. "From Apotheosis to Analysis: Some Late Renaissance Histories of Classical Astronomy." In *History and the Disciplines: The Reclassification of Knowledge in Early Modern Europe,* ed. Donald Kelley, 261–76. Rochester, NY: University of Rochester Press, 1997.

——. "Where Was Salomon's House? Ecclesiastical History and the Intellectual Origins of Bacon's *New Atlantis.*" In *Die europäische Gelehrtenrepublik im Zeitalter des Konfessionalismus,* ed. Herbert Jaumann, 21–38. Wolfenbüttler Forschungen 96. Wiesbaden, 2001.

——. "Some Uses of Eclipses in Early Modern Chronology." *JHI* 64 (2003): 213–29.

——. *What Was History? The Art of History in Early Modern Europe.* Cambridge: Cambridge University Press, 2007.

——. *Worlds Made by Words: Scholarship and Community in the Modern West.* Cambridge, MA: Harvard University Press, 2009.

Grafton, Anthony, and Lisa Jardine. *From Humanism to the Humanities: Education and the Liberal Arts in Fifteenth- and Sixteenth-Century Europe.* London: Duckworth, 1986.

——. "'Studied for Action': How Gabriel Harvey Read His Livy." *P&P* 129 (1990): 30–78.

Grafton, Anthony, with April Shelford and Nancy Siraisi. *New Worlds, Ancient Texts: The Power of Tradition and the Shock of Discovery.* Cambridge, MA: Harvard University Press, 1992.

Grafton, Anthony, and Noel M. Swerdlow. "Technical Chronology and Astrological History in Varro, Censorinus and Others." *Classical Quarterly* 35 (1985): 454–65.

——. "Calendar Dates and Ominous Days in Ancient Historiography." *JWCI* 51 (1988): 14–42.

Grafton, Anthony, and Joanna Weinberg, with Alastair Hamilton. *"I Have Always Loved the Holy Tongue": Isaac Causabon, the Jews, and a Forgotten Chapter in Renaissance Scholarship.* Cambridge, MA: Belknap Press of Harvard University Press, 2011.

Grafton, Anthony, and Megan Williams. *Christianity and the Transformation of the Book: Origen, Eusebius, and the Library of Caesarea.* Cambridge, MA: Belknap Press of Harvard University Press, 2006.

Graham, Timothy. "Matthew Parker's Manuscripts: An Elizabethan Library and Its Use." In *The Cambridge History of Libraries in Britain and Ireland,* vol. 1, *To 1640,* ed. Elizabeth Leedham-Green and Teresa Webber, 322–44. Cambridge: Cambridge University Press, 2006.

Graves, Michael A. R. *Thomas Norton: The Parliament Man.* Oxford: Blackwell, 1994.

Greenblatt, Stephen. *Sir Walter Ralegh: The Renaissance Man and His Roles.* New Haven, CT: Yale University Press, 1973.

Grendler, Paul. *Schooling in Renaissance Italy: Literacy and Learning, 1300–1600.* Baltimore: Johns Hopkins University Press, 1989.

Guy, John, ed. *The Reign of Elizabeth I: Court and Culture in the Last Decade*. Cambridge: Cambridge University Press, 1988.

———. *Politics, Law and Counsel in Tudor and Early Stuart England*. Aldershot: Ashgate, 2000.

Guy, John, and Alistair Fox. *Reassessing the Henrician Age: Humanism, Politics and Reform, 1500–1550*. New York: Blackwell, 1986.

Guyotjeannin, Olivier. "Les méthodes de travail des archivistes du roi de France (fin XIIIe–début XVie siècle)." *Archiv für Diplomatik* 42 (1996): 295–374.

Hadow, G. E., ed. *Sir Walter Raleigh: Selections from His Historie of the World, His Letters, etc.* Oxford: Clarendon, 1917.

Haigh, Christopher, ed. *The Reign of Elizabeth I*. Athens: University of Georgia Press, 1985.

Hale, J. R. *Renaissance War Studies*. London: Hambledon, 1983.

———. *War and Society in Renaissance Europe, 1450–1620*. New York: St. Martin's, 1985.

Hallam, Elizabeth. "Nine Centuries of Keeping the Public Records." In *The Records of the Nation*, ed. G. H. Martin and Peter Spufford, 9–16. Woodbridge: Boydell, 1990.

Hamilton, Alastair. *William Bedwell, the Arabist, 1563–1632*. Leiden: Thomas Browne Institute, 1985.

———. *The Apocryphal Apocalypse: The Reception of the Second Book of Esdras (4 Ezra) from the Renaissance to the Enlightenment*. Oxford: Clarendon, 1999.

Hammer, Paul E. J. "The Uses of Scholarship: The Secretariat of Robert Devereux, Second Earl of Essex, c. 1585–1601." *EHR* 109 (1994): 26–51.

———. "Essex and Europe: Evidence from Confidential Instructions by the Earl of Essex, 1595–6." *EHR* 111 (1996): 357–81.

———. "Myth-Making: Politics, Propaganda and the Capture of Cadiz in 1596." *HJ* 40 (1997): 621–42.

———. "'Absolute and Sovereign Mistress of Her Grace'? Queen Elizabeth and Her Favourites, 1581–1592." In *The World of the Favourite*, ed. J. H. Elliot and L. W. B. Brockliss, 38–53. New Haven, CT: Yale University Press, 1999.

———. *The Polarisation of Elizabethan Politics: The Political Career of Robert Devereux, 2nd Earl of Essex, 1585–1597*. Cambridge: Cambridge University Press, 1999.

———. *Elizabeth's Wars: War, Government, and Society in Tudor England, 1544–1604*. New York: Palgrave Macmillan, 2003.

Hampton, Timothy. *Writing from History: The Rhetoric of Exemplarity in Renaissance Literature*. Ithaca, NY: Cornell University Press, 1990.

Harkness, Deborah. *John Dee's Conversations with Angels: Cabala, Alchemy and the End of Nature*. Cambridge: Cambridge University Press, 1999.

———. *The Jewel House: Elizabethan London and the Scientific Revolution*. New Haven, CT: Yale University Press, 2007.

Harley, J. B. "Silences and Secrecy: The Hidden Agenda of Cartography in Early Modern Europe." *Imago Mundi* 40 (1988): 57–76.

Harley, J. B., and David Woodward, eds. *The History of Cartography*. 3 vols. to date. Chicago: University of Chicago Press, 1987–.

Harris, A. Katie. *From Muslim to Christian Granada: Inventing a City's Past in Early Modern Spain*. Baltimore: Johns Hopkins University Press, 2007.

Harris, Oliver. "Stow and the Contemporary Antiquarian Network." In *John Stow (1525–1605) and the Making of the English Past: Studies in Early Modern Culture and the History of the Book*, ed. Ian Gadd and Alexandra Gillespie, 27–36. London: BL, 2004.

Harris, Steven. "Networks of Travel, Correspondence, and Exchange." In *The Cambridge History of Science*, vol. 3, ed. Katherine Park and Lorraine Daston, 341–64. New York: Cambridge University Press, 2006.

Hay, Denys. *Europe: The Emergence of an Idea*. Edinburgh: Edinburgh University Press, 1957.

Head, Randolph. "Knowing Like a State: The Transformation of Political Knowledge in Swiss Archives, 1450–1770." *JMH* 75 (2003): 745–82.

———. "Mirroring Governance: Archives, Inventories and Political Knowledge in Early Modern Switzerland and Europe." *Archival Science* 7 (2007): 317–29.

Headley, John M. *Luther's View of Church History*. New Haven, CT: Yale University Press, 1963.

———. "Campanella, America, and World Evangelization." In *America in European Consciousness, 1493–1750*, ed. Karen Ordahl Kupperman, 243–71. Chapel Hill: University of North Carolina Press, for the Omohundro Institute of Early American History and Culture, 1995.

———. *Tommaso Campanella and the Transformation of the World*. Princeton, NJ: Princeton University Press, 1997.

———. "Geography and Empire in the Late Renaissance: Botero's Assignment, Western Universalism, and the Civilization Process." *RQ* 53 (2000): 1119–55.

Heal, Felicity. "What Can King Lucius Do for You? The Reformation and the Early British Church." *EHR* 120 (2005): 593–614.

Helgerson, Richard. *Forms of Nationhood: The Elizabethan Writing of England*. Chicago: University of Chicago Press, 1992.

Herendeen, Wyman. *William Camden: A Life in Context*. Rochester, NY: Boydell & Brewer, 2007.

Hiatt, Alfred. *The Making of Medieval Forgeries: False Documents in Fifteenth-Century England*. London: BL/University of Toronto Press, 2004.

Highley, Christopher, and John N. King, eds. *John Foxe and His World*. Aldershot: Ashgate, 2002.

Hill, Christopher. *Puritanism and Revolution*. London: Secker & Warburg, 1958.

———. *The Intellectual Origins of the English Revolution Revisited*. Oxford: Clarendon, 1997.

Hindle, Steve. *The State and Social Change in Early Modern England, c. 1550–1640*. Basingstoke: Macmillan, 2000.

Hoak, Dale. *The King's Council in the Reign of Edward VI*. Cambridge: Cambridge University Press, 1976.

Hodgen, Margaret T. *Early Anthropology in the Sixteenth and Seventeenth Centuries.* Philadelphia: University of Pennsylvania Press, 1964.

Huppert, George. *The Idea of Perfect History: Historical Erudition and Historical Philosophy in Renaissance France.* Urbana: University of Illinois Press, 1970.

Ianziti, Gary. *Humanistic Historiography under the Sforzas: Politics and Propaganda in Fifteenth-Century Milan.* Oxford: Clarendon, 1988.

———. "Challenging Chronicles: Leonardo Bruni's *History of the Florentine People.*" In *Chronicling History: Chroniclers and Historians in Medieval and Renaissance Italy*, ed. Sharon Dale, Alison Williams Lewin, and Duane J. Osheim, 249–72. University Park: Pennsylvania State University Press, 2007.

Ilardi, Vincent. "Fifteenth-Century Diplomatic Documents in Western European Archives and Libraries (1450–1494)." *Studies in the Renaissance* 9 (1962): 64–112.

Irwin, Margaret. *That Great Lucifer: A Portrait of Sir Walter Raleigh.* London: Chatto & Windus, 1960.

Jaeger, C. Stephen. *The Envy of Angels: Cathedral Schools and Social Ideas in Medieval Europe, 950–1200.* Philadelphia: University of Pennsylvania Press, 1994.

James, Mervyn. *English Politics and the Concept of Honour, 1485–1642.* Suppl. 3, *P&P* (1978).

Jardine, David, et al., eds. *The Lives and Criminal Trials of Celebrated Men.* Philadelphia, 1835.

Jardine, Lisa. "Encountering Ireland: Gabriel Harvey, Edmund Spenser and English Colonial Ventures." In *Representing Ireland: Literature and the Origins of Conflict, 1534–1660*, ed. Brendan Bradshaw, Andrew Hadfield, and Willy Maley, 60–75. Cambridge: Cambridge University Press, 1993.

Jardine, Lisa, and William Sherman. "Pragmatic Readers: Knowledge Transactions and Scholarly Services in Late Elizabethan England." In *Religion, Culture and Society in Early Modern Britain*, ed. Anthony John Fletcher and Peter Roberts, 102–24. Cambridge: Cambridge University Press, 1994.

Jardine, Nicholas. *The Birth of History and Philosophy of Science: Kepler's A Defence of Tycho against Ursus, with Essays on Its Provenance and Significance.* Cambridge: Cambridge University Press, 1984.

Jensen, Freyja Cox. "Reading Florus in Early Modern England." *Renaissance Studies* 23 (2009): 659–77.

Johannesson, Kurt. *The Renaissance of the Goths in Sixteenth-Century Sweden: Johannes and Olaus Magnus as Politicians and Historians.* Berkeley and Los Angeles: University of California Press, 1991.

Johns, Adrian. "Prudence and Pedantry in Early Modern Cosmology: The Trade of Al Ross." *History of Science* 35 (1997): 23–59.

———. *The Nature of the Book: Print and Knowledge in the Making.* Chicago: University of Chicago Press, 1998.

Johnson, Carina L. "Stone Gods and Counter-Reformation Knowledges." In *Making Knowledge in Early Modern Europe: Practices, Objects, and Texts, 1400–1800*, ed. Pamela H. Smith and Benjamin Schmidt, 233–48. Chicago: University of Chicago Press, 2007.

Johnson, Christine R. "Buying Stories: Ancient Tales, Renaissance Travelers, and the Market for the Marvelous." *JEMH* 11 (2007): 405–46.

———. *The German Discovery of the World: Renaissance Encounters with the Strange and Marvelous*. Charlottesville: University of Virginia Press, 2008.

Johnson, Dale A. "Serving Two Masters: John Knox, Scripture, and Prophecy." In *Religion and Superstition in Reformation Europe*, ed. Helen L. Parish and William G. Naphy, 133–53. Manchester: Manchester University Press, 2002.

Jones, Norman L. "Matthew Parker, John Bale, and the Magdeburg Centuriators." *SCJ* 12 (1981): 35–49.

Jotischky, Andrew. "Gerard of Nazareth, John Bale and the Origins of the Carmelite Order." *Journal of Ecclesiastical History* 46 (1995): 214–36.

———. *The Carmelites and Antiquity: Mendicants and Their Pasts in the Middle Ages*. Oxford: Oxford University Press, 2002.

Kagan, Richard L. "Clio and the Crown: Writing History in Hapsburg Spain." In *Spain, Europe, and the Atlantic World: Essays in Honour of John H. Elliot*, ed. Richard L. Kagan and Geoffrey Parker, 73–100. Cambridge: Cambridge University Press, 1995.

———. *Clio and the Crown: The Politics of History in Medieval and Early Modern Spain*. Baltimore: Johns Hopkins University Press, 2009.

Kahn, Victoria. "Reading Machiavelli: Innocent Gentillet's Discourse on Method." *Political Theory* 22 (1994): 539–60.

Kaoukji, Natalie. "Flying to Nowhere: Mathematical Magic and the Machine in the Library." Ph.D. diss., University of Cambridge, 2008.

Karrow, Robert W., Jr. *Mapmakers of the 16th Century and Their Maps: Bio-Bibliographies of the Cartographers of Abraham Ortelius, 1570*. Chicago: Speculum Orbis, for the Newberry Library, 1993.

Kassell, Lauren. *Medicine and Magic in Elizabethan London: Simon Forman: Astrologer, Alchemist, and Physician*. Oxford: Clarendon, 2005.

———. "'All Was This Land Full Fill'd of Faerie'; or, Magic and the Past in Early Modern England." *JHI* 67 (2006): 107–22.

Kelley, Donald. "Historia Integra: Francius Baudouin and His Conception of History." *JHI* 25 (1964): 35–57.

———. "Jean du Tillet, Archivist and Antiquary." *JMH* 38 (1966): 337–54.

———. *The Foundations of Modern Historical Scholarship: Language, Law and History in the French Renaissance*. New York: Columbia University Press, 1970.

———. "History as a Calling: The Case of La Popeliniere." In *Renaissance Studies in Honor of Hans Baron*, ed. Anthony Molho and John A. Tedeschi, 773–89. Firenze: G. C. Sansoni, 1971.

———. "History, English Law, and the Renaissance." *P&P* 65 (1974): 24–51.

———. "Johann Sleidan and the Origins of History as a Profession." *JMH* 52 (1980): 573–98.

———. *The Faces of History: Historical Inquiry from Herodotus to Herder*. New Haven, CT: Yale University Press, 1998.

Kelley, Donald R., and David Harris Sacks, eds. *The Historical Imagination in Early*

Modern England: History, Rhetoric, and Fiction, 1500–1800. Cambridge: Cambridge University Press, 1997.

Kendrick, T. D., *British Antiquity.* London: Methuen, 1950.

Ker, Neil R. "The Migration of Manuscripts from the English Medieval Libraries." *The Library,* 4th ser., 23 (1942): 1–11.

———. "Sir John Prise." *The Library,* 5th ser., 10 (1955): 1–24.

Kess, Alexandra. *Johann Sleidan and the Protestant Vision of History.* Aldershot: Ashgate, 2008.

Kewes, Paulina, ed. *The Uses of History in Early Modern England.* San Marino, CA: Huntington Library, 2006.

———. "Henry Savile's Tacitus and the Politics of Roman History in Late Elizabethan England." *HLQ* 74 (2011): 515–51.

Kingsley, Charles. *Sir Walter Raleigh and His Time, with Other Papers.* Boston: Ticknor & Fields, 1859.

Klempt, Adalbert. *Die Säkularisierung der universalhistorichen Auffassung: Zum Wandel des Geschichtsdenkens im 16. und 17. Jahrhundert.* Göttingen: Musterschmidt, 1960.

Kosto, Adam J., and Anders Winroth, eds. *Charters, Cartularies and Archives: The Preservation and Transmission of Documents in the Medieval West.* Toronto: Pontifical Institute of Mediaeval Studies, 2002.

Kunst, Christiane. "William Camden's *Britannia*: History and Historiography." In *Ancient History and the Antiquarian: Essays in Memory of Arnaldo Momigliano,* ed. M. H. Crawford and C. R. Ligota, 117–31. London: Warburg Institute, 1995.

Kupperman, Karen Ordahl, ed. *America in European Consciousness, 1493–1750.* Chapel Hill: University of North Carolina Press, for the Omohundro Institute of Early American History and Culture, 1995.

———. *The Jamestown Project.* Cambridge, MA: Belknap Press of Harvard University Press, 2007.

Kuriyama, Constance Brown. *Christopher Marlowe: A Renaissance Life.* Ithaca, NY: Cornell University Press, 2002.

Kusukawa, Sachiko. *The Transformation of Natural Philosophy: The Case of Philip Melanchthon.* Cambridge: Cambridge University Press, 1995.

Lacey, Robert. *Sir Walter Ralegh.* New York: Atheneum, 1973.

Lake, Peter. "Constitutional Consensus and Puritan Opposition in the 1620s: Thomas Scott and the Spanish Match." *HJ* 25 (1982): 805–25.

———. "Lancelot Andrewes, John Buckeridge, and Avant-Garde Conformity in the Court of James I." In *The Mental World of the Jacobean Court,* ed. Linda Levy Peck, 113–33. Cambridge: Cambridge University Press, 1991.

———. "The King (the Queen) and the Jesuit: James Stuart's *True Law of Free Monarchies* in Context/s." *TRHS,* 6th ser., 14 (2004): 243–60.

———. "'The Monarchical Republic of Elizabeth I' Revisited (by Its Victims) as a Conspiracy." In *Conspiracies and Conspiracy Theory in Early Modern Europe: From the Waldensians to the French Revolution,* ed. Barry Coward and Julia Swann, 87–111. Aldershot: Ashgate, 2004.

———. "'The Monarchical Republic of Queen Elizabeth I' (and the Fall of Archbishop

Grindal) Revisited." In *The Monarchical Republic of Early Modern England: Essays in Response to Patrick Collinson*, ed. John F. McDiarmid, 129–47. Aldershot: Ashgate, 2007.

———. "The Politics of 'Popularity' and the Public Sphere: The 'Monarchical Republic' of Elizabeth I Defends Itself." In *The Politics of the Public Sphere in Early Modern England*, ed. Peter Lake and Steven C. A. Pincus, 59–94. Manchester: Manchester University Press, 2007.

Lake, Peter, and Stephen C. A. Pincus, eds. *The Politics of the Public Sphere in Early Modern England*. Manchester: Manchester University Press, 2007.

Lake, Peter, and Michael C. Questier. "Puritans, Papists, and the 'Public Sphere' in Early Modern England." *JMH* 72 (2000): 587–627.

Lake, Peter, with Michael Questier. *The Anti-Christ's Lewd Hat: Protestants, Papists and Players in Post-Reformation England*. New Haven, CT: Yale University Press, 2002.

Larkum, Eleri. "Providence and Politics in Sir Walter Ralegh's *History of the World*." Ph.D. diss., University of Oxford, 1997.

Lawrence, David. *The Complete Soldier: Military Books and Military Culture in England, 1603–1645*. Leiden: Brill, 2009.

Lefranc, Pierre. "Un inédit document de Ralegh sur la conduite de la guerre." *Études anglaises* 8 (1955): 193–211.

———. *Sir Walter Raleigh, écrivain, l'oeuvre et l'idées*. Paris: Librarie Armand Colin; Quebec: Les presses de l'Université Laval, 1968.

Lestringant, Frank. *Mapping the Renaissance World: The Geographical Imagination in the Age of Discovery*. Translated by David Fausett. Cambridge: Polity, 1994.

Levine, Joseph. *Humanism and History: The Origins of Modern English Historiography*. Ithaca, NY: Cornell University Press, 1987.

———. "Latitudinarians, Neoplatonists, and the Ancient Wisdom." In *Philosophy, Science, and Religion in England, 1640–1700*, ed. Richard Kroll, Richard Ashcroft, and Perez Zagorin, 85–108. Cambridge: Cambridge University Press, 1992.

———. "Sir Walter Ralegh and the Ancient Wisdom." In *Court, Country and Culture: Essays on Early Modern British History in Honor of Perez Zagorin*, ed. Bonnelyn Young Kunze and Dwight D. Brautigam, 89–108. Rochester, NY: University of Rochester Press, 1992.

———. "Deists and Anglicans: The Ancient Wisdom and the Idea of Progress." In *The Margins of Orthodoxy: Heterodox Writing and Cultural Response, 1660–1750*, ed. Roger Lund, 219–39. Cambridge: Cambridge University Press, 1995.

Levy, F. J. *Tudor Historical Thought*. San Marino, CA: Huntington Library, 1967.

———. "Hayward, Daniel, and the Beginnings of Politic History in England." *HLQ* 50 (1987): 1–34.

Ligota, C. R. "Annius of Viterbo and Historical Method." *JWCI* 50 (1987): 44–56.

Loades, David, ed. *John Foxe and the English Reformation*. Aldershot: Scolar, 1997.

Lockhart, Rudolf A. Eliott. "Hugh of St. Victor and Twelfth-Century English Monastic Reading." In *Owners, Annotators and the Signs of Reading*, ed. Robin Myers, Michael Harris and Giles Mandelbrote, 1–18. New Castle, DE: Oak Knoll, 2005.

Lotz-Heumann, Ute. "'The Spirit of Prophecy Has Not Wholly Left the World': The

Stylisation of Archbishop James Ussher as Prophet." In *Religion and Superstition in Reformation Europe*, ed. Helen Parish and William Naphy, 119–32. Manchester: Manchester University Press, 2002.

Louthan, Howard. *The Quest for Compromise: Peacemakers in Counter-Reformation Vienna*. Cambridge: Cambridge University Press, 1997.

Luciani, Vincent. "Ralegh's 'Discourse of War' and Machiavelli's 'Discorsi.'" *Modern Philology* 46 (1948): 122–31.

Lyon, Gregory. "Baudouin, Flacius, and the Plan for the Magdeburg Centuries." *JHI* 64 (2003): 253–72.

MacCaffrey, Wallace T. *The Shaping of the Elizabethan Regime*. Princeton, NJ: Princeton University Press, 1968.

———. *Queen Elizabeth and the Making of Policy, 1572–1588*. Princeton, NJ: Princeton University Press, 1981.

———. *Elizabeth I: War and Politics*. Princeton, NJ: Princeton University Press, 1992.

MacCormack, Sabine. "Limits of Understanding: Perceptions of Greco-Roman and Amerindian Paganism in Early Modern Europe." In *America in European Consciousness, 1493–1750*, ed. Karen Ordahl Kupperman, 79–129. Chapel Hill: University of North Carolina Press, for the Omohundro Institute of Early American History and Culture, 1995.

———. *On the Wings of Time: Rome, the Incas, Spain, and Peru*. Princeton, NJ: Princeton University Press, 2007.

Malcolm, Noel. *Aspects of Hobbes*. Oxford: Clarendon, 2002.

———. "Thomas Harrison and His 'Ark of Studies': An Episode in the History of the Organization of Knowledge." *Seventeenth Century* 19 (2004): 196–232.

Mancall, Peter C., ed. *The Atlantic World and Virginia, 1550–1624*. Chapel Hill: University of North Carolina Press, for the Omohundro Institute of Early American History and Culture, 2007.

———. *Hakluyt's Promise: An Elizabethan's Obsession for an English America*. New Haven, CT: Yale University Press, 2007.

Mandelbrote, Scott. "The Religion of Thomas Harriot." In *Thomas Harriot: An Elizabethan Man of Science*, ed. Robert Fox, 246–79. Aldershot: Ashgate, 2000.

Mangani, Giorgio. *Il "mondo" di Abramo Ortelio: Misticismo, geografia e collezionismo nel Rinascimento dei Paesi Bassi*. Modena: Franco Cosimo Panini, 1998.

Manning, Roger B. *Swordsmen: The Martial Ethos in the Three Kingdoms*. New York: Oxford University Press, 2003.

Maragou, Helena. "The Potrait of Alexander the Great in Anne Bradstreet's 'The Third Monarchy.'" *Early American Literature* 23 (1988): 70–81.

Markley, Robert. "Newton, Corruption, and the Tradition of Universal History." In *Newton and Religion: Context, Nature, and Influence*, ed. James E. Force and Richard H. Popkin, 121–44. Dordrecht: Kluwer, 1999.

Markus, R. A. *Saeculum: History and Society in the Theology of Augustine*. Cambridge: Cambridge University Press, 1970.

Marshall, Alan. *Intelligence and Espionage in the Reign of Charles II*. Cambridge: Cambridge University Press, 1994.

———. "Joseph Williamson and the Conduct of Administration in Restoration England." *HR* 69 (1996): 18–41.

Martin, Julian. *Francis Bacon, the State and the Reform of Natural Philosophy.* Cambridge: Cambridge University Press, 1992.

Mattingly, Garrett. *Renaissance Diplomacy.* London: Cape, 1955.

May, Steven W. *Sir Walter Ralegh.* Boston: Twayne, 1989.

———. "How Ralegh Became a Courtier." *John Donne Journal* 27 (2008): 131–40.

Mayer, Thomas F. *Reginald Pole: Prince and Prophet.* Cambridge: Cambridge University Press, 2000.

Mayer, Thomas F., and D. R. Woolf, eds. *The Rhetorics of Life-Writing in Early Modern Europe: Forms of Biography from Cassandra Fedele to Louis XIV.* Ann Arbor: University of Michigan Press, 1995.

McCahill, Elizabeth. "Humanism in the Theater of Lies: Classical Scholarship in the Early Quattrocento Curia." Ph.D. diss., Princeton University, 2005.

McCrea, Adriana. *Constant Minds: Political Virtue and the Lipsian Paradigm in England, 1584–1650.* Toronto: University of Toronto Press, 1997.

McCuaig, William. *Carlo Sigonio: The Changing World of the Late Renaissance.* Princeton, NJ: Princeton University Press, 1989.

McCusker, Honor C. *John Bale: Dramatist and Antiquary.* Bryn Mawr, PA, 1942.

McDiarmid, John F., ed. *The Monarchical Republic of Early Modern England: Essays in Response to Patrick Collinson.* Aldershot: Ashgate, 2007.

McKisack, May. *Medieval History in the Tudor Age.* Oxford: Clarendon, 1971.

McKiterrick, Rosamond, ed. *The Uses of Literacy in Early Medieval Europe.* Cambridge: Cambridge University Press, 1990.

McLaren, A. N. "Prophecy and Providentialism in the Reign of Elizabeth I." In *Prophecy: The Power of Inspired Languages in History, 1300–2000,* ed. Bertrand Taithe and Tim Thornton, 1–30. Stroud: Sutton, 1997.

Mears, Natalie. "Counsel, Public Debate, and Queenship: John Stubbs's *The Discoverie of a Gaping Gulf,* 1579." *HJ* 44 (2001): 629–50.

———. *Queenship and Political Discourse in the Elizabethan Realms.* Cambridge: Cambridge University Press, 2005.

Meganck, Tine. "Erudite Eyes: Artists and Antiquarians in the Circle of Abraham Ortelius (1527–1598)." Ph.D. diss., Princeton University, 2003.

Melion, Walter. "Ad ductum itineris et dispositionem mansionum ostendendam: Meditation, Vocation, and Sacred History in Abraham Ortelius's Parergon." *Journal of the Walters Art Gallery* 57 (1999): 49–72.

Mellor, Ronald. "Tacitus, Academic Politics, and Regicide in the Reign of Charles I: The Tragedy of Dr. Isaac Dorislaus." *International Journal of the Classical Tradition* 11 (2004–5): 153–93.

Menn, Stephen. "The Intellectual Context." In *The Cambridge History of Seventeenth-Century Philosophy,* ed. Daniel Garber and Michael Ayers, 33–86. Cambridge: Cambridge University Press, 1998.

Meserve, Margaret. "From Samarkand to Scythia: Reinventions of Asia in Renaissance Geography and Political Thought." In *Pius II: El piu expeditivo pontifice: Selected*

Studies on Aeneas Silvius Piccolomini, ed. Z. R. W. M. von Martels and A. Vanderjagt, 13–40. Leiden: Brill, 2003.

———. *Empires of Islam in Renaissance Historical Thought*. Cambridge, MA: Harvard University Press, 2008.

Meyer, Heinrich. *The Age of the World: A Chapter in the History of Enlightenment*. Allentown, PA: Muhlenberg College, 1951.

Miller, Peter N. *Peiresc's Europe: Learning and Virtue in the Seventeenth Century*. New Haven, CT: Yale University Press, 2000.

———. "The 'Antiquarianization' of Biblical Scholarship and the London Polyglot Bible (1653–57)." *JHI* 62 (2001): 463–82.

———. "Nazis and Neo-Stoics: Otto Brunner and Gerhard Oestreich Before and After the Second World War." *P&P* 176 (2002): 144–86.

———, ed. *Momigliano and Antiquarianism: Foundations of the Modern Cultural Sciences*. Toronto: University of Toronto Press, 2007.

Milton, Anthony. *Catholic and Reformed: The Roman and Protestant Churches in English Protestant Thought, 1600–1640*. Cambridge: Cambridge University Press, 1995.

———. *Laudian and Royalist Polemic in Seventeenth-Century England: The Career and Writings of Peter Heylyn*. Manchester: Manchester University Press, 1997.

Mix, Erving R. *Marcus Atilius Regulus: Exemplum historicum*. The Hague: Mouton, 1970.

Momigliano, Arnaldo. "Ancient History and the Antiquarian." *JWCI* 13 (1950): 285–315.

———. *Sesto contributo alla storia degli studi classici e dei mondo antico*. Roma: Edizioni di storia e letteratura, 1980.

———. *Essays in Ancient and Modern Historiography*. Middletown, CT: Wesleyan University Press, 1987.

———. *The Classical Foundations of Modern Historiography*. Berkeley and Los Angeles: University of California Press, 1990.

Mommsen, Theodore. "St. Augustine and the Christian Idea of Progress." *JHI* 12 (1951): 361–74.

Morford, Mark. *Stoics and Neostoics: Rubens and the Circle of Lipsius*. Princeton, NJ: Princeton University Press, 1991.

Morrill, John. "William Dowsing: The Bureaucratic Puritan." In *Public Duty and Private Conscience in Seventeenth-Century England: Essays Presented to G. E. Aylmer*, ed. John Morrill, Paul Slack, and Daniel Woolf, 173–204. Oxford: Clarendon, 1993.

———. "William Dowsing and the Administration of Iconoclasm." In *The Journal of William Dowsing: Iconoclasm in East Anglia during the English Civil War*, ed. Trevor Cooper, 1–28. Woodbridge: Ecclesiological Society/Boydell, 2001.

Mosley, Adam. *Bearing the Heavens: Tycho Brahe and the Astronomical Community of the Late Sixteenth Century*. Cambridge: Cambridge University Press, 2007.

Moss, Ann. *Printed Commonplace-Books and the Structuring of Renaissance Thought*. Oxford: Oxford University Press, 1996.

———. "The Politica of Justus Lipsius and the Commonplace-Book." *JHI* 59 (1998): 421–36.

Mulsow, Martin. "Antiquarianism and Idolatry: The *Historia* of Religions in the Seventeenth Century." In *Historia: Empiricism and Erudition in Early Modern Europe,* ed. Gianna Pomata and Nancy Siraisi, 181–201. Cambridge: MIT Press, 2005.

Nadel, George H. "Philosophy of History Before Historicism." *History and Theory* 3 (1964): 291–315.

Neill, Donald A. "Ancestral Voices: The Influence of the Ancients on the Military Thought of the Seventeenth and Eighteenth Centuries." *Journal of Military History* 62 (1998): 487–520.

Nelles, Paul. "The Library as an Instrument of Discovery: Gabriel Naudé and the Uses of History." In *History and the Disciplines: The Reclassification of Knowledge in Early Modern Europe,* ed. Donald R. Kelley, 41–57. Rochester, NY: University of Rochester Press, 1997.

———. "The Renaissance Ancient Library Tradition and Christian Antiquity." In *Les humanistes et leur bibliothèque,* ed. Rudolf De Smet, 159–74. Brussels: Peeters, 2002.

———. "The Uses of Orthodoxy and Jacobean Erudition: Thomas James and the Bodleian Library." *History of Universities* 22 (2007): 21–70.

Nelson, Eric. *The Hebrew Republic: Jewish Sources and the Transformation of European Political Thought.* Cambridge, MA: Harvard University Press, 2010.

Niccoli, Ottavia. *Prophecy and People in Renaissance Italy.* Translated by Lydia G. Cochrane. Princeton, NJ: Princeton University Press, 1990.

Nicholl, Charles. *The Reckoning: The Murder of Christopher Marlowe.* London: J. Cape, 1992.

Nicholls, Mark. "Sir Walter Ralegh's Treason: A Prosecution Document." *EHR* 110 (1995): 902–24.

———. "Treason's Reward: The Punishment of Conspirators in the Bye Plot of 1603." *HJ* 38 (1995): 821–41.

———. "Two Winchester Trials: The Prosecution of Henry, Lord Cobham, and Thomas Lord Grey de Wilton, November 1603." *HR* 68 (1995): 26–48.

Nicholls, Mark, and Penry Williams. *Sir Walter Raleigh: In Life and Legend.* London: Continuum, 2011.

Noble, Thomas. "Literacy and the Papal Government in Late Antiquity and the Early Middle Ages." In *The Uses of Literacy in Early Medieval Europe,* ed. Rosamond McKiterrick, 82–108. Cambridge: Cambridge University Press, 1990.

Noonan, Thomas F. *The Road to Jerusalem: Pilgrimage and Travel in the Age of Discovery.* Philadelphia: University of Pennsylvania Press, 2007.

Nummedal, Tara E. *Alchemy and Authority in the Holy Roman Empire.* Chicago: University of Chicago Press, 2007.

Oakeshott, Walter. *The Queen and the Poet.* London: Faber & Faber, 1960.

———. "Sir Walter Ralegh's Library." *The Library,* 5th ser., 23 (1968): 285–327.

Oestreich, Gerhard. *Neostoicism and the Early Modern State.* Translated by David McClintock. Cambridge: Cambridge University Press, 1982.

Ogborn, Miles. *Indian Ink: Script and Print in the Making of the English East India Company.* Chicago: University of Chicago Press, 2007.

Ogilvie, Brian. "The Many Books of Nature: Renaissance Naturalists and Information Overload." *JHI* 64 (2003): 29–40.

——. *The Science of Describing: Natural History in Renaissance Europe*. Chicago: University of Chicago Press, 2006.

Olsen, Palle J. "Was John Foxe a Millenarian?" *Journal of Ecclesiastical History* 45 (1994): 600–624.

Olson, Oliver K. *Matthias Flacius and the Survival of Luther's Reform*. Wiesbaden: Harrasowitz, 2002.

Paret, Peter, and Felix Gilbert, eds. *Makers of Modern Strategy: From Machiavelli to the Nuclear Age*. Princeton, NJ: Princeton University Press, 1986.

Parker, Geoffrey. *The Army of Flanders and the Spanish Road, 1567–1659: The Logistics of Spanish Victory and Defeat in the Low Countries' Wars*. Cambridge: Cambridge University Press, 1972.

——. *The Military Revolution: Military Innovation and the Rise of the West, 1500–1800*. Cambridge: Cambridge University Press, 1988.

——, ed. *The Cambridge History of Warfare*. New York: Cambridge University Press, 2005.

——. "The Limits to Revolutions in Military Affairs: Maurice of Nassau, the Battle of Nieuwpoort (1600) and the Legacy." *Journal of Military History* 71 (2007): 331–72.

Parry, G. J. R. *A Protestant Vision: William Harrison and the Reformation of Elizabethan England*. Cambridge: Cambridge University Press, 1987.

——. "John Dee and the Elizabethan British Empire in Its European Context." *HJ* 49 (2006): 643–75.

Parry, Graham. *The Golden Age Restor'd: The Culture of the Stuart Court, 1603–42*. Manchester: Manchester University Press, 1981.

——. *The Trophies of Time: English Antiquarians in the Seventeenth Century*. Oxford: Oxford University Press, 1995.

Patrides, C. A. "Renaissance Estimates of the Year of Creation." *HLQ* 26 (1963): 315–22.

——, ed. *The History of the World*. London: Macmillan, 1971.

Patterson, W. B. *King James VI and I and the Reunion of Christendom*. Cambridge: Cambridge University Press, 1997.

Peck, Linda Levy. *Northampton, Patronage and Policy at the Court of James I*. London: Allen & Unwin, 1982.

——, ed. *The Mental World of the Jacobean Court*. Cambridge: Cambridge University Press, 1991.

Peltonen, Markku. *Classical Humanism and Republicanism in English Political Thought, 1570–1640*. Cambridge: Cambridge University Press, 1995.

Piggott, Stuart. *Ancient Britains and the Antiquarian Imagination*. London: Thames & Hudson, 1989.

Pocock, J. G. A. *The Ancient Constitution and the Feudal Law: A Study of English Historical Thought in the Seventeenth Century*. Cambridge: University Press, 1957.

——. "England." In *National Consciousness, History and Political Culture in Early-Modern Europe*, ed. Orest Ranum, 98–117. Baltimore: Johns Hopkins University Press, 1975.

——. *The Machiavellian Moment: Florentine Political Thought and the Atlantic Republican Tradition*. Princeton, NJ: Princeton University Press, 1975.

Pomata, Gianna, and Nancy Siraisi, eds. *Historia: Empiricism and Erudition in Early Modern Europe.* Cambridge, MA: MIT Press, 2005.

Popkin, Richard H. *Isaac La Peyrère (1596–1676): His Life, Work and Influence.* Leiden: Brill, 1987.

Popper, Nicholas. "The English Polydaedali: How Gabriel Harvey Read Late Tudor London." *JHI* 66 (2005): 351–81.

———. "'Abraham, Planter of Mathematics': Histories of Mathematics and Astrology in Early Modern Europe." *JHI* 67 (2006): 87–106.

———. "From Abbey to Archive: Managing Texts and Records in Early Modern England." *Archival Science* 10 (2010): 249–66.

———. "Ocean of Lies: The Problem of Historical Evidence in the Sixteenth Century." *HLQ* 74 (2011): 375–400.

Portuondo, Maria. *Secret Science: Spanish Cartography and the New World.* Chicago: University of Chicago Press, 2009.

Prothero, G. W., ed. *Select Statutes and Other Constitutional Documents Illustrative of the Reigns of Elizabeth and James I.* Oxford: Clarendon, 1913.

Pumfrey, Stephen. "The History of Science and the Renaissance Science of History." In *Science, Culture, and Popular Belief in Renaissance Europe*, ed. Stephen Pumfrey, Paolo L. Rossi, and Maurice Slawinski, 48–70. Manchester: Manchester University Press, 1991.

Pumfrey, Stephen, and Frances Dawbarn. "Science and Patronage in England, 1570–1625: A Preliminary Study." *History of Science* 42 (2004): 137–88.

Quantin, Jean-Louis. *The Church of England and Christian Antiquity: The Construction of a Confessional Identity in the 17th Century.* Oxford: Oxford University Press, 2009.

Questier, Michael. *Catholicism and Community in Early Modern England: Politics, Aristocratic Patronage and Religion, c. 1550–1640.* Cambridge: Cambridge University Press, 2006.

Quinn, David Beers. *Raleigh and the British Empire.* New York: Macmillan, 1949.

Racin, John, Jr. "The Early Editions of Sir Walter Ralegh's *History of the World*." *Studies in Bibliography* 17 (1964): 199–209.

———. *Sir Walter Raleigh as Historian.* Salzburg: Universität Salzburg, 1974.

Ranum, Orest. *Artisans of Glory: Writers and Historical Thought in Seventeenth-Century France.* Chapel Hill: University of North Carolina Press, 1980.

Rapple, Rory. *Martial Power and Elizabethan Political Culture: Military Men in England and Ireland, 1558–1594.* Cambridge: Cambridge University Press, 2009.

Rattansi, P. M. "Alchemy and Natural Magic in Raleigh's *History of the World*." *Ambix* 13 (1965–66): 122–38.

Raymond, Joad, ed. *News, Newspapers and Society in Early Modern Britain.* London: F. Cass, 1999.

Read, Conyers. *Mr. Secretary Walsingham and the Policy of Queen Elizabeth.* 3 vols. Oxford: Clarendon, 1925.

Roberts, Julian. "Extending the Frontiers: Scholar Collectors." In *The Cambridge History of Libraries in Britain and Ireland*, vol. 1, *To 1640*, ed. Elizabeth Leedham-Green and Teresa Webber, 292–321. Cambridge: Cambridge University Press, 2006.

Robertson, J. C. "Reckoning with London: Interpreting the *Bills of Mortality* before John Graunt." *Urban History* 23 (1996): 325–50.

Robinson, Benedict Scott. "'Darke Speeche': Matthew Parker and the Reforming of History." *SCJ* 29 (1998): 1061–83.

Rodgers, Clifford J., ed. *The Military Revolution Debate: Readings on the Military Transformation of Early Modern Europe*. Boulder, CO: Westview, 1995.

Romm, James. "Biblical History and the Americas: The Legend of Solomon's Ophir, 1492–1591." In *The Jews and the Expansion of Europe to the West, 1450–1800*, ed. Paolo Bernardini and Norman Fiering, 27–46. New York: Bergahn, 2001.

Rosenberg, Daniel, and Anthony Grafton. *Cartographies of Time: A History of the Timeline*. New York: Princeton Architectural Press, 2010.

Rothenberg, Gunther. "Aventinus and the Defense of the Empire against the Turks." *Studies in the Renaissance* 10 (1963): 60–67.

Rowland, Ingrid. *The Scarith of Scornello: A Tale of Renaissance Forgery*. Chicago: University of Chicago Press, 2004.

Rowse, A. L. *Ralegh and the Throckmortons*. London: Macmillan, 1962.

Rubiés, Joan-Pau. "Hugo Grotius's Dissertation on the Origin of the American Peoples and the Use of Comparative Methods." *JHI* 52 (1991): 221–44.

———. "New World and Renaissance Ethnology." *History and Anthropology* 6 (1993): 157–97.

———. "Instructions for Travellers: Teaching the Eye to See." *History and Anthropology* 9 (1996): 139–90.

———. "Travel Writing as a Genre: Facts, Fictions and the Invention of a Scientific Discourse in Early Modern Europe." *Journeys: The International Journal of Travel and Travel Writing* 1 (2000): 5–35.

———. "Travel Writing and Humanistic Culture: A Blunted Impact?" *JEMH* 10 (2006): 131–68.

Rutkin, H. Darrel. "Astrology, Natural Philosophy and the History of Science, c. 1250–1700: Studies toward an Interpretation of Giovanni Pico della Mirandola's *Disputationes adversus astrologiam divinatricem*." Ph.D. diss., Indiana University, 2002.

Sacks, David Harris. "Richard Hakluyt's Navigations in Time: History, Epic, and Empire." *Modern Language Quarterly* 67 (2006): 31–62.

———. "Discourses of Western Planting: Richard Hakluyt and the Making of the Atlantic World." In *The Atlantic World and Virginia, 1550–1624*, ed. Peter C. Mancall, 410–53. Chapel Hill: University of North Carolina Press, for the Omohundro Institute of Early American History and Culture, 2007.

Salas, Charles G. "Ralegh and the Punic Wars." *JHI* 57 (1996): 195–215.

Salmon, J. H. M. *Renaissance and Revolt: Essays in the Intellectual and Social History of Early Modern France*. Cambridge: Cambridge University Press, 1987.

———. "Seneca and Tacitus in Jacobean England." In *The Mental World of the Jacobean Court*, ed. Linda Levy Peck, 169–88. Cambridge: Cambridge University Press, 1991.

———. "Precept, Example, and Truth: Degory Wheare and the *Ars historica*." In *The Historical Imagination in Early Modern Britain: History, Rhetoric, and Fiction, 1500–1850*, ed. Donald R. Kelley and David Harris Sacks, 11–36. Cambridge: Cambridge University Press, 1997.

Scafi, Alessandro. "Mapping Eden: Cartographies of the Earthly Paradise." In *Mappings*, ed. Denis Cosgrove, 50–70. London: Reaktion, 1999.

———. *Mapping Paradise: A History of Heaven on Earth*. Chicago: University of Chicago Press, 2006.

Schaffer, Simon. "The Asiatic Enlightenments of British Astronomy." In *The Brokered World: Go-Betweens and Global Intelligence, 1770–1820*, ed. Simon Schaffer, Lissa Roberts, Kapil Raj, and James Delbourgo, 151–91. Sagamore Beach, MA: Science History, 2009.

Schiffman, Zachary Sayre. "Renaissance Historicism Reconsidered." *History and Theory* 24 (1985): 170–82.

Schmidt, Benjamin. "Space, Time, Travel: Hugo de Groot [Grotius], Johannes de Laet, and the 'Advancement' of Geographic Learning." *Lias: The Journal of Early Modern History of Ideas* 25 (1998): 177–99.

———. "Reading Ralegh's America: Texts, Books, and Readers in the Early Modern Atlantic World." In *The Atlantic World and Virginia, 1550–1624*, ed. Peter C. Mancall, 454–88. Chapel Hill: University of North Carolina Press, for the Omohundro Institute of Early American History and Culture, 2007.

Schmidt-Biggeman, Wilhelm. *Topica Universalis: Eine Modellgeschichte humanistischer und barocker Wissenschaft*. Hamburg: Meiner, 1983.

Schmitt, Charles B. "Perennial Philosophy: From Agostino Steuco to Leibniz." *JHI* 27 (1966): 505–32.

Schnapper, Antoine. "Persistance des géants." *Annales ESC* 41 (1986): 177–200.

———. *Le géant, la licorne, la tulipe: Collections et collectionneurs dans la France du XVIIe siècle*. 2 vols. Paris: Flammarion, 1988–94.

Schochet, Gordon. *The Authoritarian Family and Political Attitudes in 17th-Century England: Patriarchialism in Political Thought*. New Brunswick, NJ: Transaction, 1988.

Schwartz, Stuart B. *Implicit Understanding: Observing, Reporting, and Reflecting on the Encounters between Europeans and Other Peoples in the Early Modern Era*. Cambridge: Cambridge University Press, 1994.

Scott-Warren, Jason. "Reconstructing Manuscript Networks: The Textual Transactions of Sir Stephen Powle." In *Communities in Early Modern England: Networks, Place, Rhetoric*, ed. Alexandra Shepard and Phil Withington, 18–37. Manchester: Manchester University Press, 2000.

Selwyn, Pamela. "'Such Speciall Bookes of Mr Somersettes as Were Sould to Mr Secretary': The Fate of Robert Glover's Collections." In *Books and Collectors, 1200–1700: Essays Presented to Andrew Watson*, ed. James P. Carley and Colin G. C. Tite, 389–402. London: BL, 1996.

———. "Heralds' Libraries." In *The Cambridge History of Libraries in Britain and Ireland*, vol. 1, *To 1640*, ed. Elizabeth Leedham-Green and Teresa Webber, 472–88. Cambridge: Cambridge University Press, 2006.

Shagan, Ethan. "The Two Republics: Conflicting Views of Participatory Local Government in Early Tudor England." In *The Monarchical Republic of Early Modern England: Essays in Response to Patrick Collinson*, ed. John F. McDiarmid, 19–36. Aldershot: Ashgate, 2007.

Shalev, Zur. "Sacred Geography, Antiquarianism, and Visual Erudition: Benito Arias Montano and the Maps of the Antwerp Polyglot Bible." *Imago Mundi* 55 (2003): 56–80.

———. "Geographia Sacra: Cartography, Religion, and Scholarship in the Sixteenth and Seventeenth Centuries." Ph.D. diss., Princeton University, 2004.

Shapiro, Barbara, and Robert G. Frank Jr. *English Scientific Virtuosi in the 16th and 17th Centuries*. Los Angeles: William Andrews Clark Memorial Library, University of California, Los Angeles, 1979.

Sharpe, Kevin. *Sir Robert Cotton, 1586–1631: History and Politics in Early Modern England*. Oxford: Oxford University Press, 1979.

———. "The Foundation of the Chairs of History at Oxford and Cambridge." *History of Universities* 2 (1982): 127–52.

———. *Reading Revolutions: The Politics of Reading in Early Modern England*. New Haven, CT: Yale University Press, 2000.

———. "Reading Revelations: Prophecy, Hermeneutics and Politics in Early Modern Britain." In *Reading, Society and Politics in Early Modern England*, ed. Kevin M. Sharpe and Steven N. Zwicker, 122–63. Cambridge: Cambridge University Press, 2003.

Sharpe, Kevin M., and Peter Lake, eds. *Culture and Politics in Early Stuart England*. London: Macmillan, 1994.

Sheehan, Jonathan. "From Philology to Fossils: The Biblical Encyclopedia in Early Modern Europe." *JHI* 64 (2003): 41–60.

———. *The Enlightenment Bible: Translation, Scholarship, Culture*. Princeton, NJ: Princeton University Press, 2005.

———. "Sacred and Profane: Idolatry, Antiquarianism and the Polemics of Distinction in the Seventeenth Century." *P&P* 192 (2006): 35–66.

———. "Temple and Tabernacle: The Place of Religion in Early Modern England." In *Making Knowledge in Early Modern Europe: Practices, Objects, and Texts, 1400–1800*, ed. Pamela H. Smith and Benjamin Schmidt, 248–72. Chicago: University of Chicago Press, 2007.

Sherman, William H. *John Dee: The Politics of Reading and Writing in the Elizabethan Renaissance*. Amherst: University of Massachusetts Press, 1995.

———. "What Did Renaissance Readers Write in Their Books?" In *Books and Readers in Early Modern England: Material Studies*, ed. Jennifer Andersen and Elizabeth Sauer, 119–37. Philadelphia: University of Pennsylvania Press, 2002.

———. "John Dee's Columbian Encounter." *International Archives of the History of Ideas* 193 (2006): 131–42.

———. *Used Books: Marking Readers in Renaissance England*. Philadelphia: University of Pennsylvania Press, 2008.

Shields, David S. "The Genius of Ancient Britain." In *The Atlantic World and Virginia, 1550–1624*, ed. Peter C. Mancall, 489–509. Chapel Hill: University of North Carolina Press, for the Omohundro Institute of Early American History and Culture, 2007.

Shirley, J. W. "The Scientific Experiments of Sir Walter Ralegh, the Wizard Earl, and the Three Magi in the Tower, 1603–17." *Ambix* 1–2 (1949): 52–66.

———. "Sir Walter Raleigh's Guiana Finances." *HLQ* 13 (1949): 55–69.

———, ed. *Thomas Harriot: Renaissance Scientist*. Oxford: Clarendon, 1974.

Shuger, Debora K. *The Renaissance Bible: Scholarship, Sacrifice, and Subjectivity*. Berkeley and Los Angeles: University of California Press, 1994.

Simonetta, Marcello. *Rinascimento segreto: Il mondo del segretario da Petrarca a Machiavelli*. Milan: F. Angeli, 2004.

Siraisi, Nancy. "Girolamo Cardano and the Art of the Medical Narrative." *JHI* 52 (1991): 581–602.

———. "Anatomizing the Past: Physicians and History in Renaissance Culture." *RQ* 53 (2000): 1–30.

———. "*Historiae*, Natural History, Roman Antiquity, and Some Roman Physicians." In *Historia: Empiricism and Erudition in Early Modern Europe*, ed. Gianna Pomata and Nancy G. Siraisi, 325–54. Cambridge, MA: MIT Press, 2005.

———. *History, Medicine, and the Traditions of Renaissance Learning*. Ann Arbor: University of Michigan Press, 2007.

Skeat, T. C. "Two 'Lost' Works by John Leland." *EHR* 65 (1950): 505–8.

Skelton, Raleigh Ashlin. "Ralegh as Geographer." *Virginia Magazine of History and Biography* 71 (1963): 131–49.

Skinner, Quentin. *The Foundations of Modern Political Thought*. 2 vols. Cambridge: Cambridge University Press, 1978.

———. *Reason and Rhetoric in the Philosophy of Hobbes*. Cambridge: Cambridge University Press, 1996.

Slack, Paul. "Government and Information in Seventeenth-Century England." *P&P* 184 (2004): 33–68.

Smalley, Beryl. *English Friars and Antiquity in the Early Fourteenth Century*. New York: Barnes & Noble, 1961.

Smith, Alan G. R. "The Secretariats of the Cecils, c. 1580–1612." *EHR* 83 (1968): 481–504.

Smith, Catherine Delano, and Elizabeth Morley Ingram. *Maps in Bibles, 1500–1600: An Illustrated Catalogue*. Genève: Droz, 1991.

Smuts, R. Malcolm. *Court Culture and the Origins of a Royalist Tradition in Early Stuart England*. Philadelphia: University of Pennsylvania Press, 1987.

———. "Court-Centered Politics and the Uses of Roman Historians, c. 1590–1630." In *Culture and Politics in Early Stuart England*, ed. Kevin M. Sharpe and Peter Lake, 21–43. London: Macmillan, 1994.

Smyth, Adam. *Autobiography in Early Modern England*. Cambridge: Cambridge University Press, 2010.

Sokol, Barrett J. "Thomas Harriot—Sir Walter Ralegh's Tutor—on Population." *Annals of Science* 31 (1974): 205–12.

Soll, Jacob. "Healing the Body Politic: French Royal Doctors, History and the Birth of a Nation, 1560–1634." *RQ* 55 (2002): 1259–86.

———. *Publishing the Prince: History, Reading, and the Birth of Political Criticism*. Ann Arbor: University of Michigan Press, 2005.

———. "How to Manage an Information State: Jean-Baptiste Colbert's Letters to His Son." *Archival Science* 7 (2007): 331–42.

———. *The Information Master: Jean-Baptiste Colbert's Secret State Intelligence System*. Ann Arbor: University of Michigan Press, 2009.

Solomon, Julie Robin. *Objectivity in the Making: Francis Bacon and the Politics of Inquiry*. Baltimore: Johns Hopkins University Press, 1998.

Somerville, Johann P. "James I and the Divine Right of Kings: English Politics and Continental Theory." In *The Mental World of the Jacobean Court*, ed. Linda Levy Peck, 55–70. Cambridge: Cambridge University Press, 1991.

Southern, R. W. "Aspects of the European Tradition of Historical Writing: 3, History as Prophecy." *TRHS*, 5th ser., 22 (1972): 159–80.

Stagl, Justin. *Apodemiken: Eine räsonnierte Bibliographie der reisetheoretischen Literatur des 16., 17. und 18. Jahrhunderts*. Paderborn: F. Schöningh, 1983.

———. "The Methodising of Travel in the 16th Century: A Tale of Three Cities." *History and Anthropology* 4 (1990): 303–38.

———. *A History of Curiosity: The Theory of Travel, 1550–1800*. Chur: Harwood Academic, 1995.

Stebbing, William. *Sir Walter Ralegh, a Biography*. Oxford: Clarendon, 1891.

Stenhouse, William. "Thomas Dempster, Royal Historian to James I, and Classical and Historical Scholarship in Early Stuart England." *SCJ* 35 (2004): 397–412.

———. *Reading Inscriptions and Writing Ancient History: Historical Scholarship in the Late Renaissance*. London: Institute of Classical Studies, University of London School of Advanced Study, 2005.

Stephens, Walter. "Berosus Chaldaeus: Counterfeit and Fictive Editors of the Early Sixteenth Century." Ph.D. diss., Cornell University, 1979.

———. "The Etruscans and Ancient Theology of Annius of Viterbo." In *Umanesimo a Roma nel Quattrocento*, ed. Paolo Brezzi and Maristella de Panizza Lorch, 309–22. Roma: Istituto di studi romani, 1984.

———. *Giants in Those Days: Folklore, Ancient History, and Nationalism*. Lincoln: University of Nebraska Press, 1989.

———. "When Pope Noah Ruled the Etruscans: Annius of Viterbo and His Forged *Antiquitates*." *MLN* 119, suppl. (2004): S201–S223.

Stern, Virginia. *Sir Stephen Powle of Court and Country: Memorabilia of a Government Agent for Queen Elizabeth I, Chancery Official and English Country Gentleman*. Selinsgrove, PA: Susquehanna University Press, 1992.

Stewart, Alan. *Philip Sidney: A Double Life*. London: Chatto & Windus, 2000.

Storrs, Christopher, and H. M. Scott. "The Military Revolution and the European Nobility, c. 1600–1800." *War in History* 3 (1996): 1–41.

Strathmann, Ernest A. *Sir Walter Ralegh: A Study in Elizabethan Skepticism*. New York: Cambridge University Press, 1959.

———. "Ralegh on the Problems of Chronology." *HLQ* 11 (1948): 129–48.

Strauss, Gerald. *Sixteenth Century Germany: Its Topography and Topographers*. Madison: University of Wisconsin Press, 1959.

Summit, Jennifer. "Leland's *Itinerary* and the Remains of the Medieval Past." In *Reading the Medieval in Early Modern England*, ed. Gordan McMullan and David Matthews, 159–78. Cambridge: Cambridge University Press, 2007.

———. *Memory's Library: Medieval Books in Early Modern England*. Chicago: University of Chicago Press, 2008.

Swann, Marjorie. *Curiosities and Texts: The Culture of Collecting in Early Modern England*. Philadelphia: University of Pennsylvania Press, 2001.

Tanner, Marie. *The Last Descendant of Aeneas: The Hapsburgs and the Mythic Image of the Emperor*. New Haven, CT: Yale University Press, 1993.

Tate, Robert Brian. *Ensayos sobre la historiografía peninsular del siglo XV*. Madrid: Gredos, 1970.

Taviner, Mark. "Robert Beale and the Elizabethan Polity." Ph.D. diss., University of St. Andrews, 2000.

Tennenhouse, Leonard. "Sir Walter Raleigh and the Literature of Clientage." In *Patronage in the Renaissance*, ed. Guy Fitch Lytle and Stephen Orgel, 235–58. Princeton, NJ: Princeton University Press, 1981.

Terrill, R. J. "Humanism and Rhetoric in Legal Education: The Contribution of Sir John Dodderidge (1555–1628)." *Journal of Legal History* 2 (1981): 30–44.

Thomas, Keith. *The Perception of the Past in Early Modern England*. Creighton Trust Lecture, 1983. London: University of London, 1984.

Thompson, Edward. *Sir Walter Ralegh: Last of the Elizabethans*. New Haven, CT: Yale University Press, 1936.

Thomson, Erik. "Commerce, Law, and Erudite Culture: The Mechanics of Théodore Godefroy's Service to Cardinal Richelieu." *JHI* 68 (2007): 407–27.

Thoreau, Henry David. *Sir Walter Raleigh* (1843). New York: Gordon, 1976.

Tinguely, Frédéric. *L'écriture du Levant à la Renaissance: Enquête sur les voyageurs français dans l'empire de Soliman le Magnifique*. Geneva: Droz, 2000.

Tite, Colin. *The Manuscript Library of Sir Robert Cotton*. London: BL, 1994.

———. *The Early Records of Sir Robert Cotton's Library: Formation, Cataloguing, Use*. London: BL, 2003.

Todd, Margo. *Christian Humanism and the Puritan Social Order*. Cambridge: Cambridge University Press, 1987.

Toomer, Gerald. *John Selden: A Life in Scholarship*. 2 vols. Oxford: Oxford University Press, 2009.

Trautmann, Thomas R. *Aryans and British India*. Berkeley and Los Angeles: University of California Press, 1997.

Trevelyan, Raleigh. *Sir Walter Raleigh*. New York: Henry Holt, 2002.

Trevor-Roper, Hugh. *George Buchanan and the Ancient Scottish Constitution. EHR* suppl. 3. London: Longmans Green, 1966.

Trim, David J. B., ed. *The Chivalric Ethos and the Development of Military Professionalism*. Leiden: Brill, 2003.

Tuck, Richard. *Philosophy and Government, 1572–1651*. Cambridge: Cambridge University Press, 1993.

Tytler, Patrick Fraser. *Life of Sir Walter Raleigh, Founded on Authentic and Original Documents*. London: T. Nelson, 1853.

Vanden Broecke, Steven. *The Limits of Influence: Pico, Louvain, and the Crisis of Renaissance Astrology*. Leiden: Brill, 2003.

Van Norden, Linda. "The Elizabethan College of Antiquaries." Ph.D. diss., University of California, Los Angeles, 1949.

———. "Sir Henry Spelman on the Chronology of the Elizabethan College of Antiquaries." *HLQ* 13 (1950): 131–50.

Vaughan, Alden T. "Sir Walter Ralegh's Indian Interpreters, 1584–1618." *William and Mary Quarterly* 59 (2002): 341–76.

Vaughan, Jacqueline. "Secretaries, Statesmen, and Spies: The Clerks of the Elizabethan Privy Council." D.Phil. diss., University of St. Andrews, 2002.

Vine, Angus. *In Defiance of Time: Antiquarian Writing in Early Modern England.* Oxford: Oxford University Press, 2010.

Walker, D. P. *Spiritual and Demonic Magic from Ficino to Campanella.* London: Warburg Institute, 1958.

———. *The Ancient Theology: Studies in Christian Platonism from the Fifteenth to the Eighteenth Century.* London: Duckworth, 1972.

Wallace, Willard M. *Sir Walter Raleigh.* Princeton, NJ: Princeton University Press, 1959.

Walsham, Alexandra. *Church Papists: Catholicism, Conformity and Confessional Polemics in Early Modern England.* Woodbridge: Boydell, 1993.

———. *Providence in Early Modern England.* Oxford: Oxford University Press, 1999.

Walzer, Michael. *The Revolution of the Saints: A Study in the Origins of Radical Politics.* New York: Atheneum, 1968.

Ward, Paul L. "William Lambarde's Collections on Chancery." *Harvard Library Bulletin* 7 (1953): 271–98.

Warkentin, Germaine. "Robert Sidney and His Books." *Sidney Journal* 25 (2007): 31–42.

Warneke, Sara. *Images of the Educational Traveller in Early Modern England.* Leiden: Brill, 1995.

Watson, Andrew. "The Manuscript Collection of Walter Cope (d. 1614)." *Bodleian Library Record* 12 (1987): 262–97.

Webb, Henry J. *Elizabethan Military Science: The Books and the Practice.* Madison: University of Wisconsin Press, 1965.

Webster, Charles. *The Great Instauration: Science, Medicine, and Reform, 1626–1660.* London: Duckworth, 1975.

———. *From Paracelsus to Newton: Natural Magic in the Making of Modern Science.* Cambridge: Cambridge University Press, 1980.

Whitehead, Charles. *The Life and Times of Sir Walter Ralegh: With Copious Extracts from His* History of the World. London: N. Cooke, 1854.

Williams, Arnold. *The Common Expositor: An Account of the Commentaries on Genesis, 1527–1633.* Chapel Hill: University of North Carolina Press, 1948.

Williams, Gwyn A. *Madoc: The Making of a Myth.* London: Eyre Methuen, 1979.

Williamson, Arthur H. *Scottish National Consciousness in the Age of James VI: The Apocalypse, the Union and the Shaping of Scotland's Public Culture.* Edinburgh: John Donald, 1979.

———. "Britain and the Beast: The Apocalypse and the Seventeenth-Century Debate about the Creation of the British State." In *Millenarianism and Modernism in Early Modern European Culture,* vol. 3, *The Millenarian Turn: Millenarian Con-*

texts of Science, Politics, and Everday Anglo-American Life in the Seventeenth and Eighteenth Centuries, ed. James E. Force and Richard H. Popkin, 15–28. International Archives of the History of Ideas, 175. Dordrecht: Kluwer Academic, 2001.

———. "An Empire to End Empire: The Dynamic of Early Modern British Expansion." *HLQ* 68 (2005): 227–56. Reprinted in *The Uses of History in Early Modern England*, ed. Paulina Kewes (San Marino, CA: Huntington Library, 2006), 223–52.

Williamson, J. W. *The Myth of the Conqueror: Prince Henry Stuart, a Study of 17th Century Personation*. New York: AMS, 1978.

Wilson, Jenny. *Ralegh's History of the World: Its Purpose and Political Significance*. Durham, NC: Thomas Harriot Seminar, 1999.

Witschi-Bernz, Astrid. "Bibliography of Works in the Philosophy of History, 1500–1800." *History and Theory* 12 (1972): 3–50.

———. "Main Trends in Historical-Method Literature: Sixteenth to Eighteenth Centuries." *History and Theory* 12 (1972): 51–90.

Womersley, David. "Sir Henry Savile's Translation of Tacitus and the Political Interpretation of Elizabethan Texts." *Review of English Studies* 42 (1991): 313–42.

———. "Against the Teleology of Technique." *HLQ* 68 (2005): 95–108. Reprinted in *The Uses of History in Early Modern England*, ed. Paulina Kewes (San Marino, CA: Huntington Library, 2006), 91–104.

Woolf, D. R. *The Idea of History in Early Stuart England: Erudition, Ideology, and the "Light of Truth" from the Accession of James I to the Civil War*. Toronto: University of Toronto Press, 1990.

———. "The Power of the Past: History, Ritual and Political Authority in Tudor England." In *Political Thought and the Tudor Commonwealth: Deep Structure, Discourse and Disguise*, ed. Paul A. Fideler and T. F. Mayer, 19–49. London: Routledge, 1992.

———. *Reading History in Early Modern England*. Cambridge: Cambridge University Press, 2000.

———. "News, History, and the Construction of the Present in Early Modern England." In *The Politics of Information in Early Modern Europe*, ed. Brendan Dooley and Sabrina A. Baron, 80–118. London: Routledge, 2001.

———. *The Social Circulation of the Past: English Historical Culture, 1500–1730*. Oxford: Oxford University Press, 2003.

———. "From Hystories to the Historical: Five Transitions in Thinking about the Past, 1500–1700." *HLQ* 68 (2005): 33–70. Reprinted in *The Uses of History in Early Modern England*, ed. Paulina Kewes (San Marino: Huntington Library, 2006), 31–68.

Woolfson, Jonathan, ed. *Reassessing Tudor Humanism*. Basingstoke: Palgrave Macmillan, 2002.

Worden, Blair. "Ben Jonson among the Historians." In *Culture and Politics in Early Stuart England*, ed. Kevin Sharpe and Peter Lake, 67–89. London: Macmillan, 1994.

Wormald, Jenny. "James VI and I, *Basilikon Doron* and *The Trew Law of Free Monarchies*: The Scottish Context and the English Translation." In *The Mental World of the Jacobean Court*, ed. Linda Levy Peck, 35–54. Cambridge: Cambridge University Press, 1991.

Woudhuysen, H. R. *Sir Philip Sidney and the Circulation of Manuscripts, 1558–1640.* New York: Clarendon, 1996.

Wunder, Amanda. "Western Travelers, Eastern Antiquities, and the Image of the Turk in Early Modern Europe." *JEMH* 7 (2003): 89–119.

Yates, Frances. *Giordano Bruno and the Hermetic Tradition.* London: Routledge & Kegan Paul, 1964.

Youings, Joyce A. *Ralegh's Country: The Southwest of England in the Reign of Elizabeth I.* Raleigh: America's Four Hundredth Anniversary Committee, North Carolina Department of Cultural Resources, 1986.

Younger, Neil. "William Lambarde and the Politics of Enforcement in Early Modern England." *HR* 83 (2010): 69–82.

Zagorin, Perez. "Francis Bacon's Concept of Objectivity and the Idols of the Mind." *British Journal for the History of Science* 34 (2001): 379–93.

Zambelli, Paola, ed. *"Astrologi hallucinati": Stars and the End of the World in Luther's Time.* Berlin: de Gruyter, 1986.

Zeeberg, Peter. "Heinrich Rantzau (1526–98) and His Humanist Collaborators: The Example of Reiner Reineccius and Georg Ludwig Froben." In *Germania latina—Latinitas teutonica: Politik, Wissenschaft, humanistische Kultur vom späten Mittelalter bis in unsere Zeit,* ed. Eckhard Keßler and Heinrich C. Kuhn, 539–53. Munich: Wilhelm Fink, 2003.

Zimmerman, T. C. Price. *Paolo Giovio: The Historian and the Crisis of Sixteenth-Century Italy.* Princeton, NJ: Princeton University Press, 1995.

Zinguer, Ilana. "Les stratégies de Belon pour un représentation exotique." *Nouvelle revue du XVIe siècle* 11 (1993): 5–17.

INDEX